D1133092

SIEGE
NEW AVENGERS

WRITER: **BRIAN MICHAEL BENDIS**

THE LIST
PENCILER: **MARKO DJURDJEVIC**
INKERS: **MARK MORALES**
COLORISTS: **MARTE GRACIA**
COVER ART: **MARKO DJURDJEVIC**

ANNUAL #3
ARTIST: **MIKE MAYHEW**
COLORIST: **ANDY TROY**
COVER ART: **MIKE MAYHEW**

ISSUES #61-62
PENCILER: **STUART IMMONEN**
INKER: **WADE VON GRAWBADGER**
COLORIST: **DAVE MCCAIG**
ARTIST, SPIDER-MAN/SPIDER-WOMAN PAGES: **DANIEL ACUÑA**
COVER ART: **STUART IMMONEN, WADE VON GRAWBADGER & DAVE MCCAIG**

ISSUES #63-64
ARTIST: **MIKE MCKONE**
COLORIST: **DAVE MCCAIG**
COVER ART: **STUART IMMONEN, WADE VON GRAWBADGER & DAVE MCCAIG**

FINALE
PENCILERS: **BRYAN HITCH** WITH STUART IMMONEN
INKERS: **BUTCH GUICE** WITH ANDREW CURRIE & KARL STORY
FLASHBACK ARTISTS: **DAVID FINCH, DANNY MIKI, FRANK D'ARMATA, STEVE MCNIVEN, DEXTER VINES, MORRY HOLLOWELL, OLIVIER COIPEL, JOHN DELL, MIKE DEODATO JR., JOE PIMENTAL, DAVE STEWART, LEINIL YU, MARK MORALES, LAURA MARTIN, BRYAN HITCH, RAIN BEREDO, BILLY TAN, BATT & JUSTIN PONSOR**
COLORISTS: **PAUL MOUNTS** WITH JUSTIN PONSOR & RAIN BEREDO
COVER ART: **BRYAN HITCH & PAUL MOUNTS**

LETTERERS: **VIRTUAL CALLIGRAPHY'S JOE CARAMAGNA & CHRIS ELIOPOULOS AND RS & COMICRAFT'S ALBERT DESCHESNE**
ASSOCIATE EDITOR: **LAUREN SANKOVITCH**
EDITOR: **TOM BREVOORT**

COLLECTION EDITOR: **JENNIFER GRÜNWALD** • EDITORIAL ASSISTANTS: **JAMES EMMETT & JOE HOCKSTEIN**
ASSISTANT EDITOR: **ALEX STARBUCK** • EDITOR, SPECIAL PROJECTS: **MARK D. BEAZLEY**
SENIOR EDITOR, SPECIAL PROJECTS: **JEFF YOUNGQUIST** • SENIOR VICE PRESIDENT OF SALES: **DAVID GABRIEL**

EDITOR IN CHIEF: **JOE QUESADA** • PUBLISHER: **DAN BUCKLEY** • EXECUTIVE PRODUCER: **ALAN FINE**

SIEGE: NEW AVENGERS. Contains material originally published in magazine form as NEW AVENGERS #61-64, NEW AVENGERS ANNUAL #3, DARK REIGN: THE LIST - AVENGERS and NEW AVENGERS FINALE. First printing 2010. ISBN# 978-0-7851-4577-6. Published by MARVEL WORLDWIDE, INC., a subsidiary of MARVEL ENTERTAINMENT, LLC. OFFICE OF PUBLICATION: 417 5th Avenue, New York, NY 10016. Copyright © 2009 and 2010 Marvel Characters, Inc. All rights reserved. $29.99 per copy in the U.S. and $34.99 in Canada (GST #R127032852); Canadian Agreement #40668537. All characters featured in this issue and the distinctive names and likenesses thereof, and all related indicia are trademarks of Marvel Characters, Inc. No similarity between any of the names, characters, persons, and/or institutions in this magazine with those of any living or dead person or institution is intended, and any such similarity which may exist is purely coincidental. **Printed in the U.S.A.** ALAN FINE, EVP - Office of the President, Marvel Worldwide, Inc. and EVP & CMO Marvel Characters B.V.; DAN BUCKLEY, Chief Executive Officer and Publisher - Print, Animation & Digital Media; JIM SOKOLOWSKI, Chief Operating Officer; DAVID GABRIEL, SVP of Publishing Sales & Circulation; DAVID BOGART, SVP of Business Affairs & Talent Management; MICHAEL PASCIULLO, VP Merchandising & Communications; JIM O'KEEFE, VP of Operations & Logistics; DAN CARR, Executive Director of Publishing Technology; JUSTIN F. GABRIE, Director of Publishing & Editorial Operations; SUSAN CRESPI, Editorial Operations Manager; ALEX MORALES, Publishing Operations Manager; STAN LEE, Chairman Emeritus. For information regarding advertising in Marvel Comics or on Marvel.com, please contact Ron Stern, VP of Business Development, at rstern@marvel.com. For Marvel subscription inquiries, please call 800-217-9158. **Manufactured between 7/19/10 and 8/18/10 by R.R. DONNELLEY, INC., SALEM, VA, USA.**

10 9 8 7 6 5 4 3 2 1

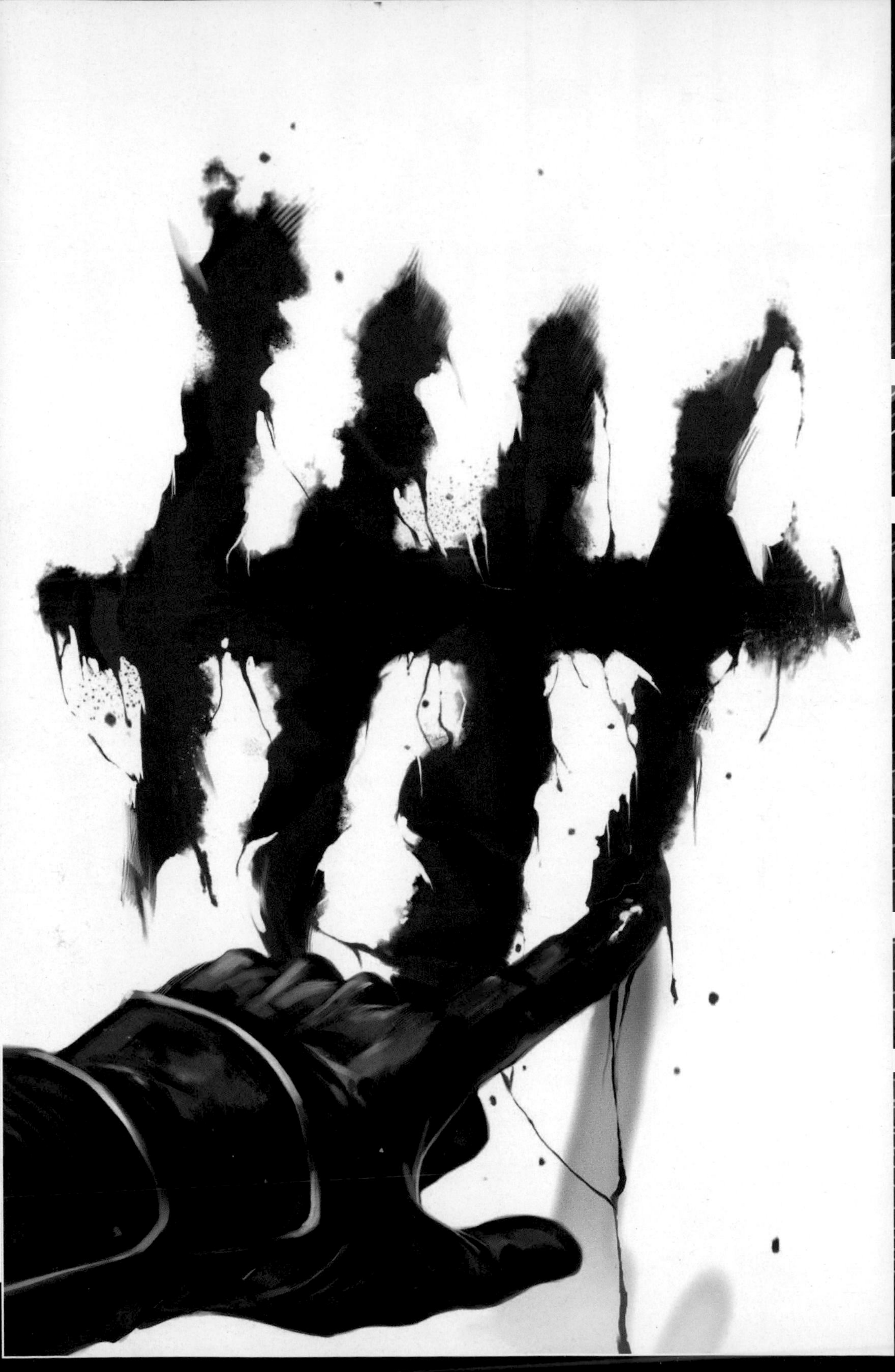

DARK REIGN: THE LIST — AVENGERS

And there came a day, a day unlike any other, when Earth's Mightiest Heroes found themselves united against a common threat! On that day, the Avengers were born, to fight the foes no single super hero could withstand!

The Avengers are on the run! Until they can be sure who's on their side, Spider-Man, Captain America, Luke Cage, Ronin, Mockingbird, Spider-Woman and Ms. Marvel are using Captain America's hideout in Brooklyn as a safe house. Collectively they try to keep the values of the Avengers name alive even though they're living on the wrong side of the law.

Norman Osborn is the new political and media darling and director of H.A.M.M.E.R., the national peacekeeping task force, which includes his own team of Avengers.

After Norman had the Hood's syndicate surprise-attack the New Avengers, Clint Barton – aka Hawkeye – aka Ronin went to the media and outed Norman as the twisted Green Goblin…

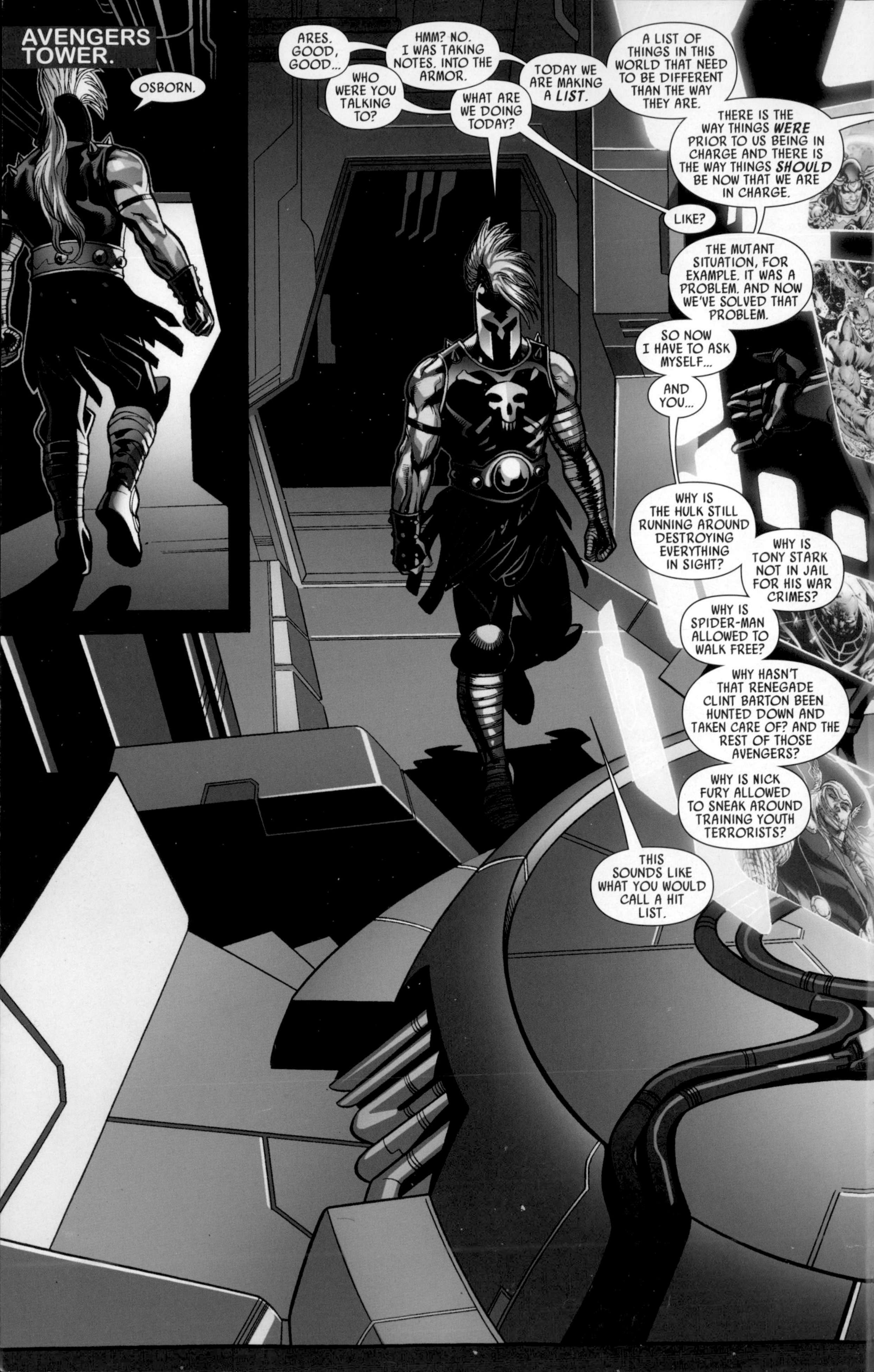
AVENGERS TOWER.
OSBORN.
ARES. GOOD, GOOD...
WHO WERE YOU TALKING TO?
HMM? NO. I WAS TAKING NOTES. INTO THE ARMOR.
WHAT ARE WE DOING TODAY?
TODAY WE ARE MAKING A LIST.
A LIST OF THINGS IN THIS WORLD THAT NEED TO BE DIFFERENT THAN THE WAY THEY ARE.
THERE IS THE WAY THINGS WERE PRIOR TO US BEING IN CHARGE AND THERE IS THE WAY THINGS SHOULD BE NOW THAT WE ARE IN CHARGE.
LIKE?
THE MUTANT SITUATION, FOR EXAMPLE. IT WAS A PROBLEM. AND NOW WE'VE SOLVED THAT PROBLEM.
SO NOW I HAVE TO ASK MYSELF...
AND YOU...
WHY IS THE HULK STILL RUNNING AROUND DESTROYING EVERYTHING IN SIGHT?
WHY IS TONY STARK NOT IN JAIL FOR HIS WAR CRIMES?
WHY IS SPIDER-MAN ALLOWED TO WALK FREE?
WHY HASN'T THAT RENEGADE CLINT BARTON BEEN HUNTED DOWN AND TAKEN CARE OF? AND THE REST OF THOSE AVENGERS?
WHY IS NICK FURY ALLOWED TO SNEAK AROUND TRAINING YOUTH TERRORISTS?
THIS SOUNDS LIKE WHAT YOU WOULD CALL A HIT LIST.

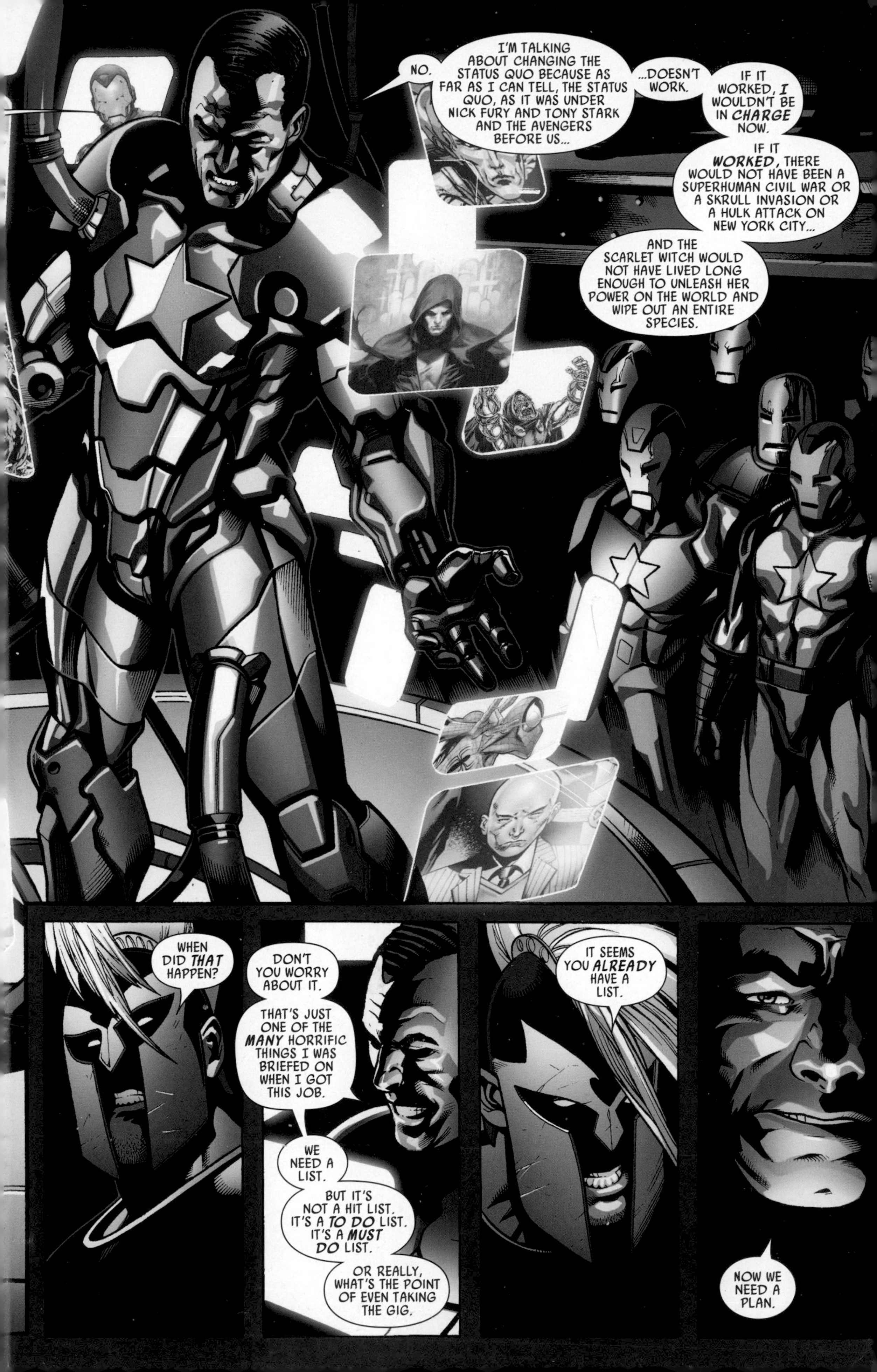
NO.
I'M TALKING ABOUT CHANGING THE STATUS QUO BECAUSE AS FAR AS I CAN TELL, THE STATUS QUO, AS IT WAS UNDER NICK FURY AND TONY STARK AND THE AVENGERS BEFORE US...
...DOESN'T WORK.
IF IT WORKED, I WOULDN'T BE IN CHARGE NOW.
IF IT WORKED, THERE WOULD NOT HAVE BEEN A SUPERHUMAN CIVIL WAR OR A SKRULL INVASION OR A HULK ATTACK ON NEW YORK CITY...
AND THE SCARLET WITCH WOULD NOT HAVE LIVED LONG ENOUGH TO UNLEASH HER POWER ON THE WORLD AND WIPE OUT AN ENTIRE SPECIES.
WHEN DID THAT HAPPEN?
DON'T YOU WORRY ABOUT IT.
THAT'S JUST ONE OF THE MANY HORRIFIC THINGS I WAS BRIEFED ON WHEN I GOT THIS JOB.
WE NEED A LIST.
BUT IT'S NOT A HIT LIST. IT'S A TO DO LIST. IT'S A MUST DO LIST.
OR REALLY, WHAT'S THE POINT OF EVEN TAKING THE GIG.
IT SEEMS YOU ALREADY HAVE A LIST.
NOW WE NEED A PLAN.

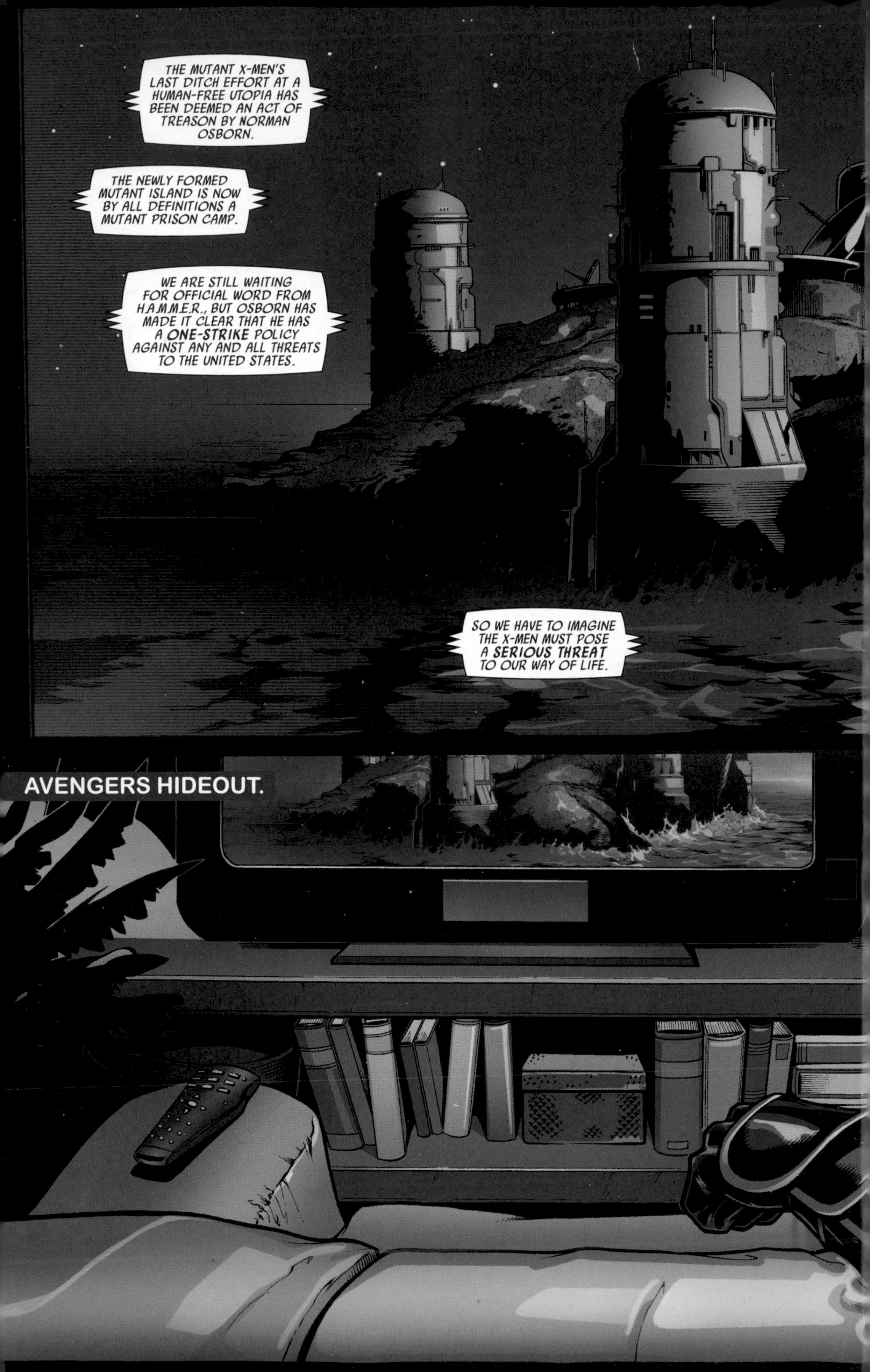
THE MUTANT X-MEN'S LAST DITCH EFFORT AT A HUMAN-FREE UTOPIA HAS BEEN DEEMED AN ACT OF TREASON BY NORMAN OSBORN.
THE NEWLY FORMED MUTANT ISLAND IS NOW BY ALL DEFINITIONS A MUTANT PRISON CAMP.
WE ARE STILL WAITING FOR OFFICIAL WORD FROM H.A.M.M.E.R., BUT OSBORN HAS MADE IT CLEAR THAT HE HAS A ONE-STRIKE POLICY AGAINST ANY AND ALL THREATS TO THE UNITED STATES.
SO WE HAVE TO IMAGINE THE X-MEN MUST POSE A SERIOUS THREAT TO OUR WAY OF LIFE.
AVENGERS HIDEOUT.

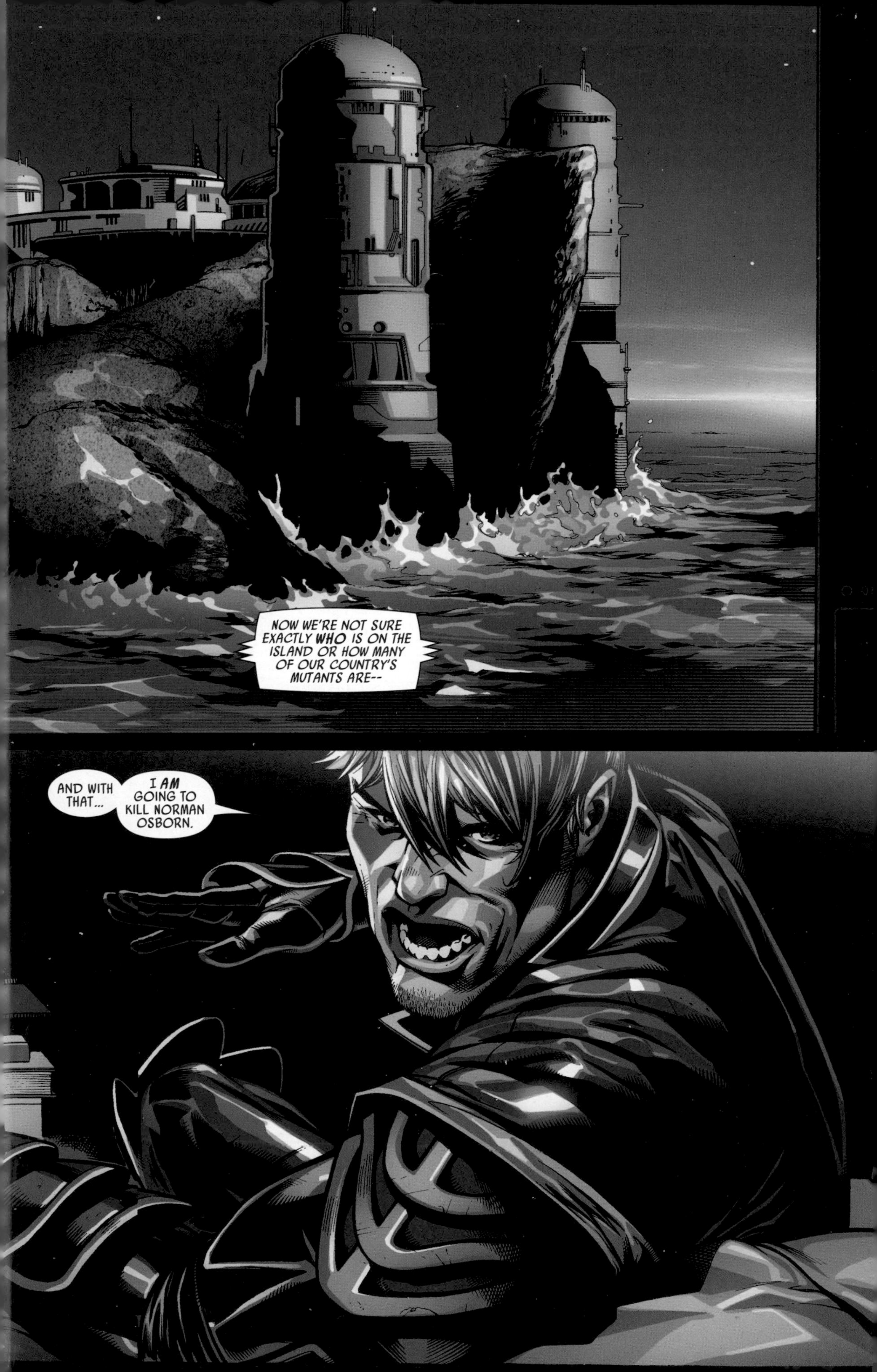
NOW WE'RE NOT SURE EXACTLY WHO IS ON THE ISLAND OR HOW MANY OF OUR COUNTRY'S MUTANTS ARE--
AND WITH THAT...
I AM GOING TO KILL NORMAN OSBORN.

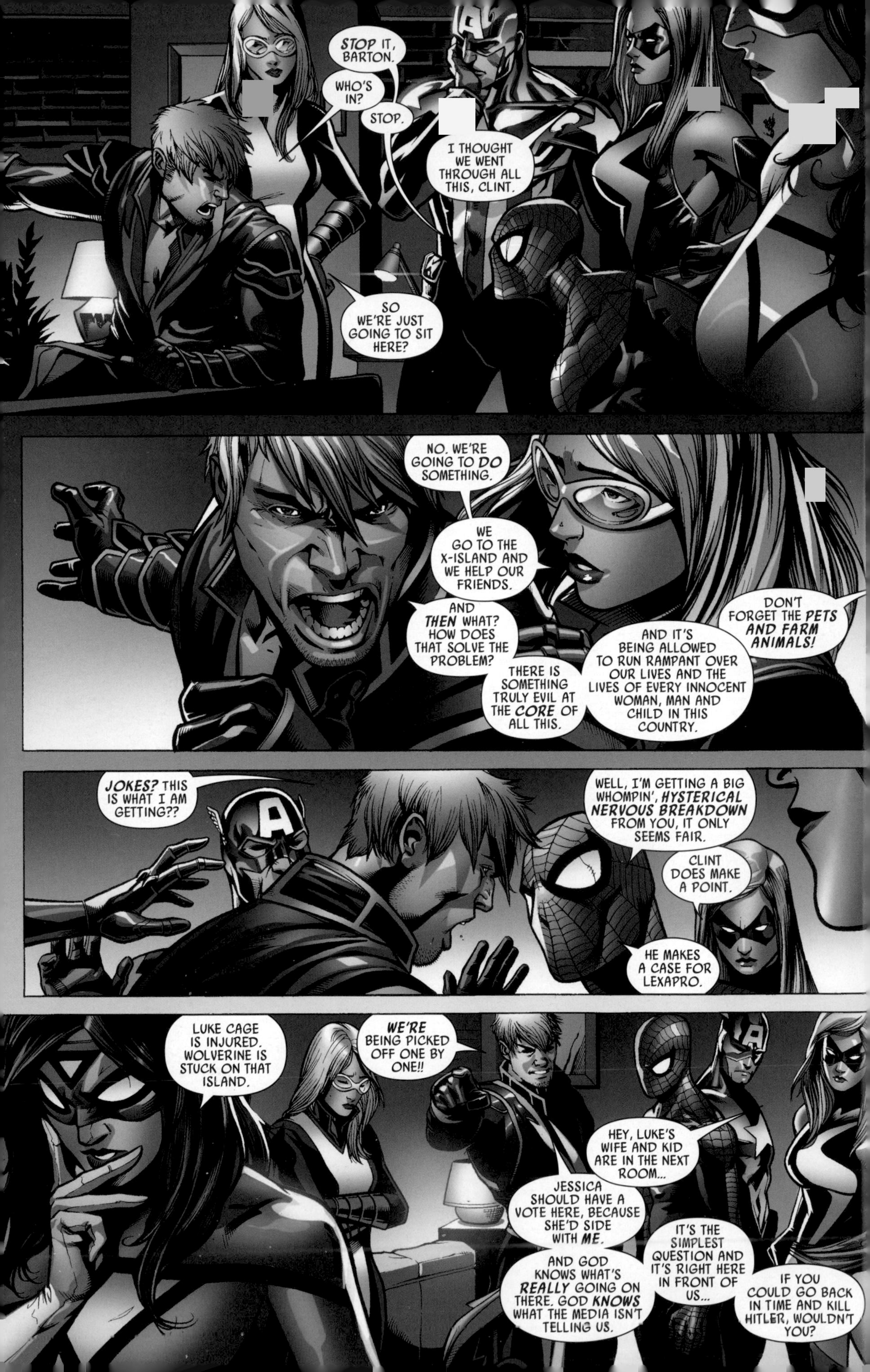
WHO'S IN?
STOP IT, BARTON.
STOP.
I THOUGHT WE WENT THROUGH ALL THIS, CLINT.
SO WE'RE JUST GOING TO SIT HERE?
NO. WE'RE GOING TO DO SOMETHING.
WE GO TO THE X-ISLAND AND WE HELP OUR FRIENDS.
AND THEN WHAT? HOW DOES THAT SOLVE THE PROBLEM?
THERE IS SOMETHING TRULY EVIL AT THE CORE OF ALL THIS.
AND IT'S BEING ALLOWED TO RUN RAMPANT OVER OUR LIVES AND THE LIVES OF EVERY INNOCENT WOMAN, MAN AND CHILD IN THIS COUNTRY.
DON'T FORGET THE PETS AND FARM ANIMALS!
JOKES? THIS IS WHAT I AM GETTING??
WELL, I'M GETTING A BIG WHOMPIN', HYSTERICAL NERVOUS BREAKDOWN FROM YOU, IT ONLY SEEMS FAIR.
CLINT DOES MAKE A POINT.
HE MAKES A CASE FOR LEXAPRO.
LUKE CAGE IS INJURED. WOLVERINE IS STUCK ON THAT ISLAND.
WE'RE BEING PICKED OFF ONE BY ONE!!
HEY, LUKE'S WIFE AND KID ARE IN THE NEXT ROOM...
JESSICA SHOULD HAVE A VOTE HERE, BECAUSE SHE'D SIDE WITH ME.
AND GOD KNOWS WHAT'S REALLY GOING ON THERE. GOD KNOWS WHAT THE MEDIA ISN'T TELLING US.
IT'S THE SIMPLEST QUESTION AND IT'S RIGHT HERE IN FRONT OF US...
IF YOU COULD GO BACK IN TIME AND KILL HITLER, WOULDN'T YOU?

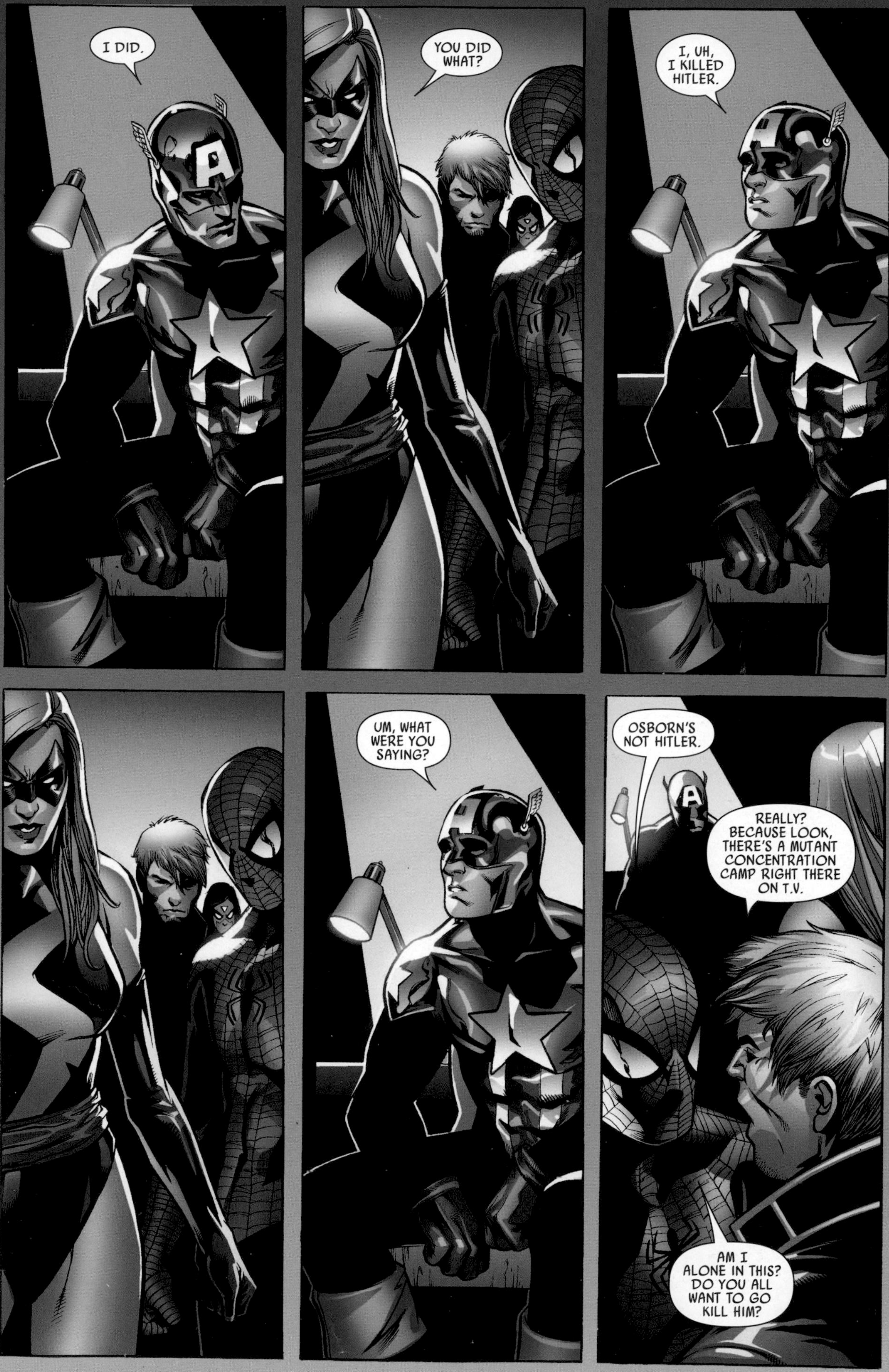
I DID.
YOU DID WHAT?
I, UH, I KILLED HITLER.
UM, WHAT WERE YOU SAYING?
OSBORN'S NOT HITLER.
REALLY? BECAUSE LOOK, THERE'S A MUTANT CONCENTRATION CAMP RIGHT THERE ON T.V.
AM I ALONE IN THIS? DO YOU ALL WANT TO GO KILL HIM?

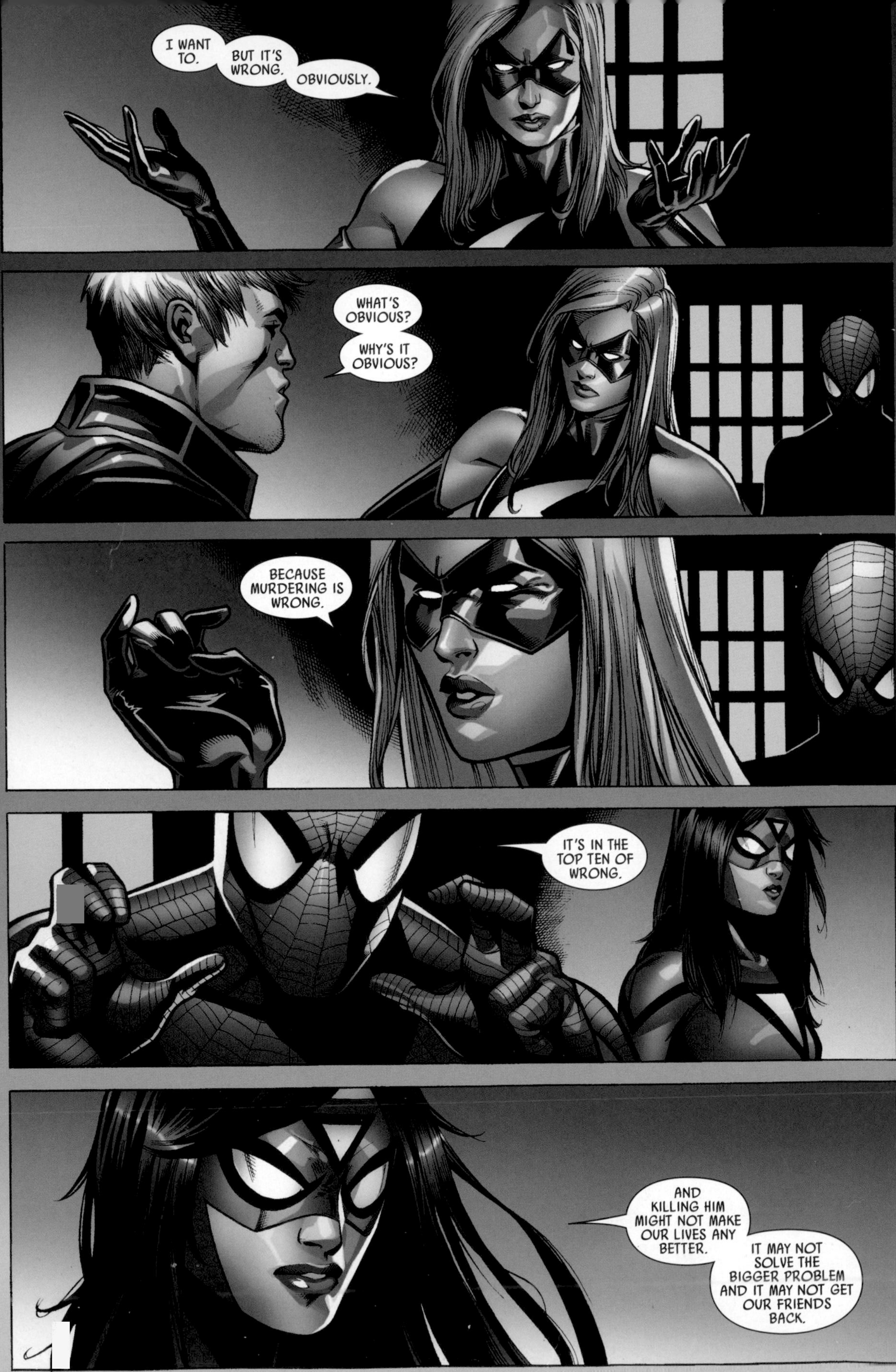
I WANT TO.
BUT IT'S WRONG.
OBVIOUSLY.
WHAT'S OBVIOUS?
WHY'S IT OBVIOUS?
BECAUSE MURDERING IS WRONG.
IT'S IN THE TOP TEN OF WRONG.
AND KILLING HIM MIGHT NOT MAKE OUR LIVES ANY BETTER.
IT MAY NOT SOLVE THE BIGGER PROBLEM AND IT MAY NOT GET OUR FRIENDS BACK.

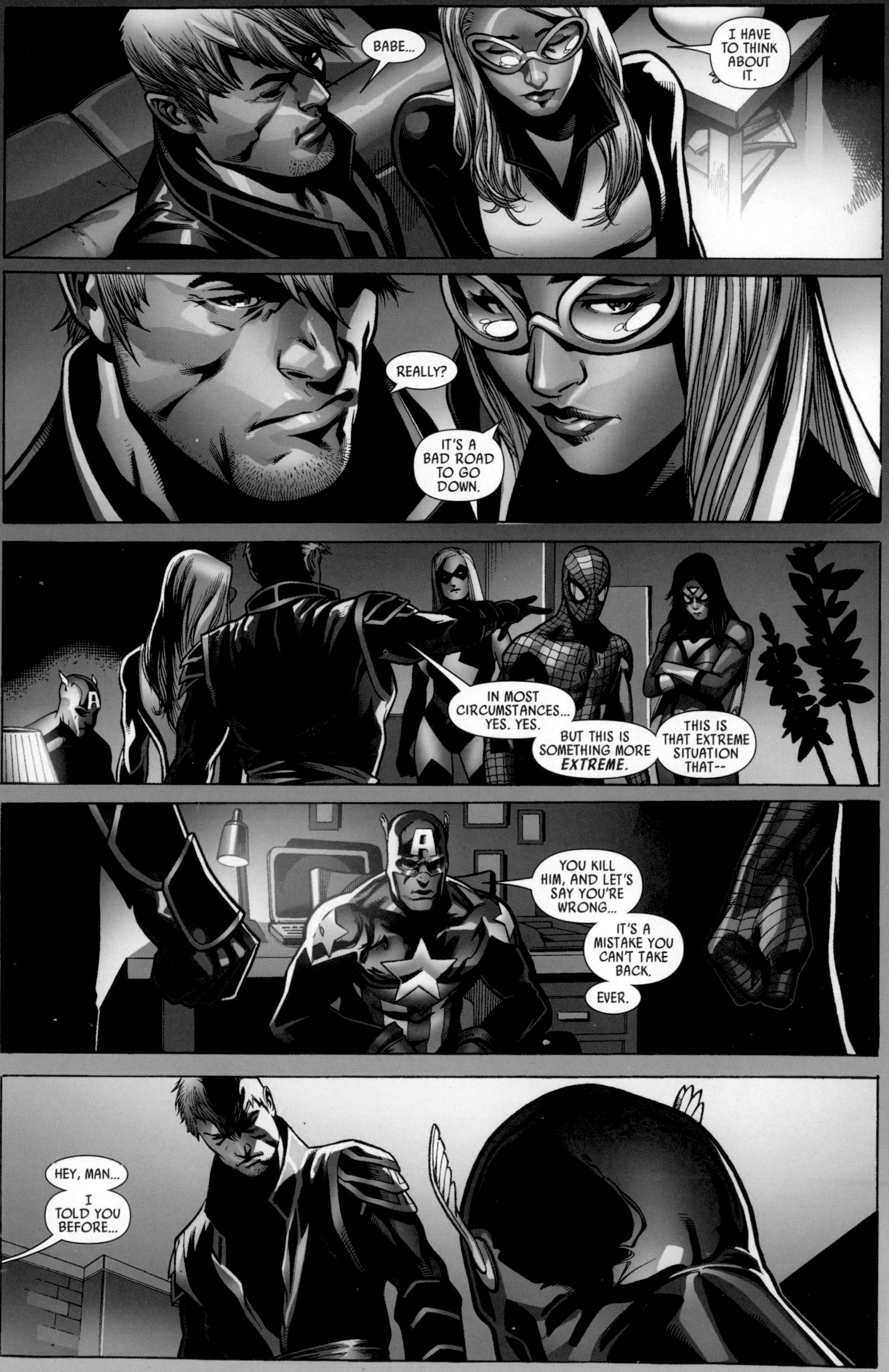
BABE...
I HAVE TO THINK ABOUT IT.
REALLY?
IT'S A BAD ROAD TO GO DOWN.
IN MOST CIRCUMSTANCES... YES. YES.
BUT THIS IS SOMETHING MORE *EXTREME.*
THIS IS THAT EXTREME SITUATION THAT--
YOU KILL HIM, AND LET'S SAY YOU'RE WRONG...
IT'S A MISTAKE YOU CAN'T TAKE BACK.
EVER.
HEY, MAN...
I TOLD YOU BEFORE...

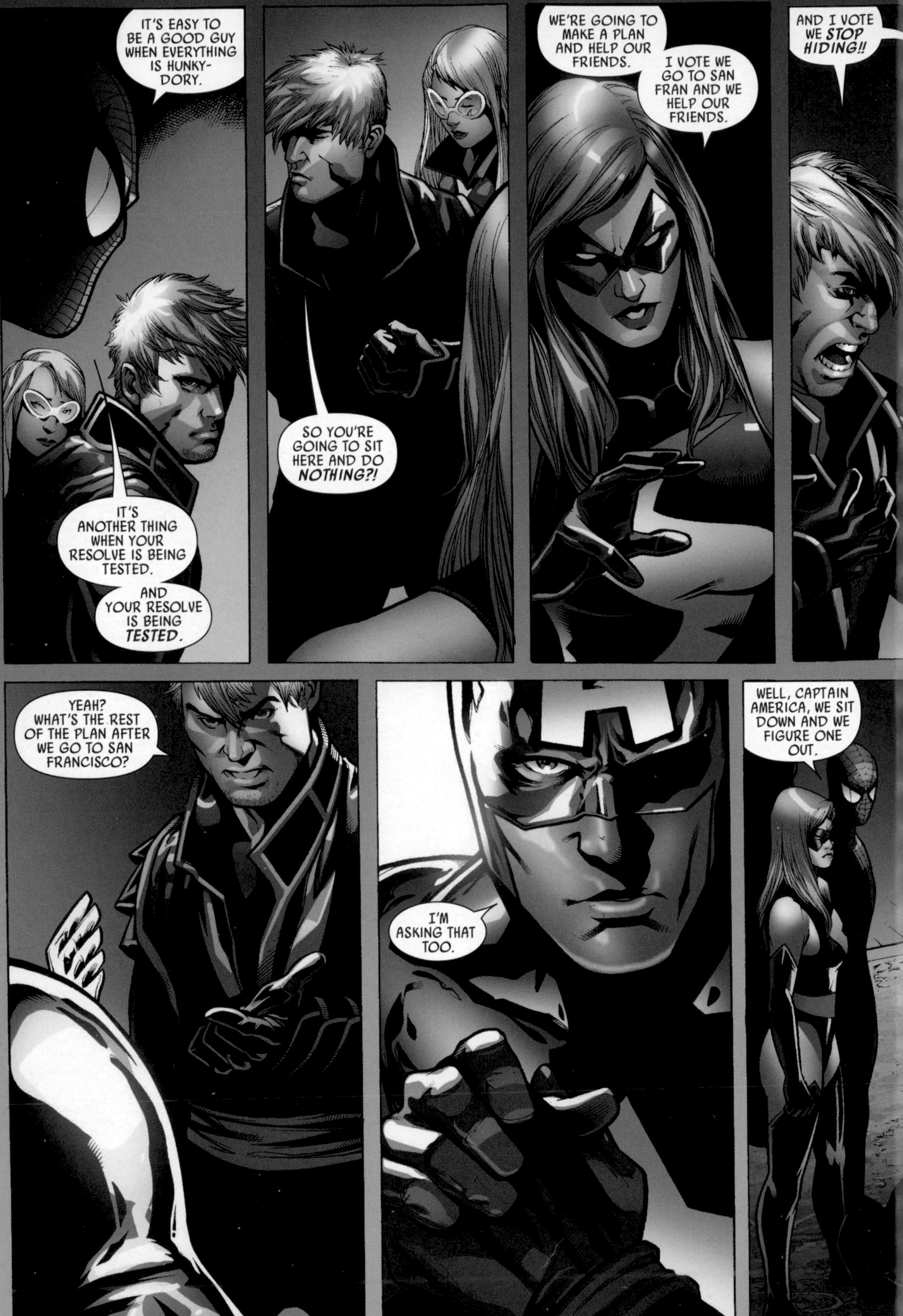
IT'S EASY TO BE A GOOD GUY WHEN EVERYTHING IS HUNKY-DORY.
IT'S ANOTHER THING WHEN YOUR RESOLVE IS BEING TESTED.
AND YOUR RESOLVE IS BEING TESTED.
SO YOU'RE GOING TO SIT HERE AND DO NOTHING?!
WE'RE GOING TO MAKE A PLAN AND HELP OUR FRIENDS.
I VOTE WE GO TO SAN FRAN AND WE HELP OUR FRIENDS.
AND I VOTE WE STOP HIDING!!
YEAH? WHAT'S THE REST OF THE PLAN AFTER WE GO TO SAN FRANCISCO?
I'M ASKING THAT TOO.
WELL, CAPTAIN AMERICA, WE SIT DOWN AND WE FIGURE ONE OUT.

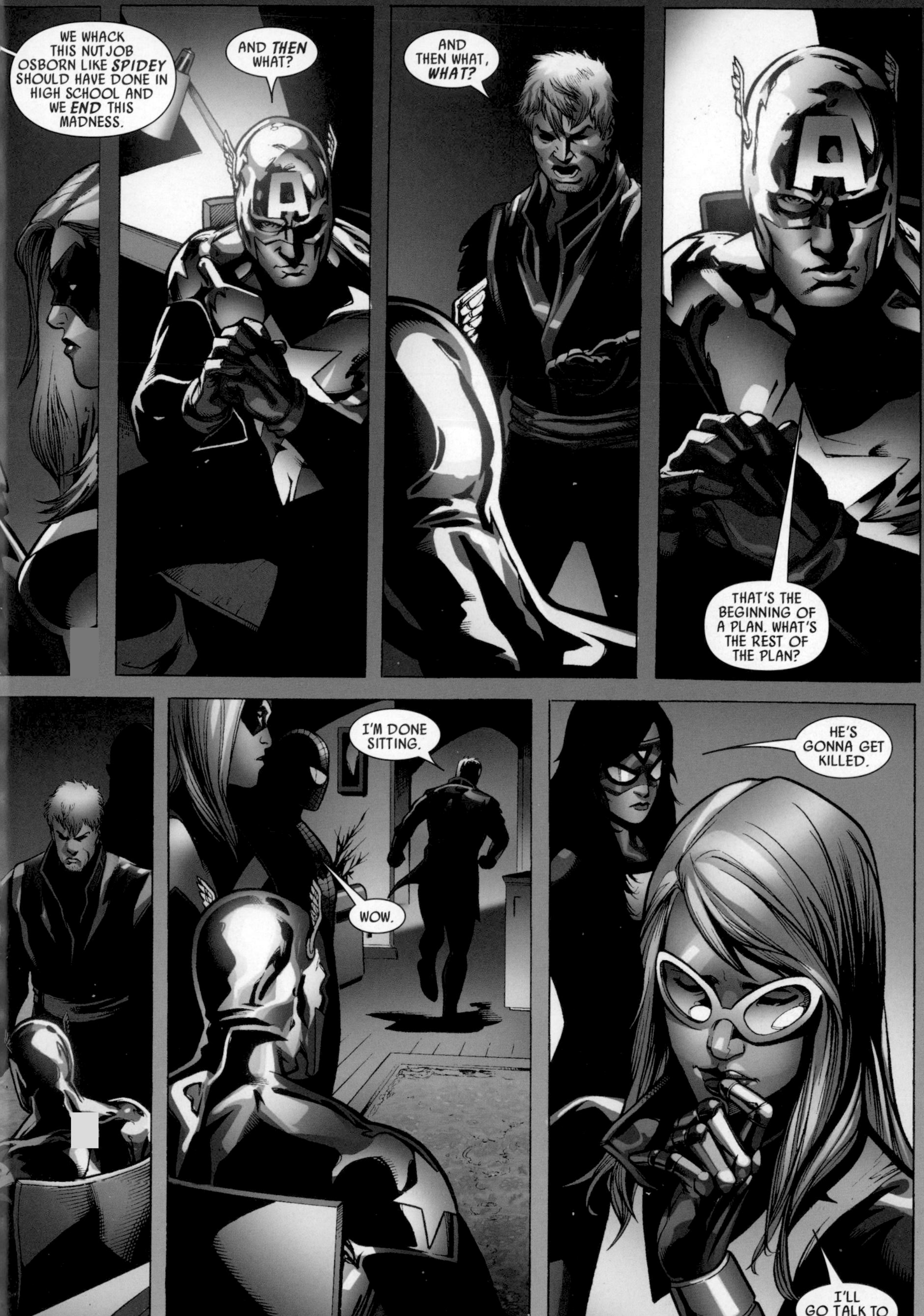
WE WHACK THIS NUTJOB OSBORN LIKE SPIDEY SHOULD HAVE DONE IN HIGH SCHOOL AND WE END THIS MADNESS.
AND THEN WHAT?
AND THEN WHAT, WHAT?
THAT'S THE BEGINNING OF A PLAN. WHAT'S THE REST OF THE PLAN?
I'M DONE SITTING.
WOW.
HE'S GONNA GET KILLED.
I'LL GO TALK TO HIM.

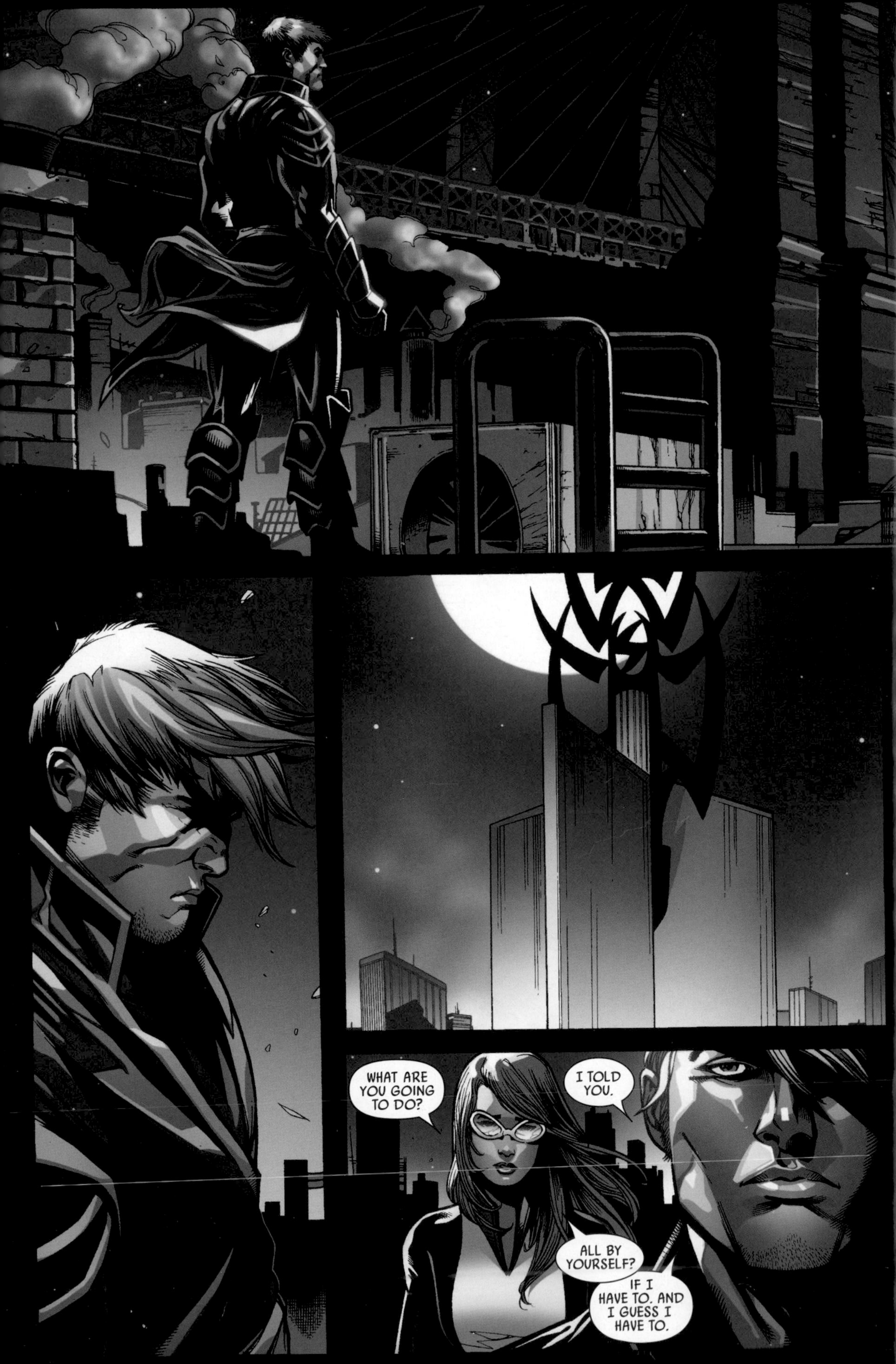
WHAT ARE YOU GOING TO DO?
I TOLD YOU.
ALL BY YOURSELF?
IF I HAVE TO. AND I GUESS I HAVE TO.

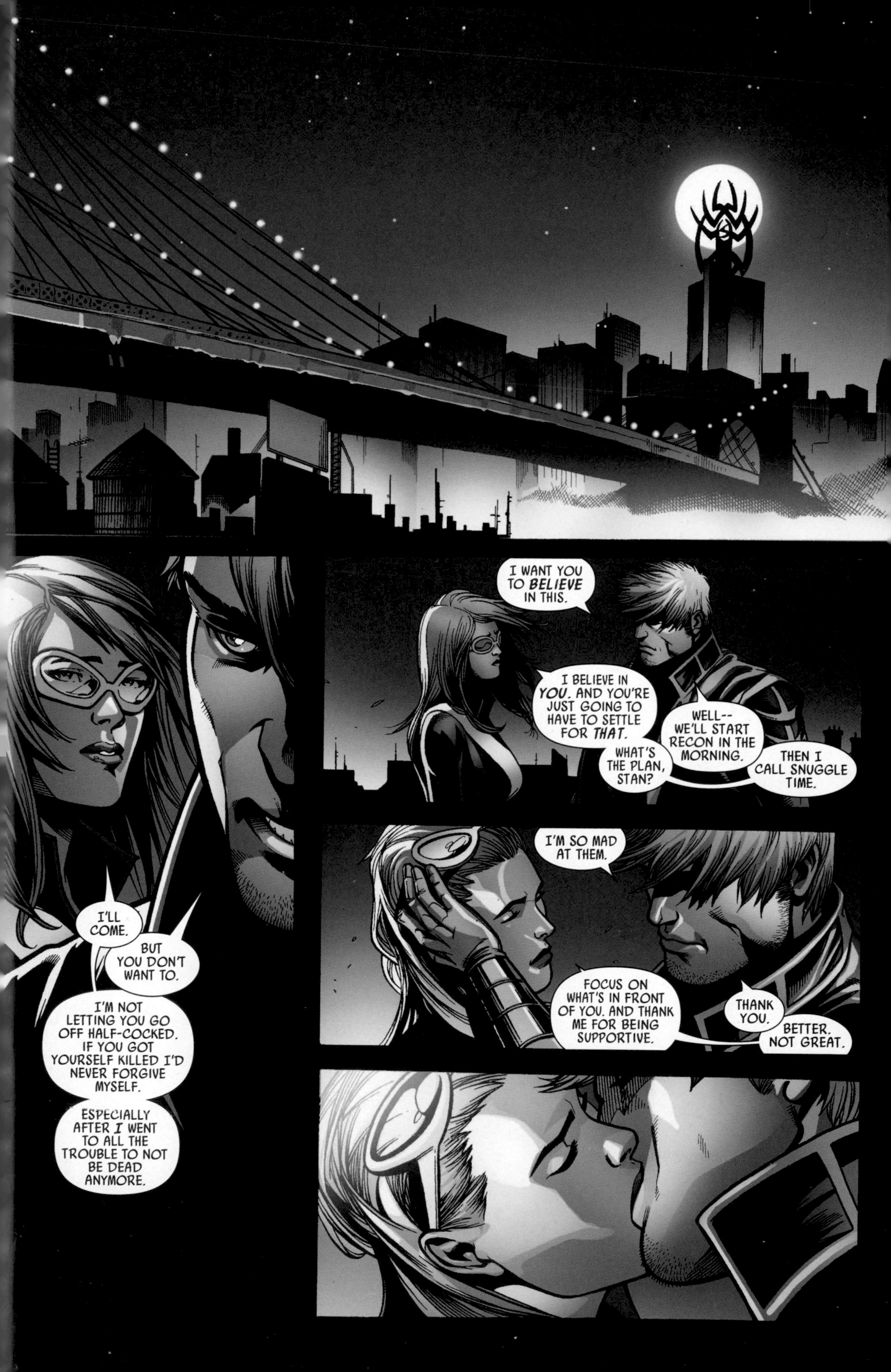
I'LL COME.
BUT YOU DON'T WANT TO.
I'M NOT LETTING YOU GO OFF HALF-COCKED. IF YOU GOT YOURSELF KILLED I'D NEVER FORGIVE MYSELF.
ESPECIALLY AFTER *I* WENT TO ALL THE TROUBLE TO NOT BE DEAD ANYMORE.
I WANT YOU TO ***BELIEVE*** IN THIS.
I BELIEVE IN ***YOU.*** AND YOU'RE JUST GOING TO HAVE TO SETTLE FOR ***THAT***.
WHAT'S THE PLAN, STAN?
WELL-- WE'LL START RECON IN THE MORNING.
THEN I CALL SNUGGLE TIME.
I'M SO MAD AT THEM.
FOCUS ON WHAT'S IN FRONT OF YOU. AND THANK ME FOR BEING SUPPORTIVE.
THANK YOU.
BETTER. NOT GREAT.

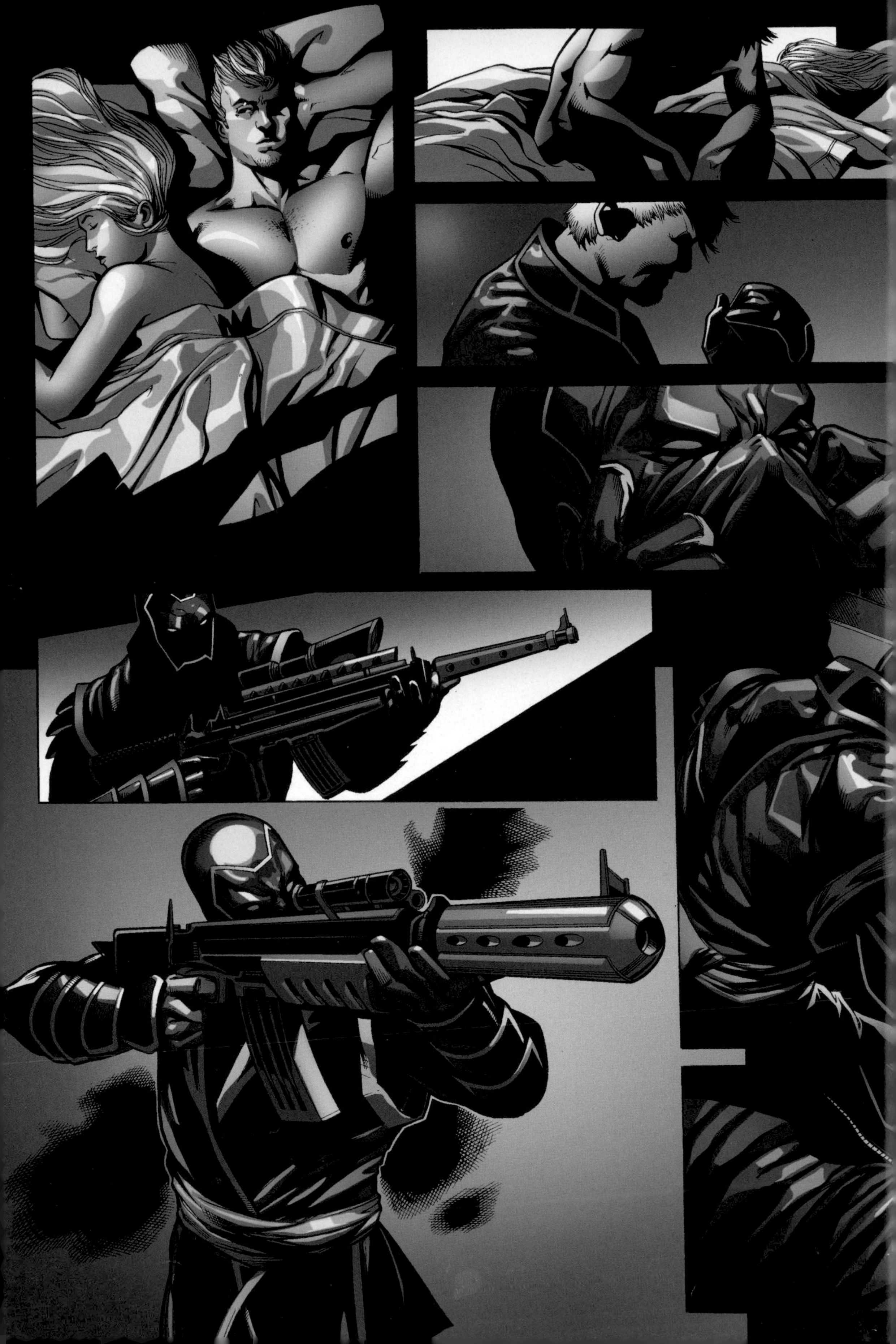

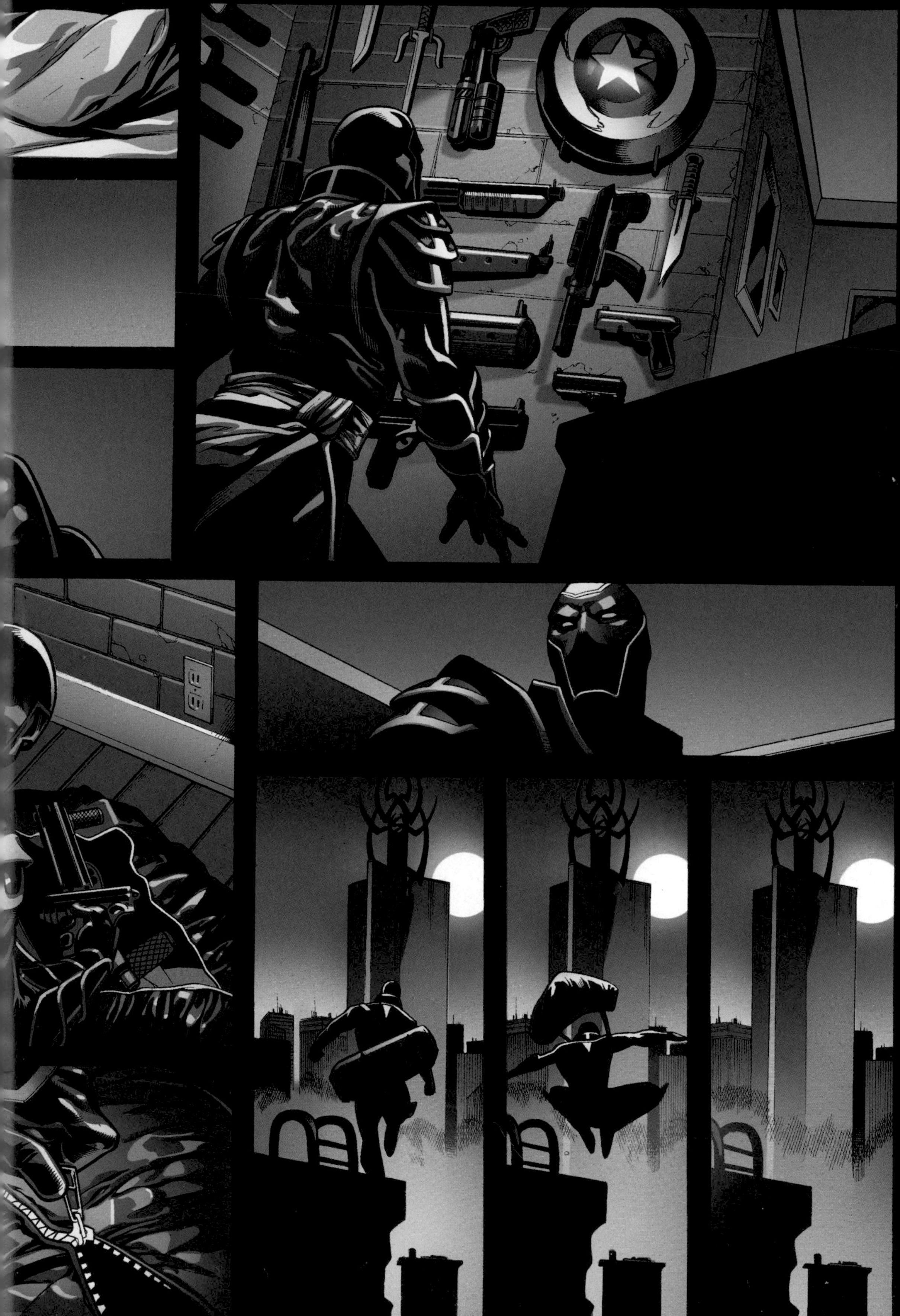

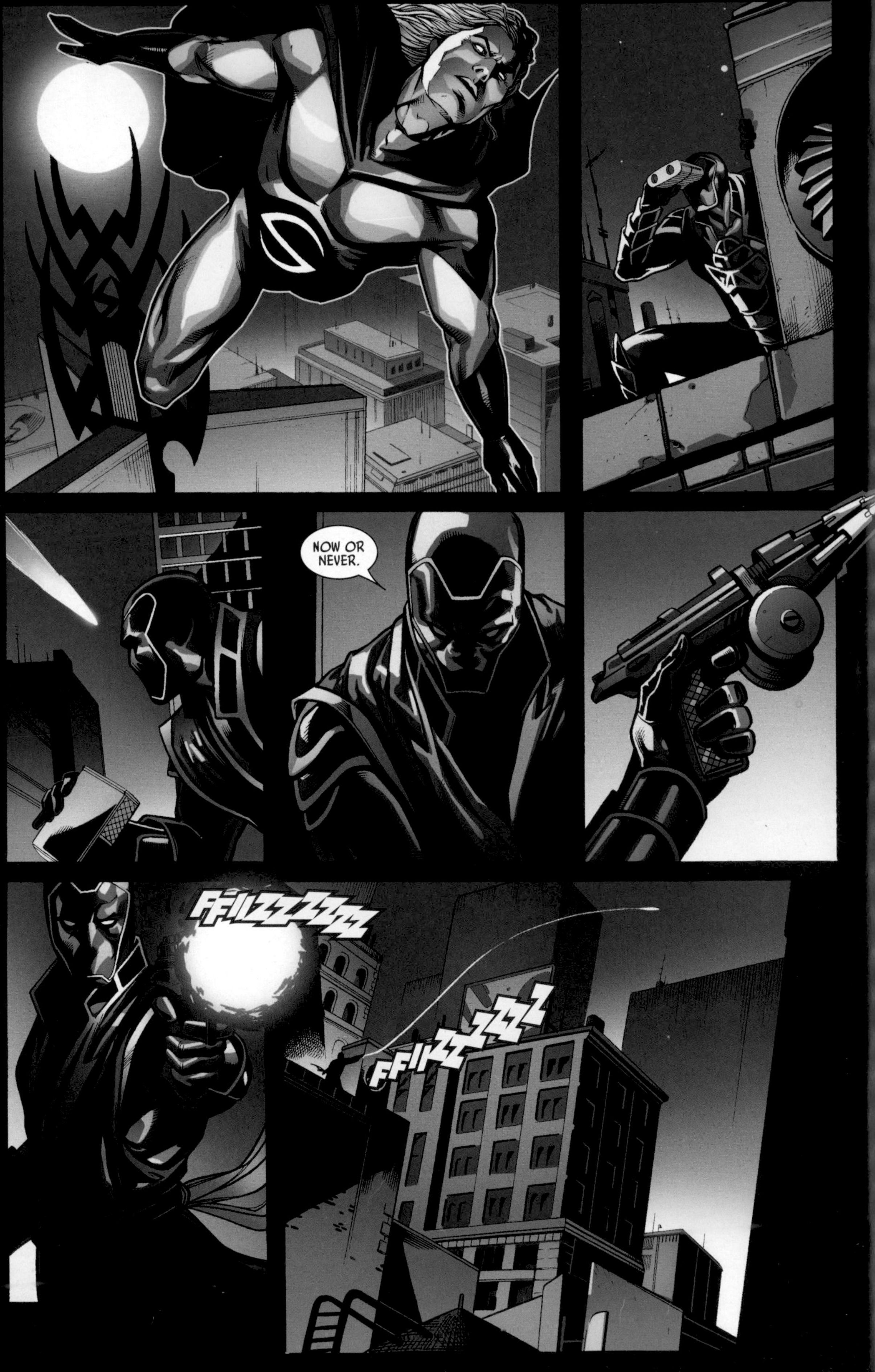
NOW OR NEVER.
FFIIZZZZZZZ
FFIIZZZZZZZ

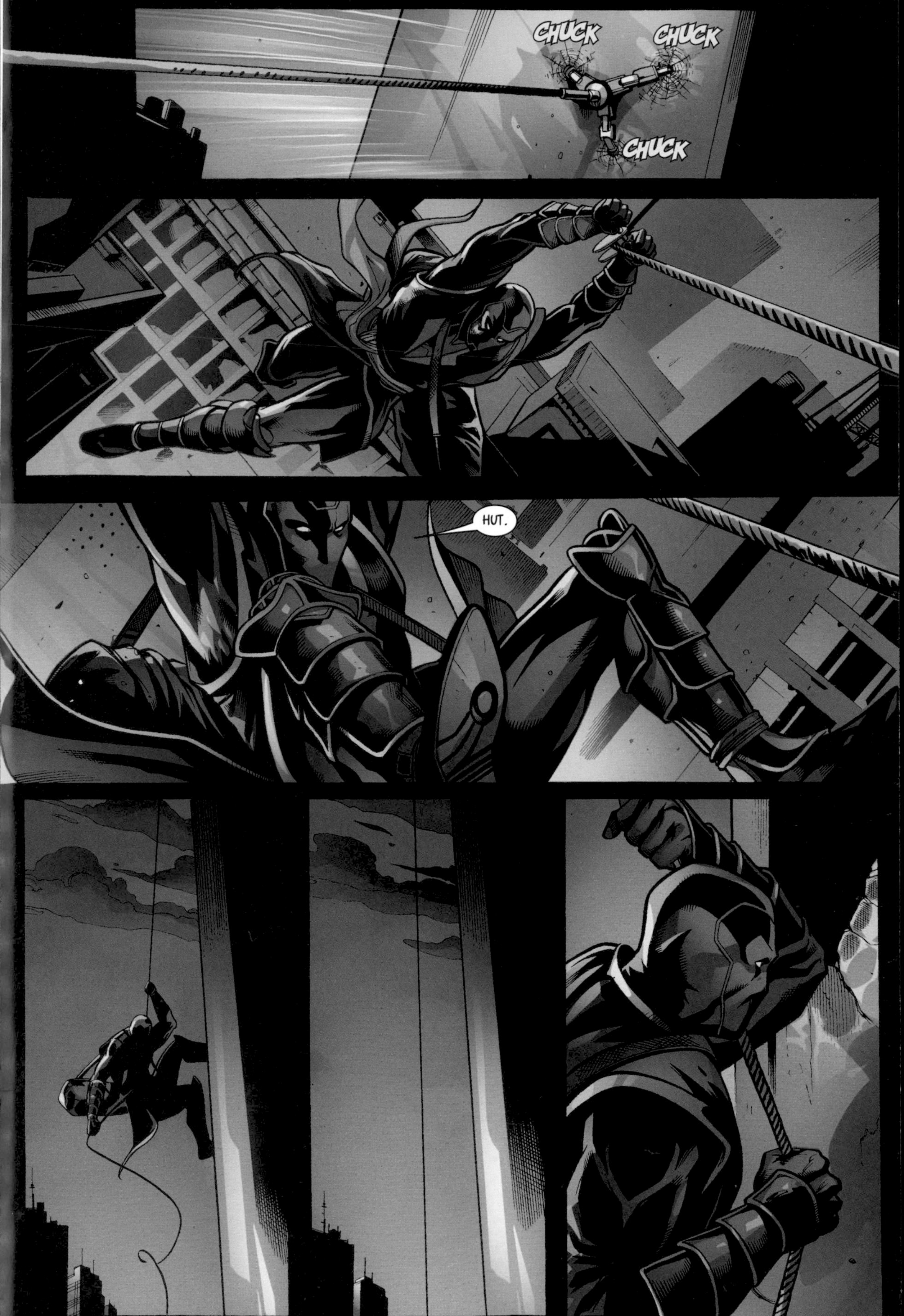
CHUCK
CHUCK
CHUCK
HUT.

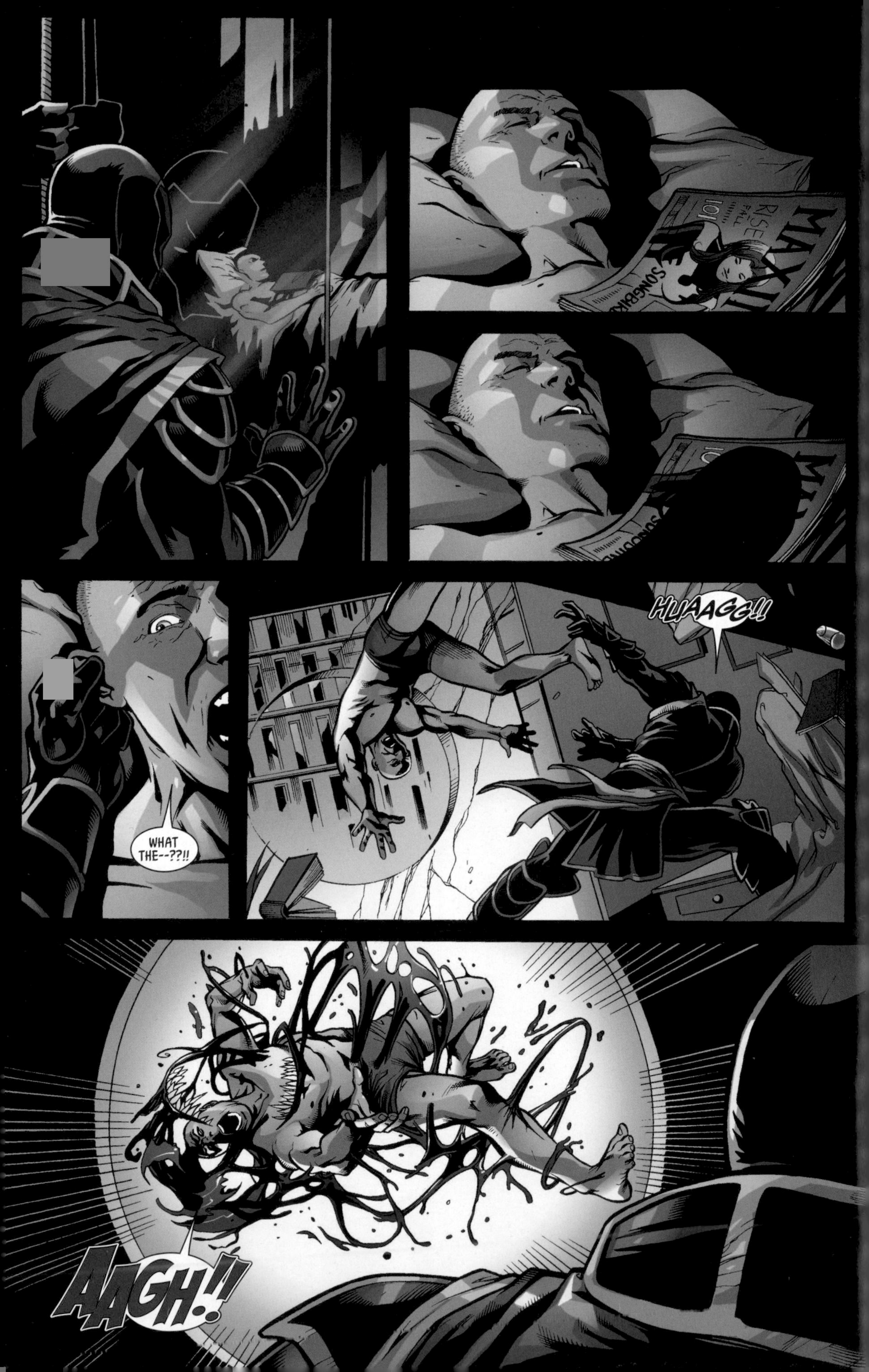
WHAT THE--??!!
HUAAGG!!
AAGH!!

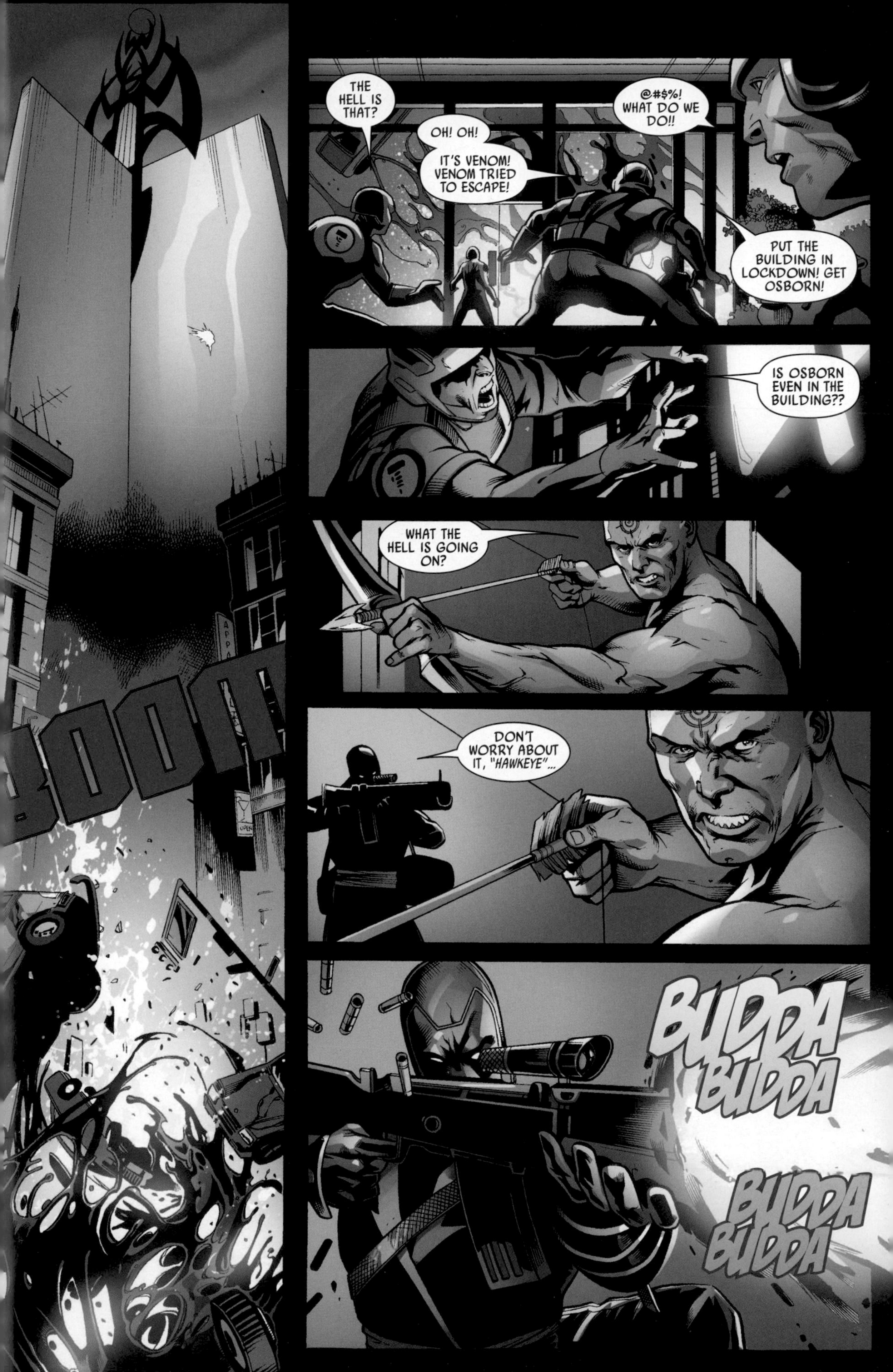
BOOM
THE HELL IS THAT?
OH! OH!
IT'S VENOM! VENOM TRIED TO ESCAPE!
@#$%! WHAT DO WE DO!!
PUT THE BUILDING IN LOCKDOWN! GET OSBORN!
IS OSBORN EVEN IN THE BUILDING??
WHAT THE HELL IS GOING ON?
DON'T WORRY ABOUT IT, "HAWKEYE"...
BUDDA BUDDA
BUDDA BUDDA

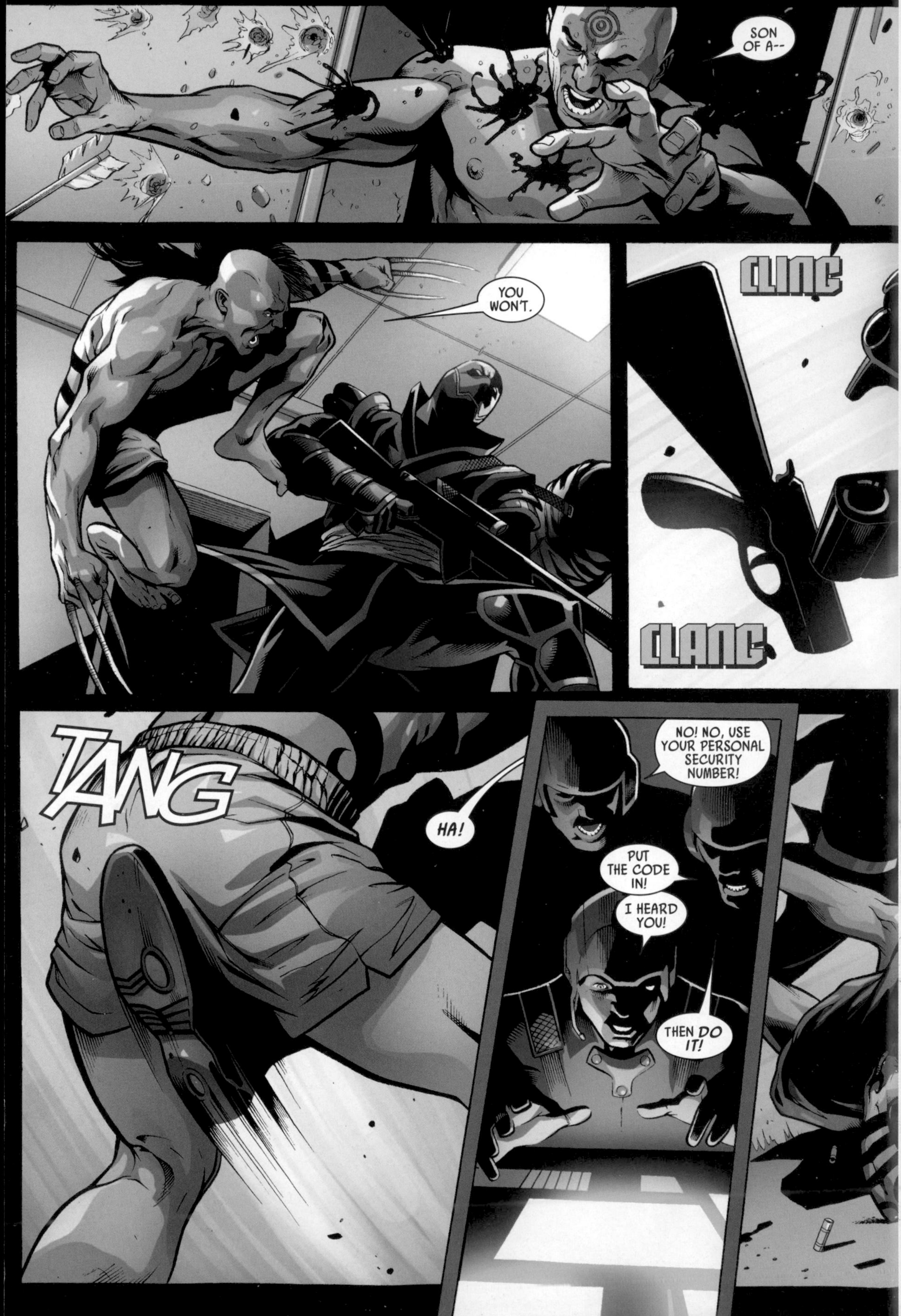
SON OF A--
YOU WON'T.
CLING
CLANG
TANG
HA!
NO! NO, USE YOUR PERSONAL SECURITY NUMBER!
PUT THE CODE IN!
I HEARD YOU!
THEN DO IT!

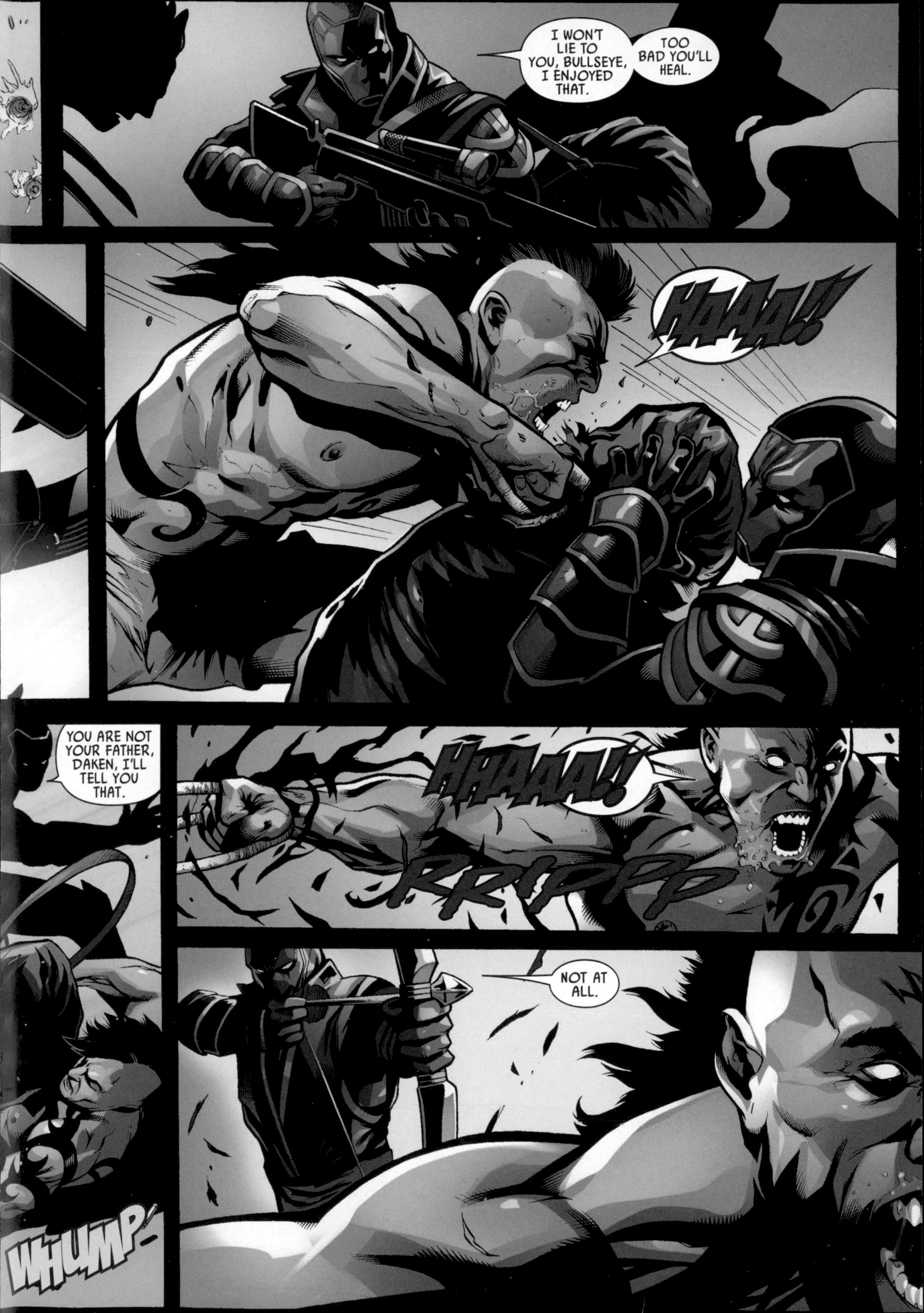
I WON'T LIE TO YOU, BULLSEYE, I ENJOYED THAT.
TOO BAD YOU'LL HEAL.
HAAA!!
YOU ARE NOT YOUR FATHER, DAKEN, I'LL TELL YOU THAT.
HHAAAA!!
RRIPPP
NOT AT ALL.
WHUMP!

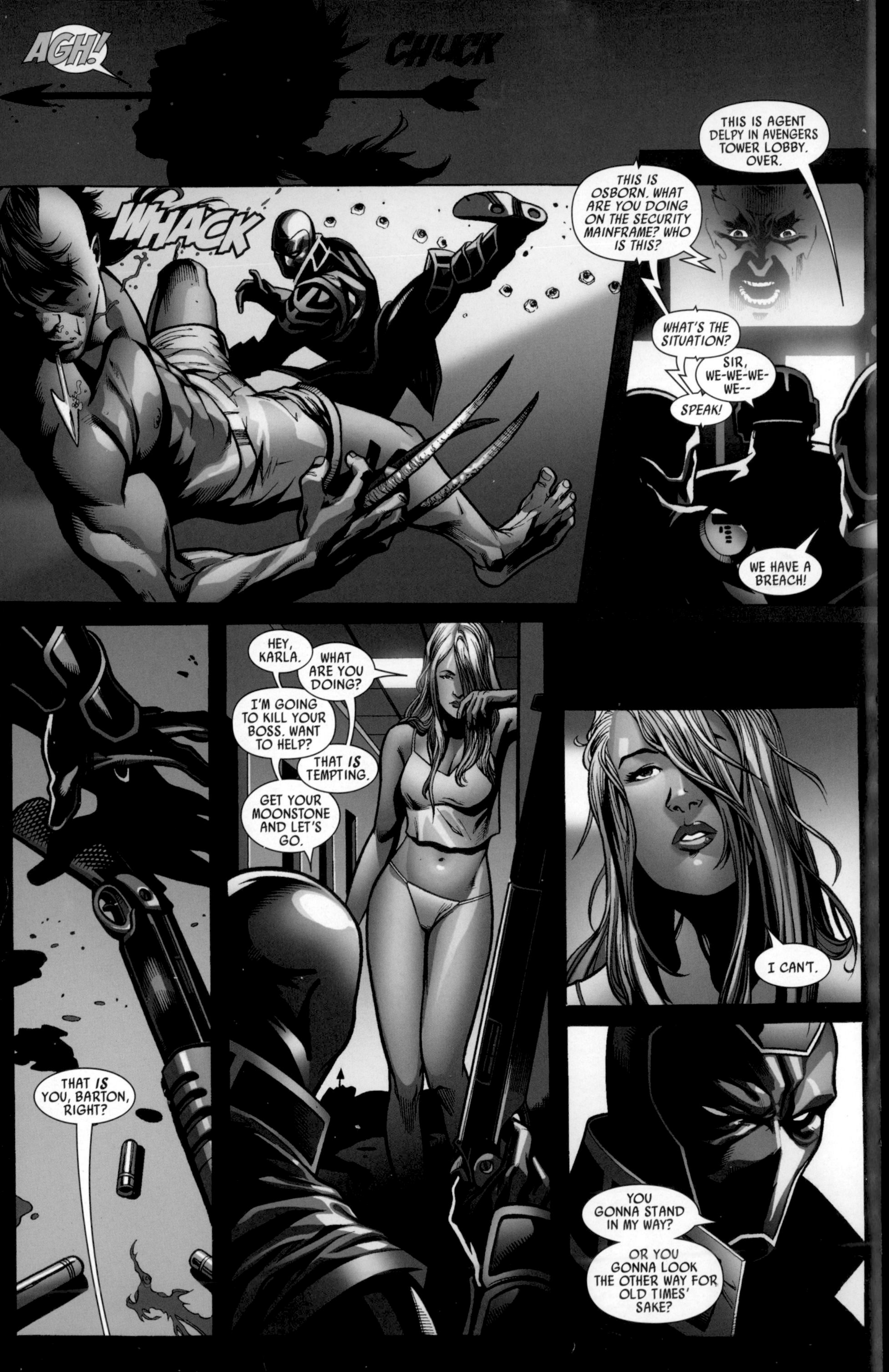
AGH!
CHUCK
WHACK
THIS IS AGENT DELPY IN AVENGERS TOWER LOBBY. OVER.
THIS IS OSBORN. WHAT ARE YOU DOING ON THE SECURITY MAINFRAME? WHO IS THIS?
WHAT'S THE SITUATION?
SIR, WE-WE-WE-WE--
SPEAK!
WE HAVE A BREACH!
THAT IS YOU, BARTON, RIGHT?
HEY, KARLA.
WHAT ARE YOU DOING?
I'M GOING TO KILL YOUR BOSS. WANT TO HELP?
THAT IS TEMPTING.
GET YOUR MOONSTONE AND LET'S GO.
I CAN'T.
YOU GONNA STAND IN MY WAY?
OR YOU GONNA LOOK THE OTHER WAY FOR OLD TIMES' SAKE?

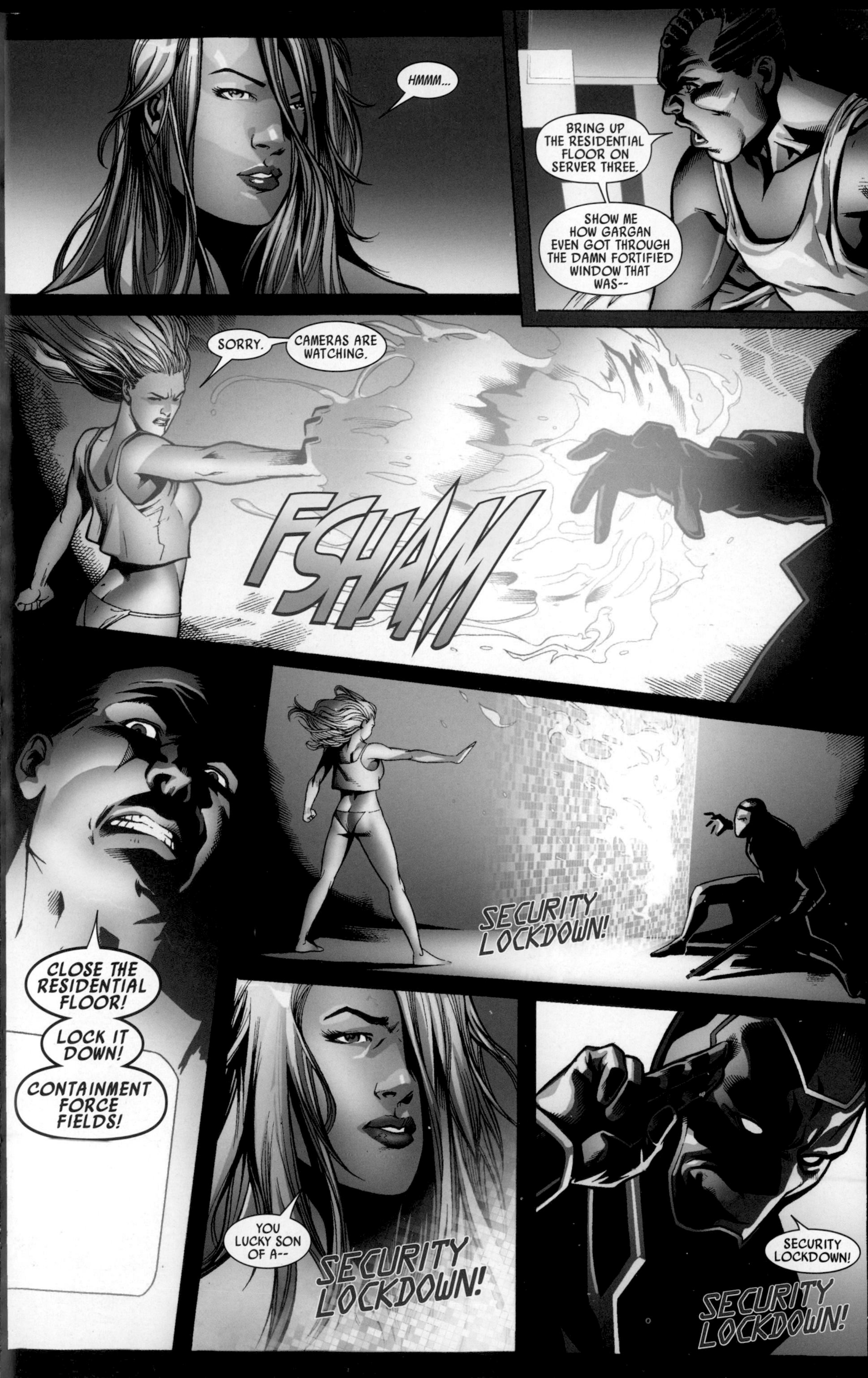
HMMM...
BRING UP THE RESIDENTIAL FLOOR ON SERVER THREE.
SHOW ME HOW GARGAN EVEN GOT THROUGH THE DAMN FORTIFIED WINDOW THAT WAS--
SORRY.
CAMERAS ARE WATCHING.
FSHAM
SECURITY LOCKDOWN!
CLOSE THE RESIDENTIAL FLOOR!
LOCK IT DOWN!
CONTAINMENT FORCE FIELDS!
YOU LUCKY SON OF A--
SECURITY LOCKDOWN!
SECURITY LOCKDOWN!
SECURITY LOCKDOWN!

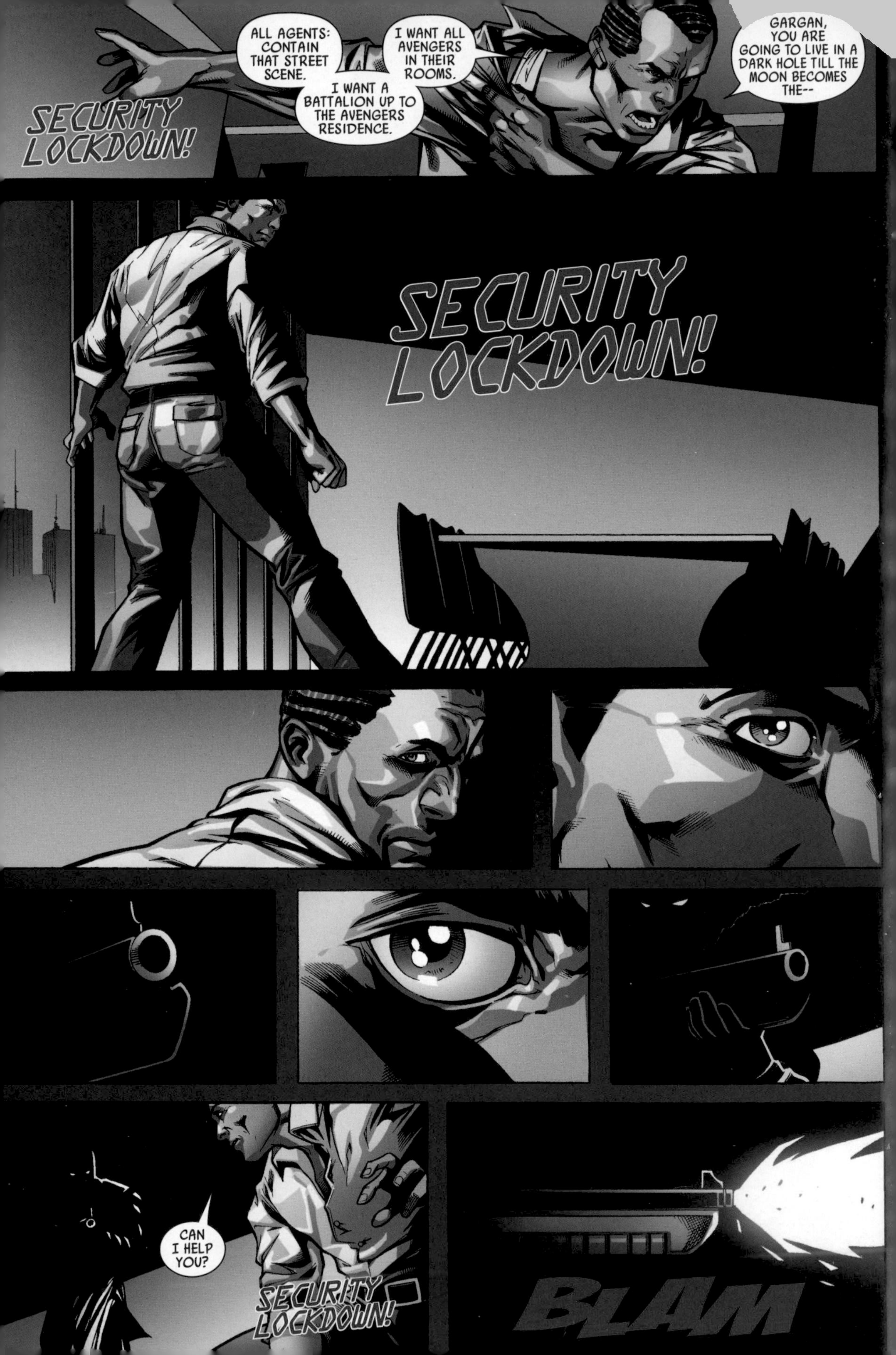
SECURITY LOCKDOWN!
ALL AGENTS: CONTAIN THAT STREET SCENE.
I WANT ALL AVENGERS IN THEIR ROOMS.
I WANT A BATTALION UP TO THE AVENGERS RESIDENCE.
GARGAN, YOU ARE GOING TO LIVE IN A DARK HOLE TILL THE MOON BECOMES THE--
SECURITY LOCKDOWN!
CAN I HELP YOU?
SECURITY LOCKDOWN!
BLAM

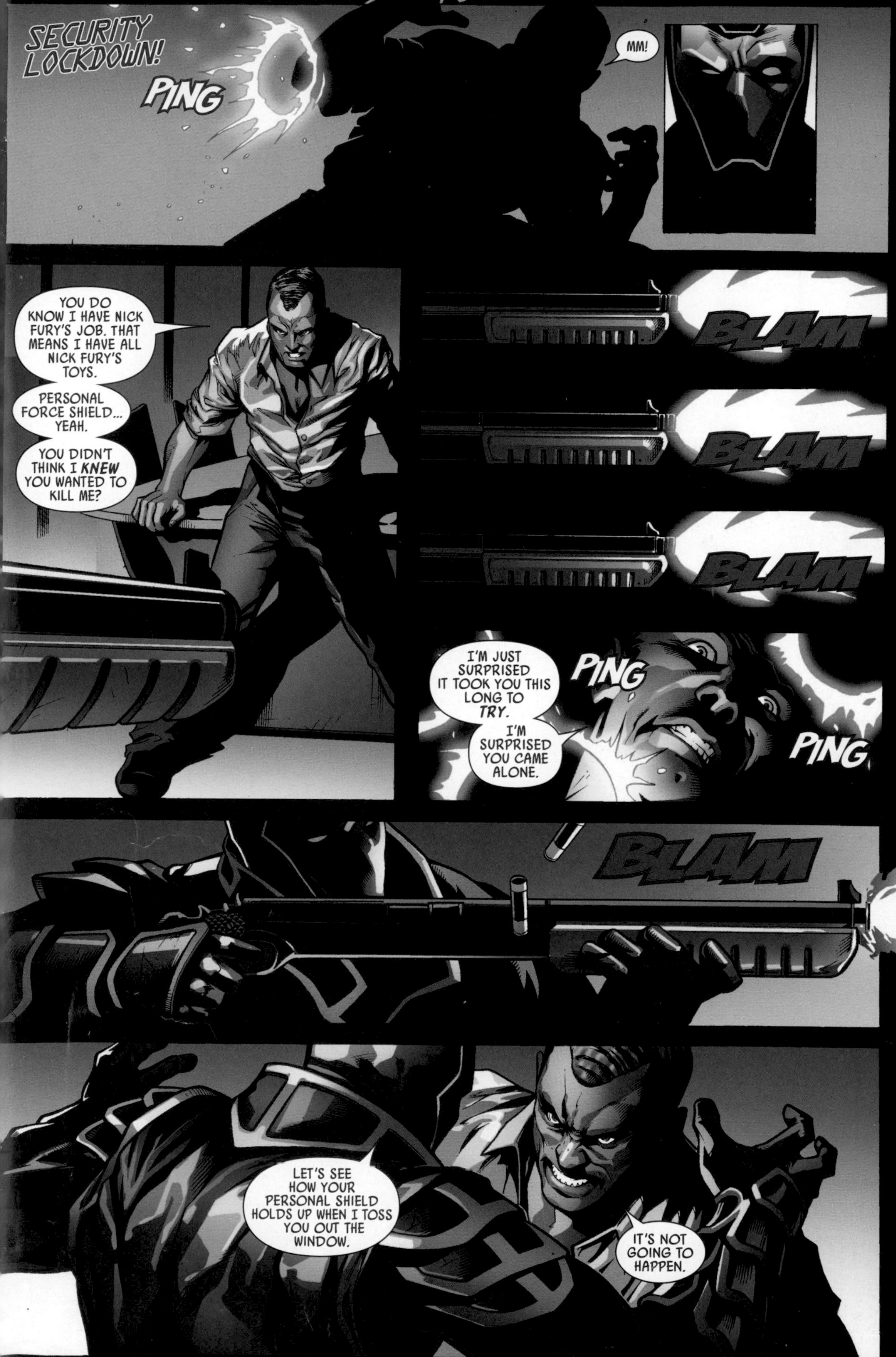
SECURITY LOCKDOWN!
PING
MM!
YOU DO KNOW I HAVE NICK FURY'S JOB. THAT MEANS I HAVE ALL NICK FURY'S TOYS.
PERSONAL FORCE SHIELD... YEAH.
YOU DIDN'T THINK I *KNEW* YOU WANTED TO KILL ME?
BLAM
BLAM
BLAM
I'M JUST SURPRISED IT TOOK YOU THIS LONG TO *TRY*.
I'M SURPRISED YOU CAME ALONE.
PING
PING
BLAM
LET'S SEE HOW YOUR PERSONAL SHIELD HOLDS UP WHEN I TOSS YOU OUT THE WINDOW.
IT'S NOT GOING TO HAPPEN.

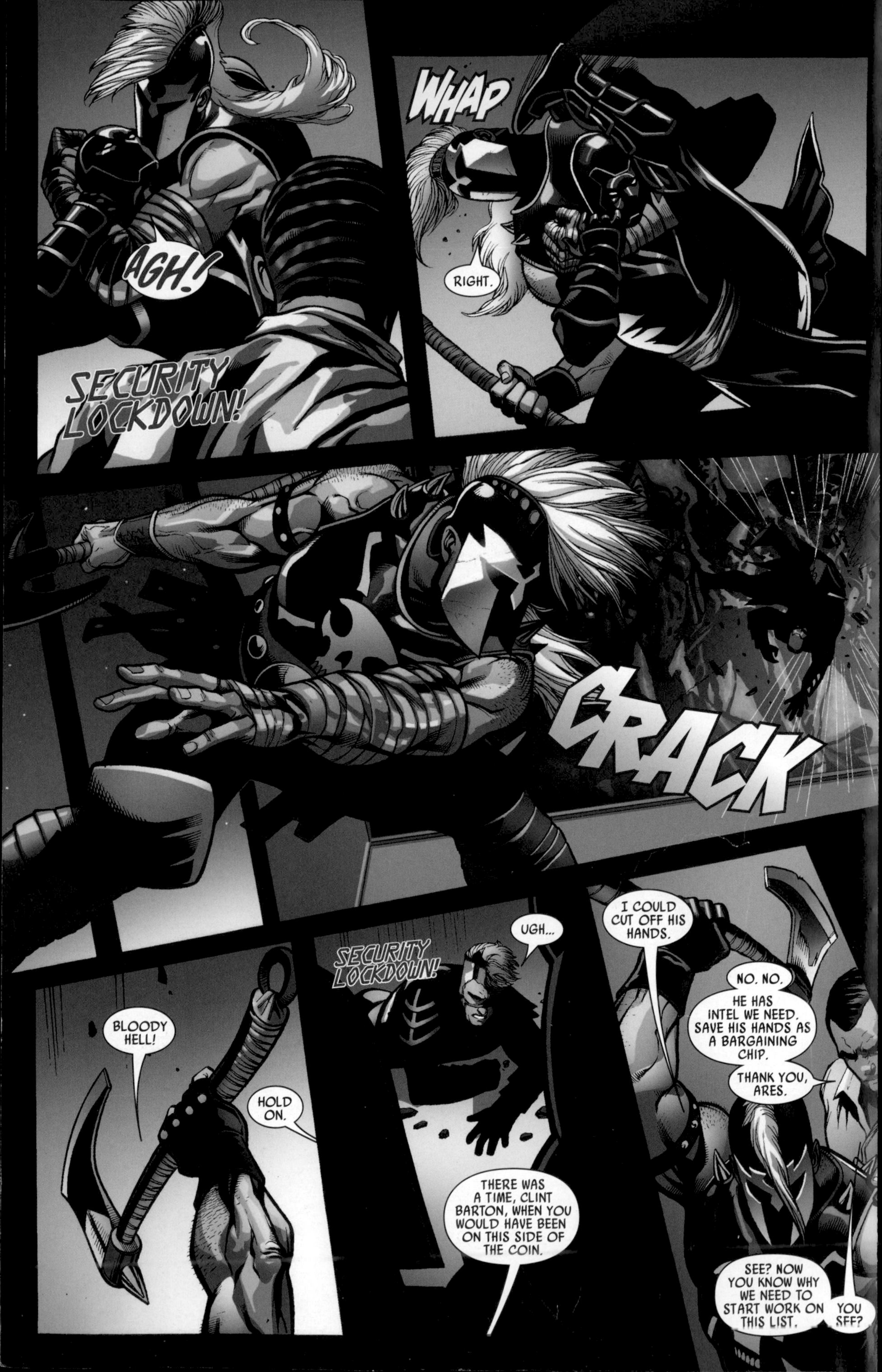
AGH!
SECURITY LOCKDOWN!
WHAP
RIGHT.
CRACK
BLOODY HELL!
HOLD ON.
SECURITY LOCKDOWN!
UGH...
THERE WAS A TIME, CLINT BARTON, WHEN YOU WOULD HAVE BEEN ON THIS SIDE OF THE COIN.
I COULD CUT OFF HIS HANDS.
NO. NO.
HE HAS INTEL WE NEED. SAVE HIS HANDS AS A BARGAINING CHIP.
THANK YOU, ARES.
SEE? NOW YOU KNOW WHY WE NEED TO START WORK ON THIS LIST.
YOU SEE?

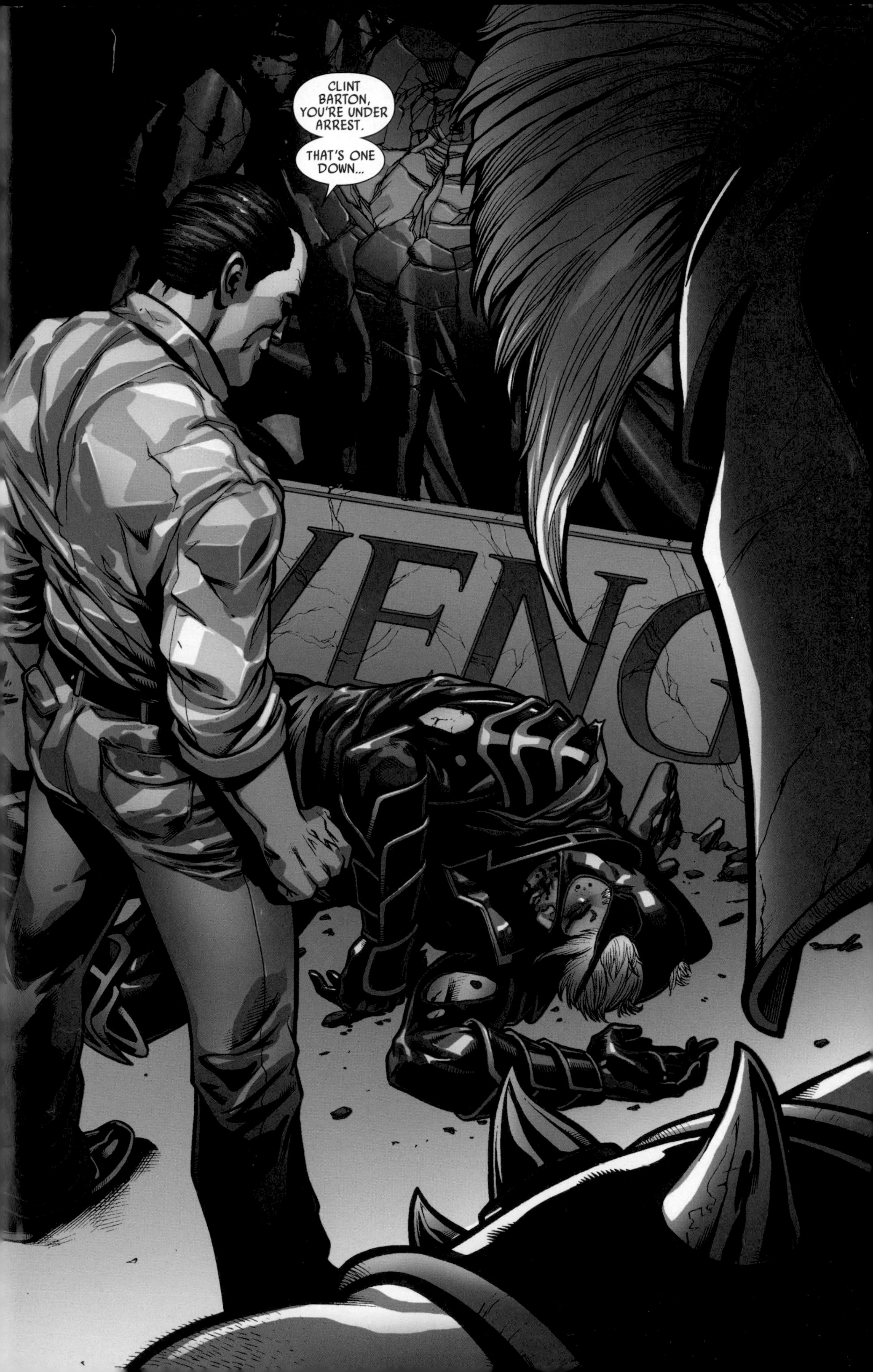
CLINT BARTON, YOU'RE UNDER ARREST.
THAT'S ONE DOWN...

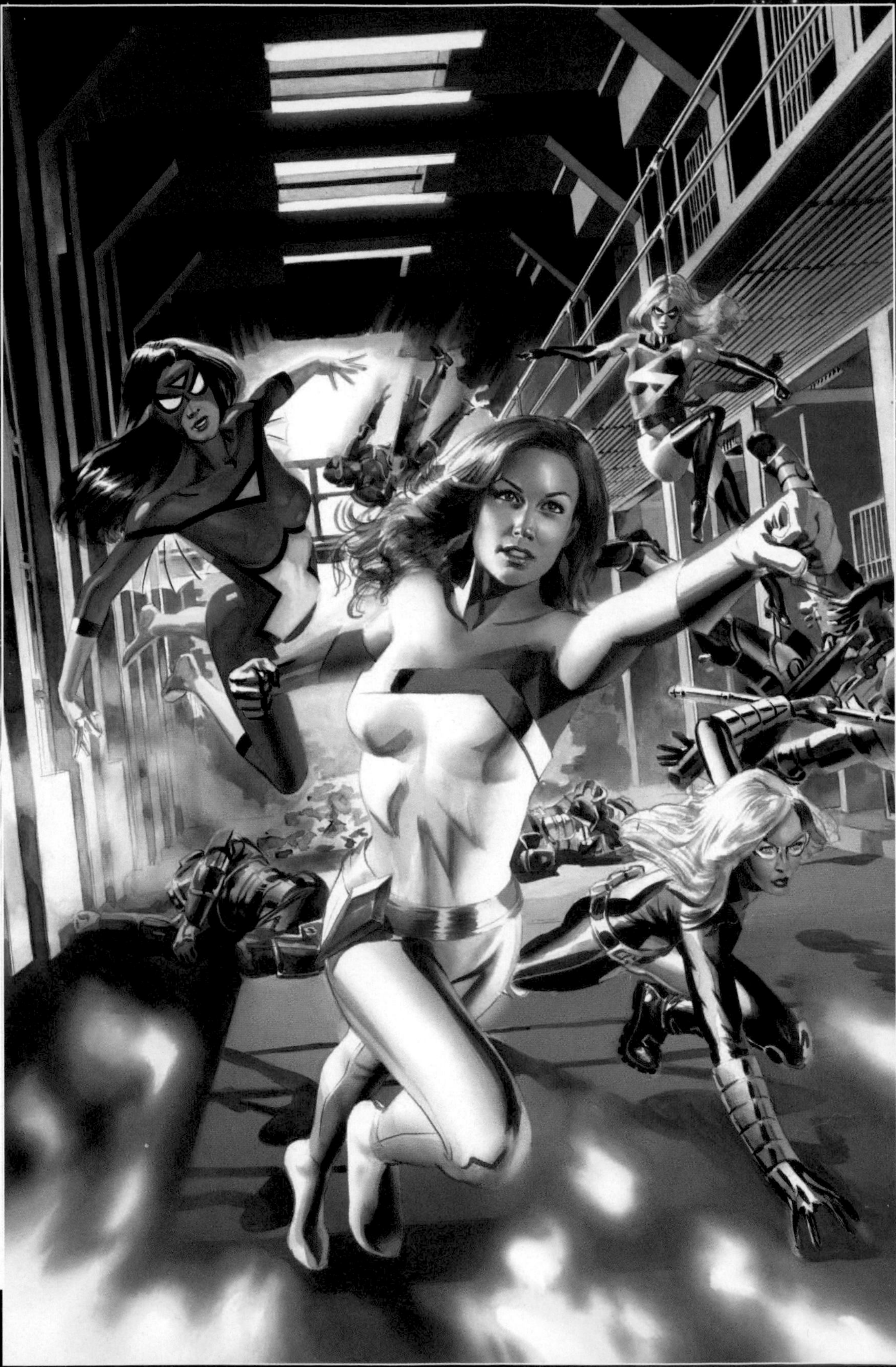

NEW AVENGERS ANNUAL #3

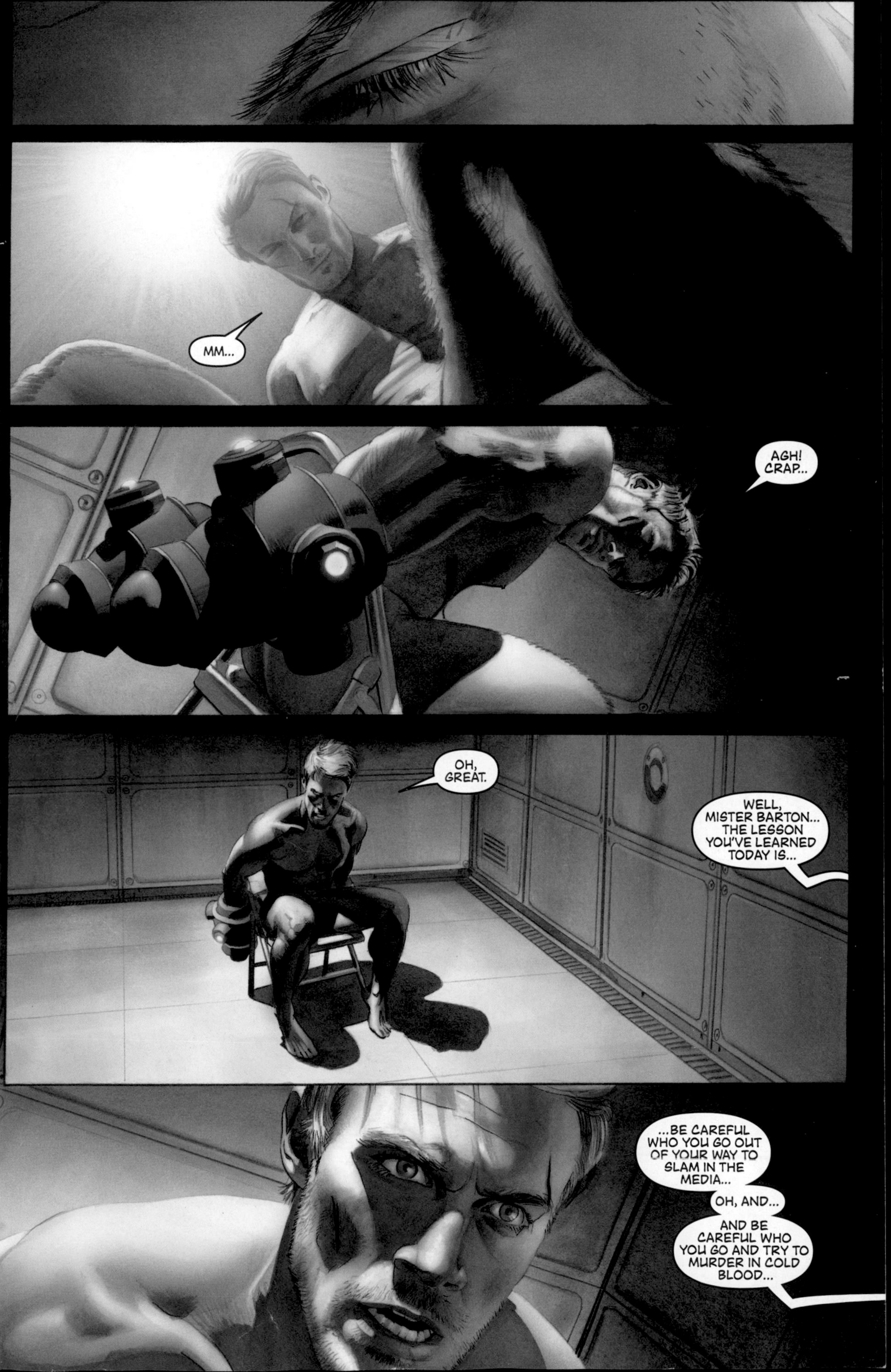
MM...
AGH! CRAP...
OH, GREAT.
WELL, MISTER BARTON... THE LESSON YOU'VE LEARNED TODAY IS...
...BE CAREFUL WHO YOU GO OUT OF YOUR WAY TO SLAM IN THE MEDIA...
OH, AND...
AND BE CAREFUL WHO YOU GO AND TRY TO MURDER IN COLD BLOOD...

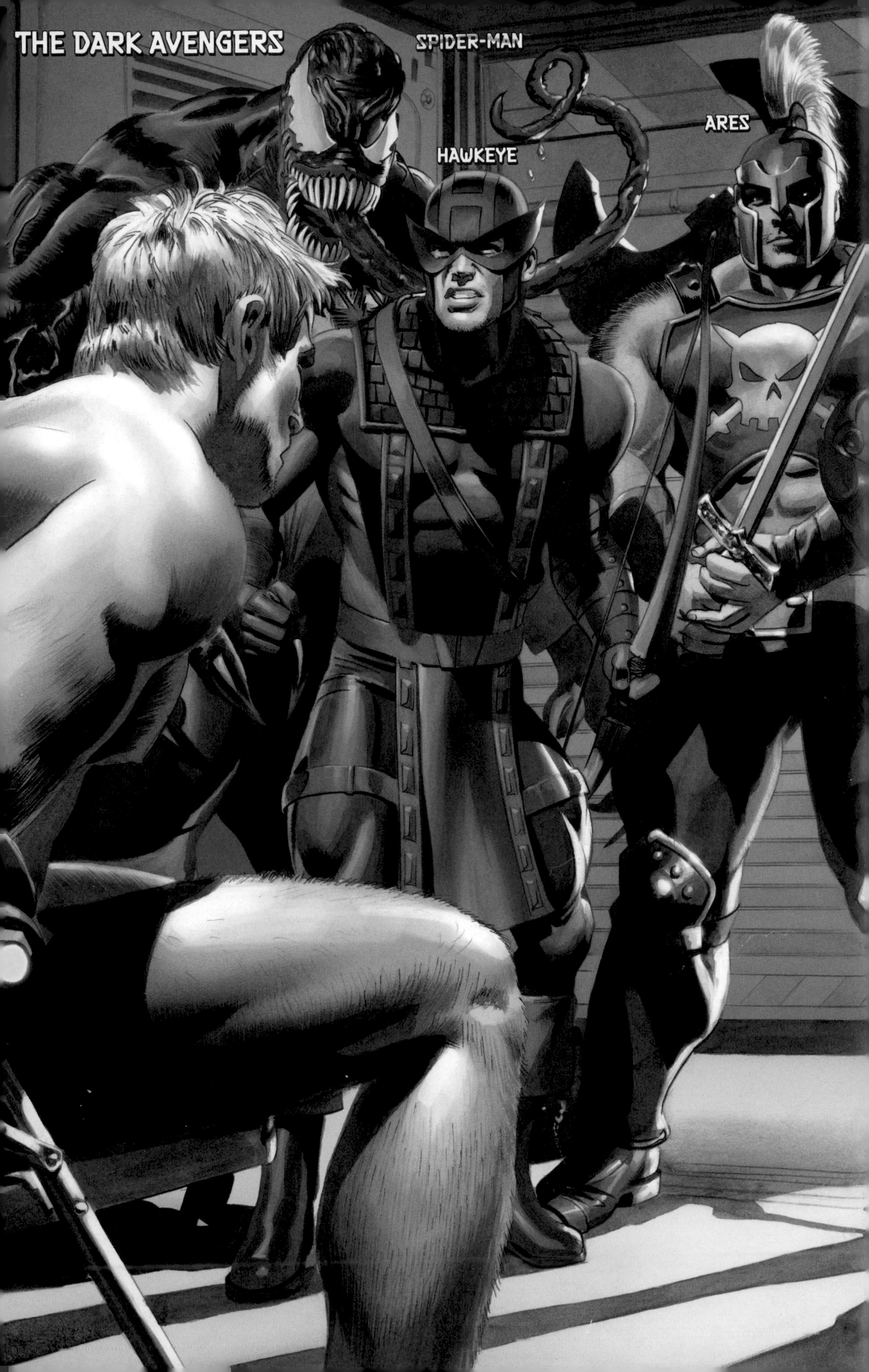
THE DARK AVENGERS
SPIDER-MAN
HAWKEYE
ARES

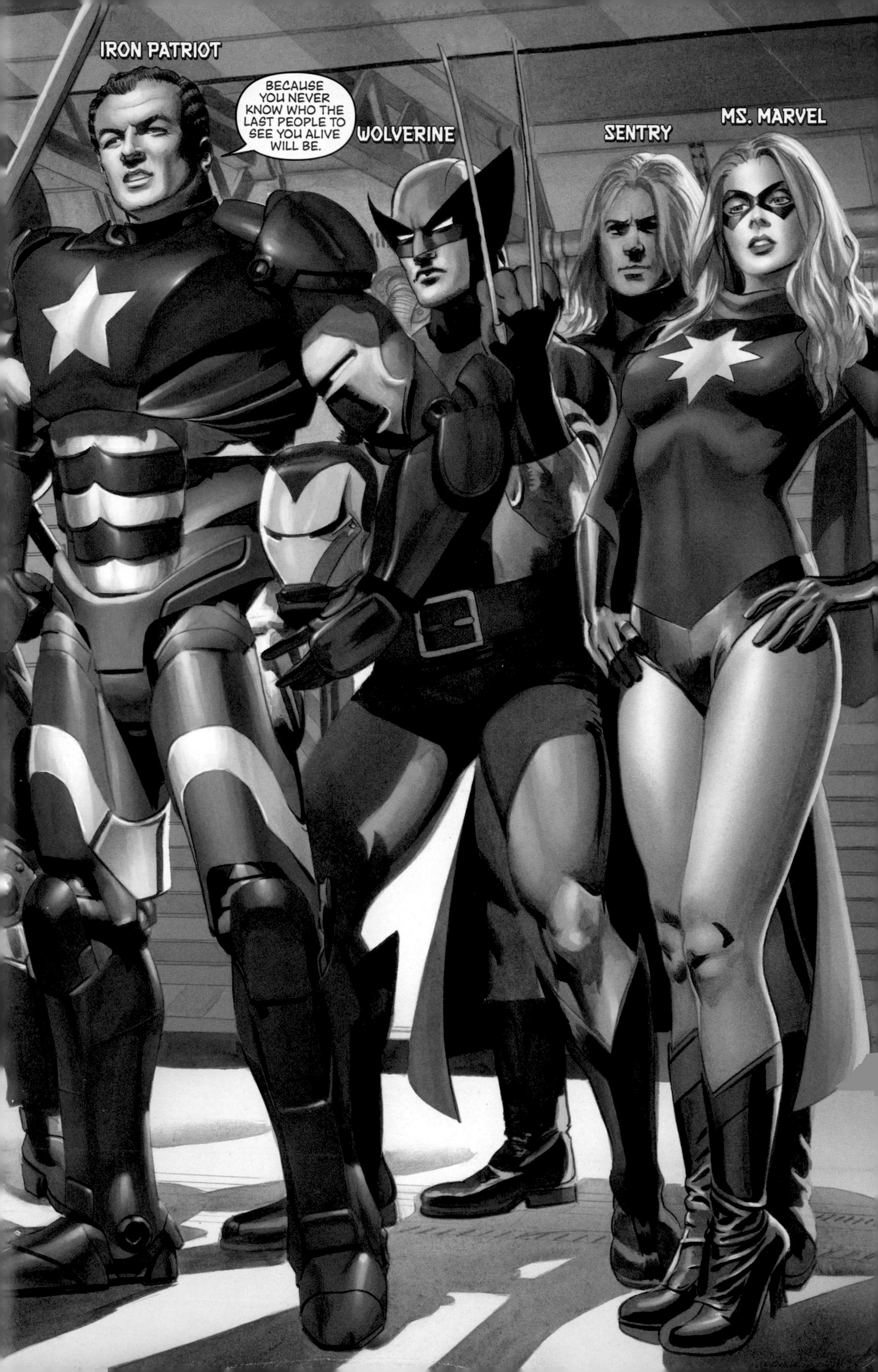
IRON PATRIOT
BECAUSE YOU NEVER KNOW WHO THE LAST PEOPLE TO SEE YOU ALIVE WILL BE.
WOLVERINE
SENTRY
MS. MARVEL

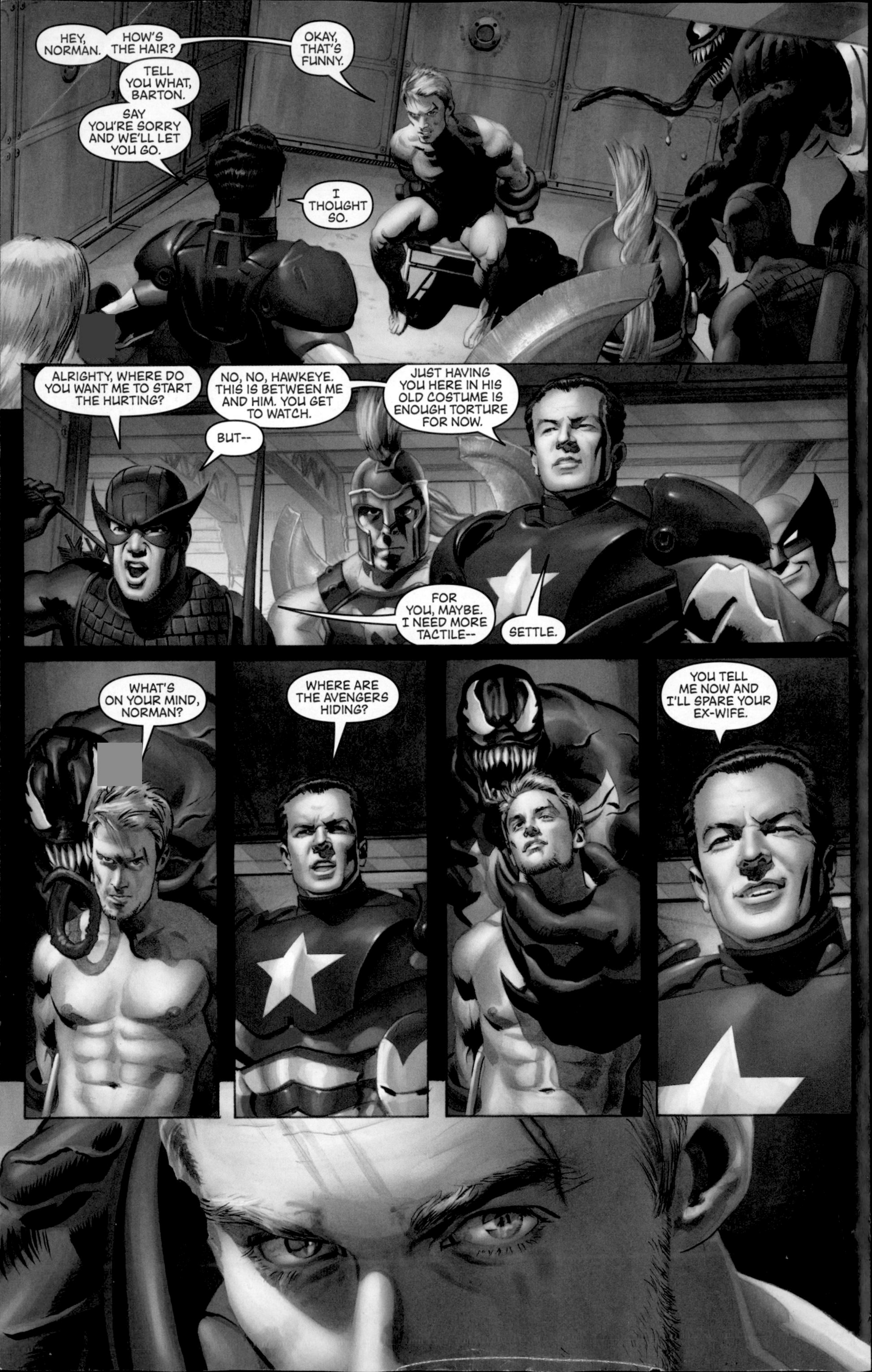
HEY, NORMAN.
HOW'S THE HAIR?
OKAY, THAT'S FUNNY.
TELL YOU WHAT, BARTON.
SAY YOU'RE SORRY AND WE'LL LET YOU GO.
I THOUGHT SO.
ALRIGHTY, WHERE DO YOU WANT ME TO START THE HURTING?
NO, NO, HAWKEYE. THIS IS BETWEEN ME AND HIM. YOU GET TO WATCH.
BUT--
JUST HAVING YOU HERE IN HIS OLD COSTUME IS ENOUGH TORTURE FOR NOW.
FOR YOU, MAYBE. I NEED MORE TACTILE--
SETTLE.
WHAT'S ON YOUR MIND, NORMAN?
WHERE ARE THE AVENGERS HIDING?
YOU TELL ME NOW AND I'LL SPARE YOUR EX-WIFE.

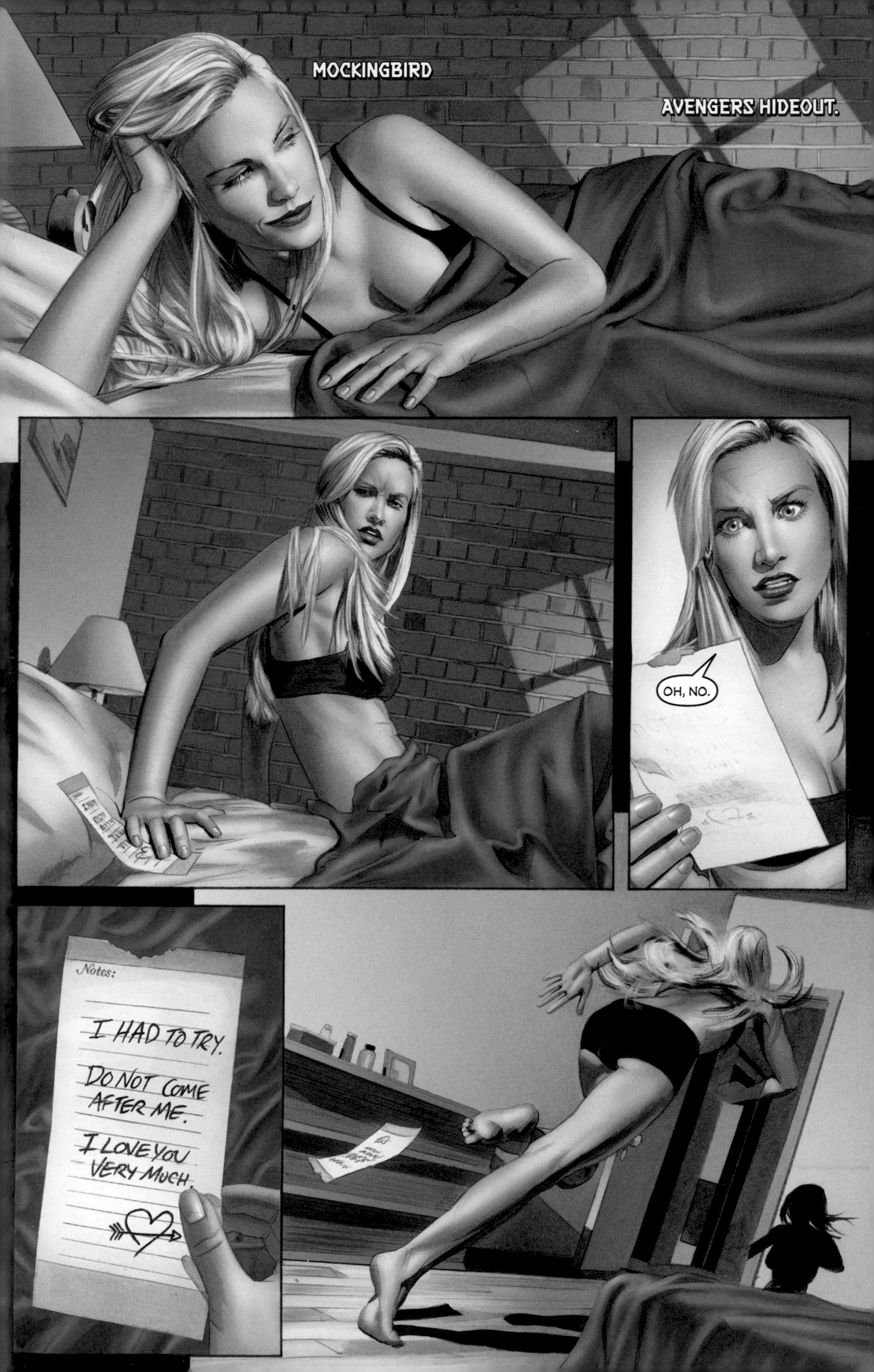
MOCKINGBIRD
AVENGERS HIDEOUT.
OH, NO.
Notes:
I HAD TO TRY.
DO NOT COME AFTER ME.
I LOVE YOU VERY MUCH.

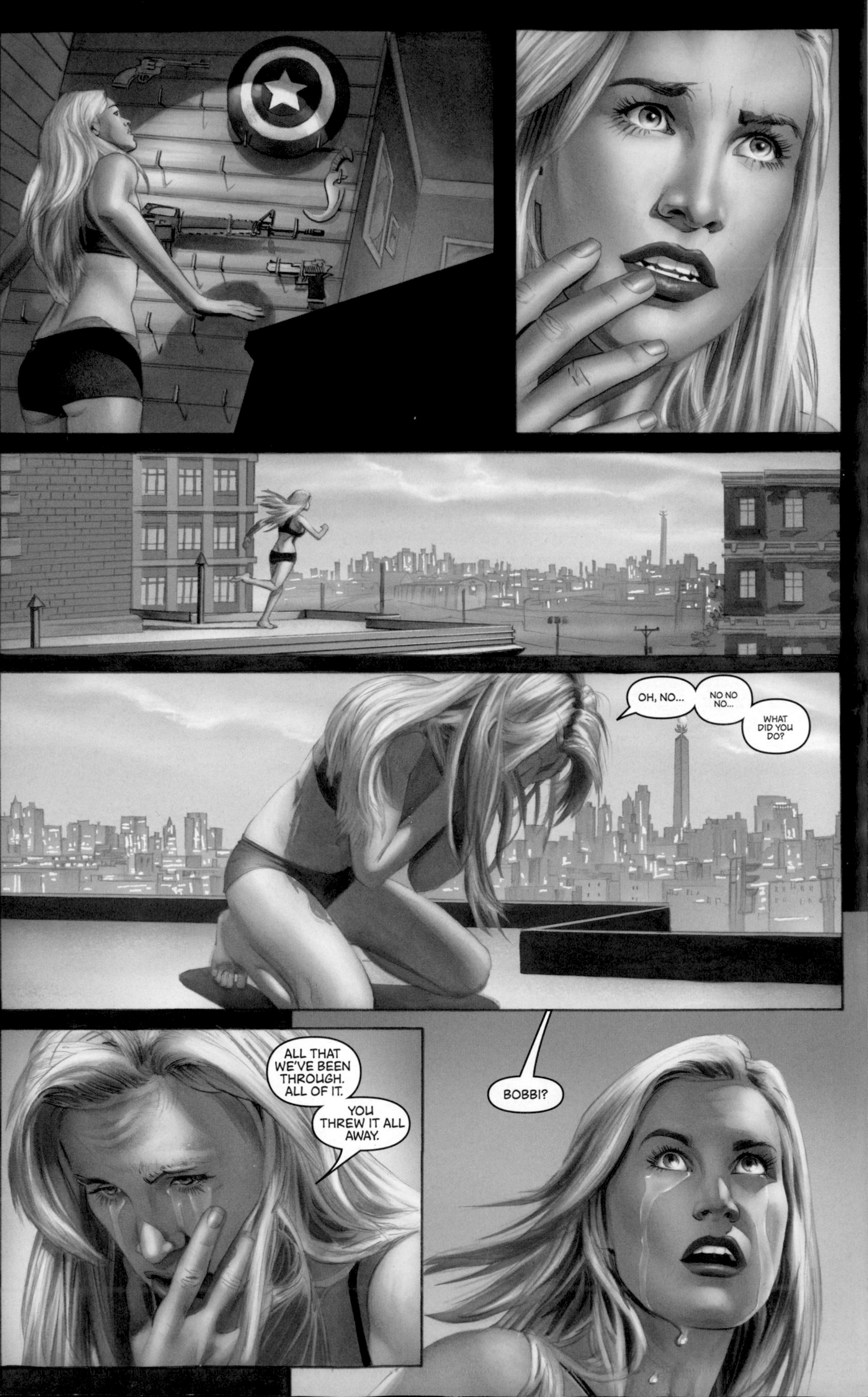
OH, NO...
NO NO NO...
WHAT DID YOU DO?
BOBBI?
ALL THAT WE'VE BEEN THROUGH. ALL OF IT.
YOU THREW IT ALL AWAY.

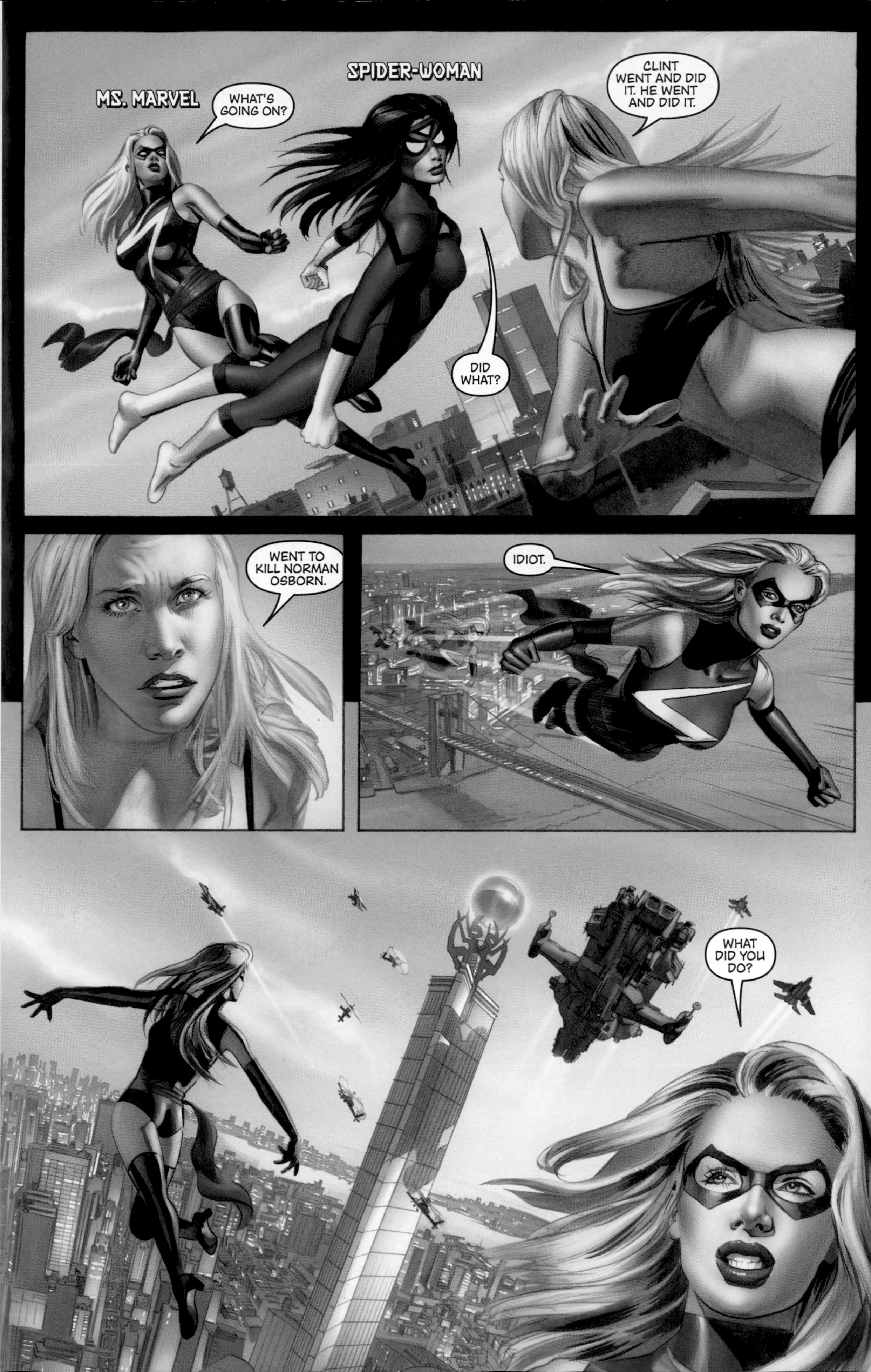
SPIDER-WOMAN
MS. MARVEL
WHAT'S GOING ON?
CLINT WENT AND DID IT. HE WENT AND DID IT.
DID WHAT?
WENT TO KILL NORMAN OSBORN.
IDIOT.
WHAT DID YOU DO?

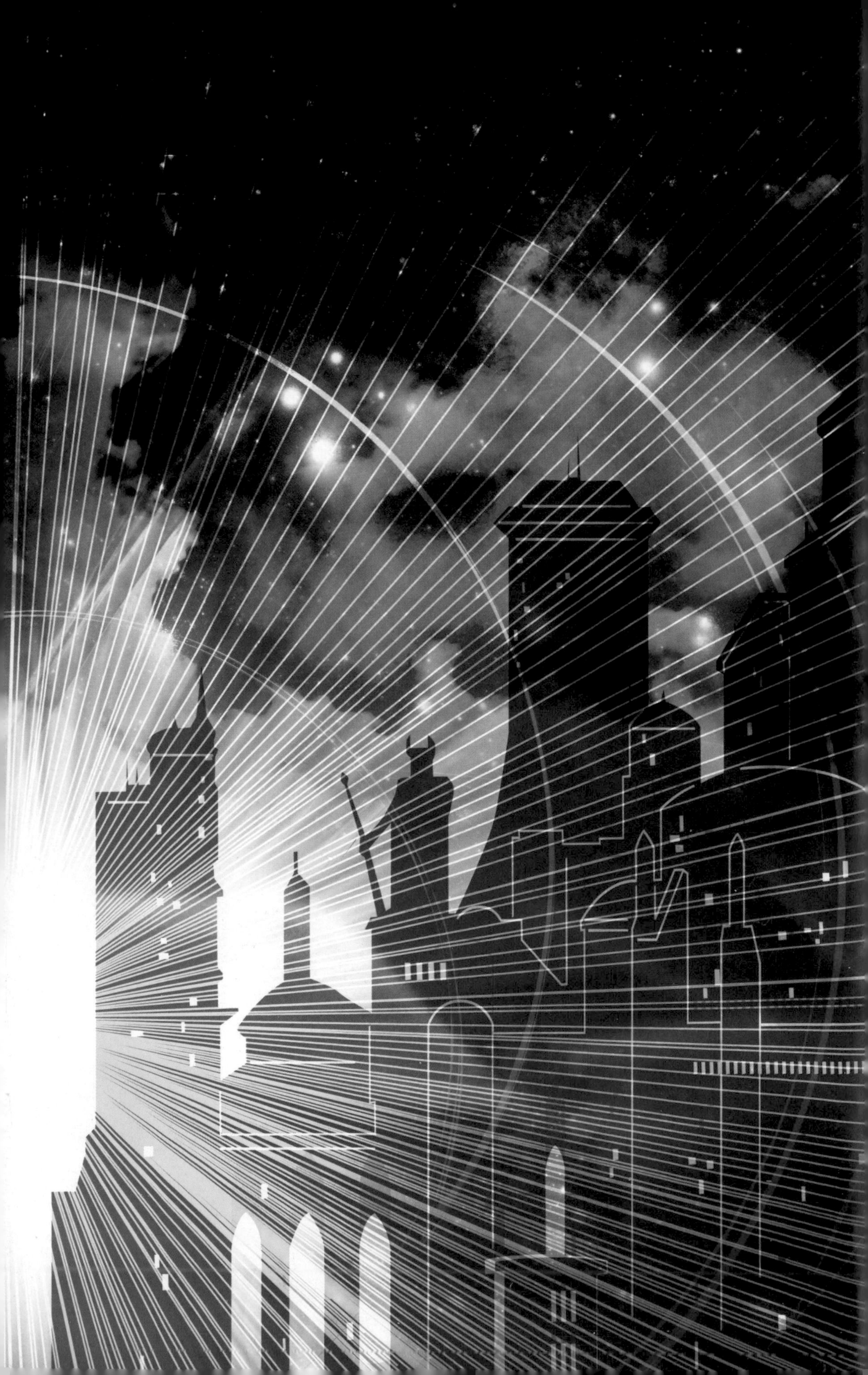

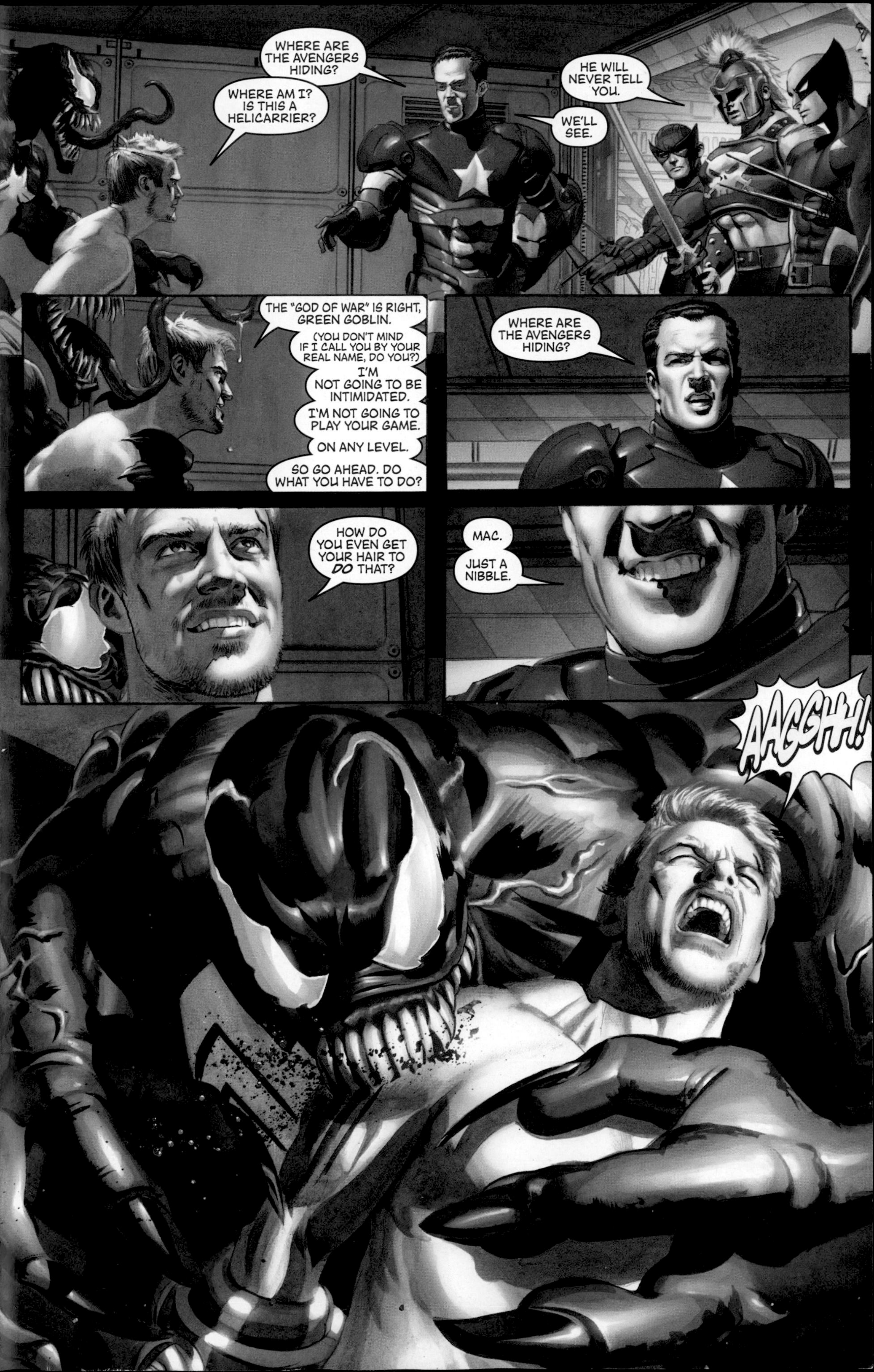
WHERE ARE THE AVENGERS HIDING?
WHERE AM I? IS THIS A HELICARRIER?
HE WILL NEVER TELL YOU.
WE'LL SEE.
THE "GOD OF WAR" IS RIGHT, GREEN GOBLIN.
(YOU DON'T MIND IF I CALL YOU BY YOUR REAL NAME, DO YOU?)
I'M NOT GOING TO BE INTIMIDATED.
I'M NOT GOING TO PLAY YOUR GAME.
ON ANY LEVEL.
SO GO AHEAD. DO WHAT YOU HAVE TO DO?
WHERE ARE THE AVENGERS HIDING?
HOW DO YOU EVEN GET YOUR HAIR TO DO THAT?
MAC.
JUST A NIBBLE.
AAGGHH!

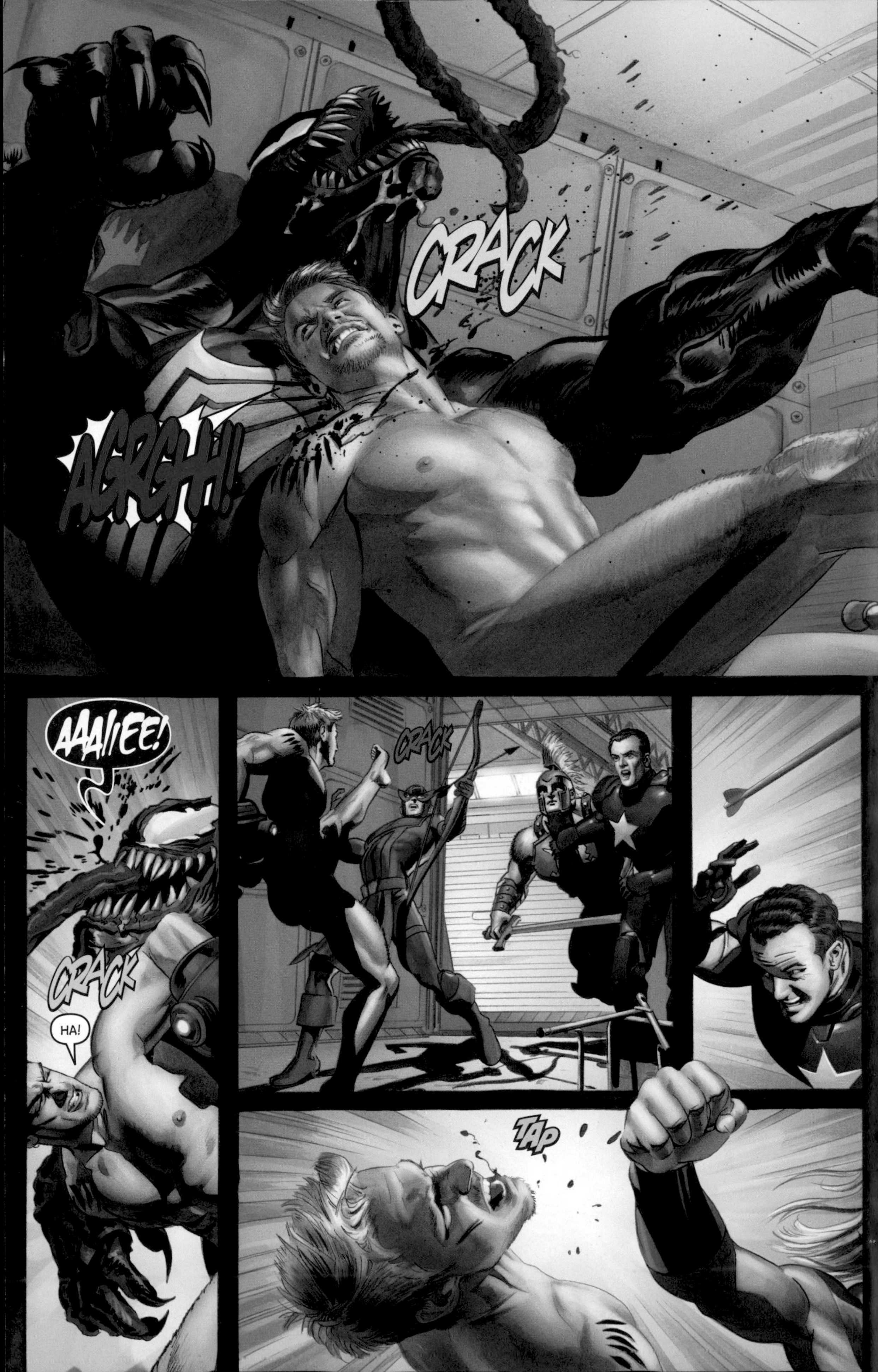
CRACK
AGRGH!
AAAIIEE!
CRACK
HA!
CRACK
TAP

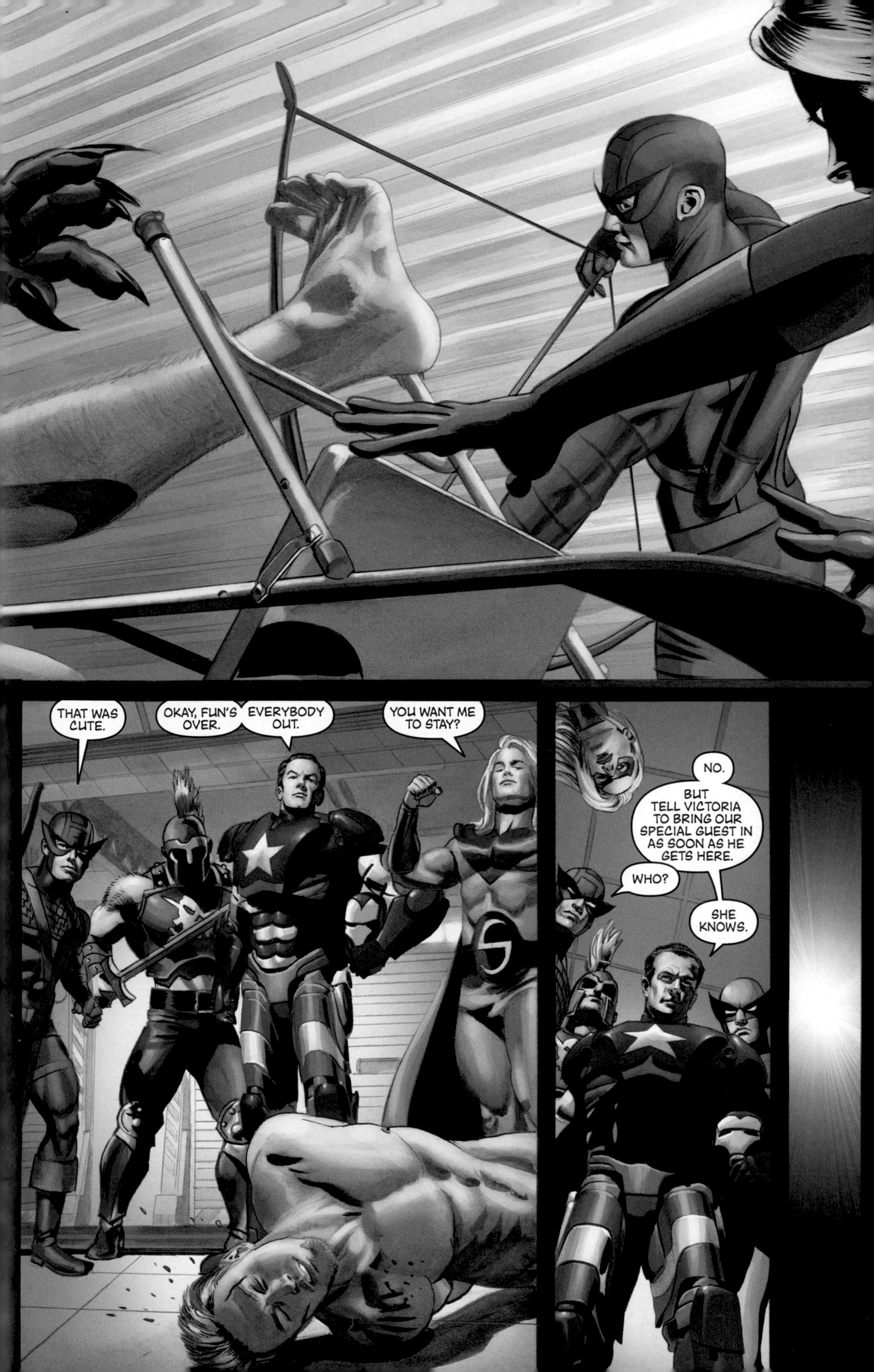
THAT WAS CUTE.
OKAY, FUN'S OVER.
EVERYBODY OUT.
YOU WANT ME TO STAY?
NO.
BUT TELL VICTORIA TO BRING OUR SPECIAL GUEST IN AS SOON AS HE GETS HERE.
WHO?
SHE KNOWS.

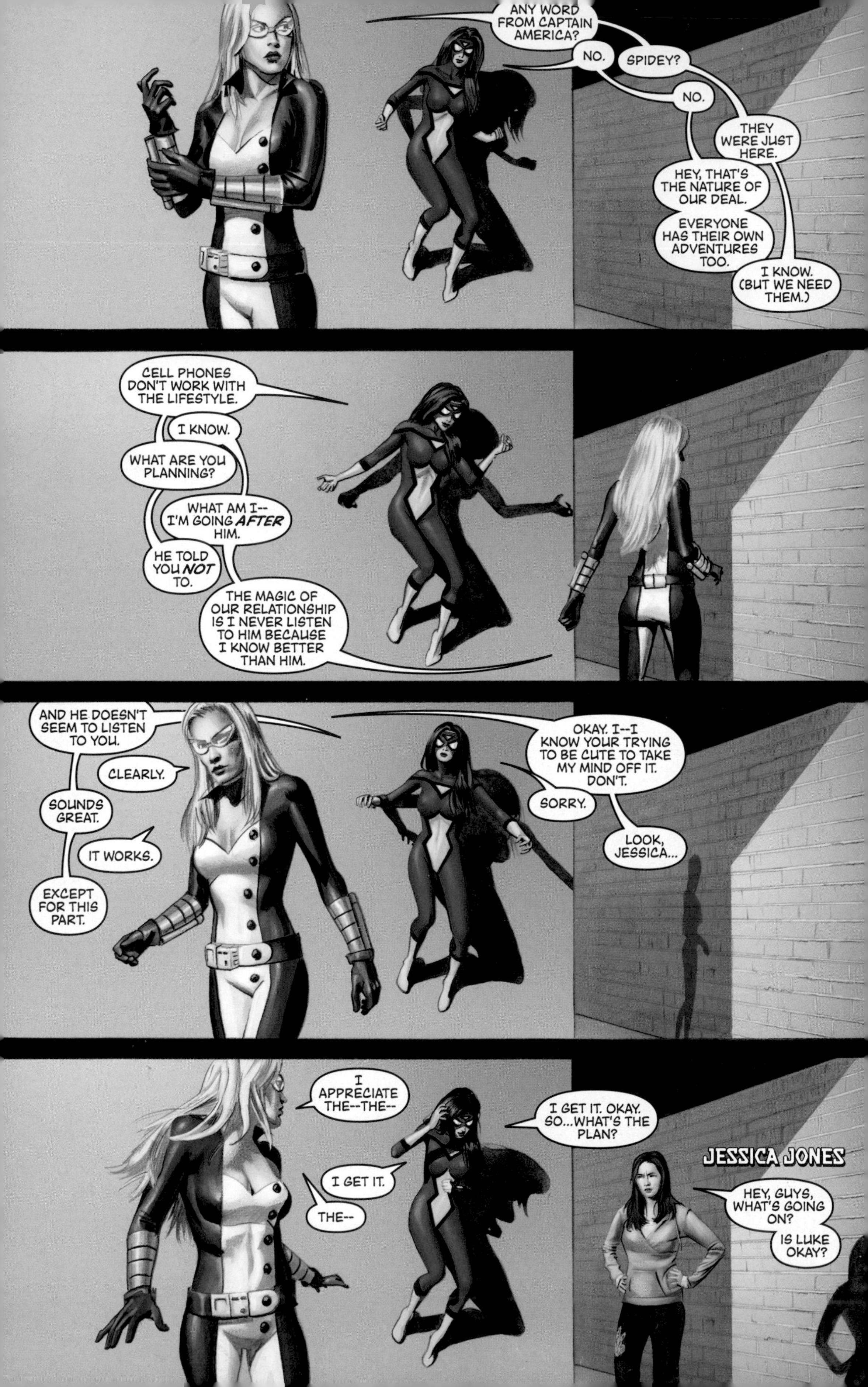
ANY WORD FROM CAPTAIN AMERICA?
NO.
SPIDEY?
NO.
THEY WERE JUST HERE.
HEY, THAT'S THE NATURE OF OUR DEAL.
EVERYONE HAS THEIR OWN ADVENTURES TOO.
I KNOW. (BUT WE NEED THEM.)
CELL PHONES DON'T WORK WITH THE LIFESTYLE.
I KNOW.
WHAT ARE YOU PLANNING?
WHAT AM I-- I'M GOING AFTER HIM.
HE TOLD YOU NOT TO.
THE MAGIC OF OUR RELATIONSHIP IS I NEVER LISTEN TO HIM BECAUSE I KNOW BETTER THAN HIM.
AND HE DOESN'T SEEM TO LISTEN TO YOU.
CLEARLY.
SOUNDS GREAT.
IT WORKS.
EXCEPT FOR THIS PART.
OKAY. I--I KNOW YOUR TRYING TO BE CUTE TO TAKE MY MIND OFF IT. DON'T.
SORRY.
LOOK, JESSICA...
I APPRECIATE THE--THE--
I GET IT.
THE--
I GET IT. OKAY. SO...WHAT'S THE PLAN?
JESSICA JONES
HEY, GUYS, WHAT'S GOING ON?
IS LUKE OKAY?

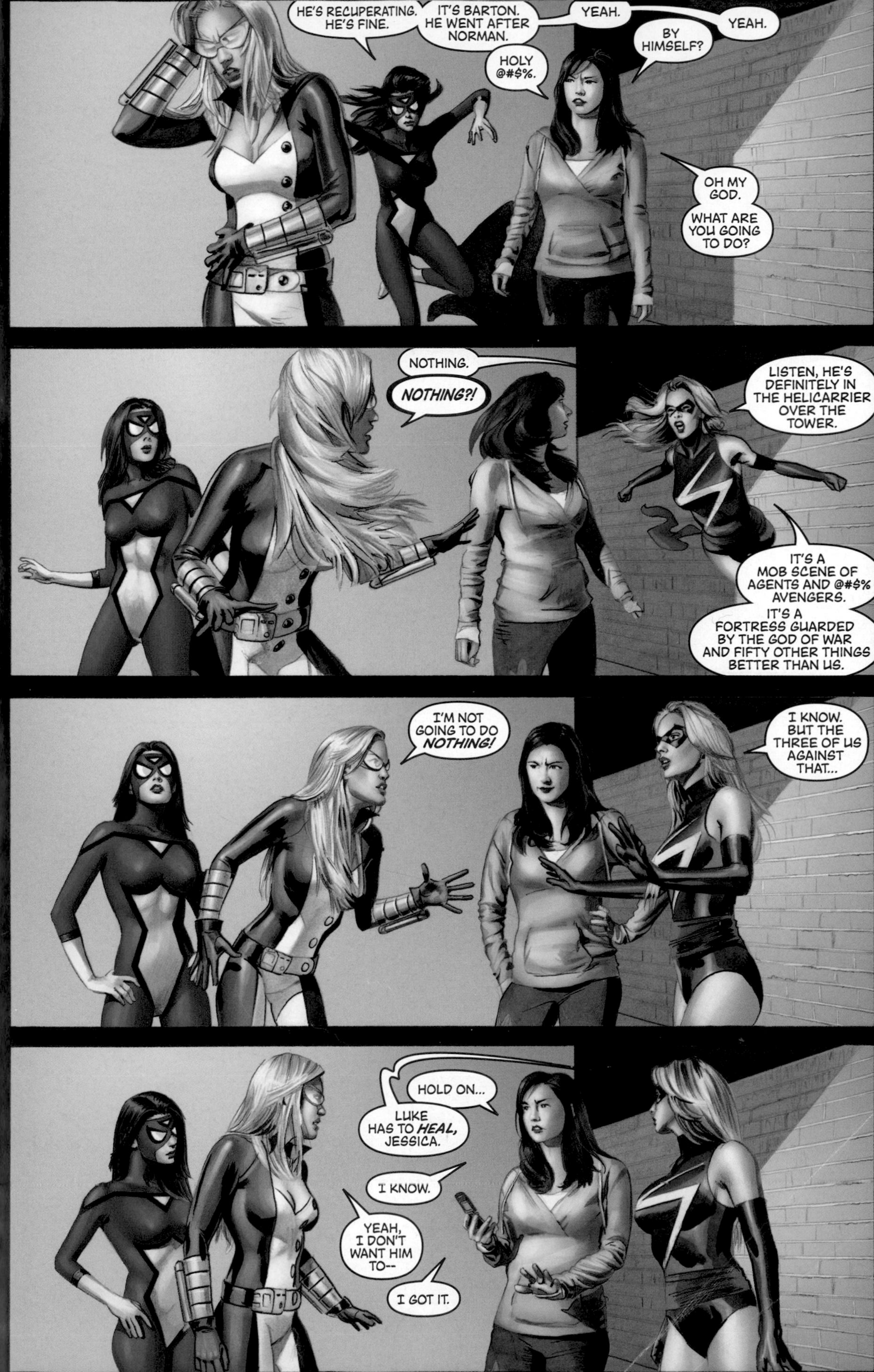

HE'S RECUPERATING. HE'S FINE.
IT'S BARTON. HE WENT AFTER NORMAN.
YEAH.
YEAH.
BY HIMSELF?
HOLY @#$%.
OH MY GOD.
WHAT ARE YOU GOING TO DO?
NOTHING.
NOTHING?!
LISTEN, HE'S DEFINITELY IN THE HELICARRIER OVER THE TOWER.
IT'S A MOB SCENE OF AGENTS AND @#$% AVENGERS.
IT'S A FORTRESS GUARDED BY THE GOD OF WAR AND FIFTY OTHER THINGS BETTER THAN US.
I'M NOT GOING TO DO NOTHING!
I KNOW. BUT THE THREE OF US AGAINST THAT...
HOLD ON...
LUKE HAS TO HEAL, JESSICA.
I KNOW.
YEAH, I DON'T WANT HIM TO--
I GOT IT.

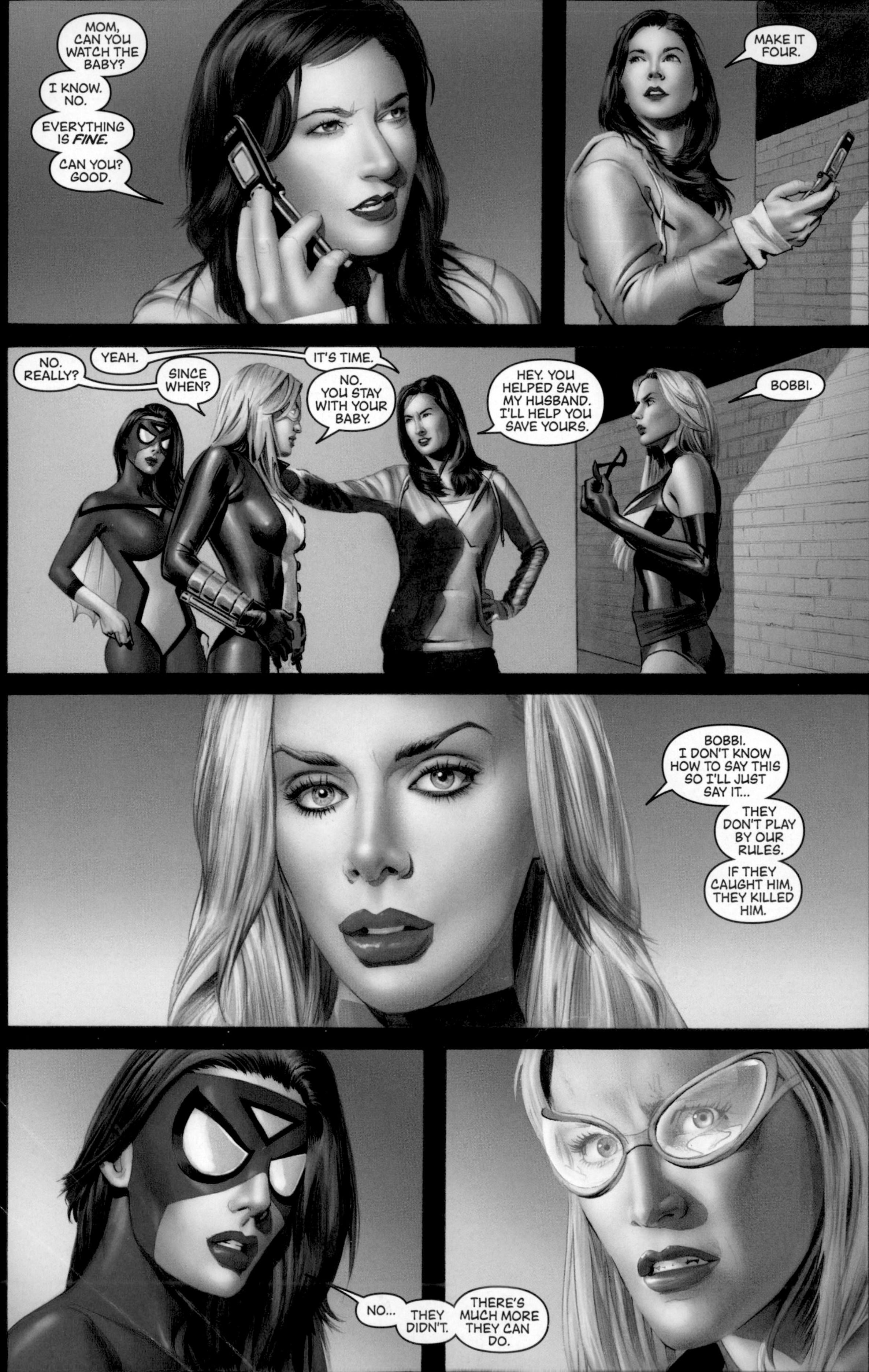
MOM, CAN YOU WATCH THE BABY?
I KNOW. NO.
EVERYTHING IS *FINE.*
CAN YOU? GOOD.
MAKE IT FOUR.
YEAH.
NO. REALLY?
SINCE WHEN?
IT'S TIME.
NO. YOU STAY WITH YOUR BABY.
HEY. YOU HELPED SAVE MY HUSBAND. I'LL HELP YOU SAVE YOURS.
BOBBI.
BOBBI. I DON'T KNOW HOW TO SAY THIS SO I'LL JUST SAY IT...
THEY DON'T PLAY BY OUR RULES.
IF THEY CAUGHT HIM, THEY KILLED HIM.
NO...
THEY DIDN'T.
THERE'S MUCH MORE THEY CAN DO.

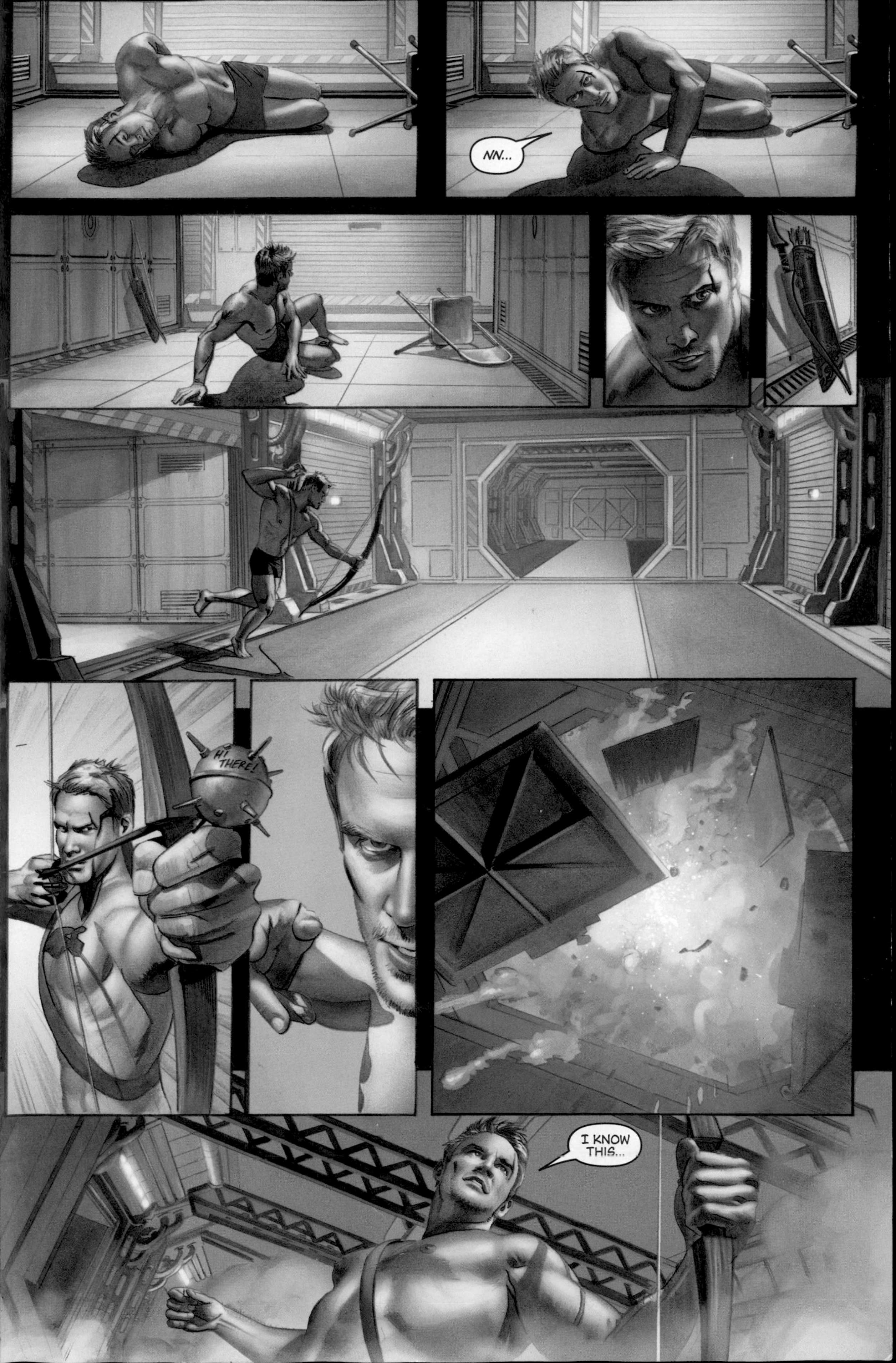
NN...
HI THERE!
I KNOW THIS...

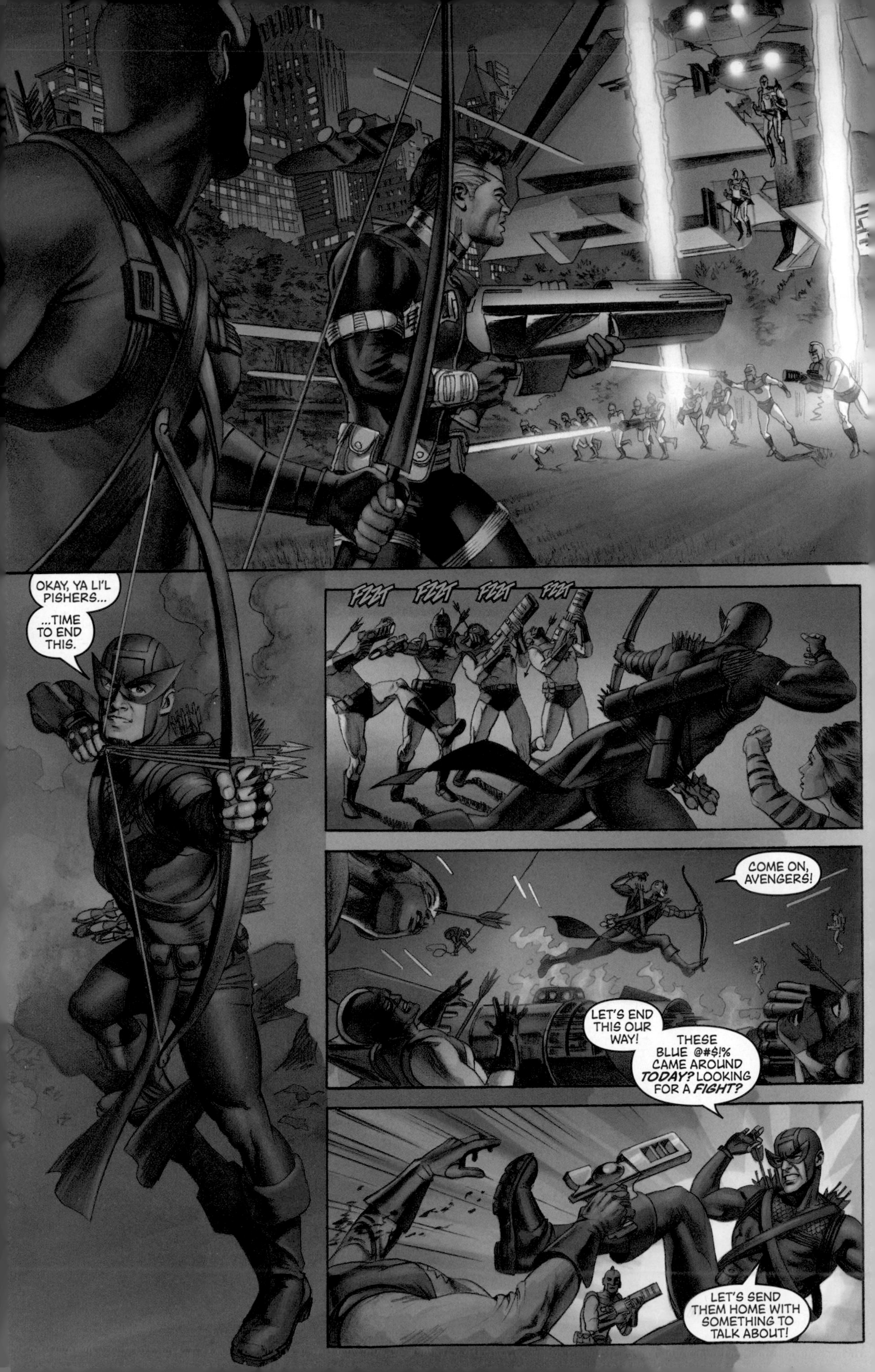
OKAY, YA LI'L PISHERS...
...TIME TO END THIS.
FZZT FZZT FZZT FZZT
COME ON, AVENGERS!
LET'S END THIS OUR WAY!
THESE BLUE @#$!% CAME AROUND *TODAY?* LOOKING FOR A *FIGHT?*
LET'S SEND THEM HOME WITH SOMETHING TO TALK ABOUT!

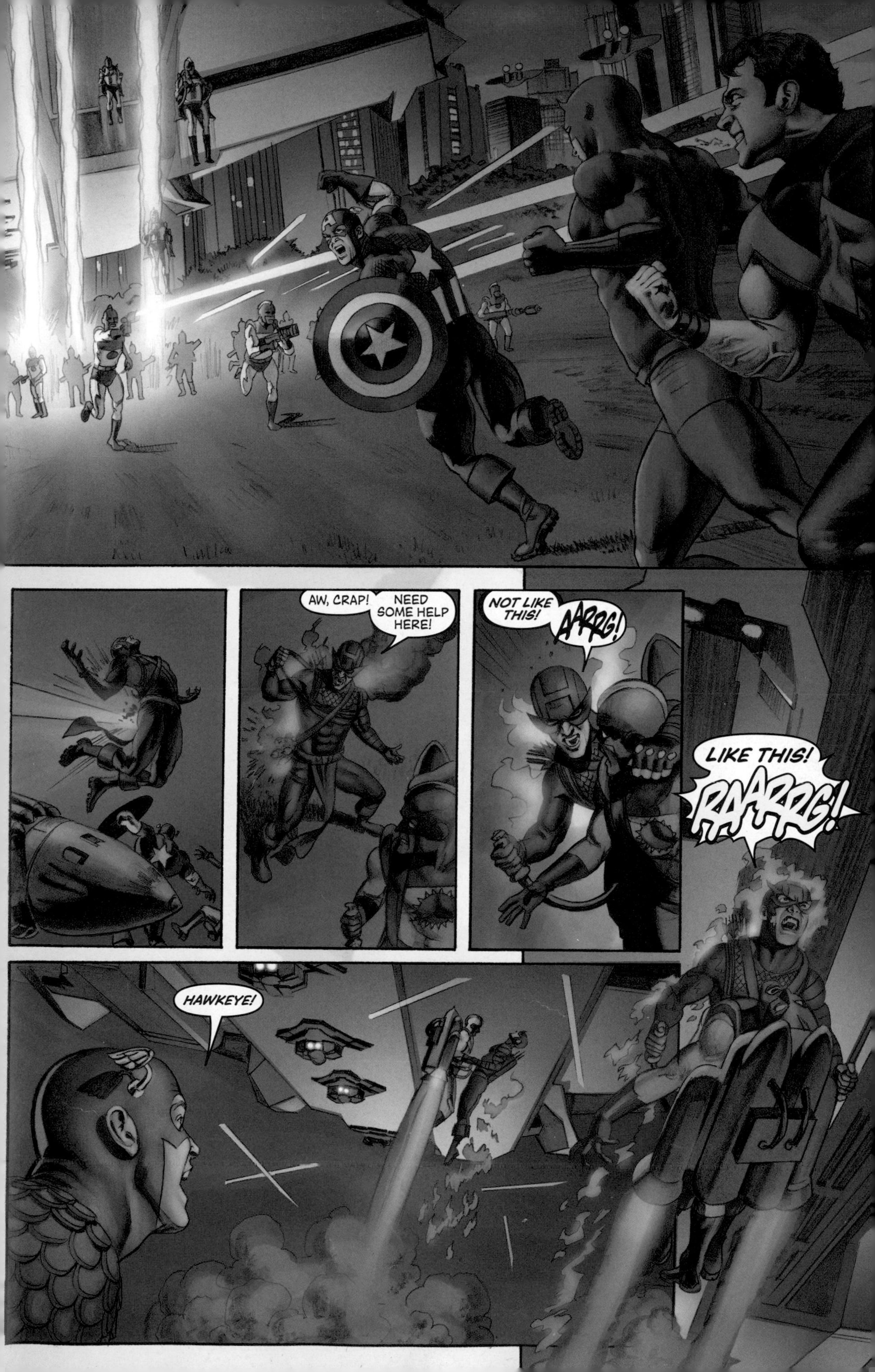
AW, CRAP!
NEED SOME HELP HERE!
NOT LIKE THIS!
AARRG!
LIKE THIS!
RAARRG!
HAWKEYE!

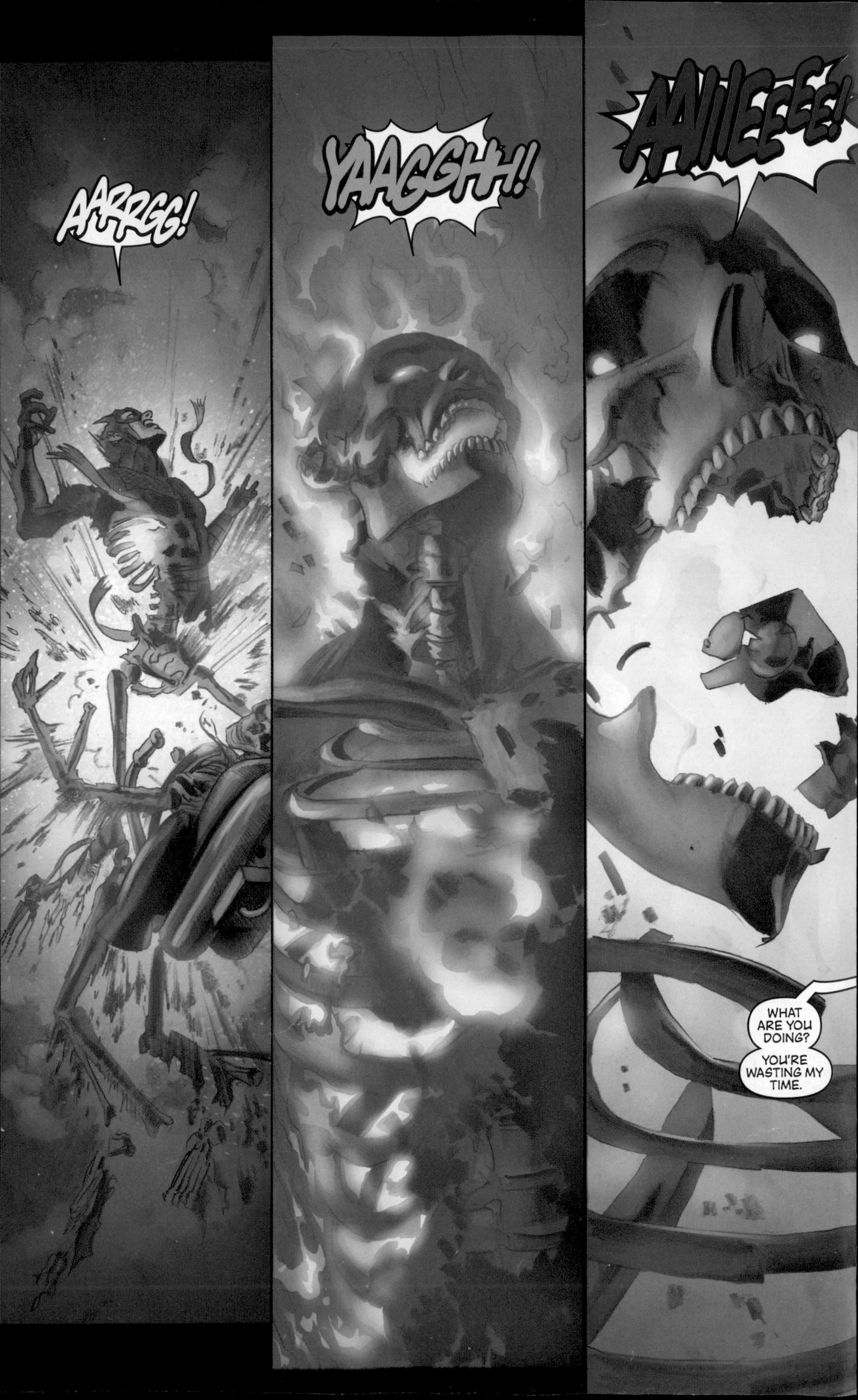
AARRGG!
YAAGGHH!
AAIIIEEEEE!
WHAT ARE YOU DOING?
YOU'RE WASTING MY TIME.

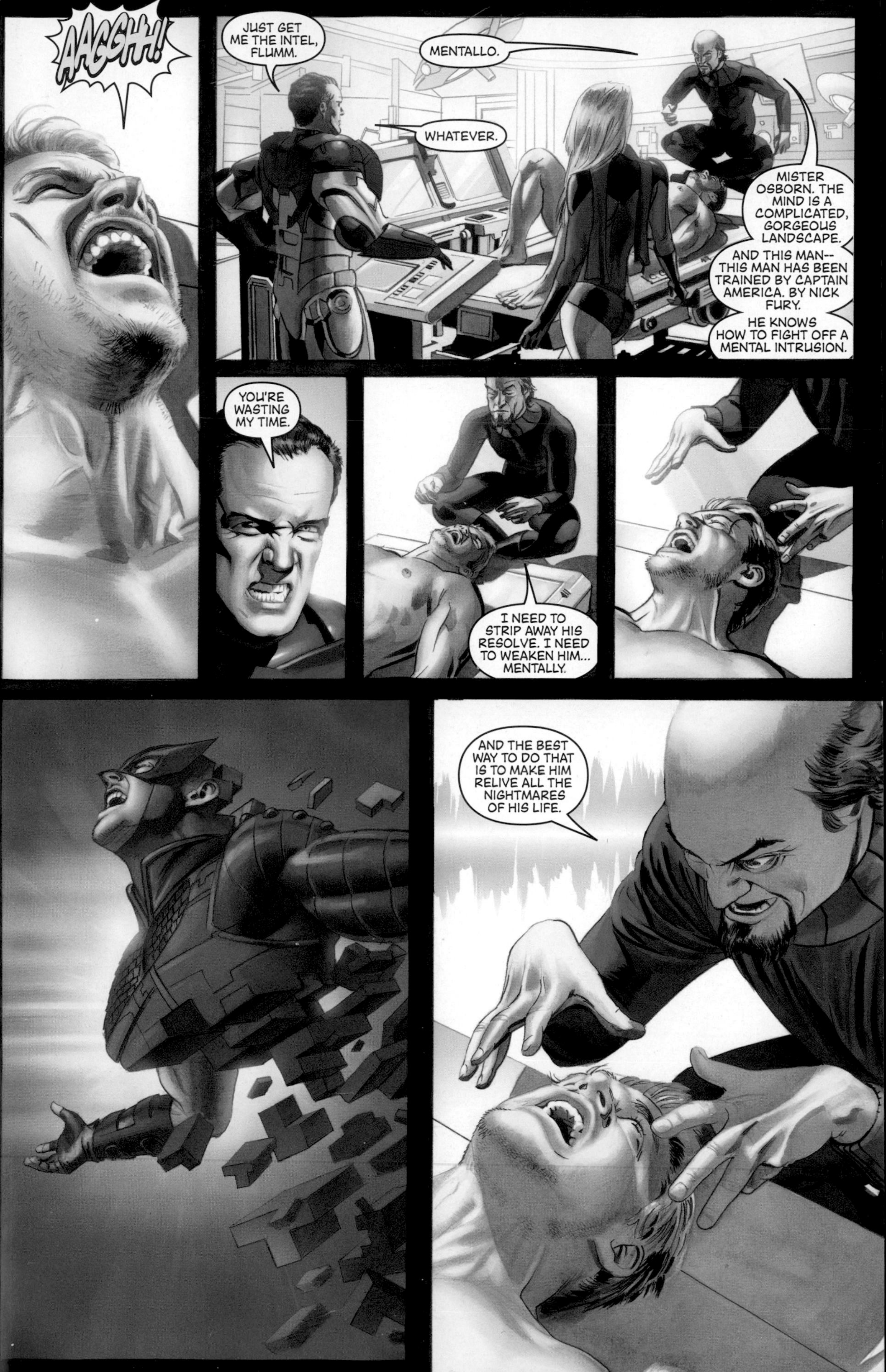
AAGGHH!
JUST GET ME THE INTEL, FLUMM.
MENTALLO.
WHATEVER.
MISTER OSBORN. THE MIND IS A COMPLICATED, GORGEOUS LANDSCAPE.
AND THIS MAN-- THIS MAN HAS BEEN TRAINED BY CAPTAIN AMERICA. BY NICK FURY.
HE KNOWS HOW TO FIGHT OFF A MENTAL INTRUSION.
YOU'RE WASTING MY TIME.
I NEED TO STRIP AWAY HIS RESOLVE. I NEED TO WEAKEN HIM... MENTALLY.
AND THE BEST WAY TO DO THAT IS TO MAKE HIM RELIVE ALL THE NIGHTMARES OF HIS LIFE.

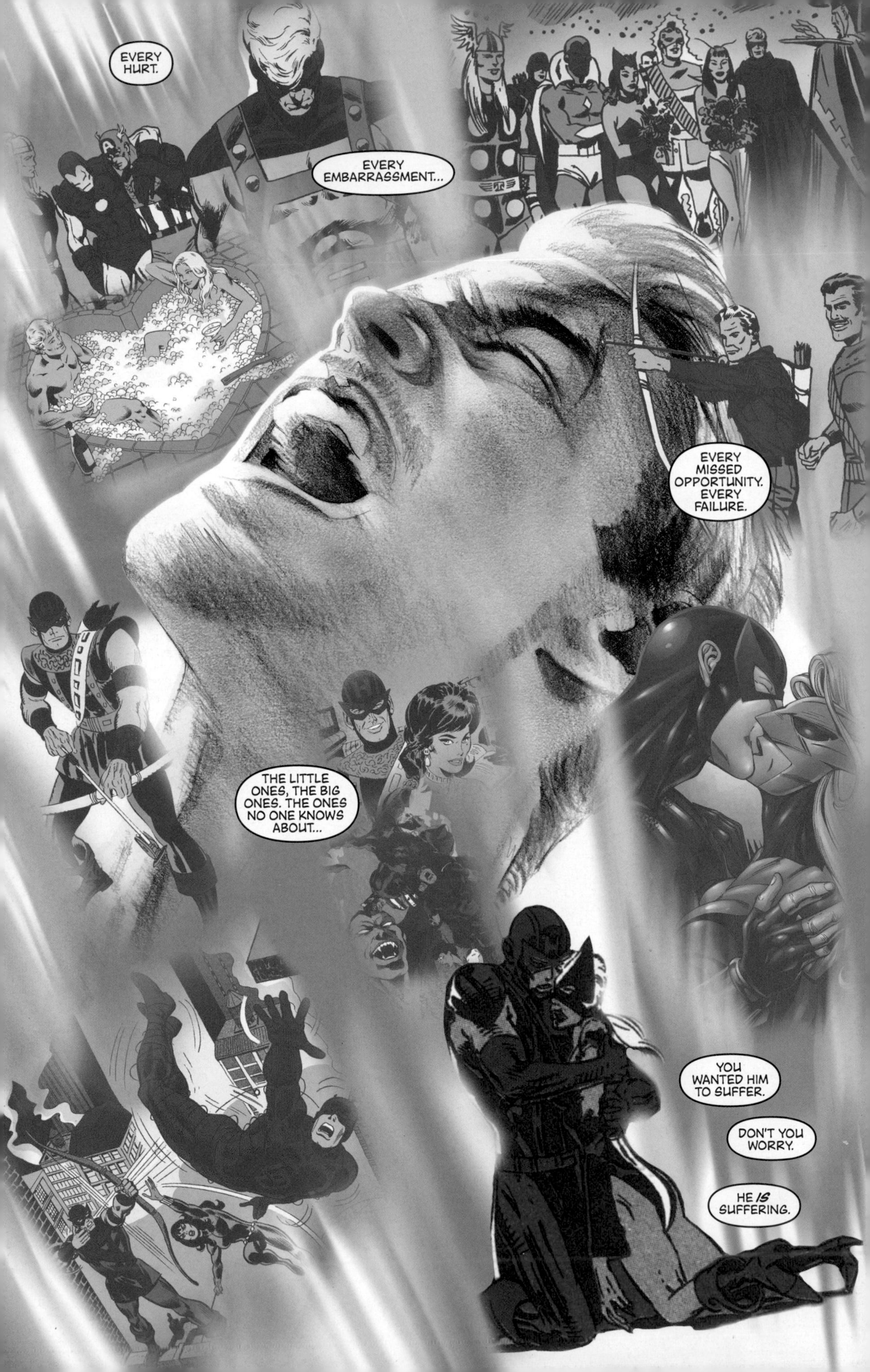
EVERY HURT.
EVERY EMBARRASSMENT...
EVERY MISSED OPPORTUNITY. EVERY FAILURE.
THE LITTLE ONES, THE BIG ONES. THE ONES NO ONE KNOWS ABOUT...
YOU WANTED HIM TO SUFFER.
DON'T YOU WORRY.
HE *IS* SUFFERING.

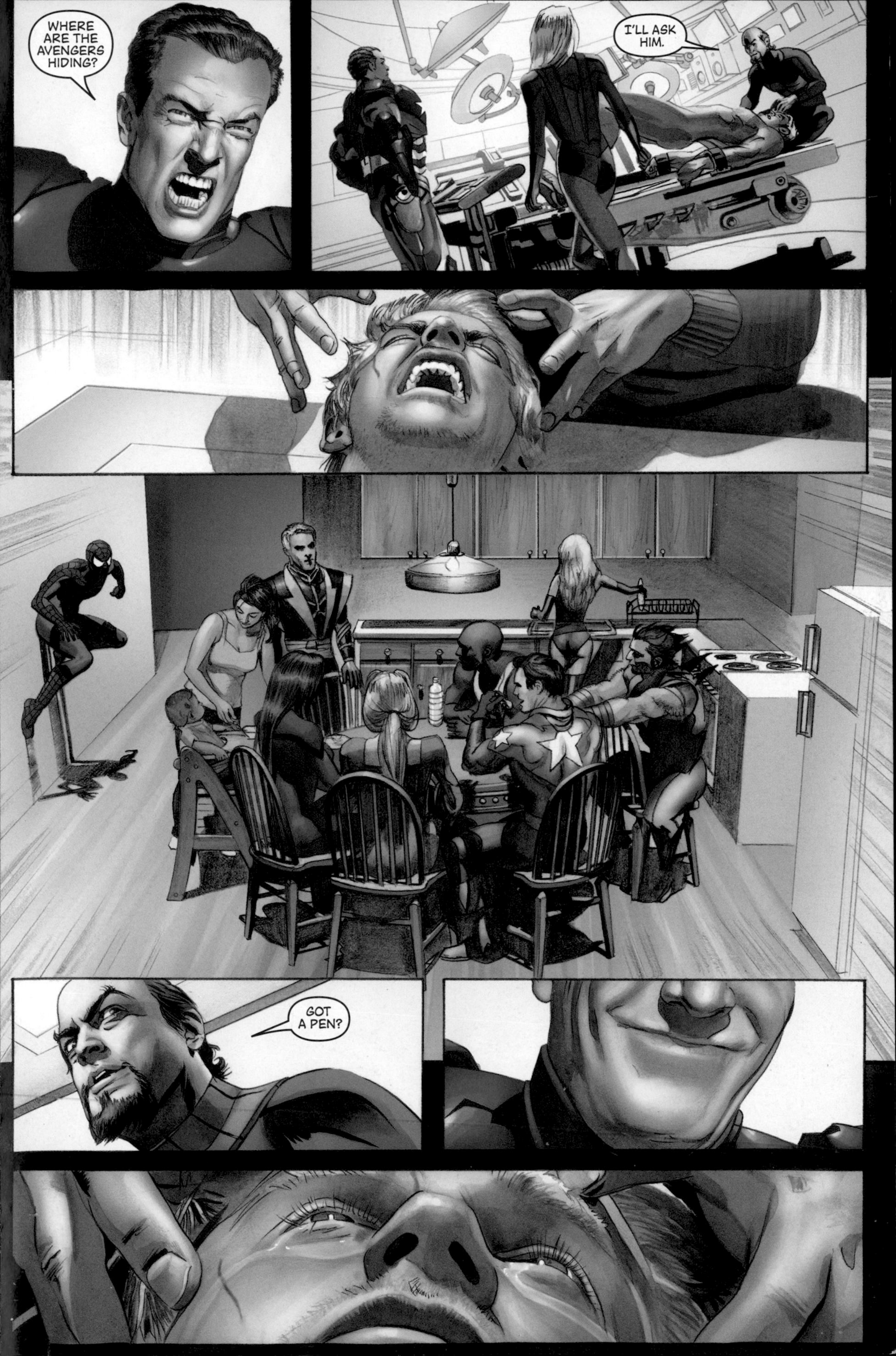
WHERE ARE THE AVENGERS HIDING?
I'LL ASK HIM.
GOT A PEN?

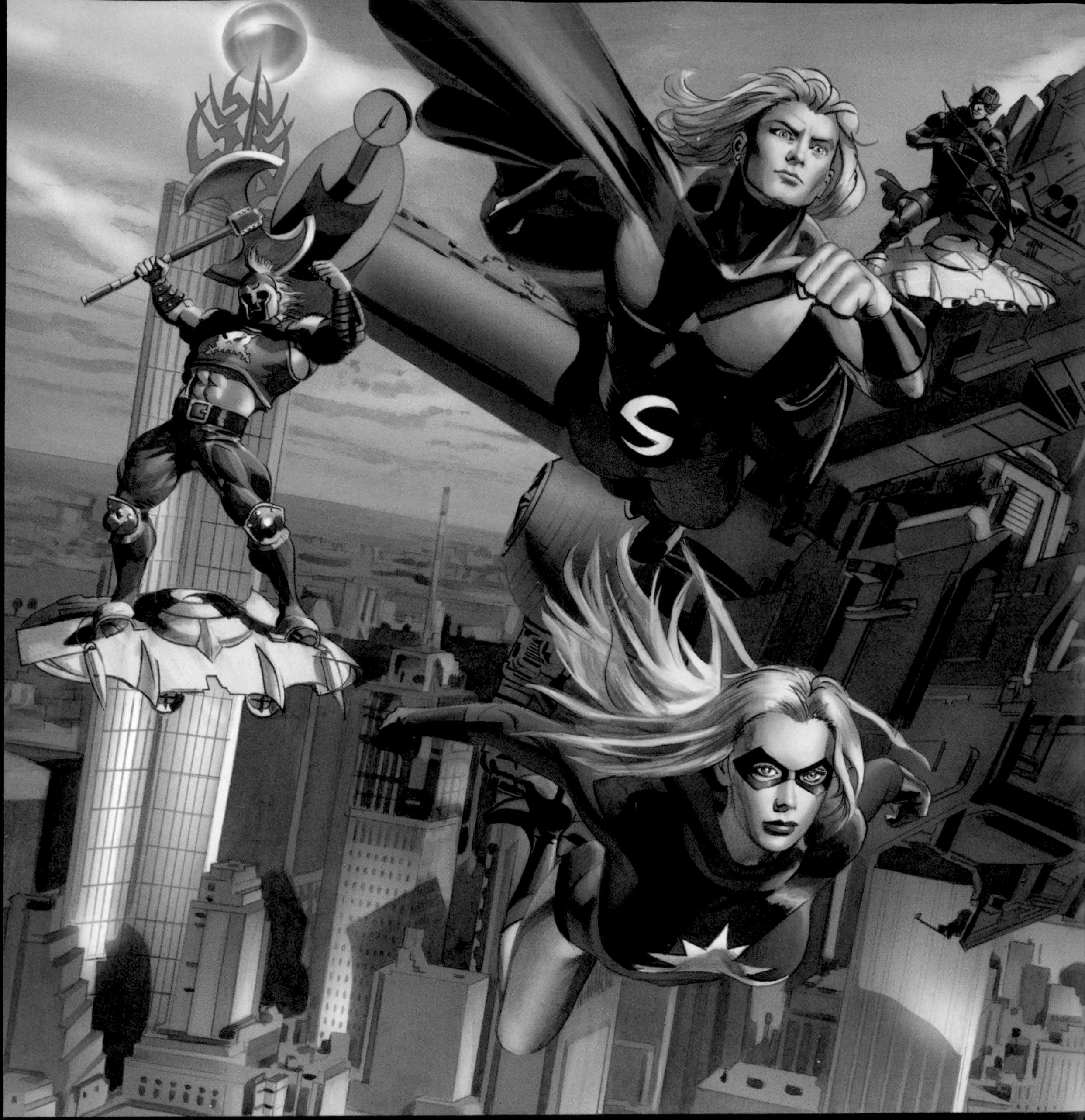

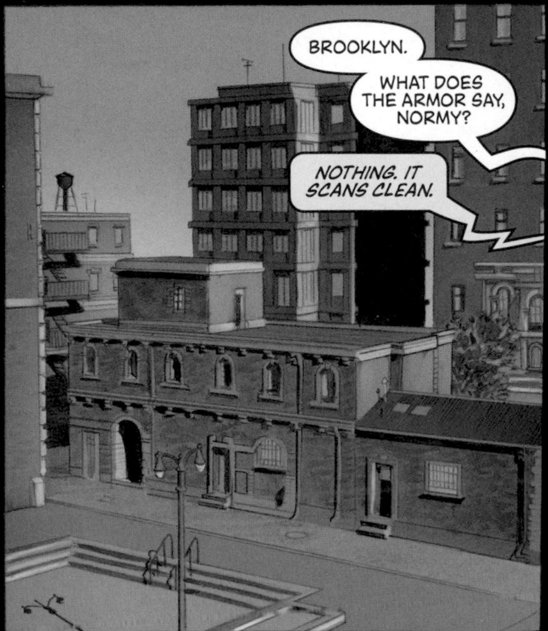
BROOKLYN.
WHAT DOES THE ARMOR SAY, NORMY?
NOTHING. IT SCANS CLEAN.

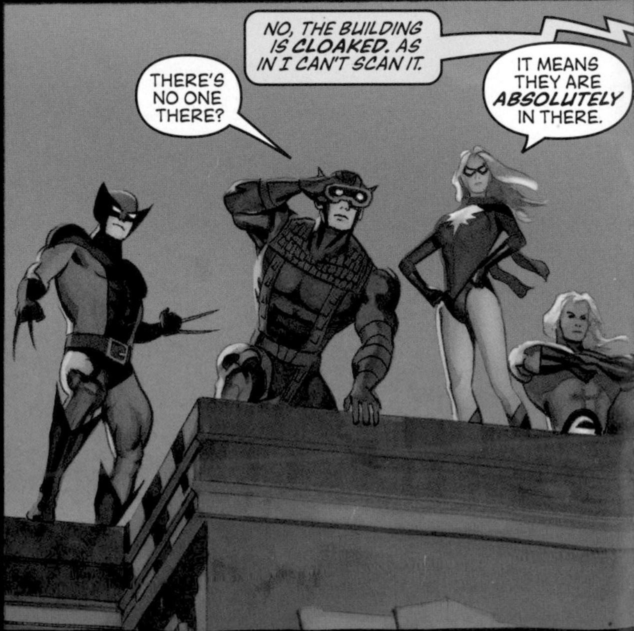
THERE'S NO ONE THERE?
NO, THE BUILDING IS CLOAKED. AS IN I CAN'T SCAN IT.
IT MEANS THEY ARE ABSOLUTELY IN THERE.

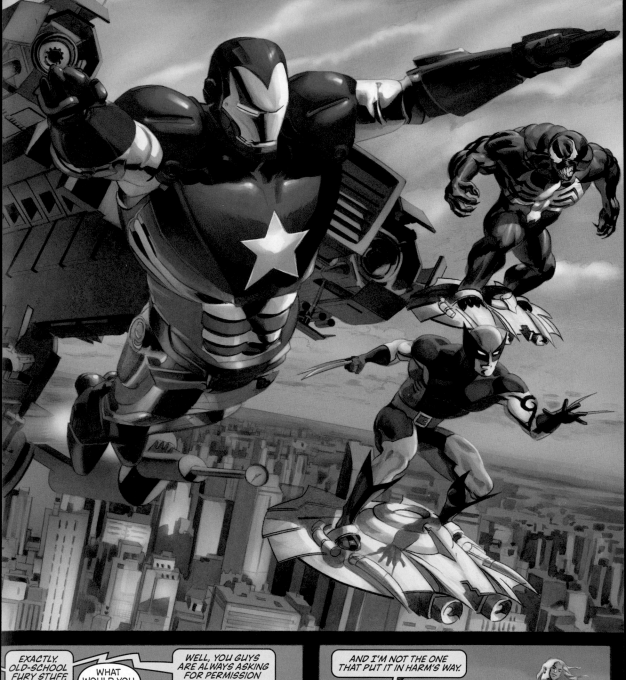

EXACTLY. OLD-SCHOOL FURY STUFF.

WHAT WOULD YOU HAVE US DO?

WELL, YOU GUYS ARE ALWAYS ASKING FOR PERMISSION TO LET LOOSE.

ON MY WORD. HAVE AT IT.

THERE'S A BABY IN THERE. LIKE CAGE'S BABY...

AND I'M NOT THE ONE THAT PUT IT IN HARM'S WAY.

BOB, RIP THE NORTH SIDE OF THE BUILDING OFF.

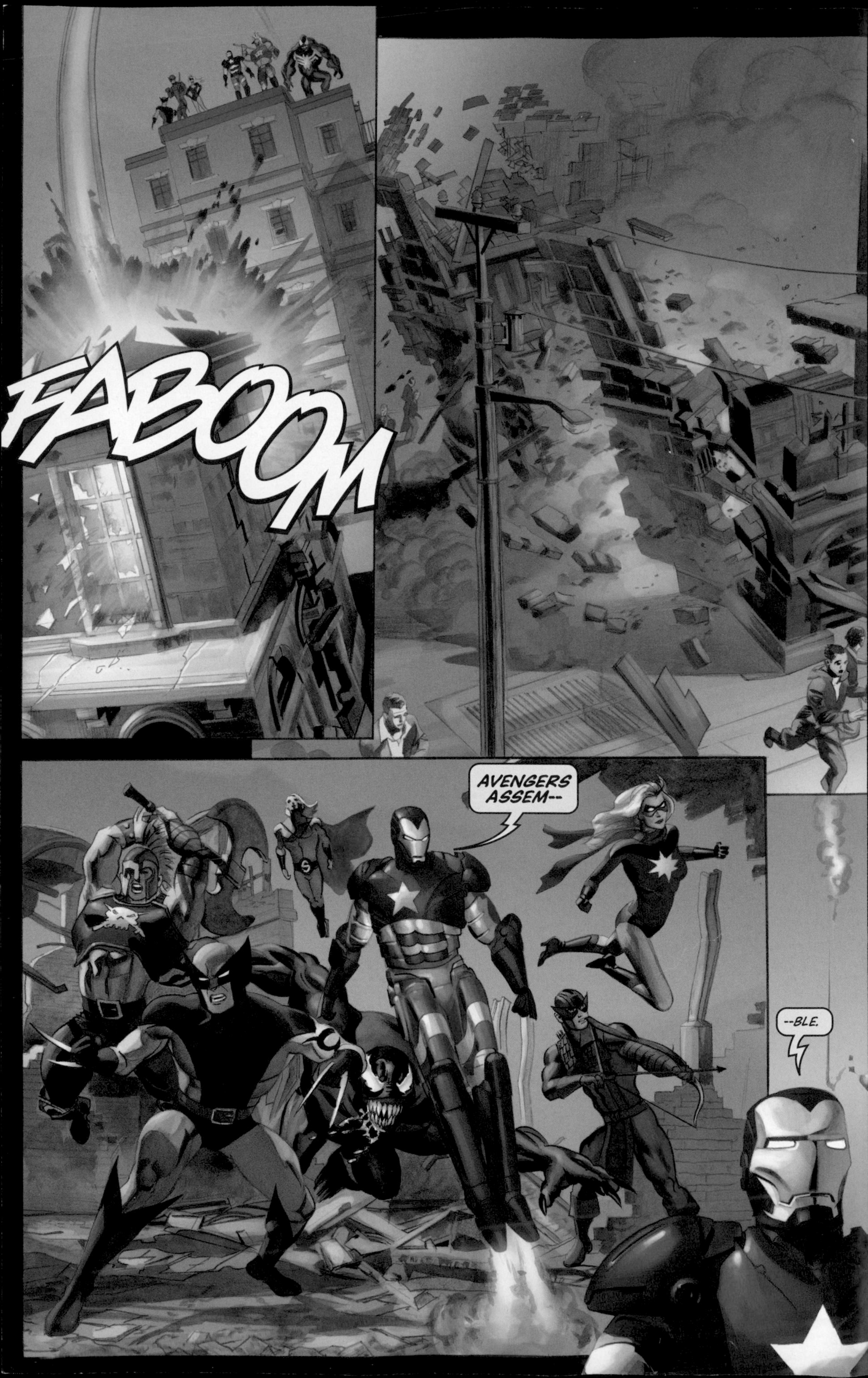
FABOOM
AVENGERS ASSEM--
--BLE.

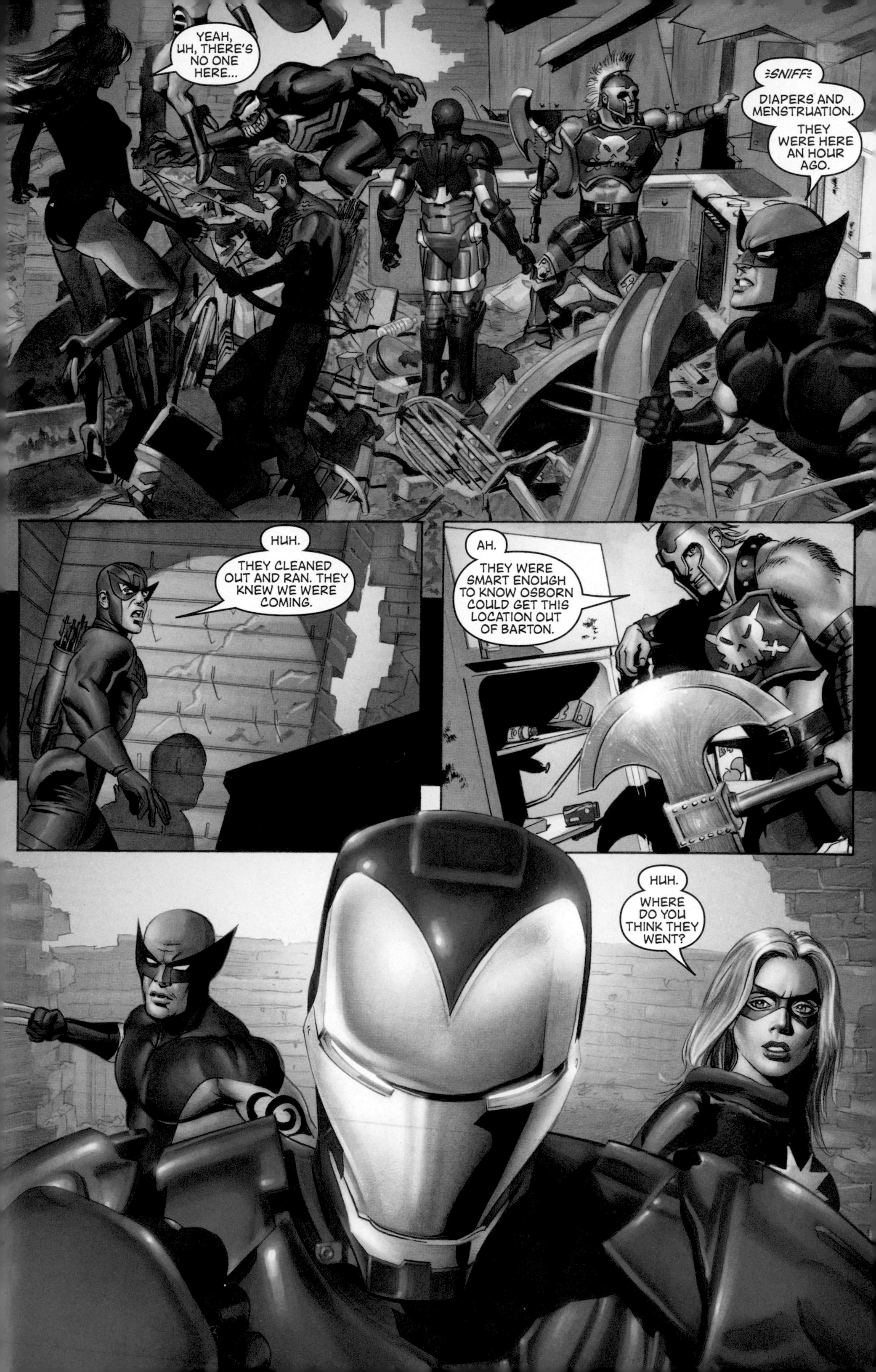
YEAH, UH, THERE'S NO ONE HERE...
SNIFF
DIAPERS AND MENSTRUATION.
THEY WERE HERE AN HOUR AGO.
HUH.
THEY CLEANED OUT AND RAN. THEY KNEW WE WERE COMING.
AH.
THEY WERE SMART ENOUGH TO KNOW OSBORN COULD GET THIS LOCATION OUT OF BARTON.
HUH.
WHERE DO YOU THINK THEY WENT?

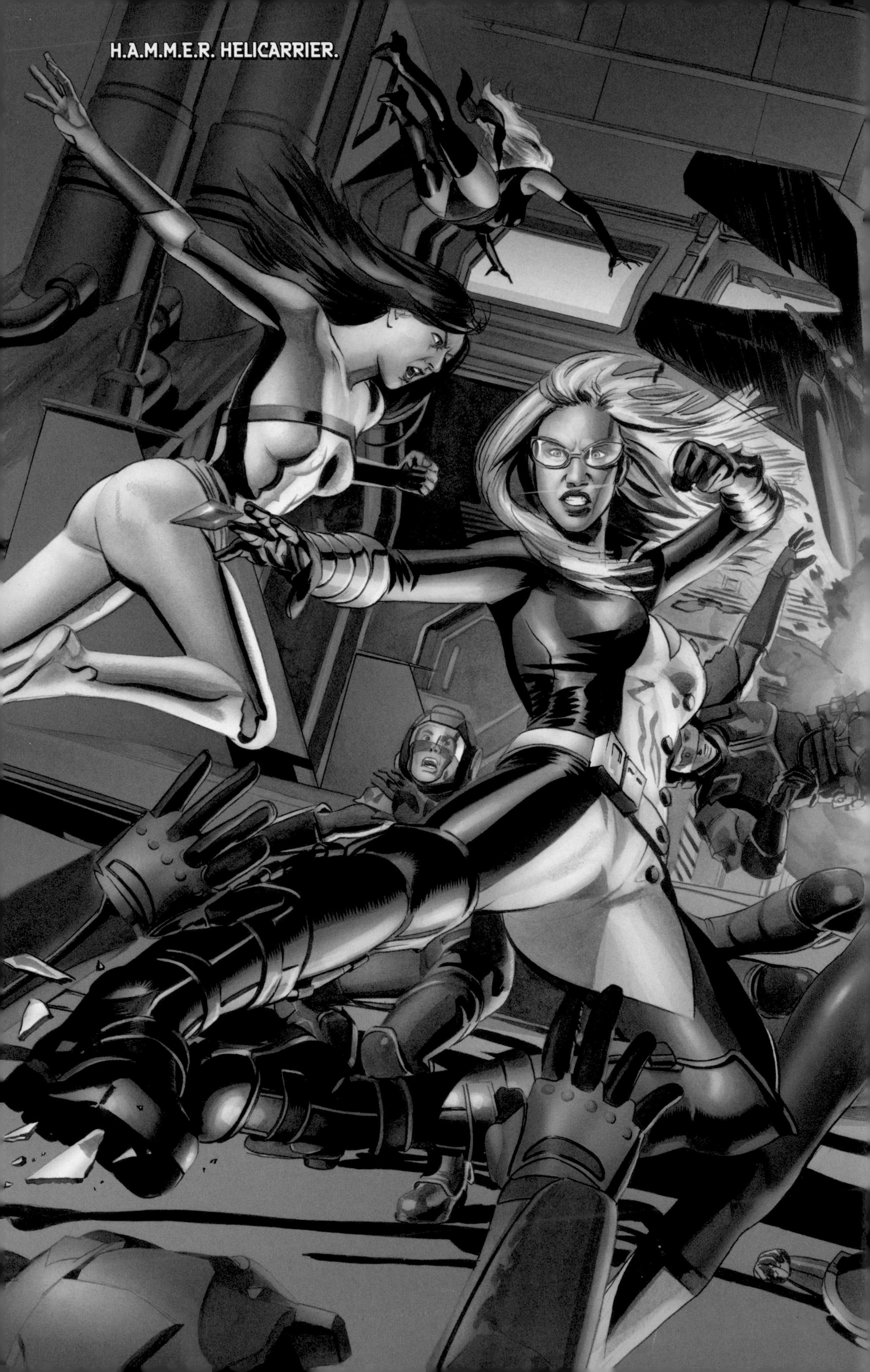
H.A.M.M.E.R. HELICARRIER.

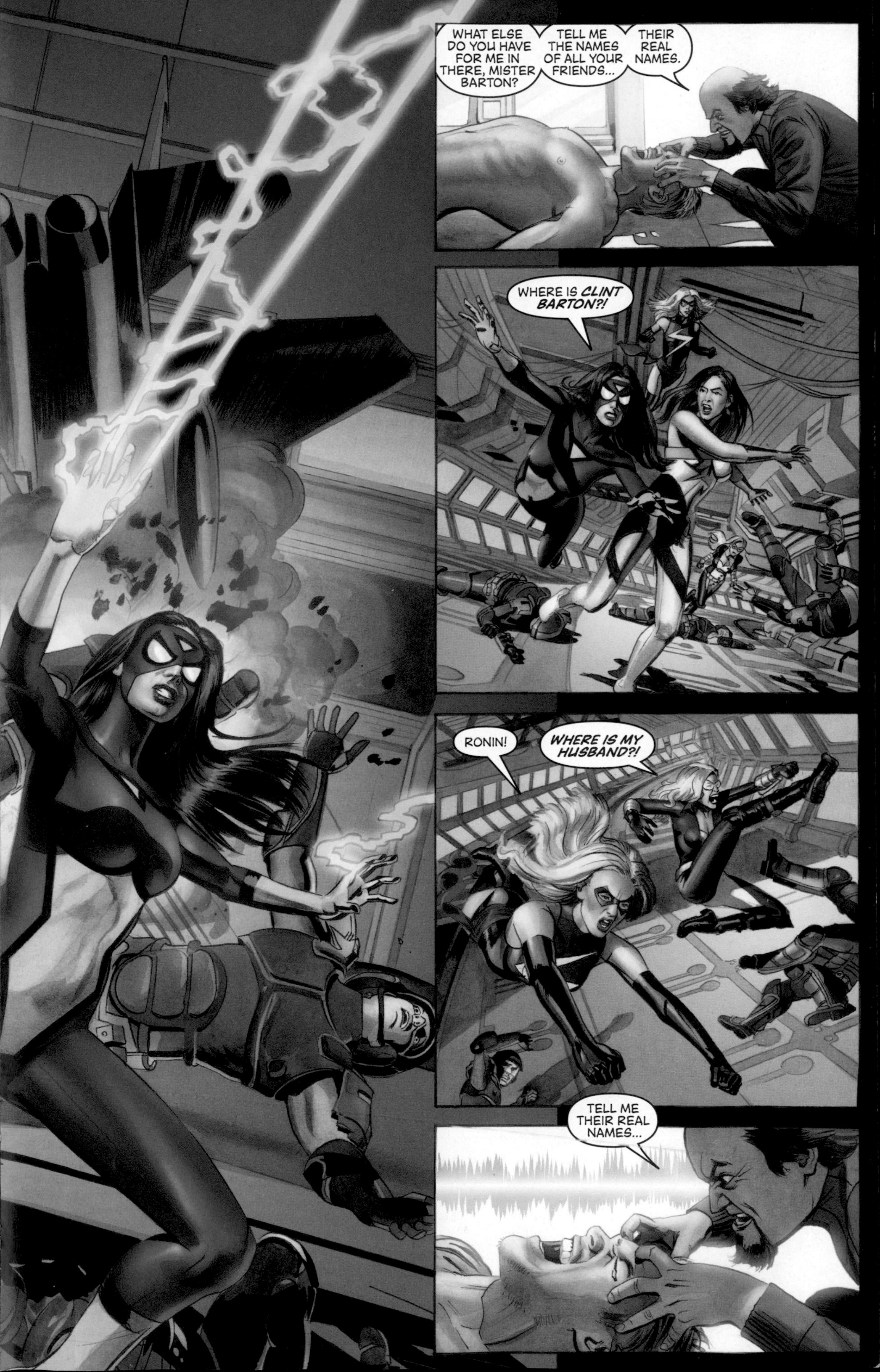
WHAT ELSE DO YOU HAVE FOR ME IN THERE, MISTER BARTON?
TELL ME THE NAMES OF ALL YOUR FRIENDS...
THEIR REAL NAMES.
WHERE IS *CLINT BARTON?!*
RONIN!
WHERE IS MY HUSBAND?!
TELL ME THEIR REAL NAMES...

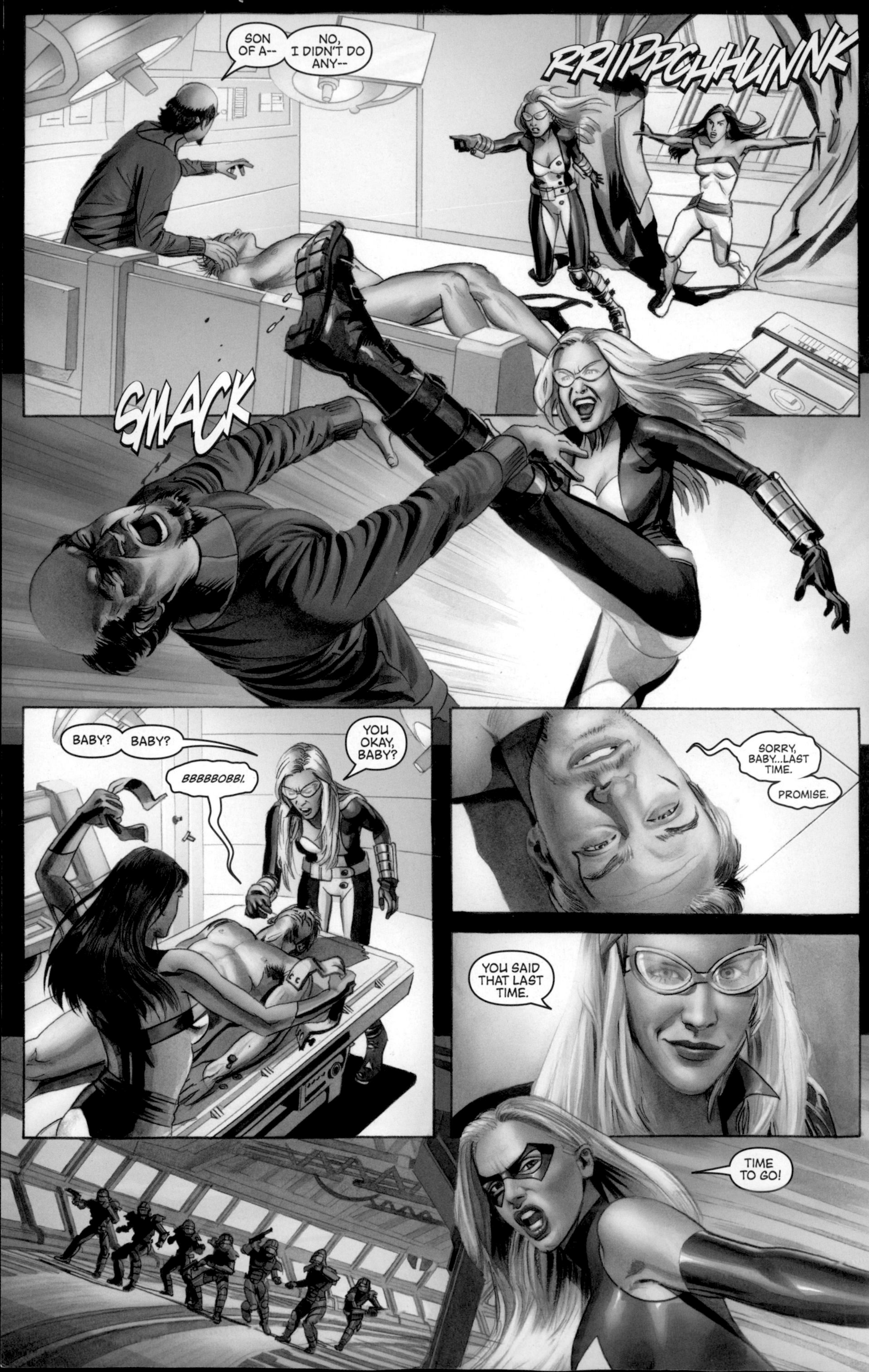
SON OF A--
NO, I DIDN'T DO ANY--
RRIIPPCHHUNNK
SMACK
BABY? BABY?
BBBBBOBBI.
YOU OKAY, BABY?
SORRY, BABY...LAST TIME.
PROMISE.
YOU SAID THAT LAST TIME.
TIME TO GO!

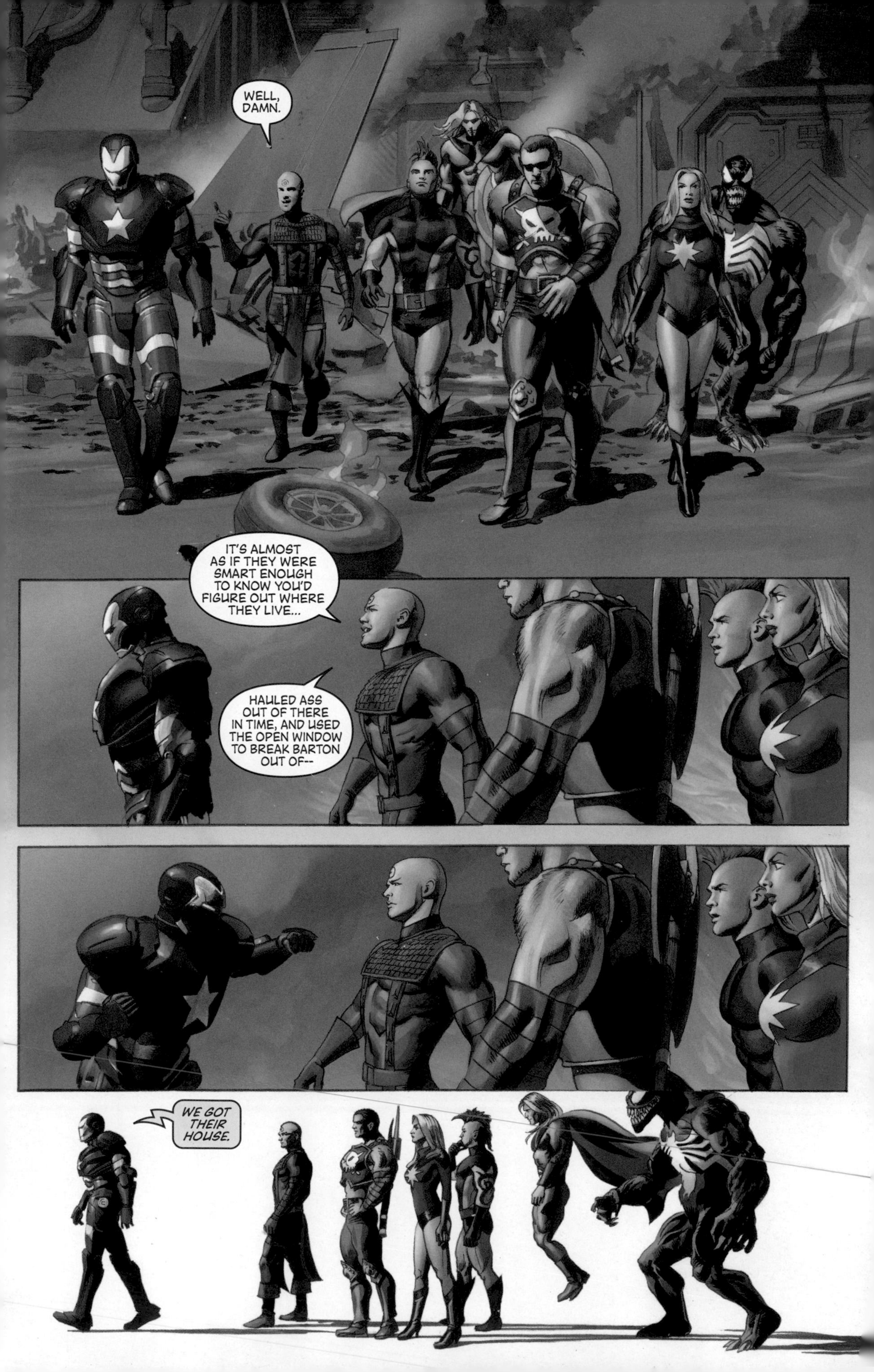
WELL, DAMN.
IT'S ALMOST AS IF THEY WERE SMART ENOUGH TO KNOW YOU'D FIGURE OUT WHERE THEY LIVE...
HAULED ASS OUT OF THERE IN TIME, AND USED THE OPEN WINDOW TO BREAK BARTON OUT OF--
WE GOT THEIR HOUSE.

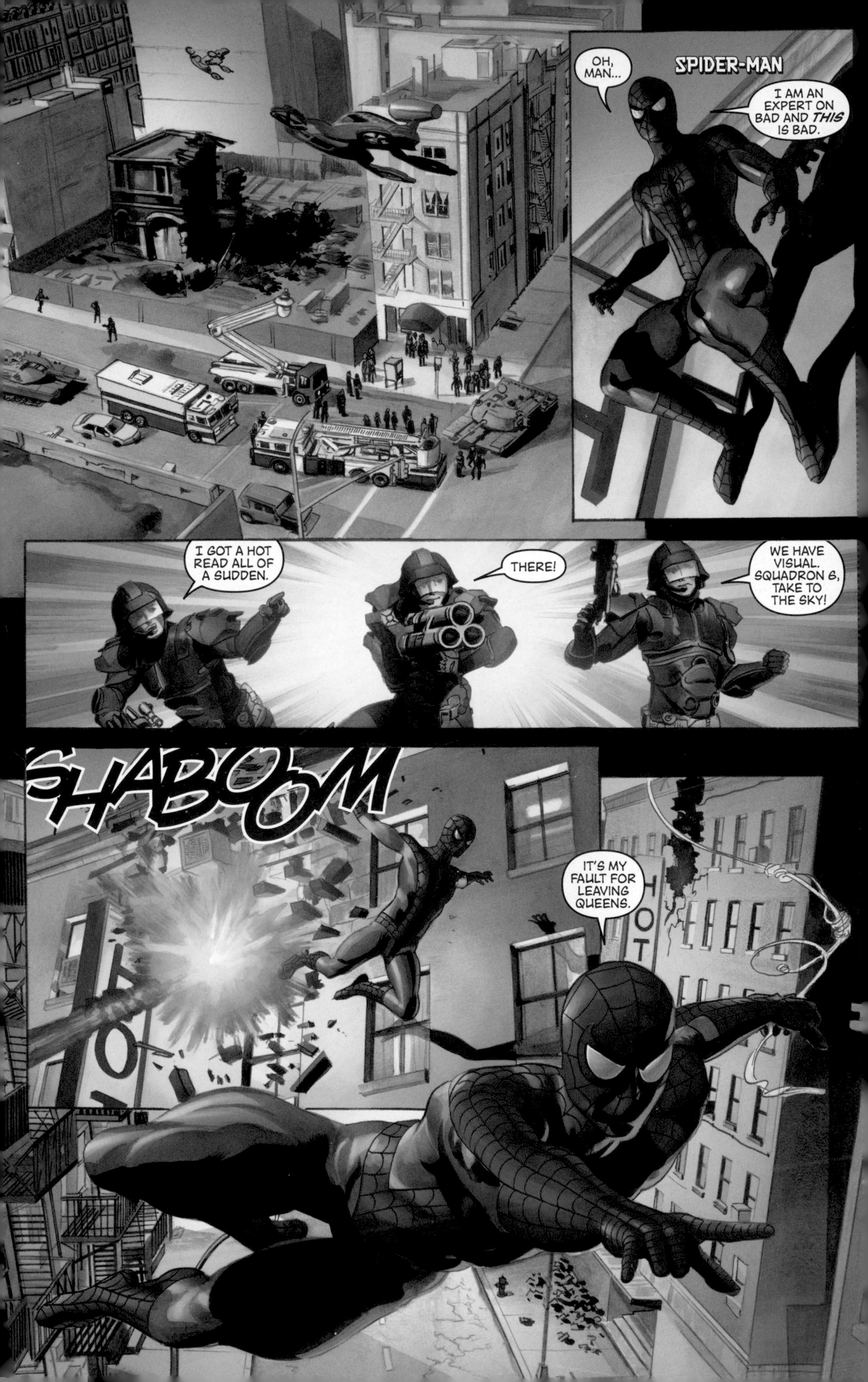
OH, MAN...
SPIDER-MAN
I AM AN EXPERT ON BAD AND *THIS* IS BAD.
I GOT A HOT READ ALL OF A SUDDEN.
THERE!
WE HAVE VISUAL. SQUADRON 6, TAKE TO THE SKY!
SHABOOM
IT'S MY FAULT FOR LEAVING QUEENS.

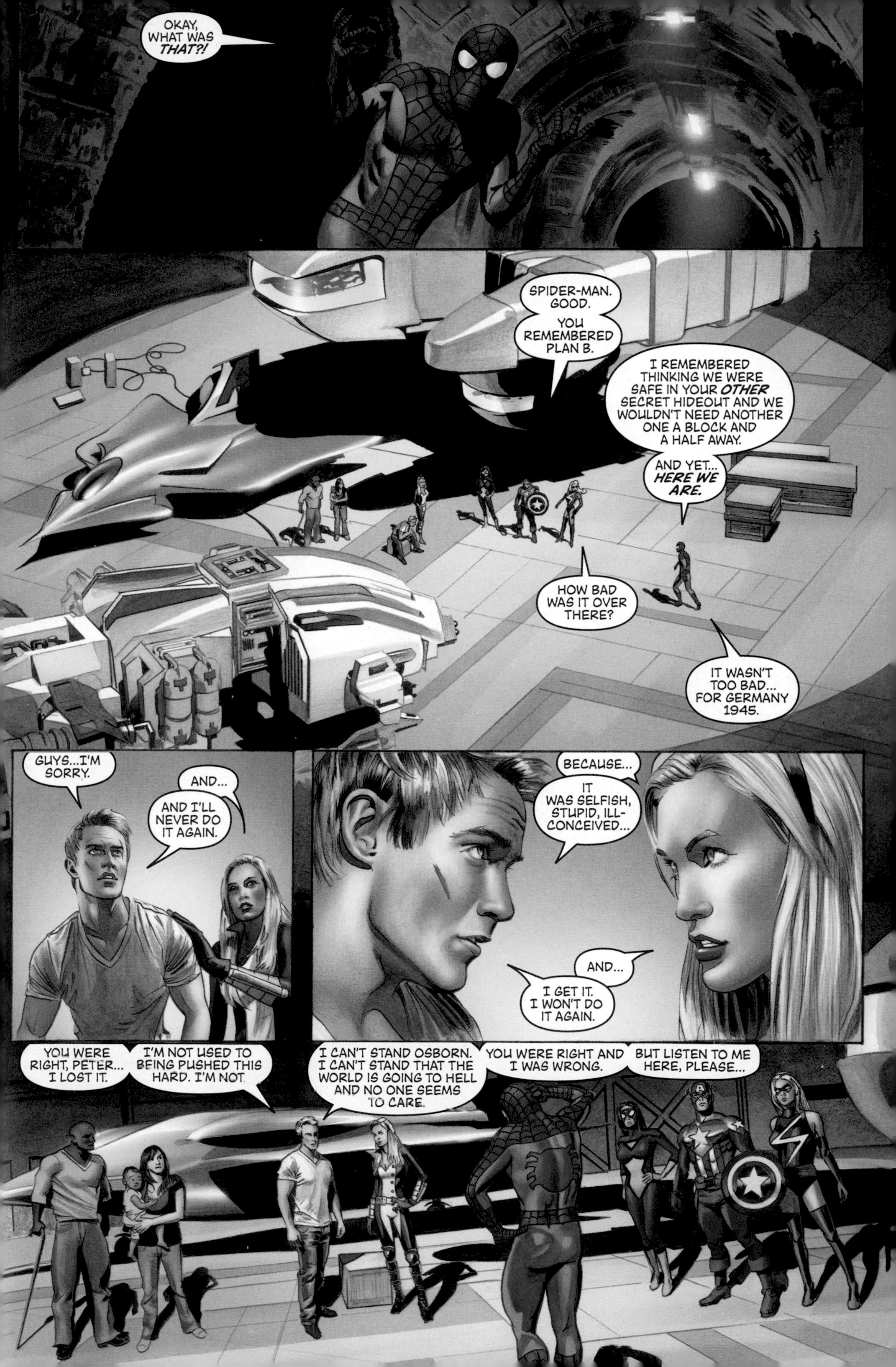
OKAY, WHAT WAS *THAT?!*
SPIDER-MAN. GOOD.
YOU REMEMBERED PLAN B.
I REMEMBERED THINKING WE WERE SAFE IN YOUR *OTHER* SECRET HIDEOUT AND WE WOULDN'T NEED ANOTHER ONE A BLOCK AND A HALF AWAY.
AND YET... ***HERE WE ARE.***
HOW BAD WAS IT OVER THERE?
IT WASN'T TOO BAD... FOR GERMANY 1945.
GUYS...I'M SORRY.
AND...
AND I'LL NEVER DO IT AGAIN.
BECAUSE...
IT WAS SELFISH, STUPID, ILL-CONCEIVED...
AND...
I GET IT. I WON'T DO IT AGAIN.
YOU WERE RIGHT, PETER... I LOST IT.
I'M NOT USED TO BEING PUSHED THIS HARD. I'M NOT.
I CAN'T STAND OSBORN. I CAN'T STAND THAT THE WORLD IS GOING TO HELL AND NO ONE SEEMS TO CARE.
YOU WERE RIGHT AND I WAS WRONG.
BUT LISTEN TO ME HERE, PLEASE...

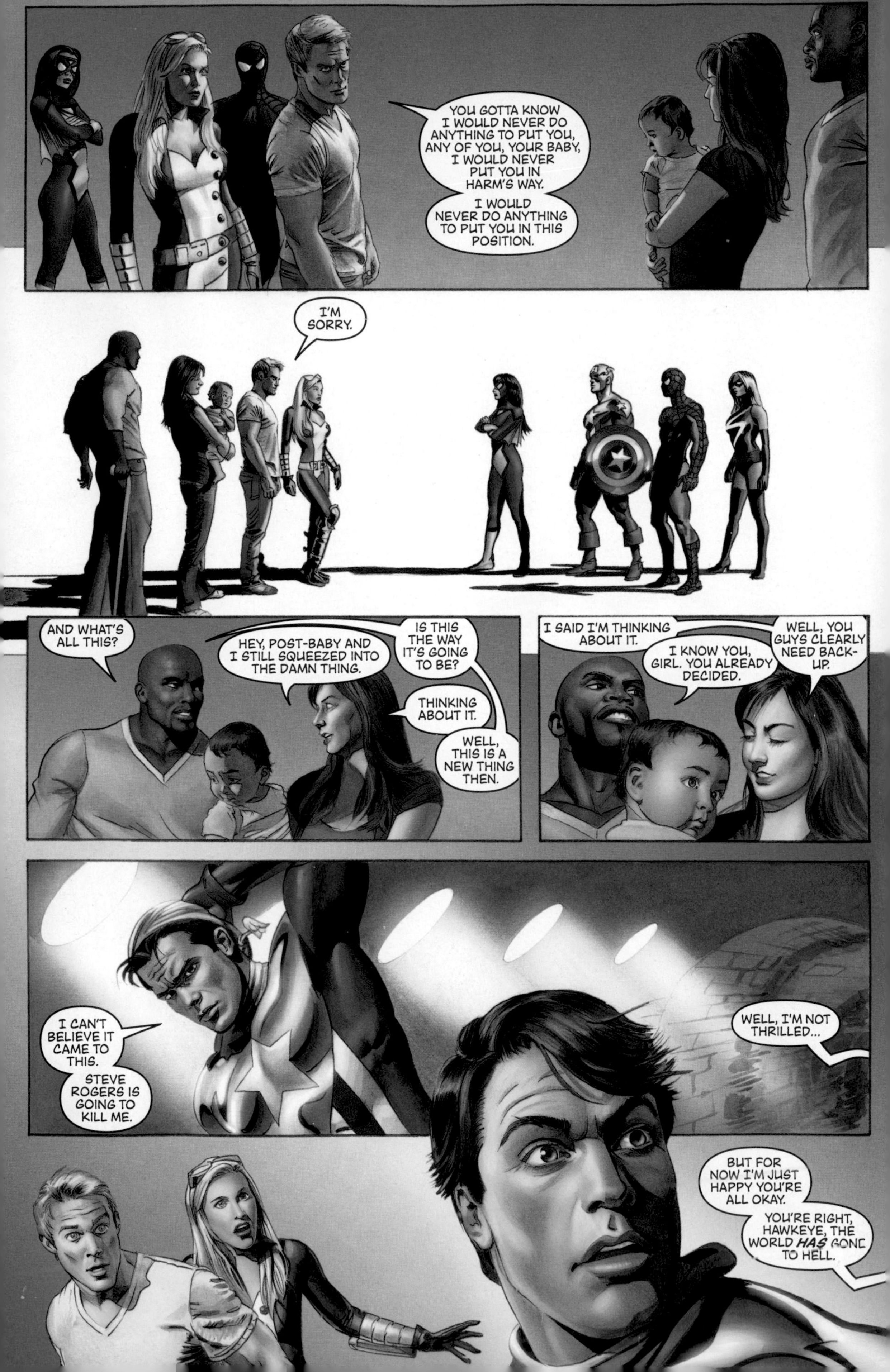
YOU GOTTA KNOW I WOULD NEVER DO ANYTHING TO PUT YOU, ANY OF YOU, YOUR BABY, I WOULD NEVER PUT YOU IN HARM'S WAY.
I WOULD NEVER DO ANYTHING TO PUT YOU IN THIS POSITION.
I'M SORRY.
AND WHAT'S ALL THIS?
HEY, POST-BABY AND I STILL SQUEEZED INTO THE DAMN THING.
IS THIS THE WAY IT'S GOING TO BE?
THINKING ABOUT IT.
WELL, THIS IS A NEW THING THEN.
I SAID I'M THINKING ABOUT IT.
I KNOW YOU, GIRL. YOU ALREADY DECIDED.
WELL, YOU GUYS CLEARLY NEED BACK-UP.
I CAN'T BELIEVE IT CAME TO THIS.
STEVE ROGERS IS GOING TO KILL ME.
WELL, I'M NOT THRILLED...
BUT FOR NOW I'M JUST HAPPY YOU'RE ALL OKAY.
YOU'RE RIGHT, HAWKEYE, THE WORLD HAS GONE TO HELL.

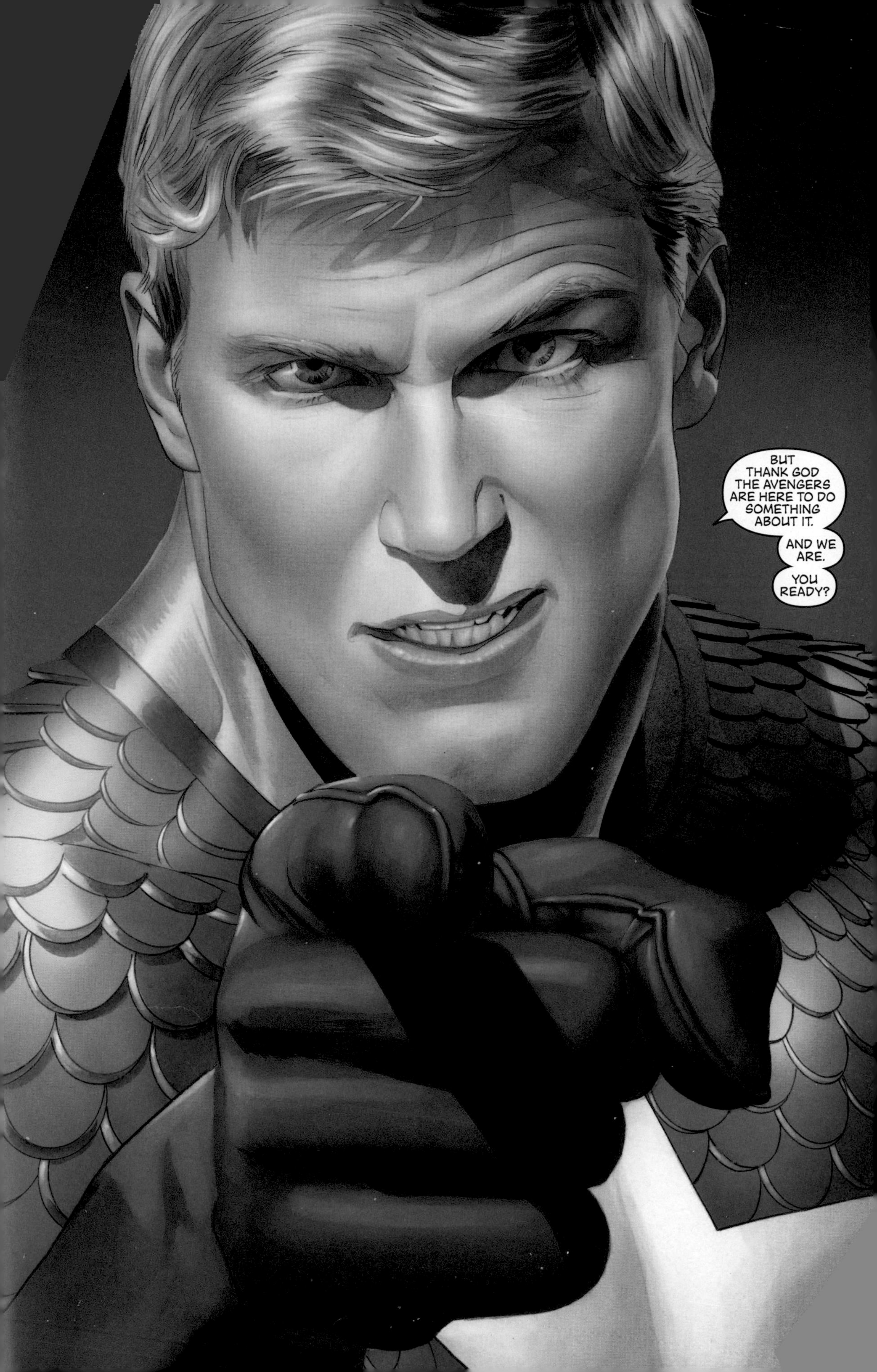
BUT THANK GOD THE AVENGERS ARE HERE TO DO SOMETHING ABOUT IT.
AND WE ARE.
YOU READY?

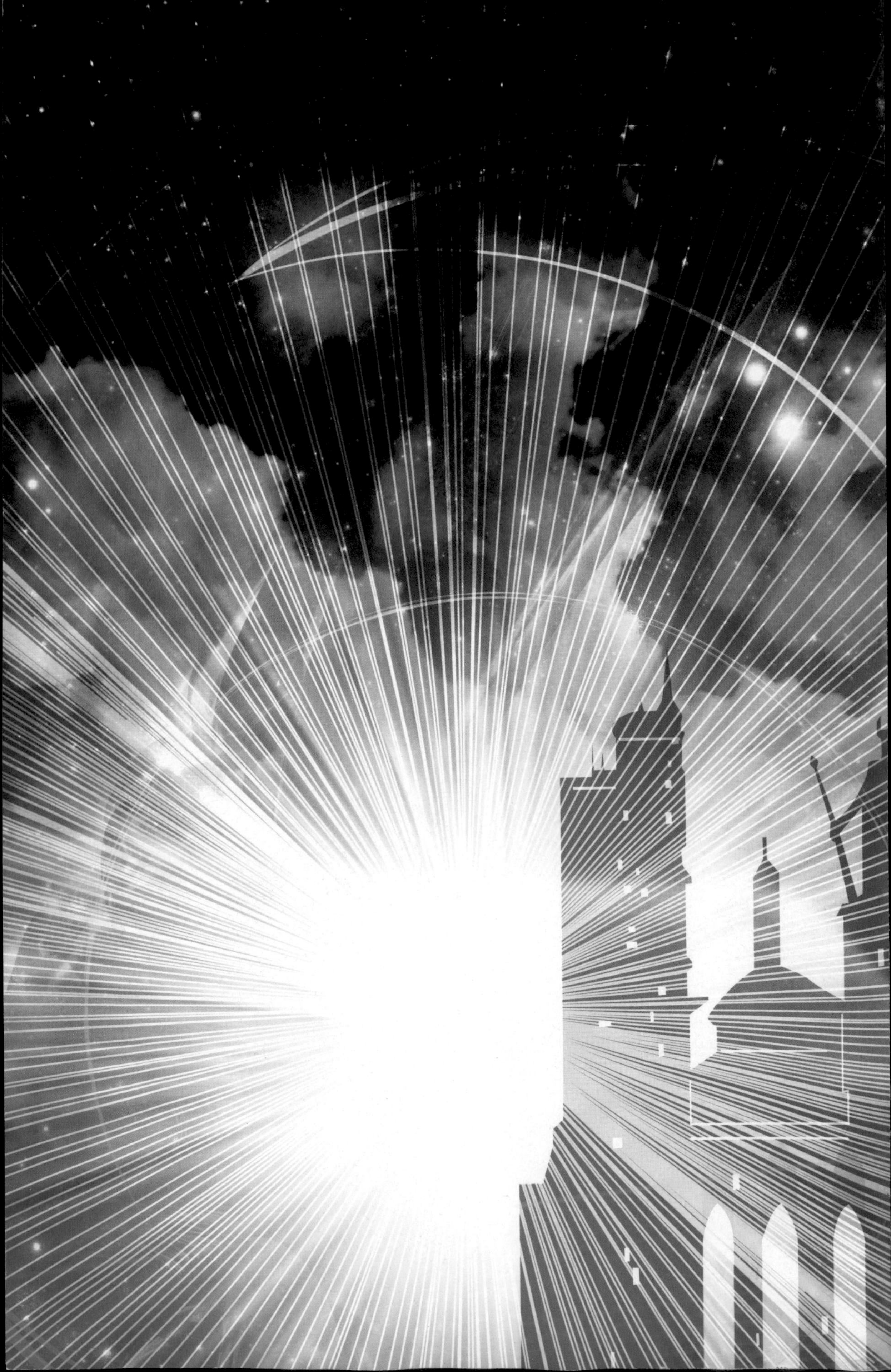

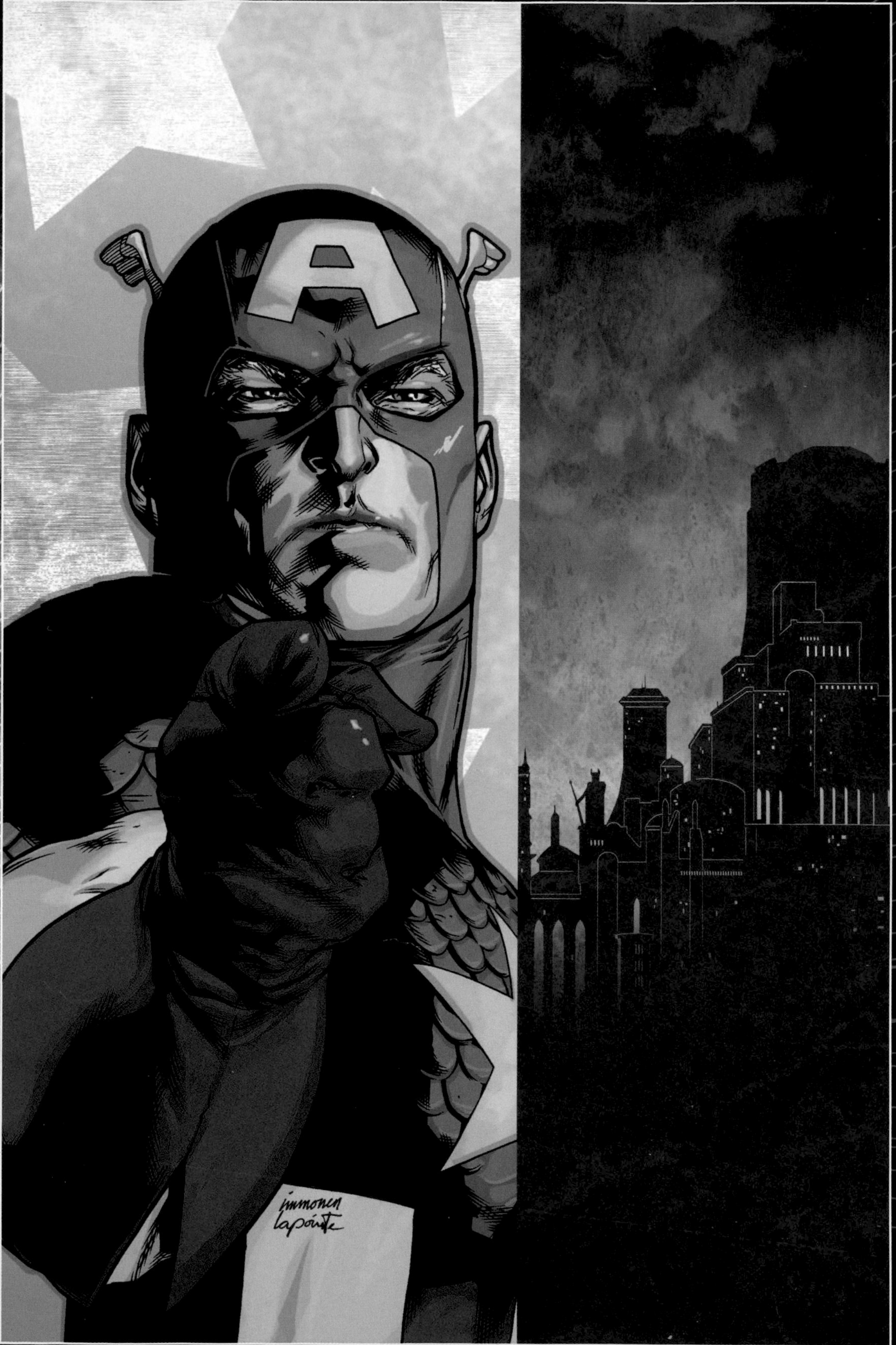

NEW AVENGERS #61

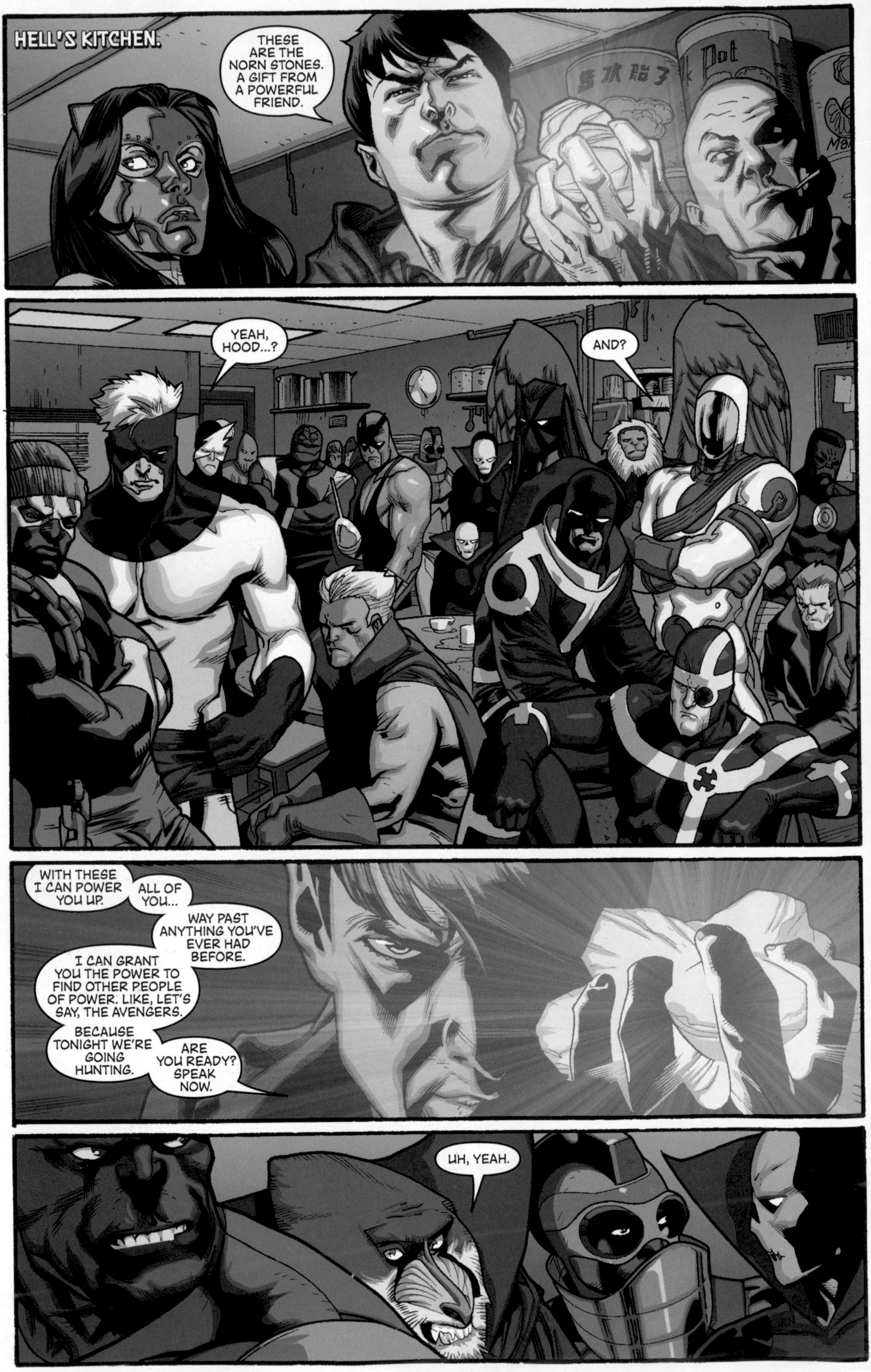
HELL'S KITCHEN.
THESE ARE THE NORN STONES. A GIFT FROM A POWERFUL FRIEND.
YEAH, HOOD...?
AND?
WITH THESE I CAN POWER YOU UP.
ALL OF YOU...
WAY PAST ANYTHING YOU'VE EVER HAD BEFORE.
I CAN GRANT YOU THE POWER TO FIND OTHER PEOPLE OF POWER. LIKE, LET'S SAY, THE AVENGERS.
BECAUSE TONIGHT WE'RE GOING HUNTING.
ARE YOU READY? SPEAK NOW.
UH, YEAH.

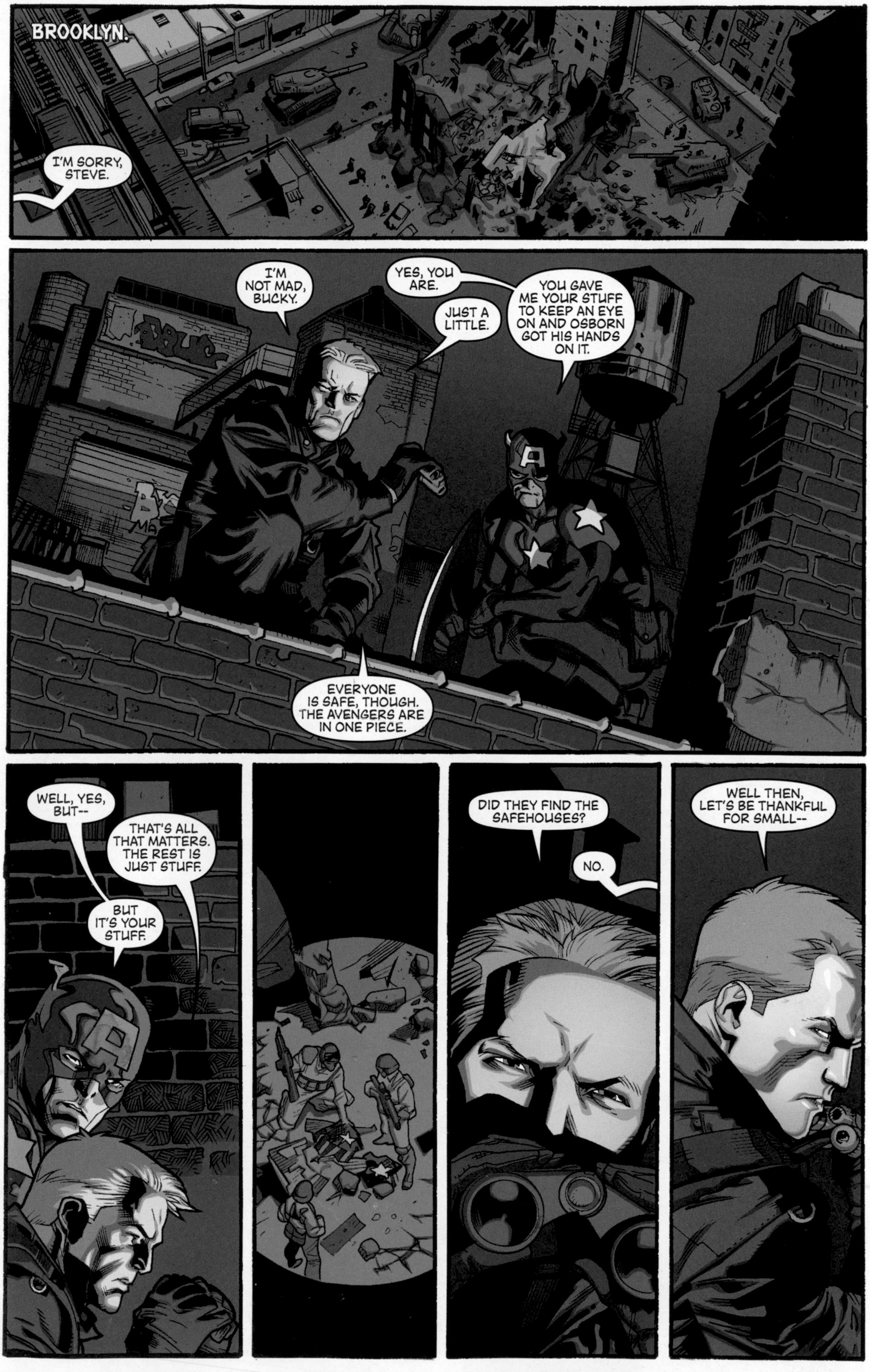
BROOKLYN.
I'M SORRY, STEVE.
I'M NOT MAD, BUCKY.
YES, YOU ARE.
JUST A LITTLE.
YOU GAVE ME YOUR STUFF TO KEEP AN EYE ON AND OSBORN GOT HIS HANDS ON IT.
EVERYONE IS SAFE, THOUGH. THE AVENGERS ARE IN ONE PIECE.
WELL, YES, BUT--
THAT'S ALL THAT MATTERS. THE REST IS JUST STUFF.
BUT IT'S YOUR STUFF.
DID THEY FIND THE SAFEHOUSES?
NO.
WELL THEN, LET'S BE THANKFUL FOR SMALL--

NRAAKNBOOM

DAMN, SO CLOSE.

BAM

BAM

BAM

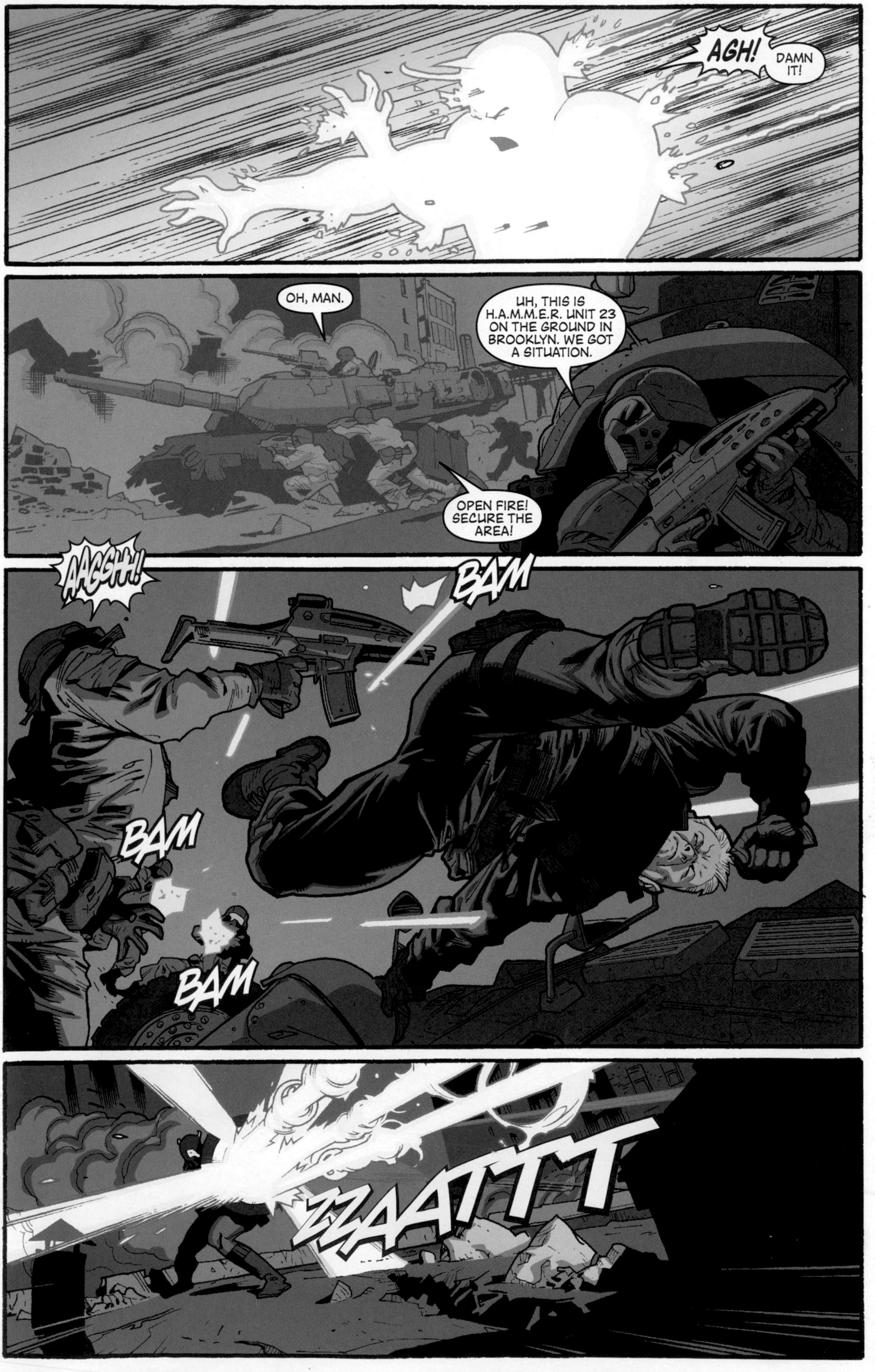
AGH!
DAMN IT!
OH, MAN.
UH, THIS IS H.A.M.M.E.R. UNIT 23 ON THE GROUND IN BROOKLYN. WE GOT A SITUATION.
OPEN FIRE! SECURE THE AREA!
AAGGHH!
BAM
BAM
BAM
ZZAATTTT

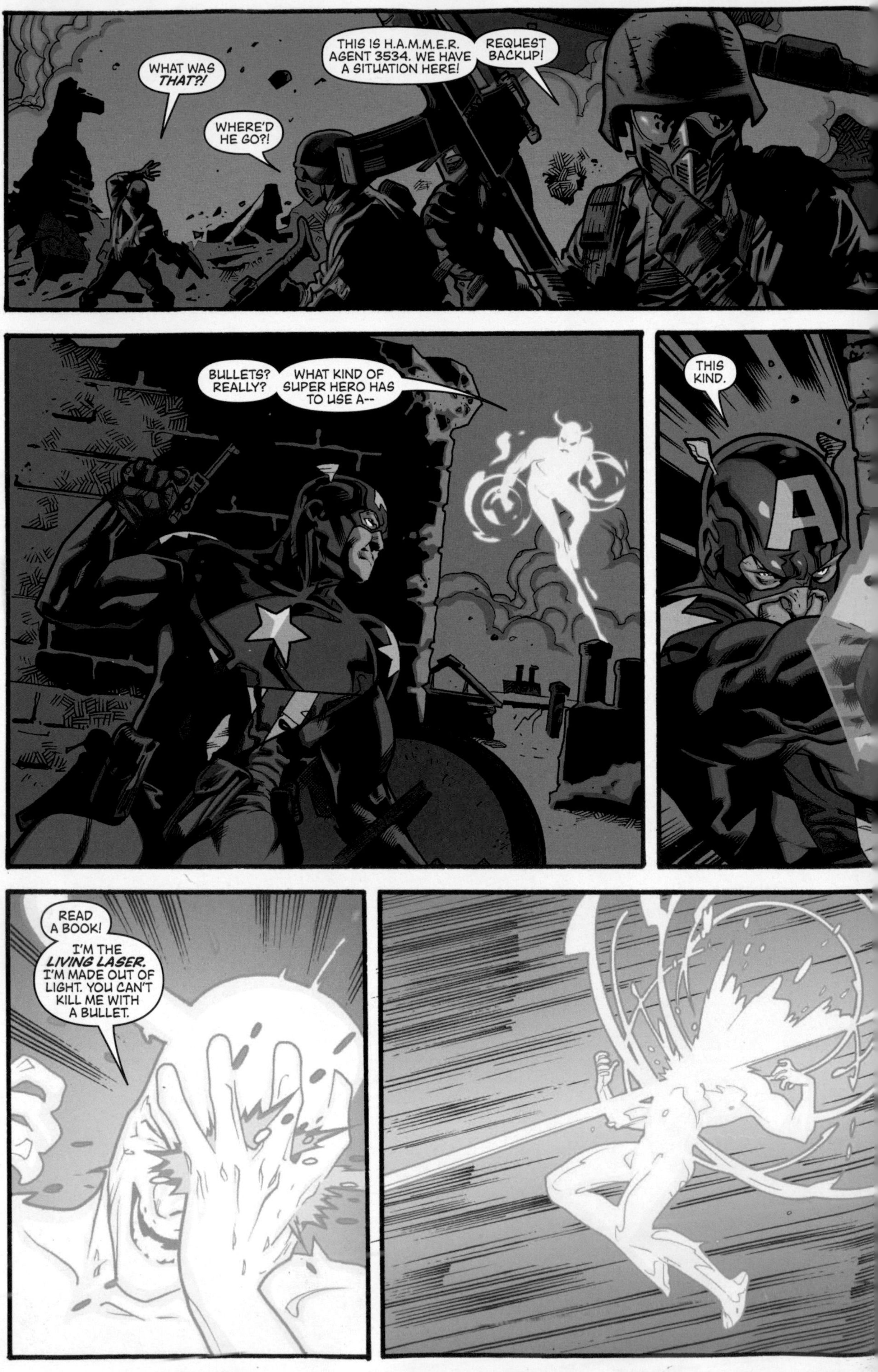
WHAT WAS THAT?!
WHERE'D HE GO?!
THIS IS H.A.M.M.E.R. AGENT 3534. WE HAVE A SITUATION HERE!
REQUEST BACKUP!
BULLETS? REALLY?
WHAT KIND OF SUPER HERO HAS TO USE A--
THIS KIND.
READ A BOOK!
I'M THE LIVING LASER. I'M MADE OUT OF LIGHT. YOU CAN'T KILL ME WITH A BULLET.

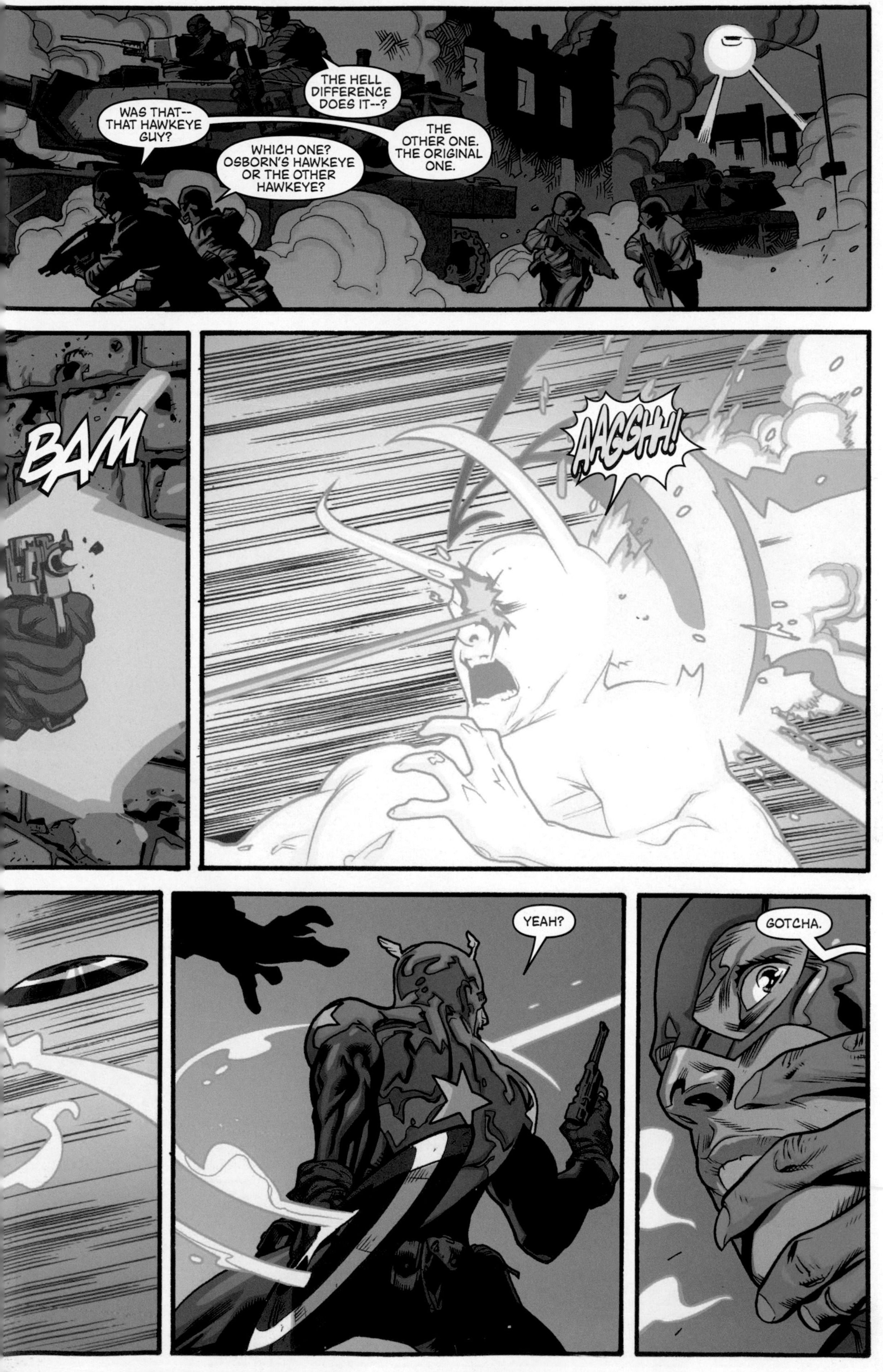
WAS THAT--
THAT HAWKEYE GUY?
THE HELL DIFFERENCE DOES IT--?
WHICH ONE? OSBORN'S HAWKEYE OR THE OTHER HAWKEYE?
THE OTHER ONE. THE ORIGINAL ONE.
BAM
AAGGHH!
YEAH?
GOTCHA.

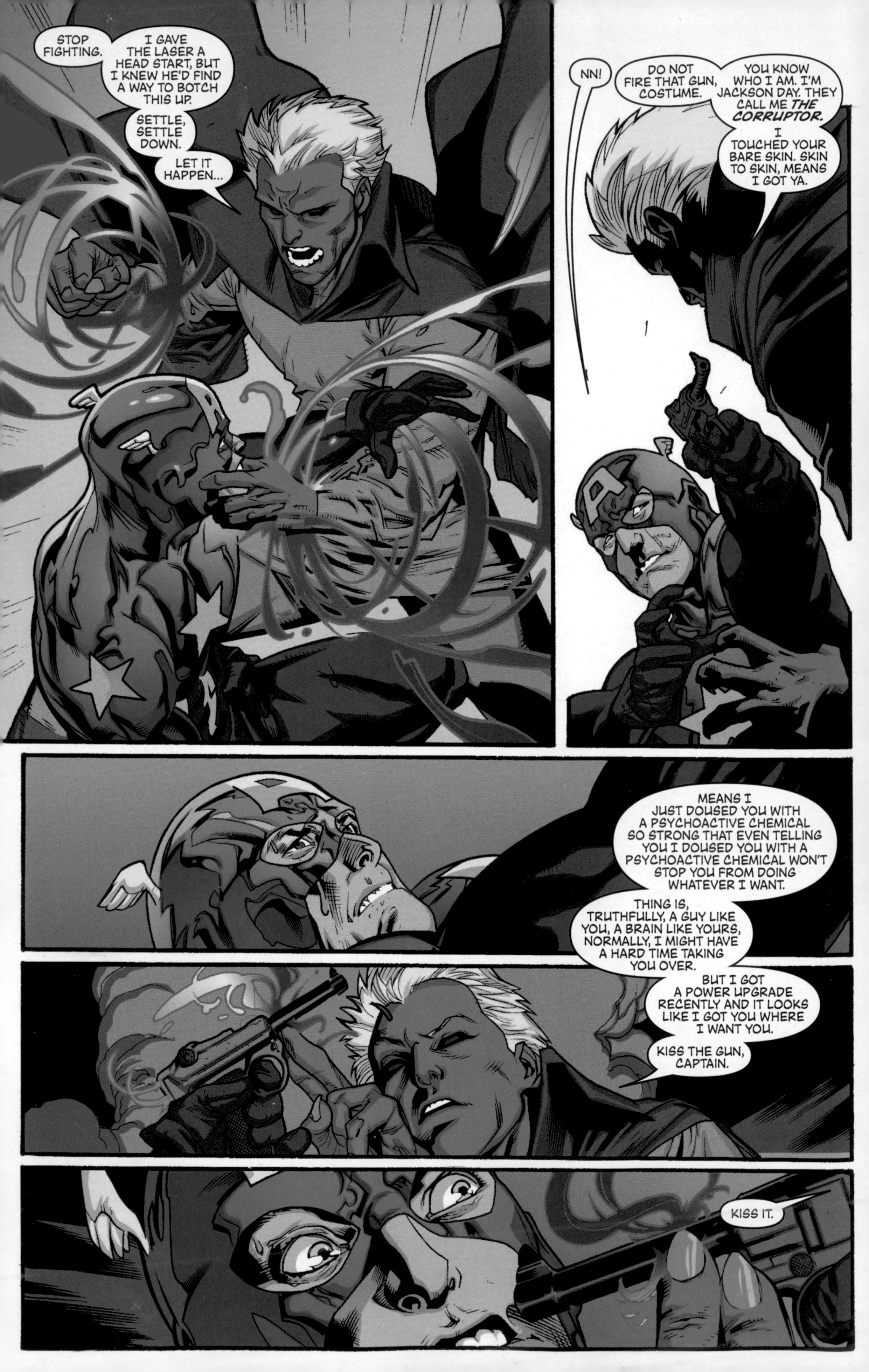
STOP FIGHTING.
I GAVE THE LASER A HEAD START, BUT I KNEW HE'D FIND A WAY TO BOTCH THIS UP.
SETTLE, SETTLE DOWN.
LET IT HAPPEN...
NN!
DO NOT FIRE THAT GUN, COSTUME.
YOU KNOW WHO I AM. I'M JACKSON DAY. THEY CALL ME THE CORRUPTOR.
I TOUCHED YOUR BARE SKIN. SKIN TO SKIN, MEANS I GOT YA.
MEANS I JUST DOUSED YOU WITH A PSYCHOACTIVE CHEMICAL SO STRONG THAT EVEN TELLING YOU I DOUSED YOU WITH A PSYCHOACTIVE CHEMICAL WON'T STOP YOU FROM DOING WHATEVER I WANT.
THING IS, TRUTHFULLY, A GUY LIKE YOU, A BRAIN LIKE YOURS, NORMALLY, I MIGHT HAVE A HARD TIME TAKING YOU OVER.
BUT I GOT A POWER UPGRADE RECENTLY AND IT LOOKS LIKE I GOT YOU WHERE I WANT YOU.
KISS THE GUN, CAPTAIN.
KISS IT.

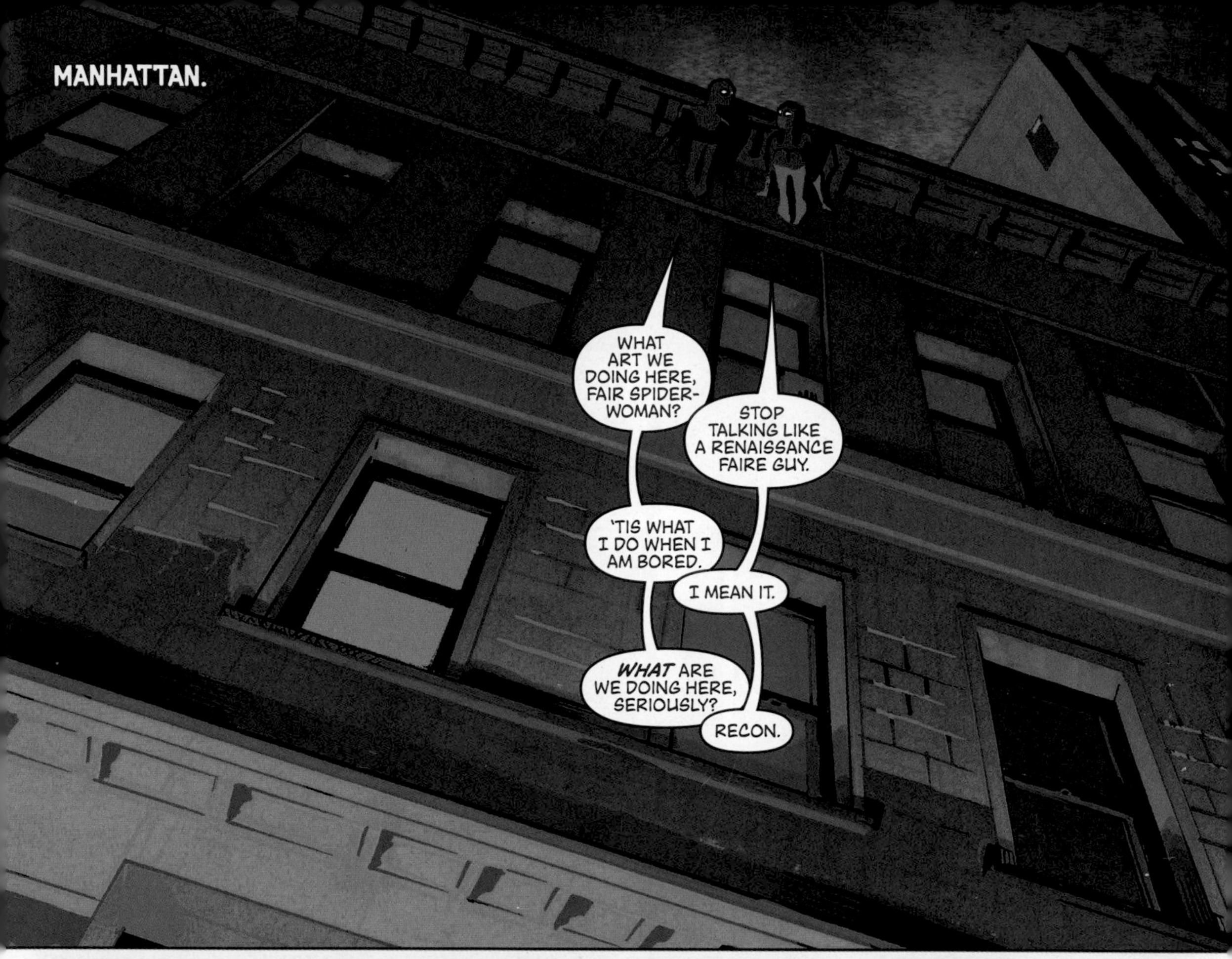
MANHATTAN.
WHAT ART WE DOING HERE, FAIR SPIDER-WOMAN?
STOP TALKING LIKE A RENAISSANCE FAIRE GUY.
'TIS WHAT I DO WHEN I AM BORED.
I MEAN IT.
WHAT ARE WE DOING HERE, SERIOUSLY?
RECON.

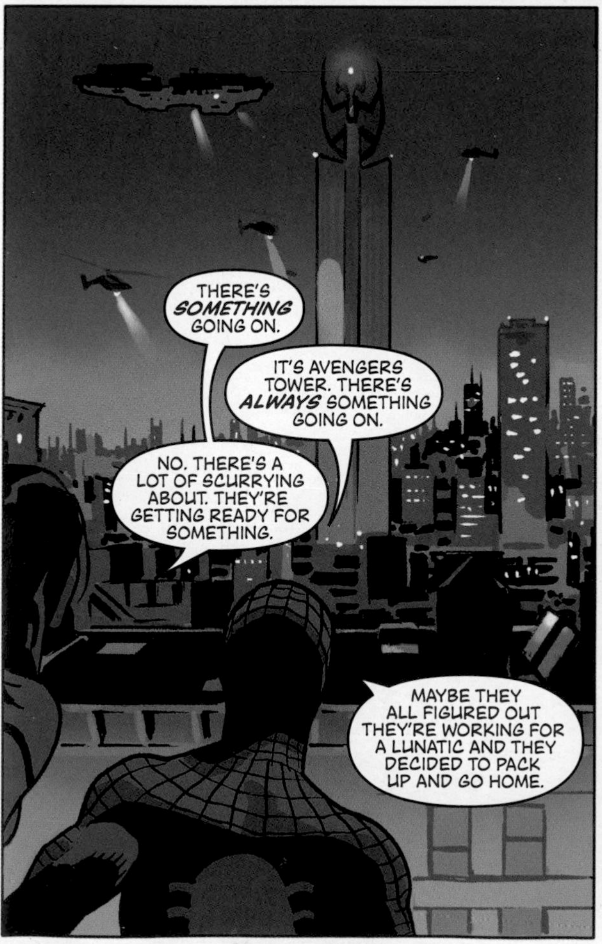
THERE'S *SOMETHING* GOING ON.
IT'S AVENGERS TOWER. THERE'S *ALWAYS* SOMETHING GOING ON.
NO. THERE'S A LOT OF SCURRYING ABOUT. THEY'RE GETTING READY FOR SOMETHING.
MAYBE THEY ALL FIGURED OUT THEY'RE WORKING FOR A LUNATIC AND THEY DECIDED TO PACK UP AND GO HOME.

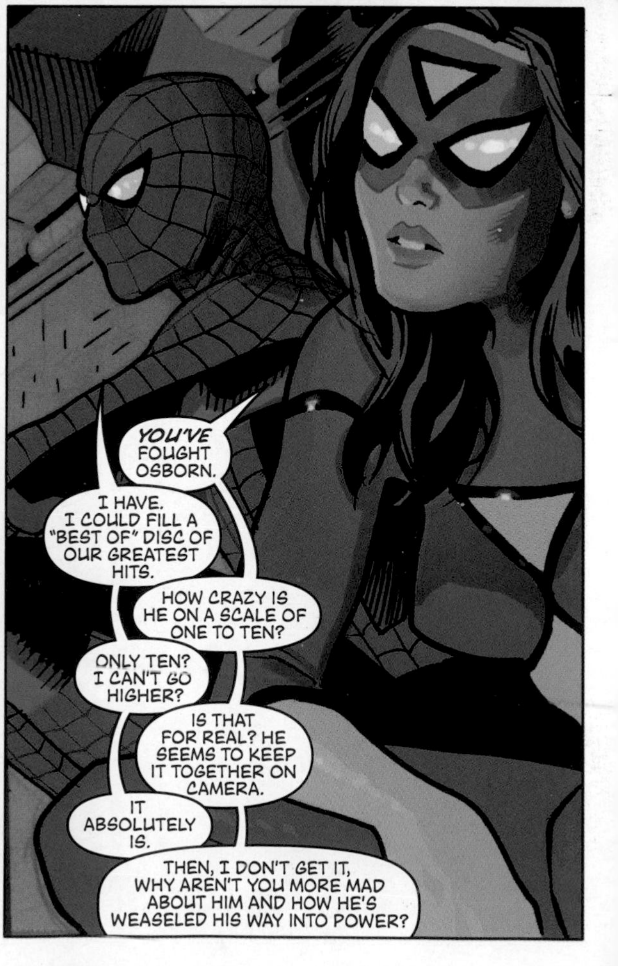
YOU'VE FOUGHT OSBORN.
I HAVE. I COULD FILL A "BEST OF" DISC OF OUR GREATEST HITS.
HOW CRAZY IS HE ON A SCALE OF ONE TO TEN?
ONLY TEN? I CAN'T GO HIGHER?
IS THAT FOR REAL? HE SEEMS TO KEEP IT TOGETHER ON CAMERA.
IT ABSOLUTELY IS.
THEN, I DON'T GET IT, WHY AREN'T YOU MORE MAD ABOUT HIM AND HOW HE'S WEASELED HIS WAY INTO POWER?

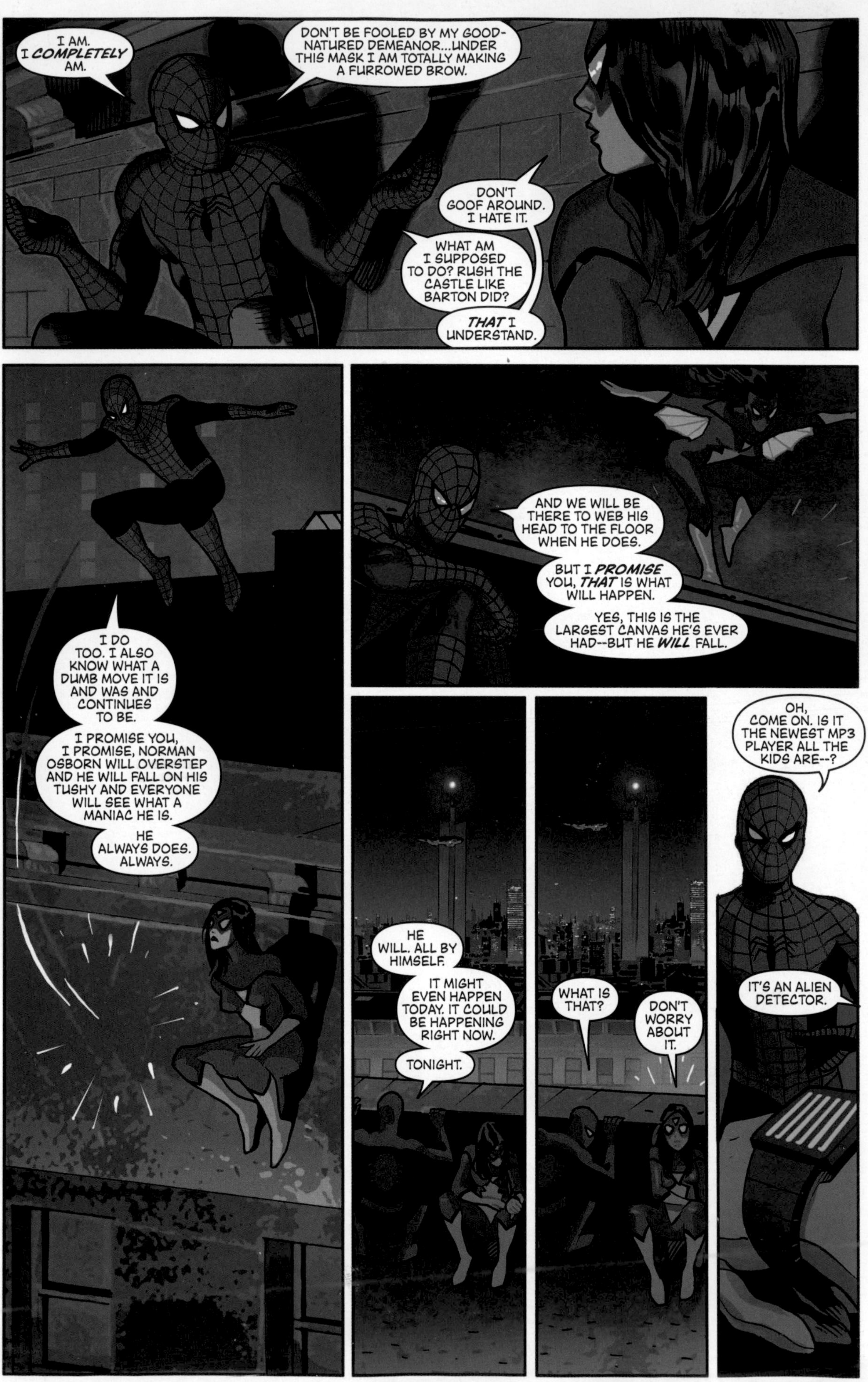
I AM. I *COMPLETELY* AM.
DON'T BE FOOLED BY MY GOOD-NATURED DEMEANOR...UNDER THIS MASK I AM TOTALLY MAKING A FURROWED BROW.
DON'T GOOF AROUND. I HATE IT.
WHAT AM I SUPPOSED TO DO? RUSH THE CASTLE LIKE BARTON DID?
THAT I UNDERSTAND.
I DO TOO. I ALSO KNOW WHAT A DUMB MOVE IT IS AND WAS AND CONTINUES TO BE.
I PROMISE YOU, I PROMISE, NORMAN OSBORN WILL OVERSTEP AND HE WILL FALL ON HIS TUSHY AND EVERYONE WILL SEE WHAT A MANIAC HE IS.
HE ALWAYS DOES. ALWAYS.
AND WE WILL BE THERE TO WEB HIS HEAD TO THE FLOOR WHEN HE DOES.
BUT I *PROMISE* YOU, *THAT* IS WHAT WILL HAPPEN.
YES, THIS IS THE LARGEST CANVAS HE'S EVER HAD--BUT HE *WILL* FALL.
HE WILL. ALL BY HIMSELF.
IT MIGHT EVEN HAPPEN TODAY. IT COULD BE HAPPENING RIGHT NOW.
TONIGHT.
WHAT IS THAT?
DON'T WORRY ABOUT IT.
OH, COME ON. IS IT THE NEWEST MP3 PLAYER ALL THE KIDS ARE--?
IT'S AN ALIEN DETECTOR.

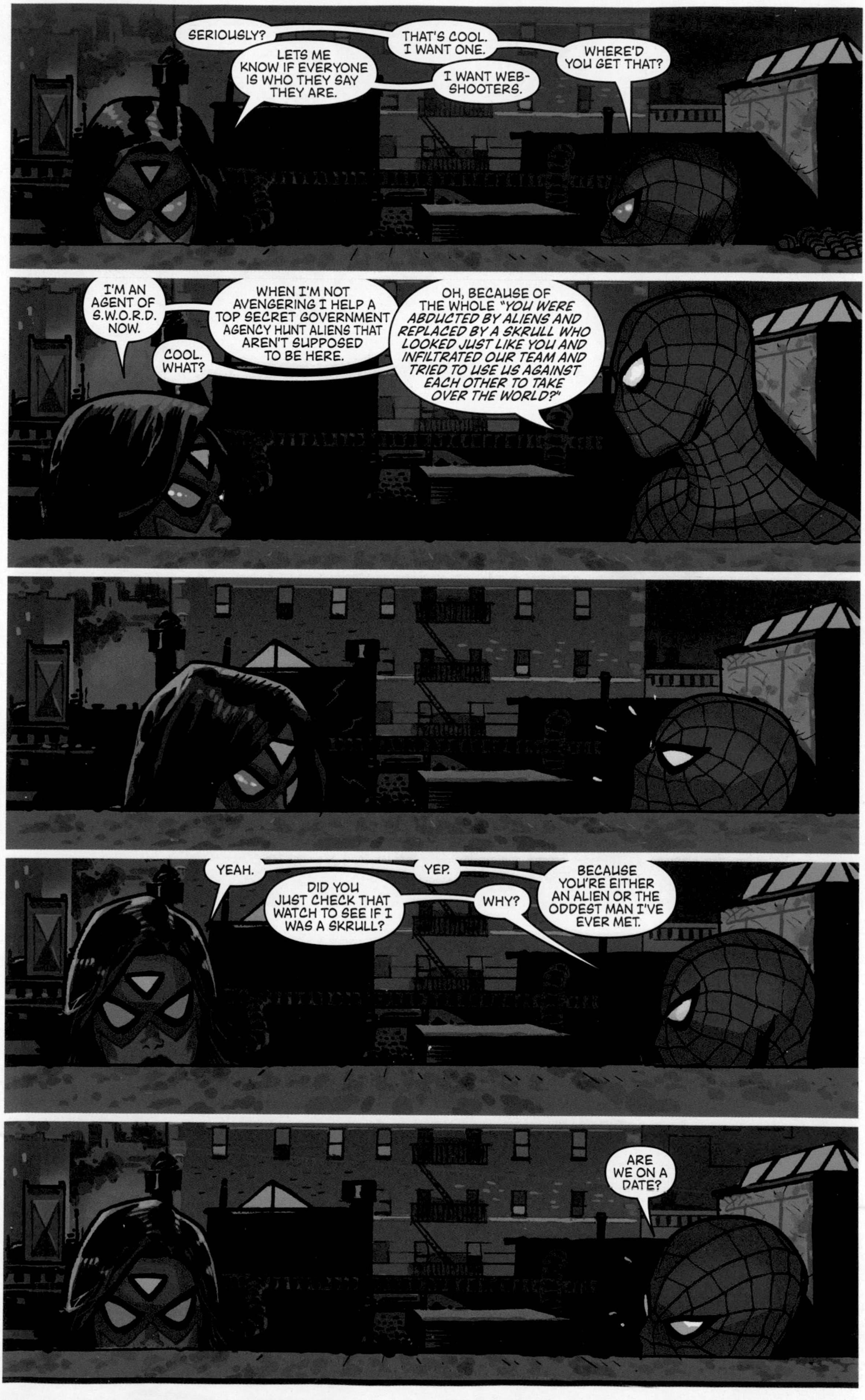
SERIOUSLY?
LETS ME KNOW IF EVERYONE IS WHO THEY SAY THEY ARE.
THAT'S COOL. I WANT ONE.
I WANT WEB-SHOOTERS.
WHERE'D YOU GET THAT?
I'M AN AGENT OF S.W.O.R.D. NOW.
WHEN I'M NOT AVENGERING I HELP A TOP SECRET GOVERNMENT AGENCY HUNT ALIENS THAT AREN'T SUPPOSED TO BE HERE.
COOL. WHAT?
OH, BECAUSE OF THE WHOLE *"YOU WERE ABDUCTED BY ALIENS AND REPLACED BY A SKRULL WHO LOOKED JUST LIKE YOU AND INFILTRATED OUR TEAM AND TRIED TO USE US AGAINST EACH OTHER TO TAKE OVER THE WORLD?"*
YEAH.
DID YOU JUST CHECK THAT WATCH TO SEE IF I WAS A SKRULL?
YEP.
WHY?
BECAUSE YOU'RE EITHER AN ALIEN OR THE ODDEST MAN I'VE EVER MET.
ARE WE ON A DATE?

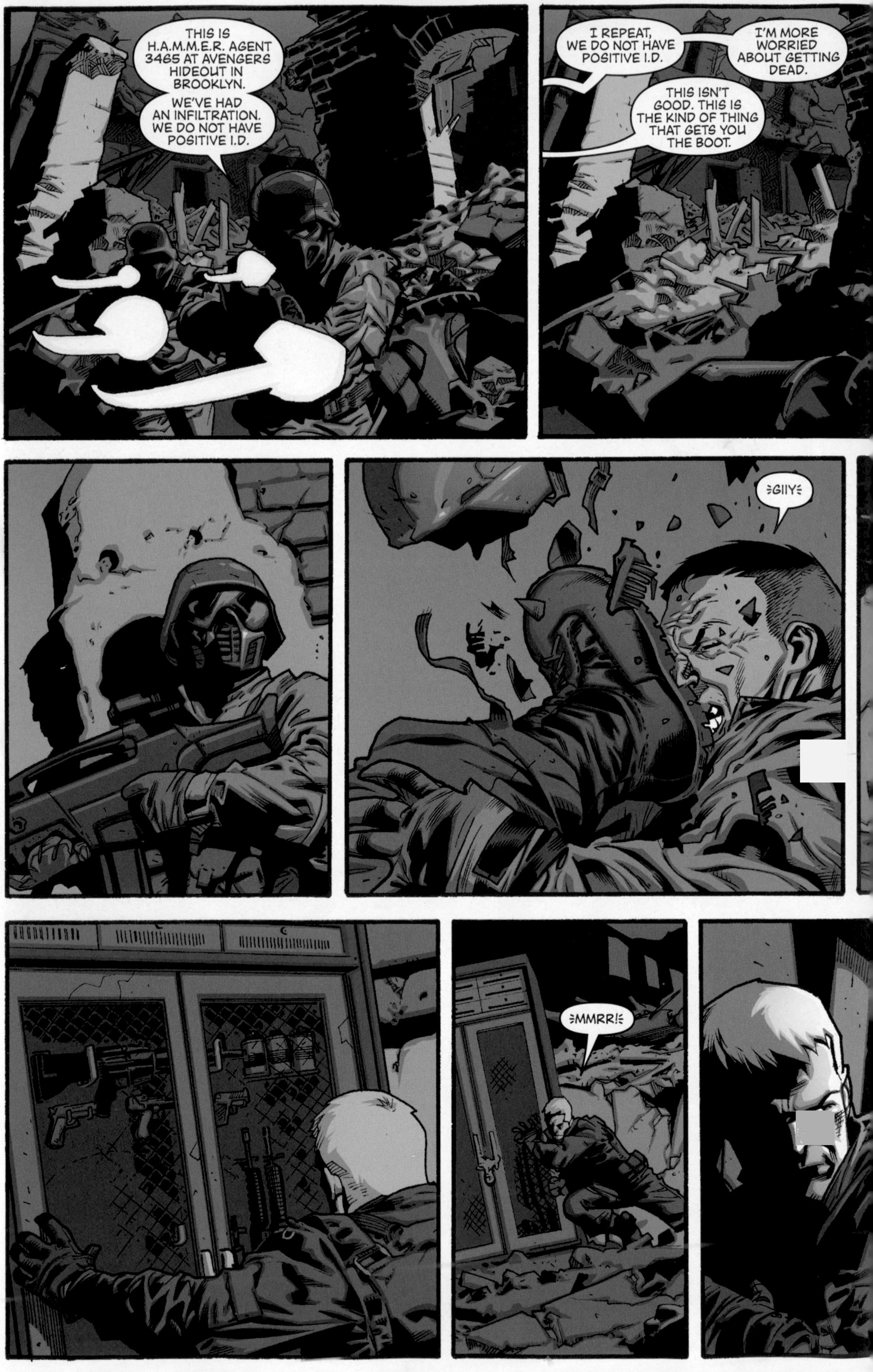
THIS IS H.A.M.M.E.R. AGENT 3465 AT AVENGERS HIDEOUT IN BROOKLYN.
WE'VE HAD AN INFILTRATION. WE DO NOT HAVE POSITIVE I.D.
I REPEAT, WE DO NOT HAVE POSITIVE I.D.
I'M MORE WORRIED ABOUT GETTING DEAD.
THIS ISN'T GOOD. THIS IS THE KIND OF THING THAT GETS YOU THE BOOT.
GIIY
MMRR!

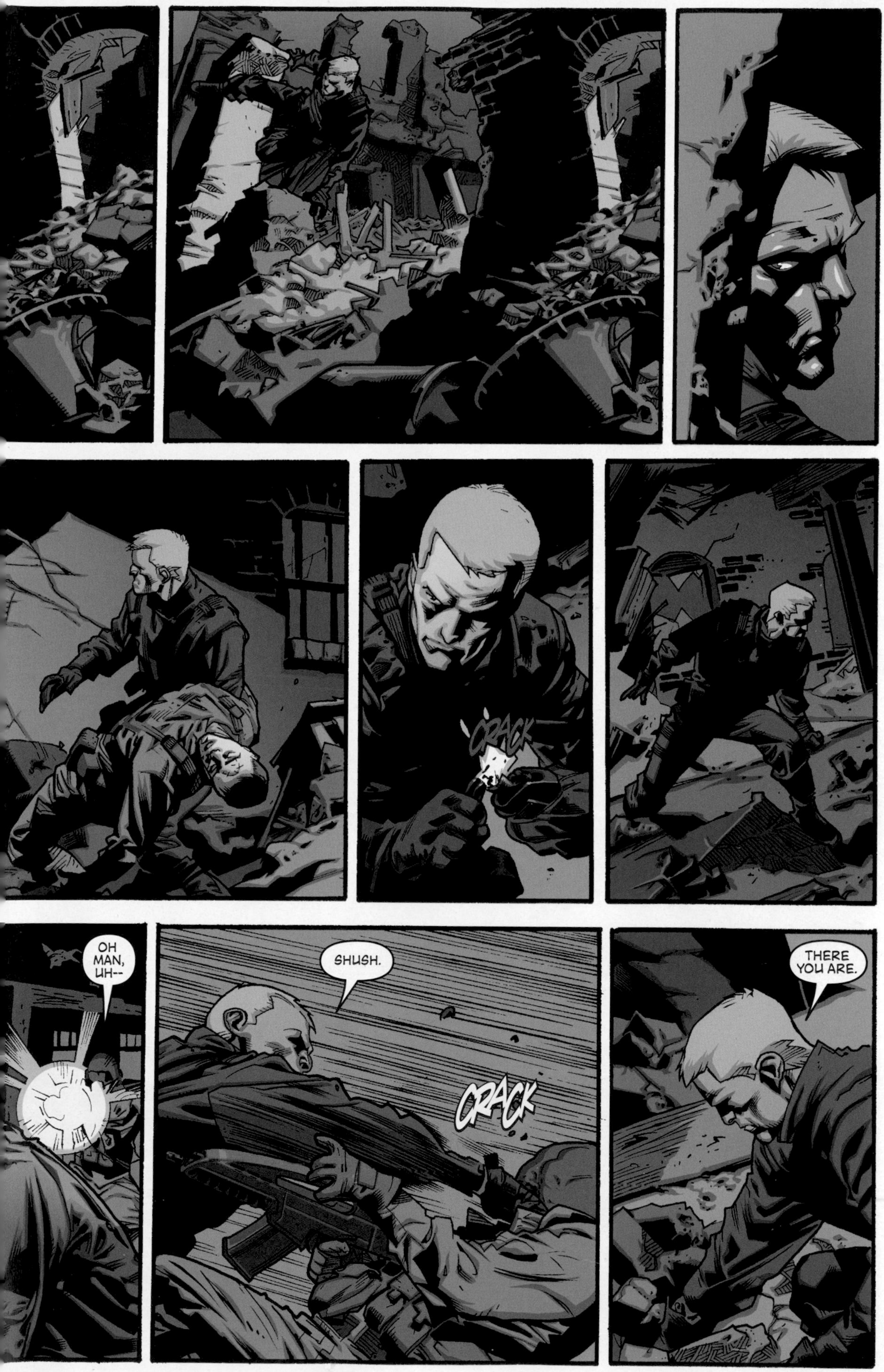
CRACK
OH MAN, UH--
SHUSH.
CRACK
THERE YOU ARE.

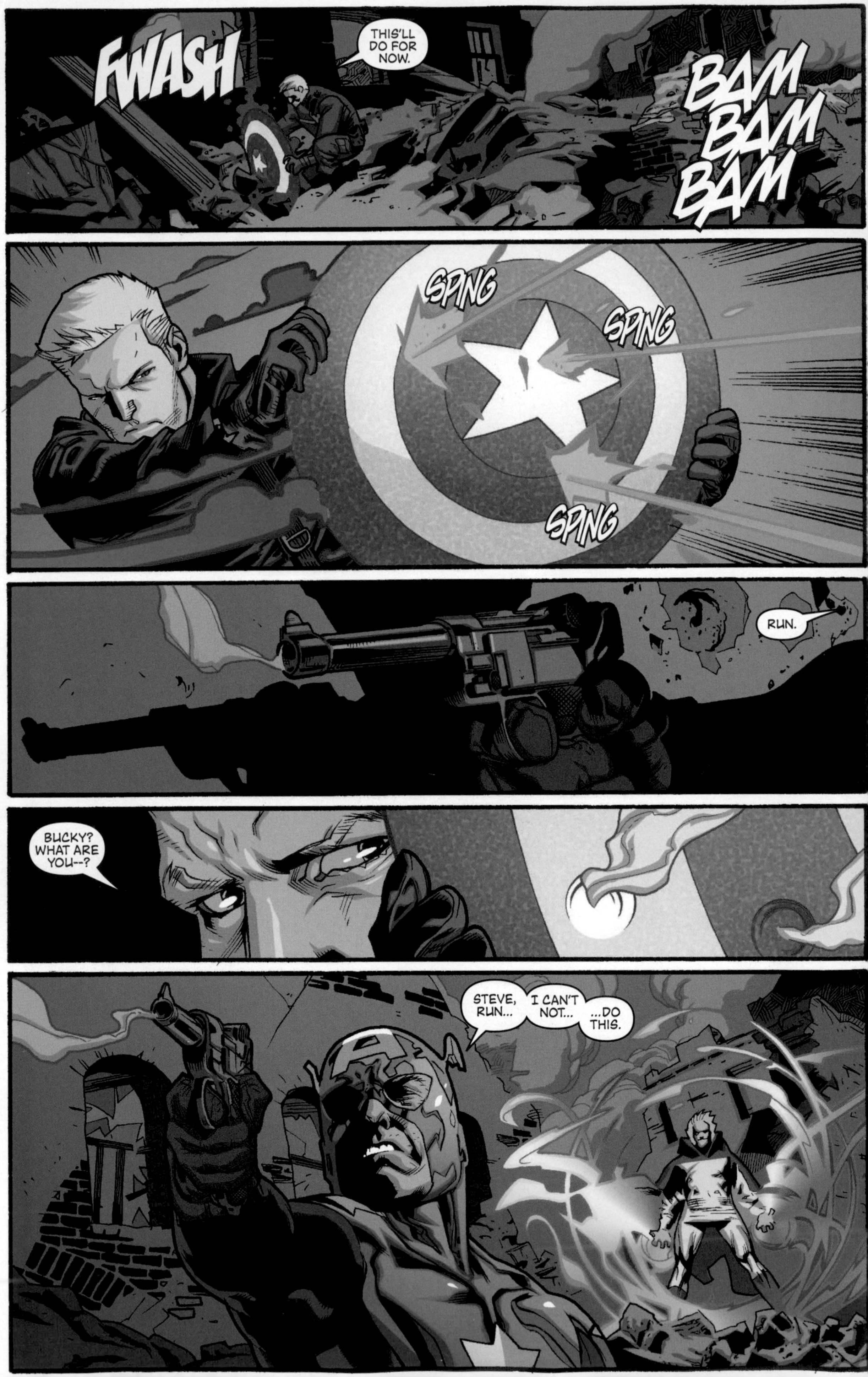
FWASH
THIS'LL DO FOR NOW.
BAM BAM BAM
SPING
SPING
SPING
RUN.
BUCKY? WHAT ARE YOU--?
STEVE, RUN...
I CAN'T NOT...
...DO THIS.

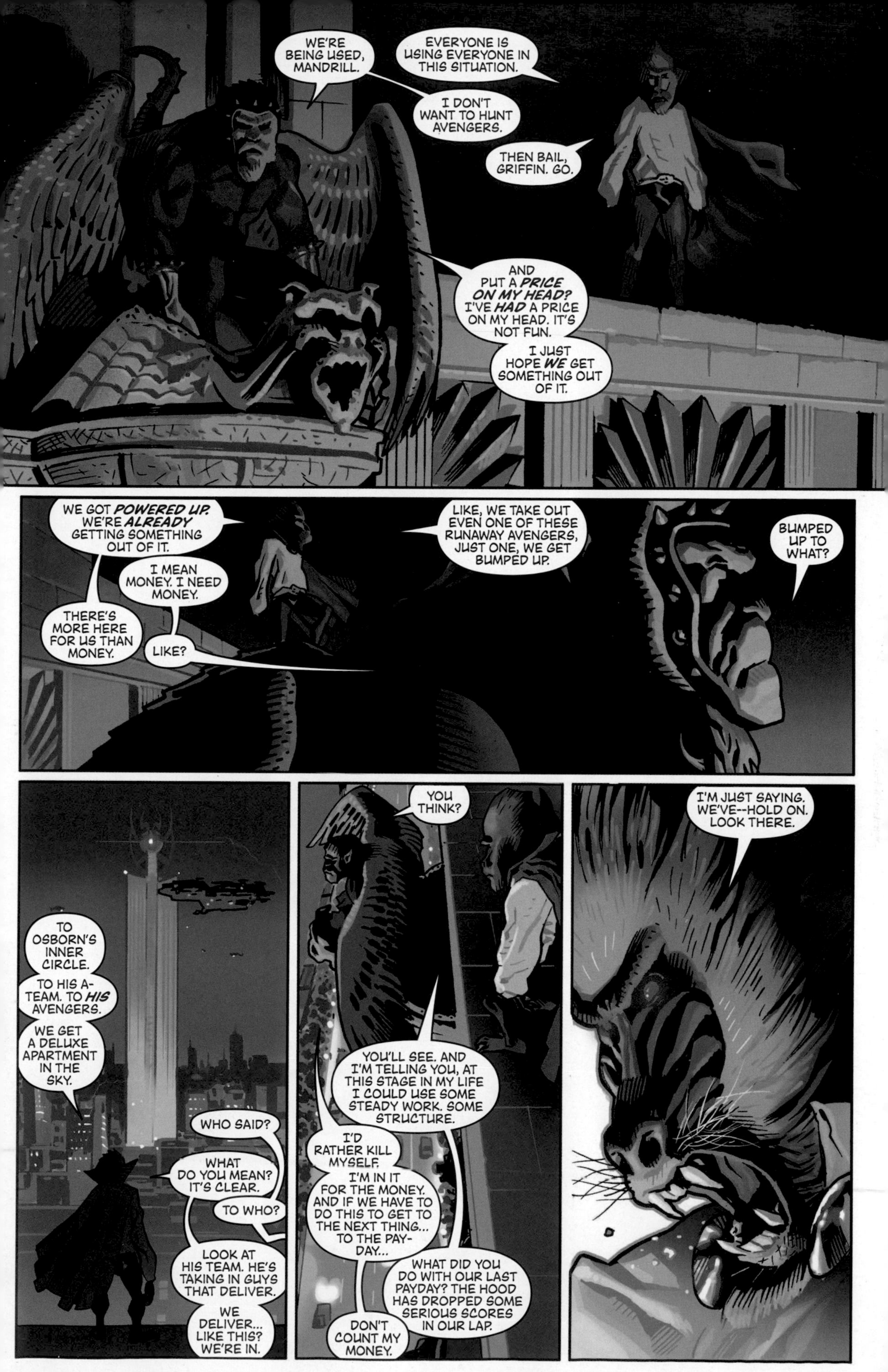
WE'RE BEING USED, MANDRILL.
EVERYONE IS USING EVERYONE IN THIS SITUATION.
I DON'T WANT TO HUNT AVENGERS.
THEN BAIL, GRIFFIN. GO.
AND PUT A PRICE ON MY HEAD? I'VE HAD A PRICE ON MY HEAD. IT'S NOT FUN.
I JUST HOPE WE GET SOMETHING OUT OF IT.
WE GOT POWERED UP. WE'RE ALREADY GETTING SOMETHING OUT OF IT.
I MEAN MONEY. I NEED MONEY.
THERE'S MORE HERE FOR US THAN MONEY.
LIKE?
LIKE, WE TAKE OUT EVEN ONE OF THESE RUNAWAY AVENGERS, JUST ONE, WE GET BUMPED UP.
BUMPED UP TO WHAT?
TO OSBORN'S INNER CIRCLE.
TO HIS A-TEAM. TO HIS AVENGERS.
WE GET A DELUXE APARTMENT IN THE SKY.
WHO SAID?
WHAT DO YOU MEAN? IT'S CLEAR.
TO WHO?
LOOK AT HIS TEAM. HE'S TAKING IN GUYS THAT DELIVER.
WE DELIVER... LIKE THIS? WE'RE IN.
YOU THINK?
YOU'LL SEE. AND I'M TELLING YOU, AT THIS STAGE IN MY LIFE I COULD USE SOME STEADY WORK. SOME STRUCTURE.
I'D RATHER KILL MYSELF.
I'M IN IT FOR THE MONEY. AND IF WE HAVE TO DO THIS TO GET TO THE NEXT THING... TO THE PAY-DAY...
WHAT DID YOU DO WITH OUR LAST PAYDAY? THE HOOD HAS DROPPED SOME SERIOUS SCORES IN OUR LAP.
DON'T COUNT MY MONEY.
I'M JUST SAYING. WE'VE--HOLD ON. LOOK THERE.

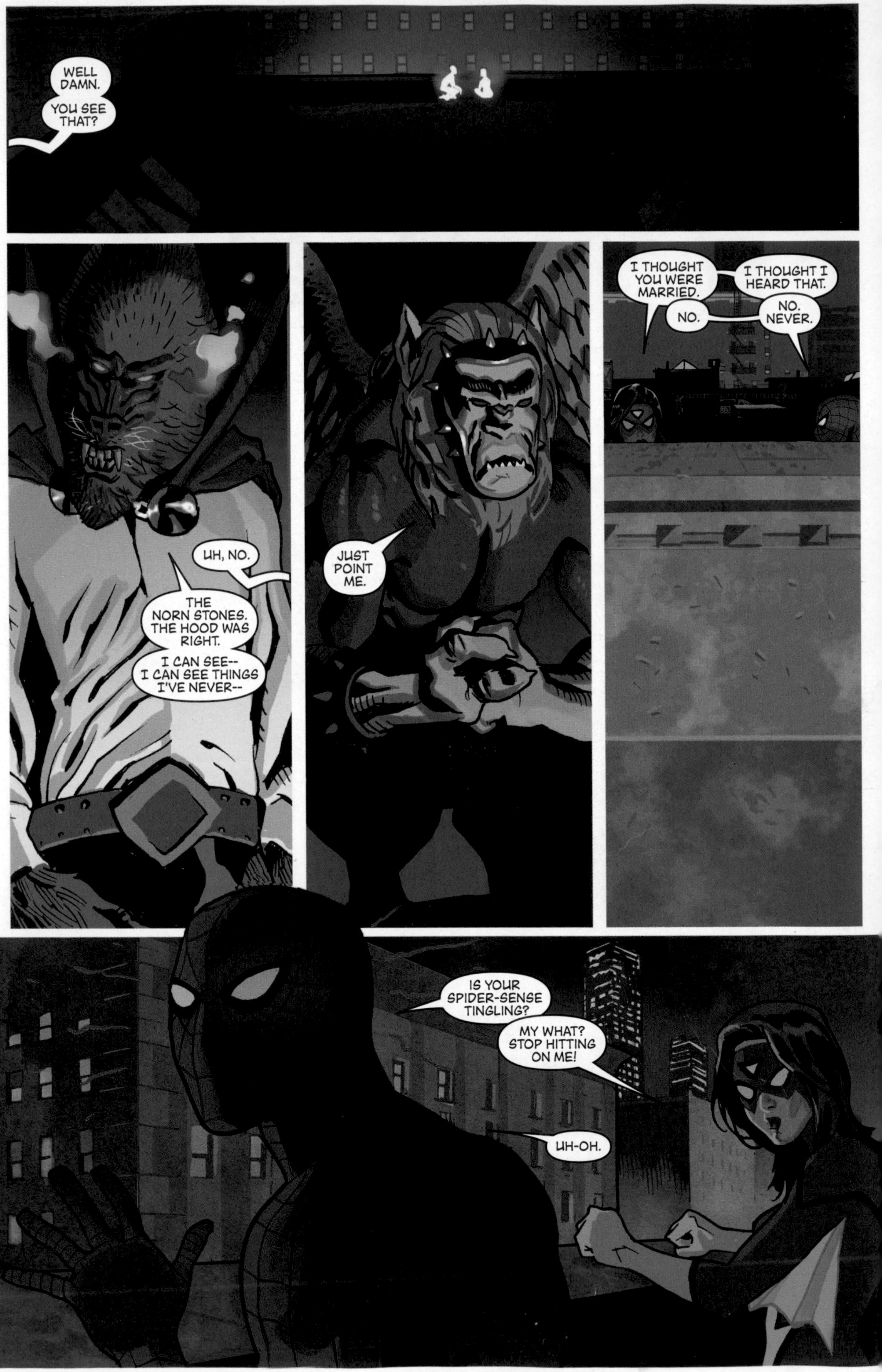
WELL DAMN.
YOU SEE THAT?
UH, NO.
THE NORN STONES. THE HOOD WAS RIGHT.
I CAN SEE-- I CAN SEE THINGS I'VE NEVER--
JUST POINT ME.
I THOUGHT YOU WERE MARRIED.
I THOUGHT I HEARD THAT.
NO.
NO. NEVER.
IS YOUR SPIDER-SENSE TINGLING?
MY WHAT? STOP HITTING ON ME!
UH-OH.

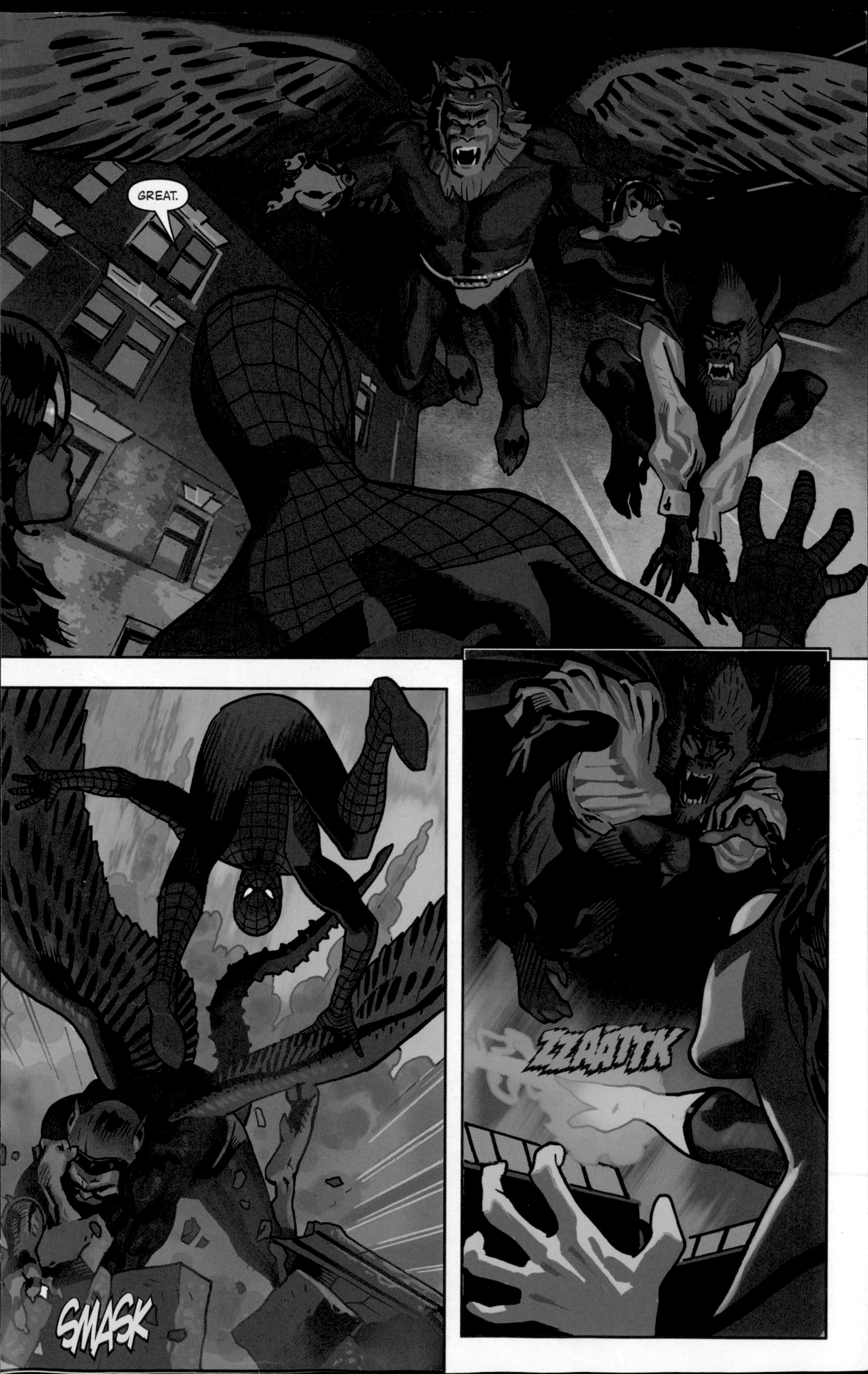
GREAT.
SMASK
ZZAATTK

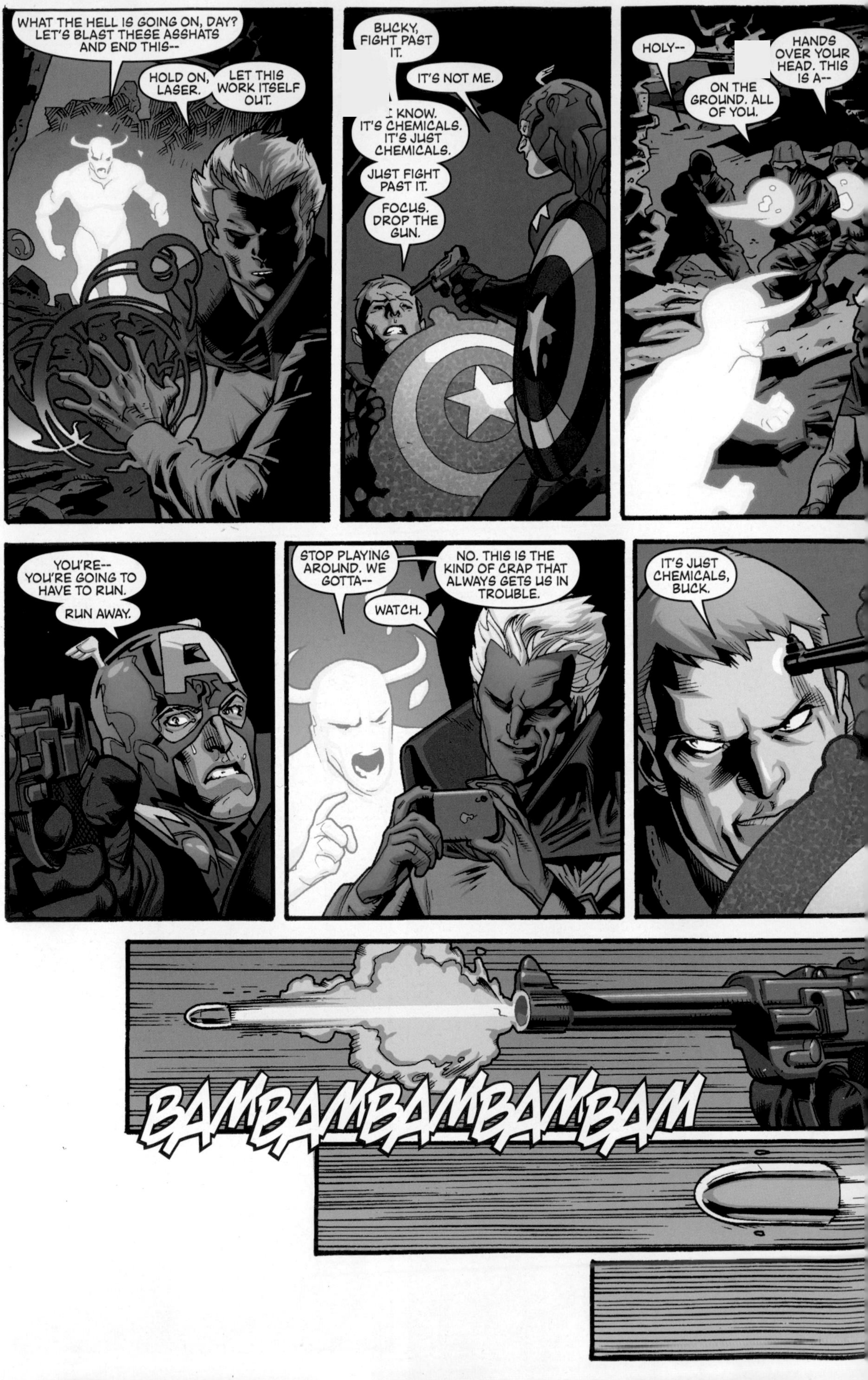
WHAT THE HELL IS GOING ON, DAY? LET'S BLAST THESE ASSHATS AND END THIS--
HOLD ON, LASER.
LET THIS WORK ITSELF OUT.
BUCKY, FIGHT PAST IT.
IT'S NOT ME.
KNOW. IT'S CHEMICALS. IT'S JUST CHEMICALS.
JUST FIGHT PAST IT.
FOCUS. DROP THE GUN.
HOLY--
HANDS OVER YOUR HEAD. THIS IS A--
ON THE GROUND. ALL OF YOU.
YOU'RE-- YOU'RE GOING TO HAVE TO RUN.
RUN AWAY.
STOP PLAYING AROUND. WE GOTTA--
NO. THIS IS THE KIND OF CRAP THAT ALWAYS GETS US IN TROUBLE.
WATCH.
IT'S JUST CHEMICALS, BUCK.
BAMBAMBAMBAMBAM

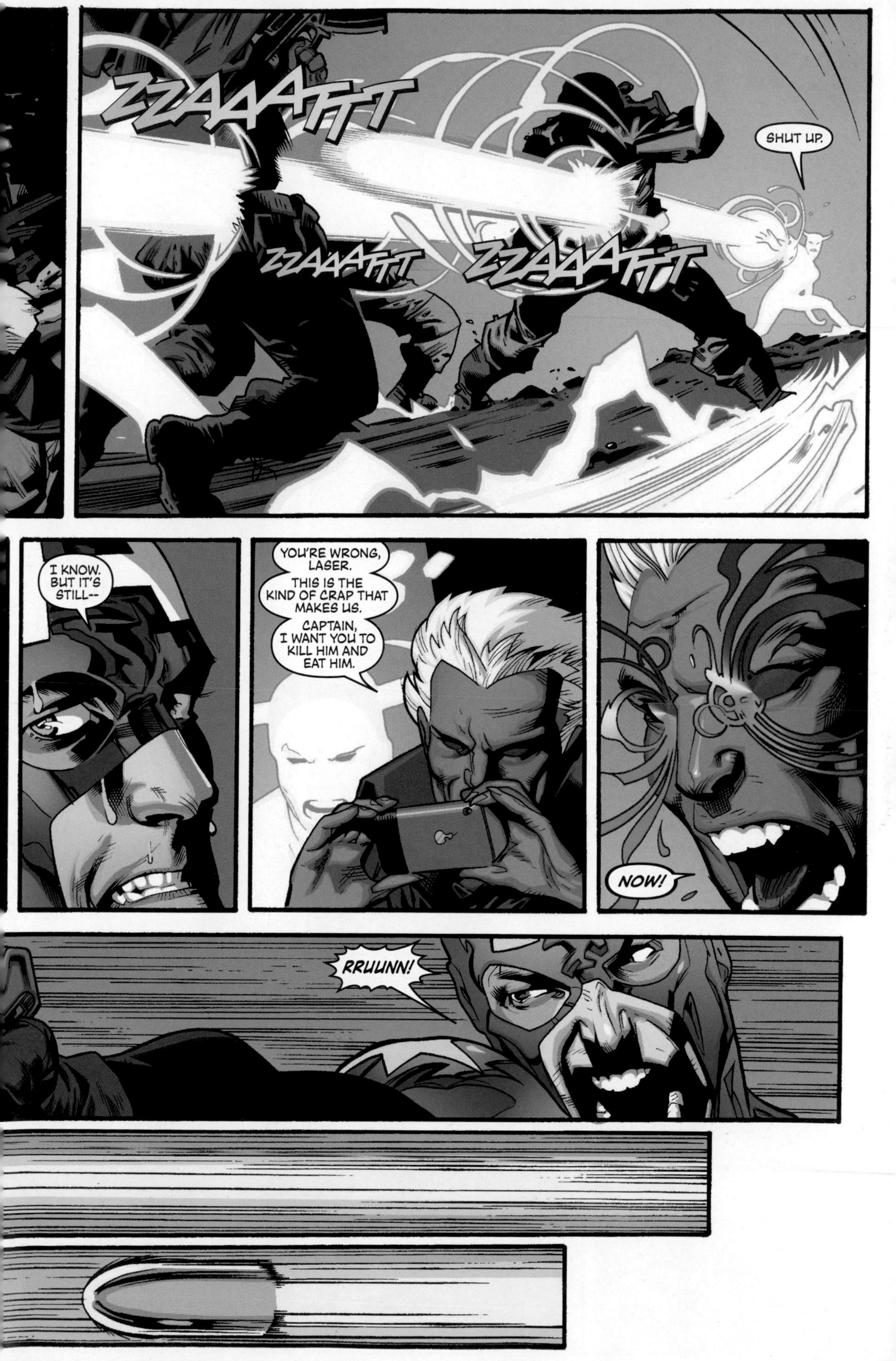
ZZAAAFTTT
SHUT UP.
ZZAAAFTTT
ZZAAAFTTT
I KNOW. BUT IT'S STILL--
YOU'RE WRONG, LASER.
THIS IS THE KIND OF CRAP THAT MAKES US.
CAPTAIN, I WANT YOU TO KILL HIM AND EAT HIM.
NOW!
RRUUNN!

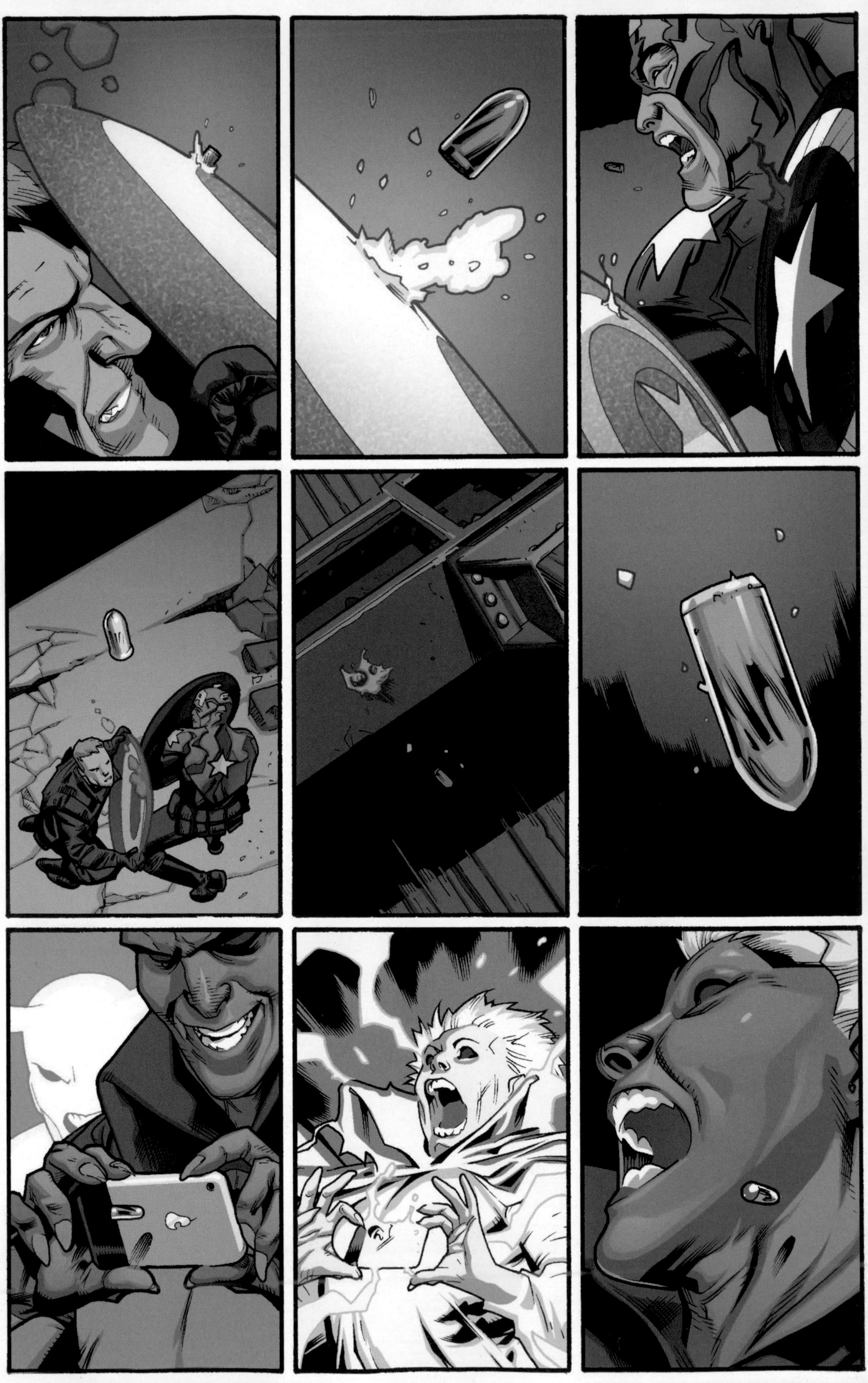

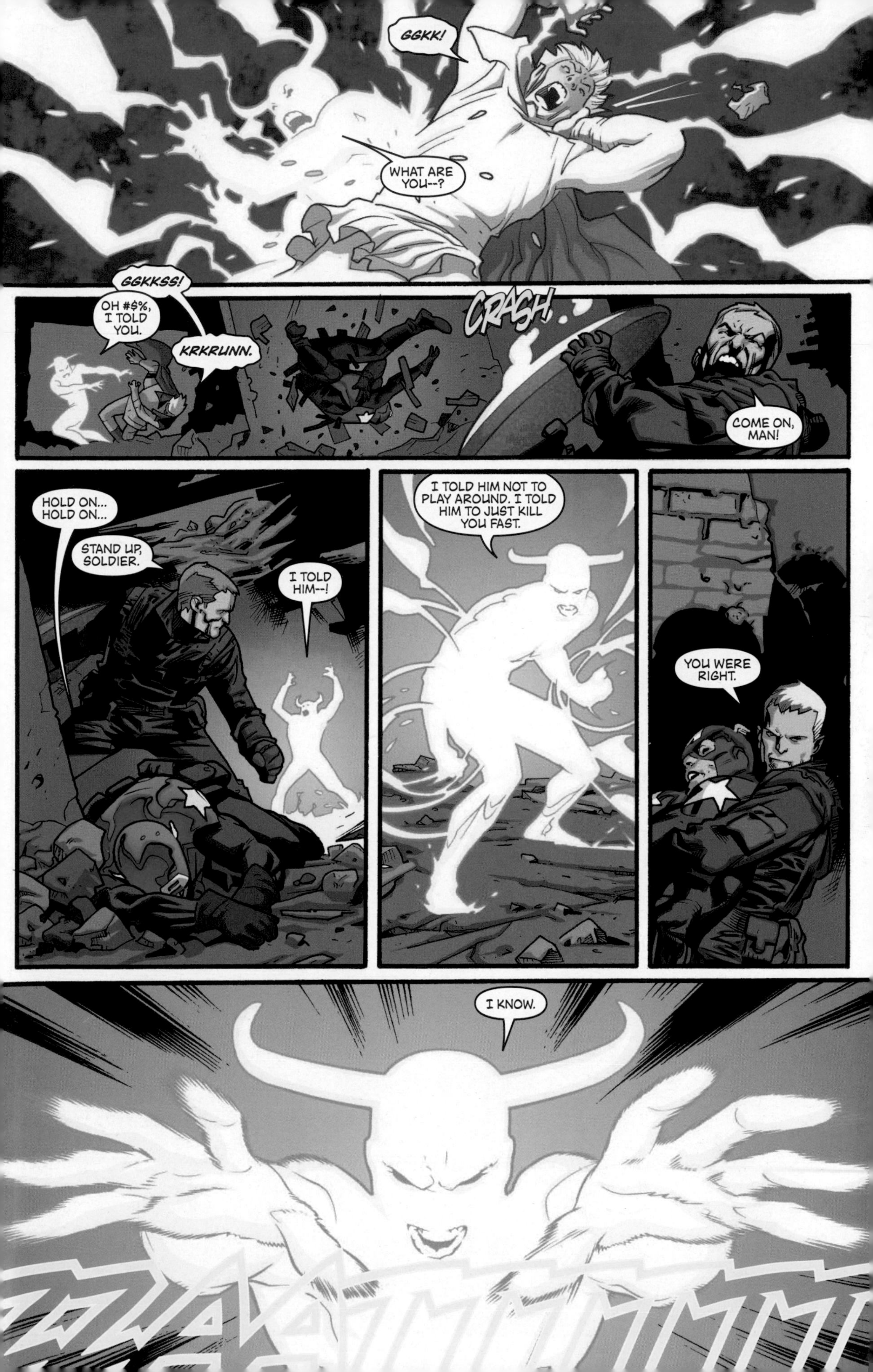
GGKK!
WHAT ARE YOU--?
GGKKSS!
OH #$%, I TOLD YOU.
KRKRUNN.
CRASH
COME ON, MAN!
HOLD ON... HOLD ON...
STAND UP, SOLDIER.
I TOLD HIM--!
I TOLD HIM NOT TO PLAY AROUND. I TOLD HIM TO JUST KILL YOU FAST.
YOU WERE RIGHT.
I KNOW.

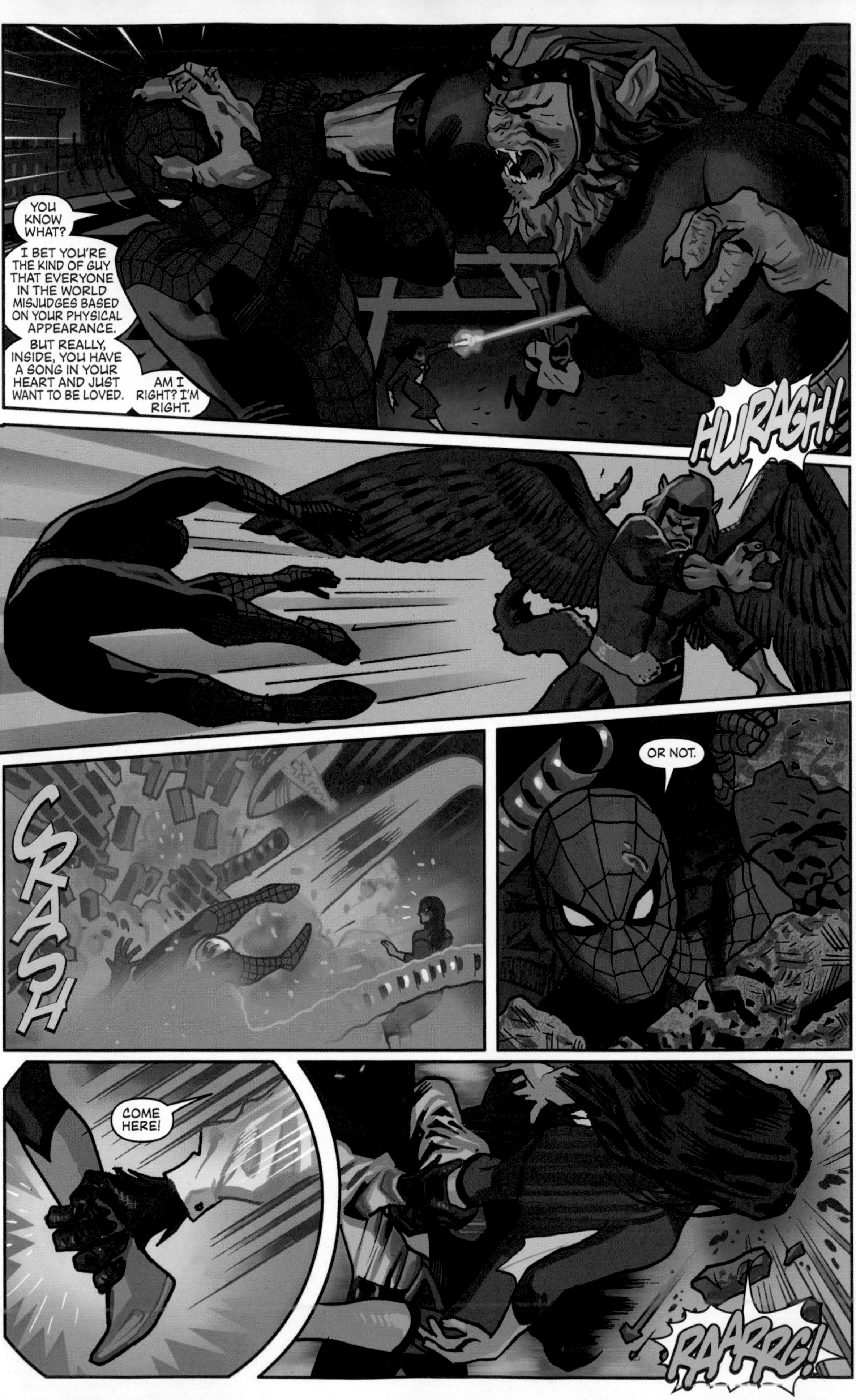

YOU KNOW WHAT?
I BET YOU'RE THE KIND OF GUY THAT EVERYONE IN THE WORLD MISJUDGES BASED ON YOUR PHYSICAL APPEARANCE.
BUT REALLY, INSIDE, YOU HAVE A SONG IN YOUR HEART AND JUST WANT TO BE LOVED.
AM I RIGHT? I'M RIGHT.
HURAGH!
CRASH
OR NOT.
COME HERE!
RAARRG!

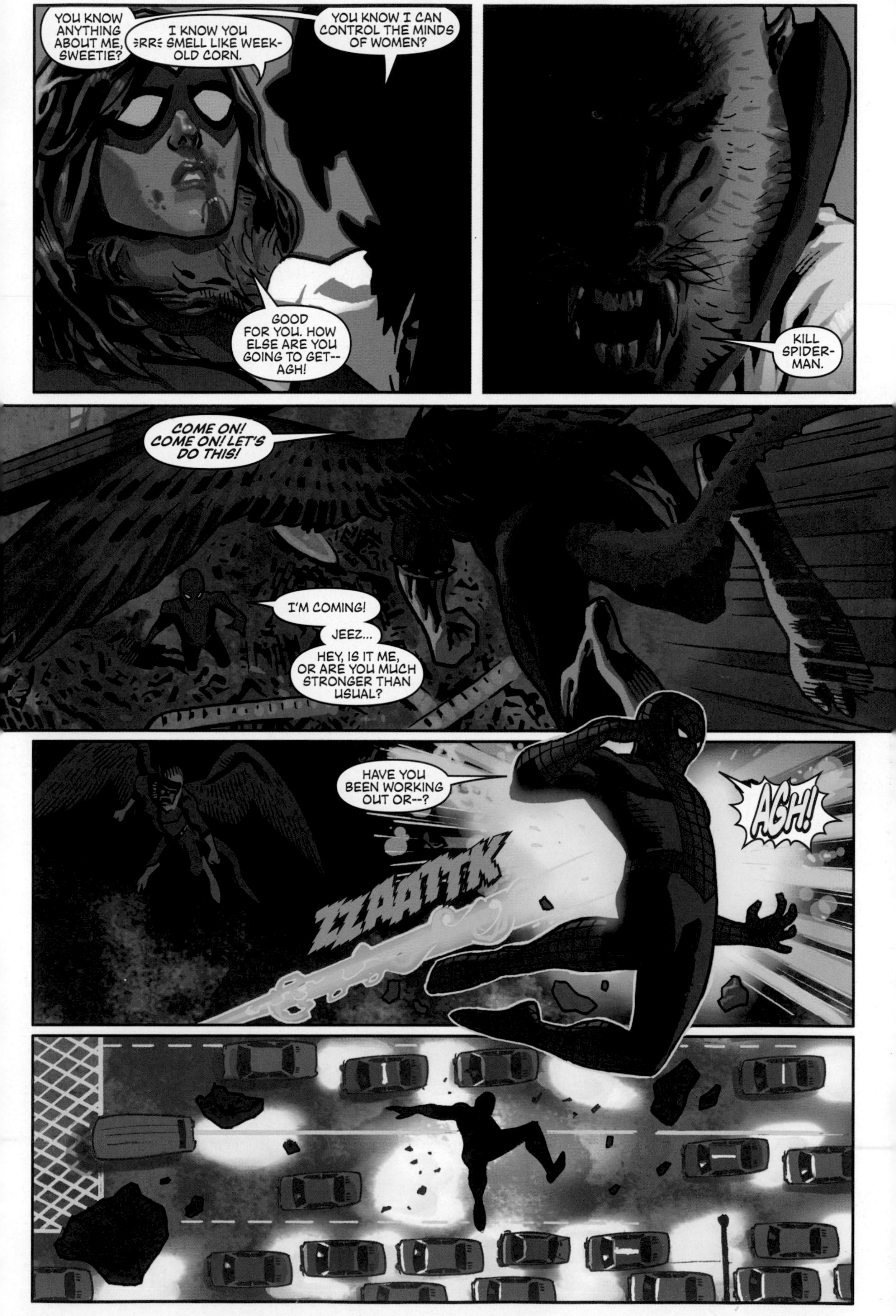

YOU KNOW ANYTHING ABOUT ME, SWEETIE?
I KNOW YOU SMELL LIKE WEEK-OLD CORN.
YOU KNOW I CAN CONTROL THE MINDS OF WOMEN?
GOOD FOR YOU. HOW ELSE ARE YOU GOING TO GET-- AGH!
KILL SPIDER-MAN.
COME ON! COME ON! LET'S DO THIS!
I'M COMING!
JEEZ...
HEY, IS IT ME, OR ARE YOU MUCH STRONGER THAN USUAL?
HAVE YOU BEEN WORKING OUT OR--?
AGH!
ZZAATTK

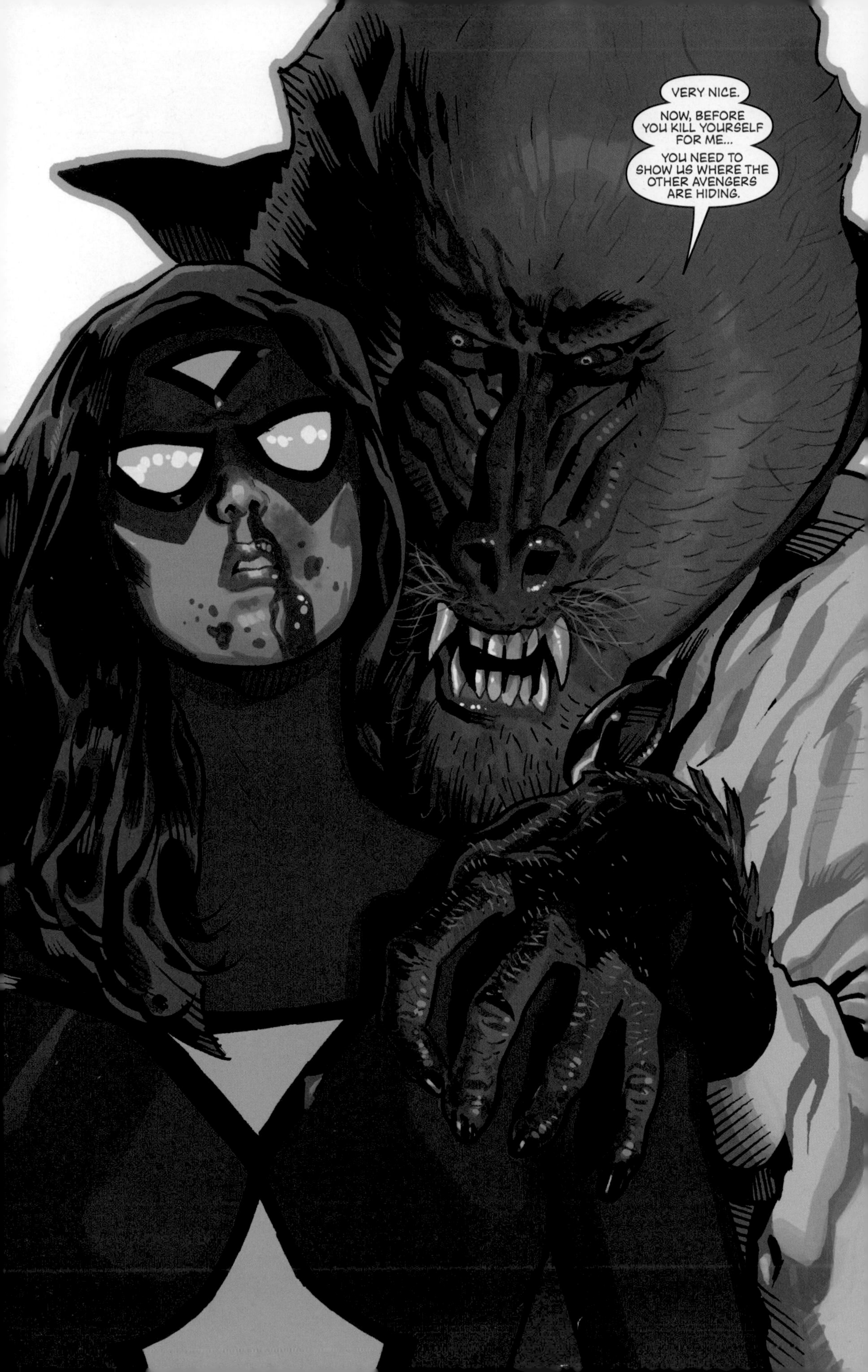
VERY NICE.
NOW, BEFORE YOU KILL YOURSELF FOR ME...
YOU NEED TO SHOW US WHERE THE OTHER AVENGERS ARE HIDING.

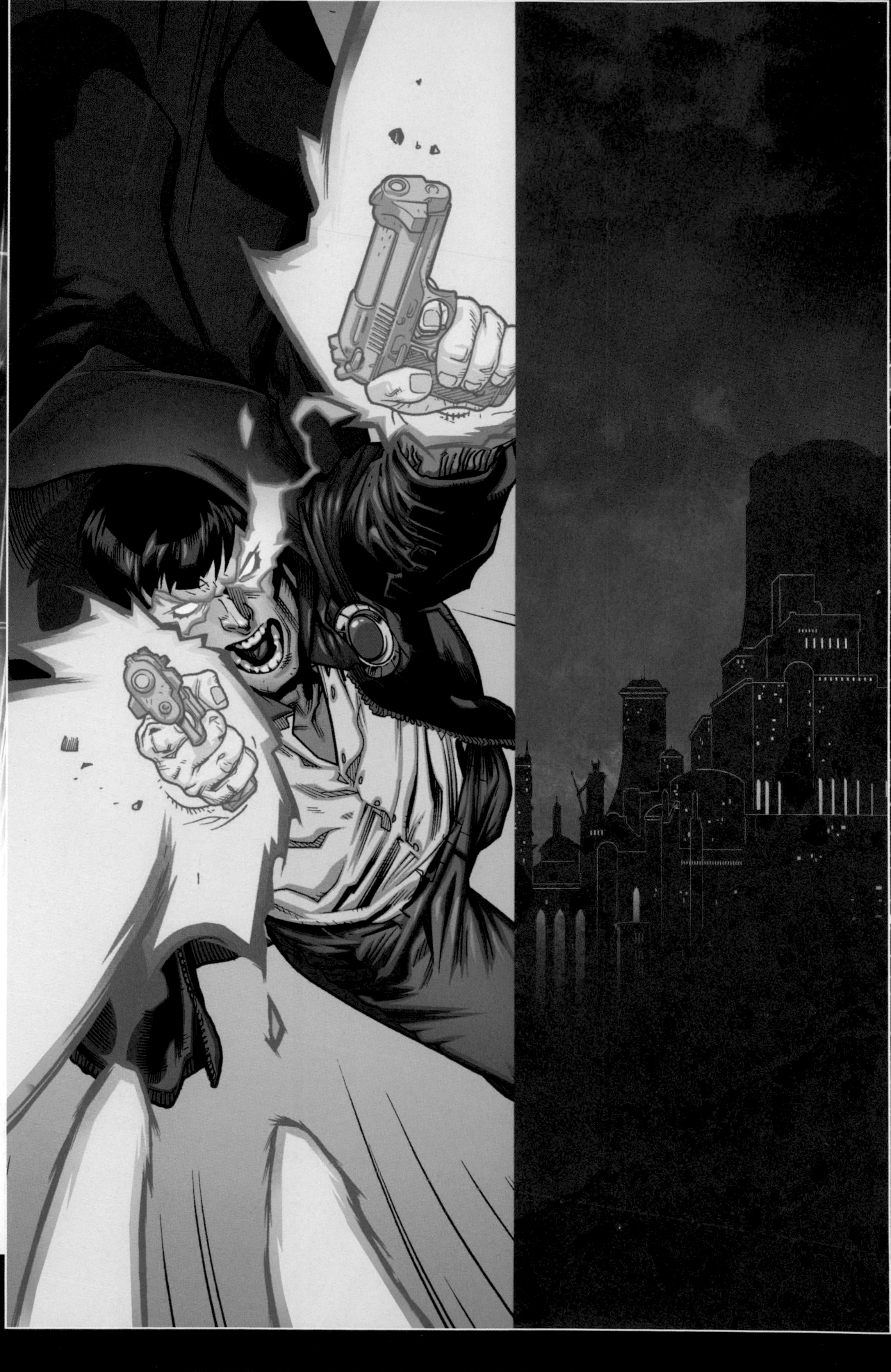

NEW AVENGERS #62

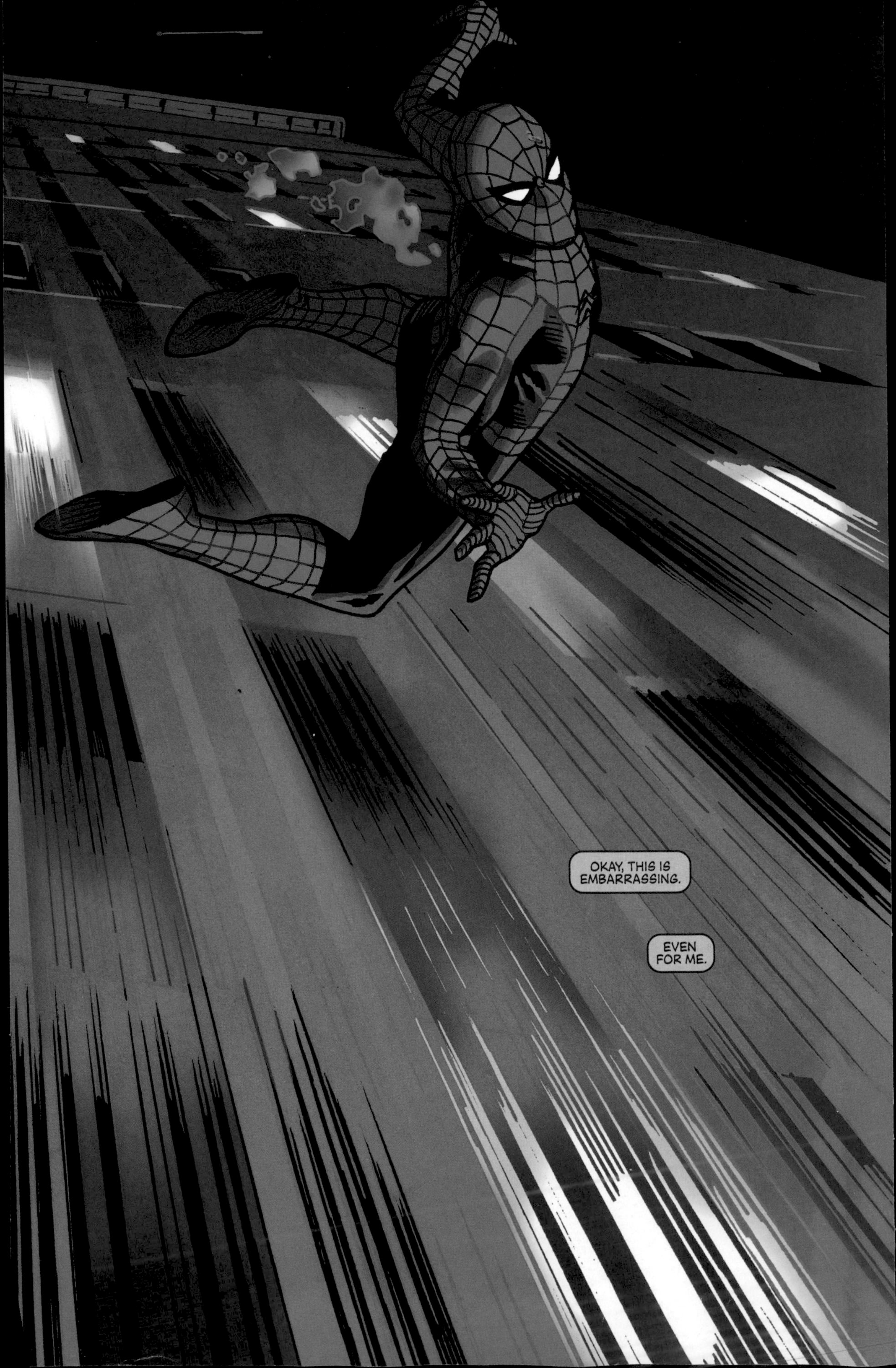
OKAY, THIS IS EMBARRASSING.
EVEN FOR ME.

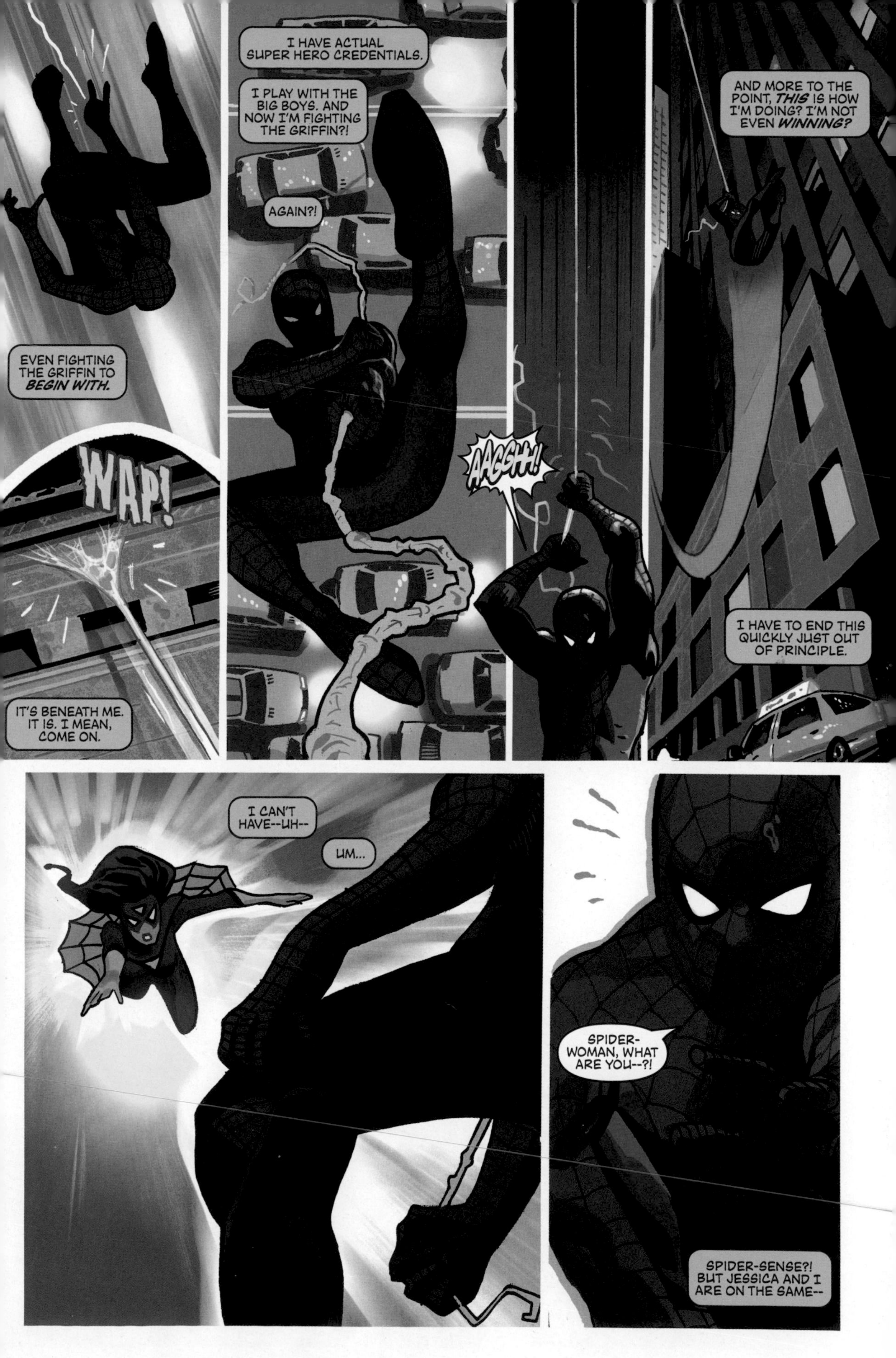

EVEN FIGHTING THE GRIFFIN TO BEGIN WITH.
WAP!
IT'S BENEATH ME. IT IS. I MEAN, COME ON.
I HAVE ACTUAL SUPER HERO CREDENTIALS.
I PLAY WITH THE BIG BOYS. AND NOW I'M FIGHTING THE GRIFFIN?!
AGAIN?!
AAGGH!
AND MORE TO THE POINT, THIS IS HOW I'M DOING? I'M NOT EVEN WINNING?
I HAVE TO END THIS QUICKLY JUST OUT OF PRINCIPLE.
I CAN'T HAVE--UH--
UM...
SPIDER-WOMAN, WHAT ARE YOU--?!
SPIDER-SENSE?! BUT JESSICA AND I ARE ON THE SAME--

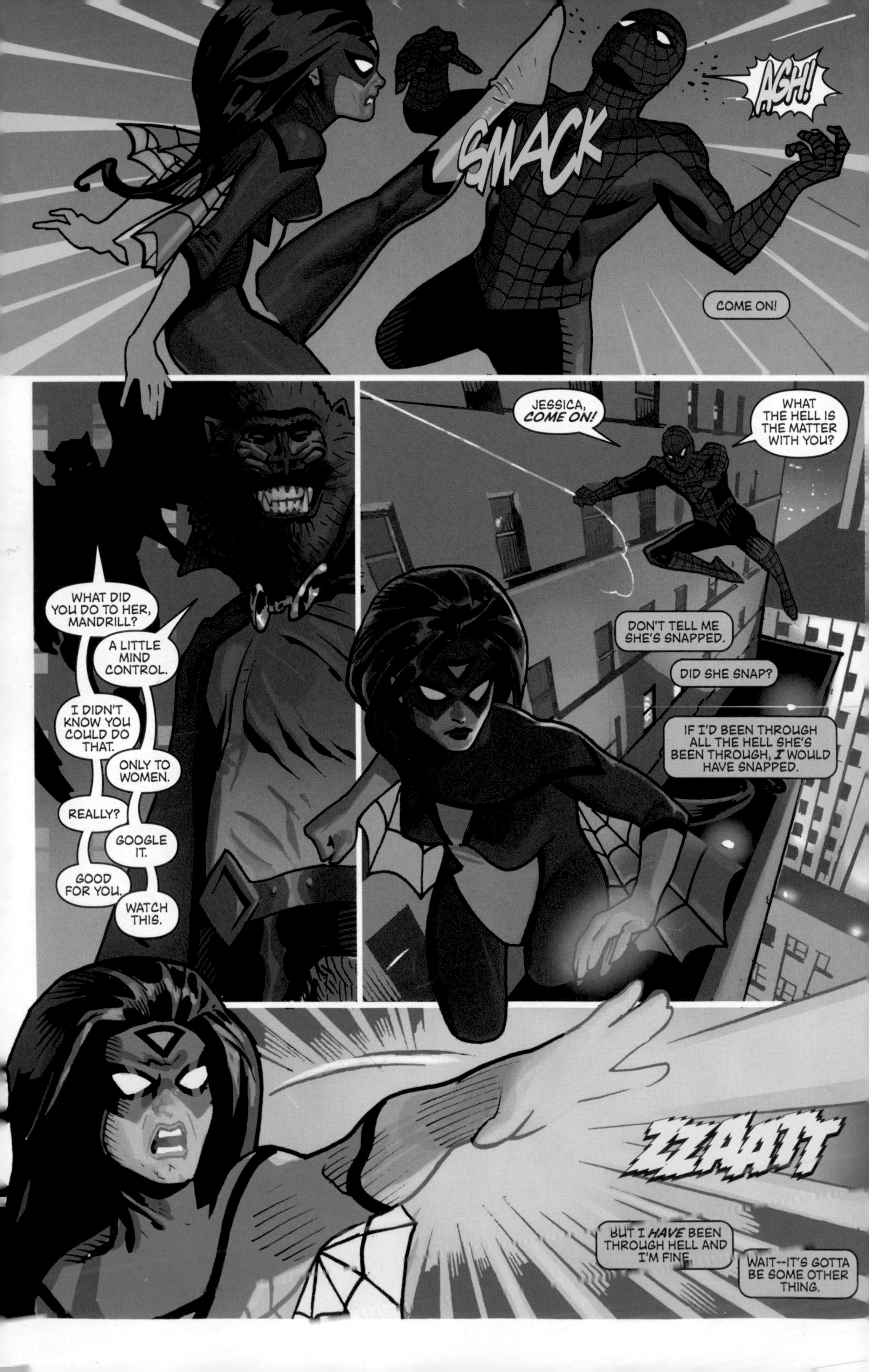
SMACK
AGH!
COME ON!
WHAT DID YOU DO TO HER, MANDRILL?
A LITTLE MIND CONTROL.
I DIDN'T KNOW YOU COULD DO THAT.
ONLY TO WOMEN.
REALLY?
GOOGLE IT.
GOOD FOR YOU.
WATCH THIS.
JESSICA, COME ON!
WHAT THE HELL IS THE MATTER WITH YOU?
DON'T TELL ME SHE'S SNAPPED.
DID SHE SNAP?
IF I'D BEEN THROUGH ALL THE HELL SHE'S BEEN THROUGH, I WOULD HAVE SNAPPED.
ZZAATT
BUT I HAVE BEEN THROUGH HELL AND I'M FINE.
WAIT--IT'S GOTTA BE SOME OTHER THING.

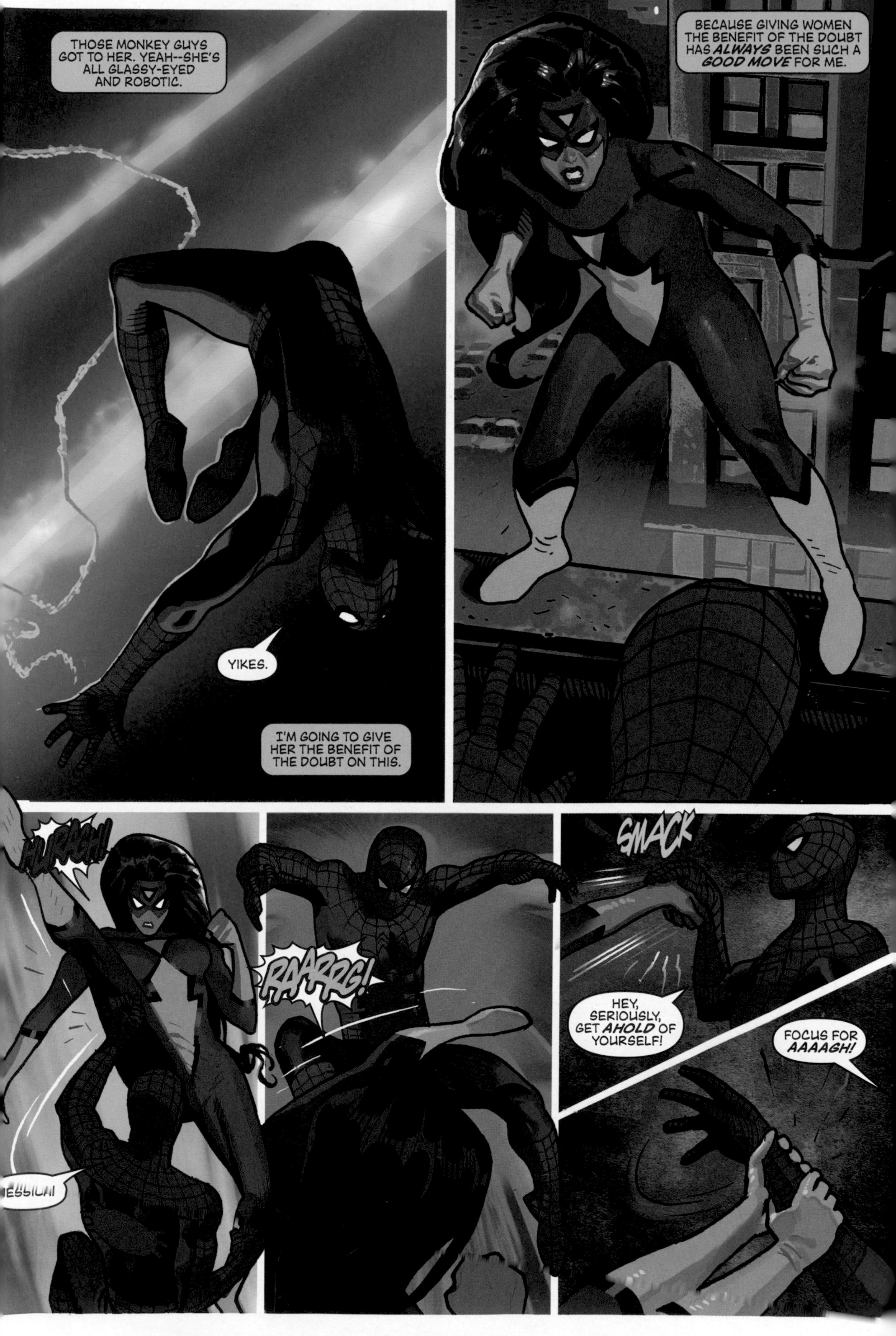
THOSE MONKEY GUYS GOT TO HER. YEAH--SHE'S ALL GLASSY-EYED AND ROBOTIC.
YIKES.
I'M GOING TO GIVE HER THE BENEFIT OF THE DOUBT ON THIS.
BECAUSE GIVING WOMEN THE BENEFIT OF THE DOUBT HAS ALWAYS BEEN SUCH A GOOD MOVE FOR ME.
HURACH!
RAARRG!
SMACK
HEY, SERIOUSLY, GET AHOLD OF YOURSELF!
FOCUS FOR AAAAGH!

AAGH!

OH, THAT'S GREAT.

I SHOULD HAVE BROUGHT MY CAMERA. I ALWAYS MISS IT.

SHOULD WE GO IN AND FINISH IT?

NO, NO, LET IT PLAY OUT.

YOU SURE?

IT'LL BE OVER IN TWO MINUTES. WHY DENY YOURSELF?

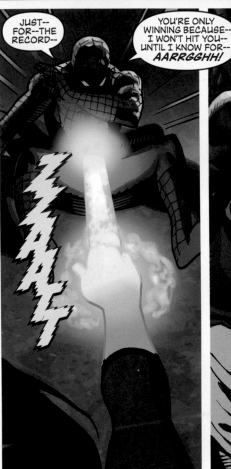

JUST-- FOR--THE RECORD--

YOU'RE ONLY WINNING BECAUSE-- I WON'T HIT YOU-- UNTIL I KNOW FOR-- AARRGGHH!

OKAY, THAT WAS GREAT.

SEE?

JESSICA. COME ON.

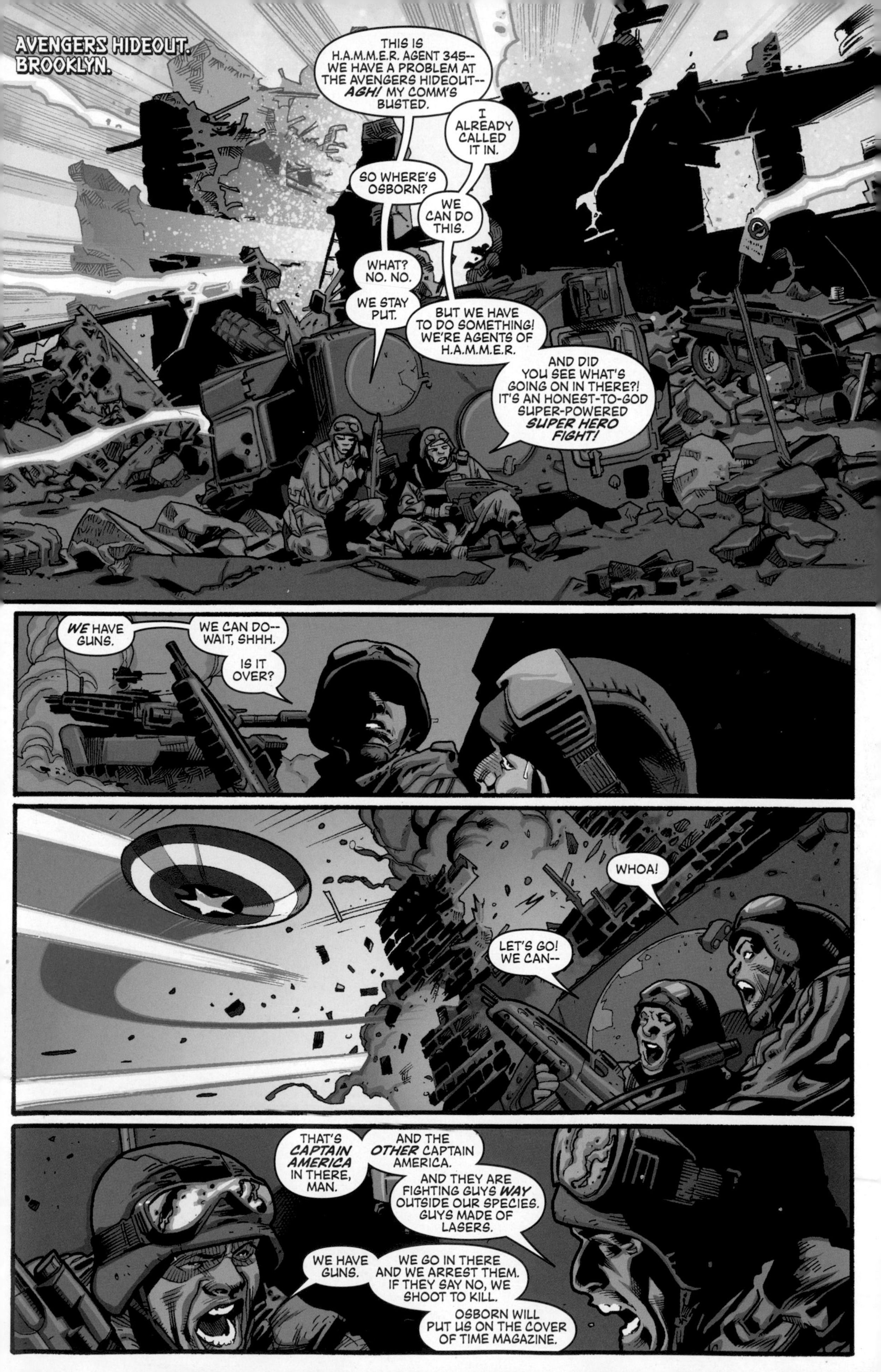
AVENGERS HIDEOUT. BROOKLYN.
THIS IS H.A.M.M.E.R. AGENT 345-- WE HAVE A PROBLEM AT THE AVENGERS HIDEOUT-- AGH! MY COMM'S BUSTED.
I ALREADY CALLED IT IN.
SO WHERE'S OSBORN?
WE CAN DO THIS.
WHAT? NO. NO.
WE STAY PUT.
BUT WE HAVE TO DO SOMETHING! WE'RE AGENTS OF H.A.M.M.E.R.
AND DID YOU SEE WHAT'S GOING ON IN THERE?! IT'S AN HONEST-TO-GOD SUPER-POWERED SUPER HERO FIGHT!
WE HAVE GUNS.
WE CAN DO-- WAIT, SHHH.
IS IT OVER?
WHOA!
LET'S GO! WE CAN--
THAT'S CAPTAIN AMERICA IN THERE, MAN.
AND THE OTHER CAPTAIN AMERICA.
AND THEY ARE FIGHTING GUYS WAY OUTSIDE OUR SPECIES. GUYS MADE OF LASERS.
WE HAVE GUNS.
WE GO IN THERE AND WE ARREST THEM. IF THEY SAY NO, WE SHOOT TO KILL.
OSBORN WILL PUT US ON THE COVER OF TIME MAGAZINE.

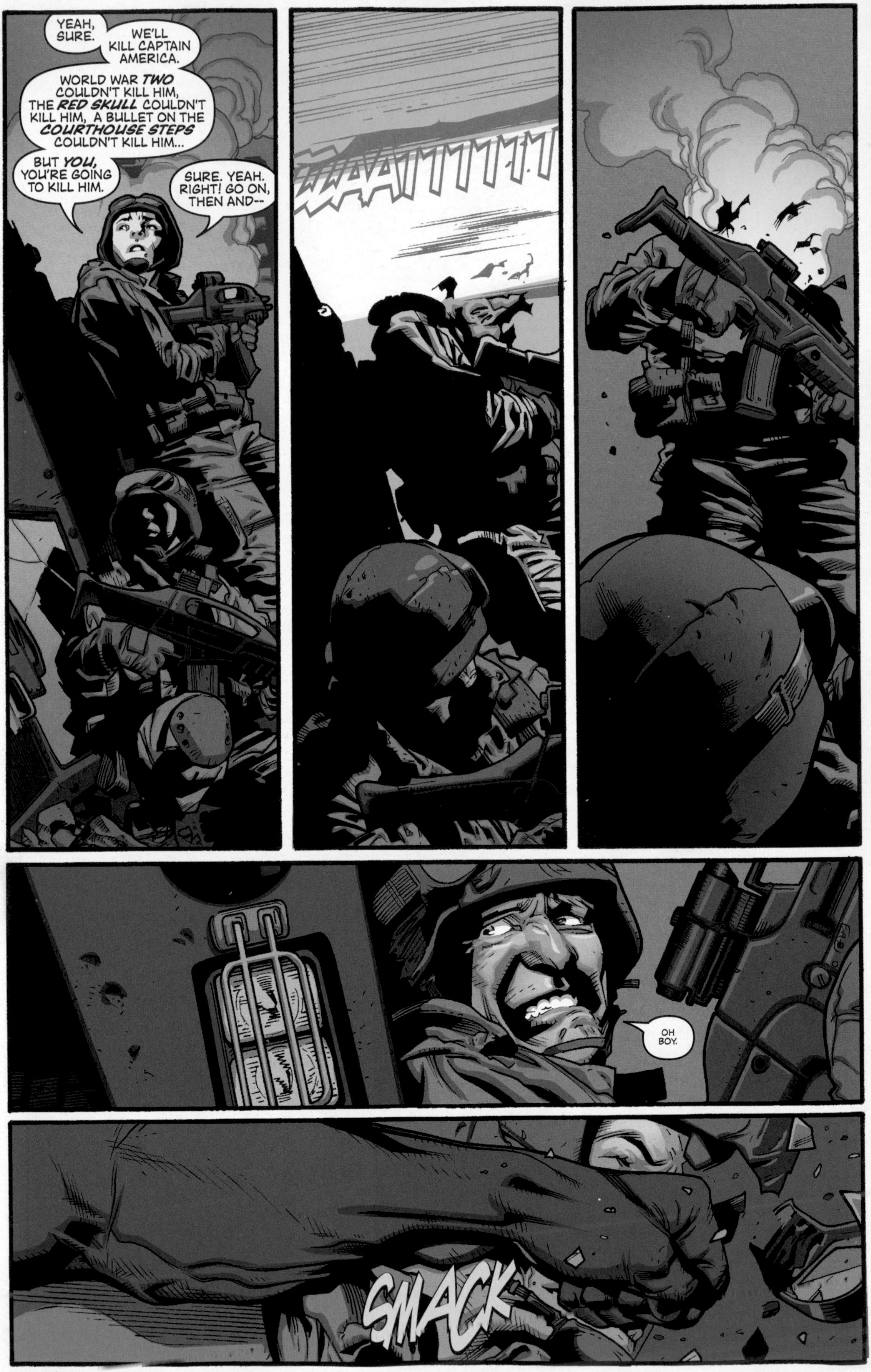
YEAH, SURE.
WE'LL KILL CAPTAIN AMERICA.
WORLD WAR *TWO* COULDN'T KILL HIM, THE *RED SKULL* COULDN'T KILL HIM, A BULLET ON THE *COURTHOUSE STEPS* COULDN'T KILL HIM...
BUT *YOU*, YOU'RE GOING TO KILL HIM.
SURE. YEAH. RIGHT! GO ON, THEN AND--
OH BOY.
SMACK

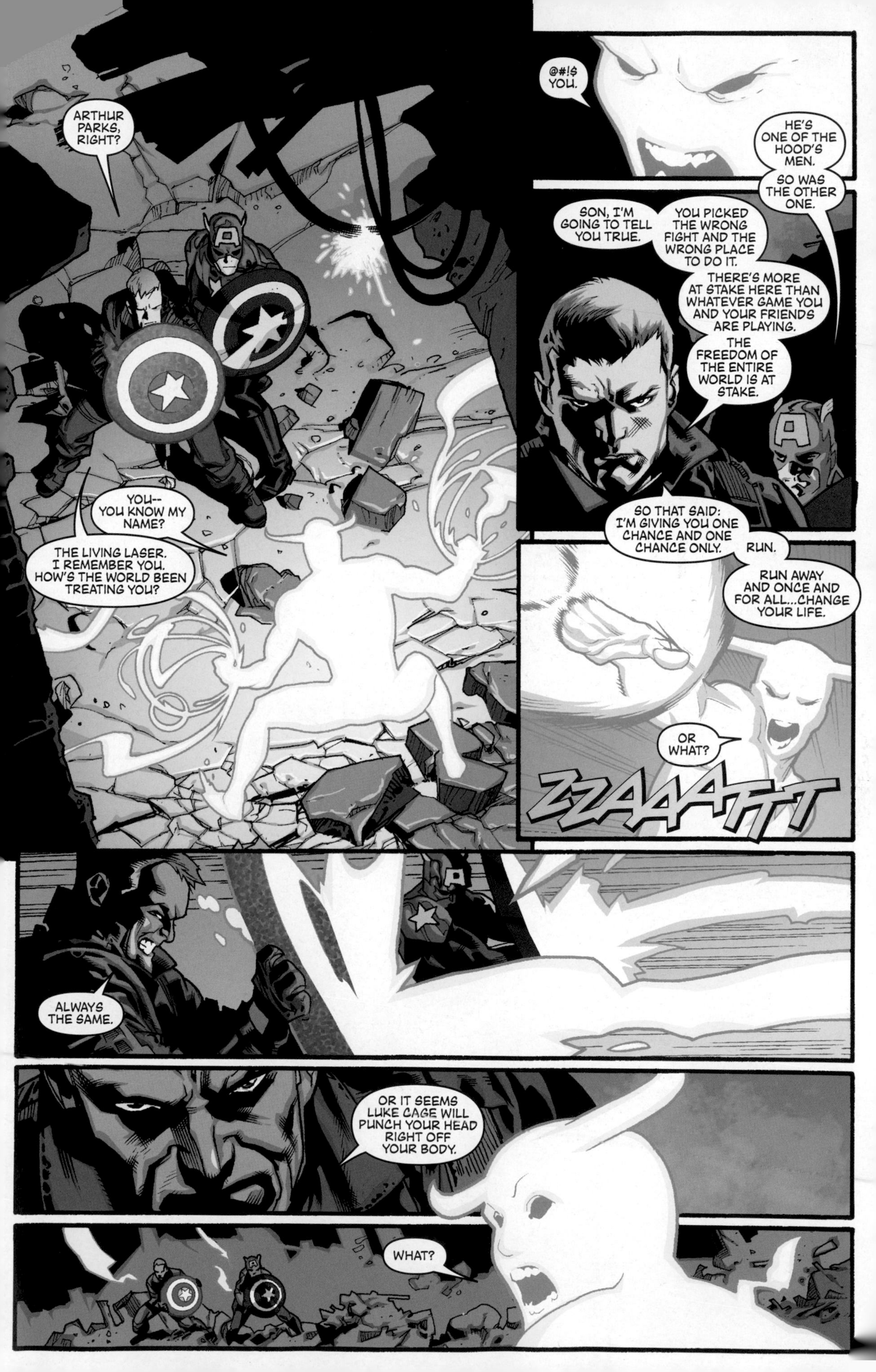
ARTHUR PARKS, RIGHT?
YOU-- YOU KNOW MY NAME?
THE LIVING LASER. I REMEMBER YOU. HOW'S THE WORLD BEEN TREATING YOU?
@#!$ YOU.
HE'S ONE OF THE HOOD'S MEN.
SO WAS THE OTHER ONE.
SON, I'M GOING TO TELL YOU TRUE.
YOU PICKED THE WRONG FIGHT AND THE WRONG PLACE TO DO IT.
THERE'S MORE AT STAKE HERE THAN WHATEVER GAME YOU AND YOUR FRIENDS ARE PLAYING.
THE FREEDOM OF THE ENTIRE WORLD IS AT STAKE.
SO THAT SAID: I'M GIVING YOU ONE CHANCE AND ONE CHANCE ONLY.
RUN.
RUN AWAY AND ONCE AND FOR ALL...CHANGE YOUR LIFE.
OR WHAT?
ZZAAAATTT
ALWAYS THE SAME.
OR IT SEEMS LUKE CAGE WILL PUNCH YOUR HEAD RIGHT OFF YOUR BODY.
WHAT?

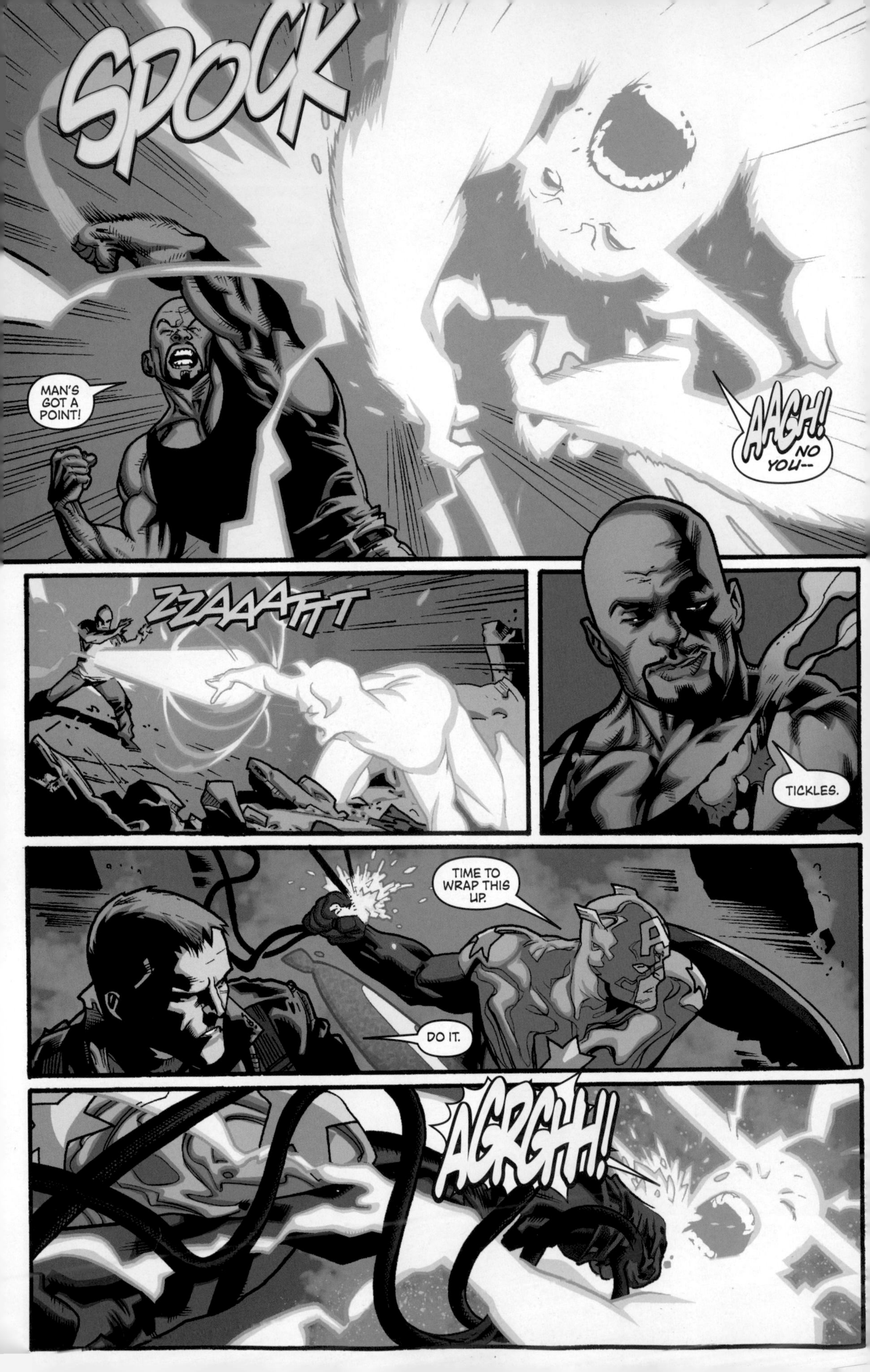
SPOCK
MAN'S GOT A POINT!
AAGH! NO YOU--
ZZAAAATTTT
TICKLES.
TIME TO WRAP THIS UP.
DO IT.
AGRGH!

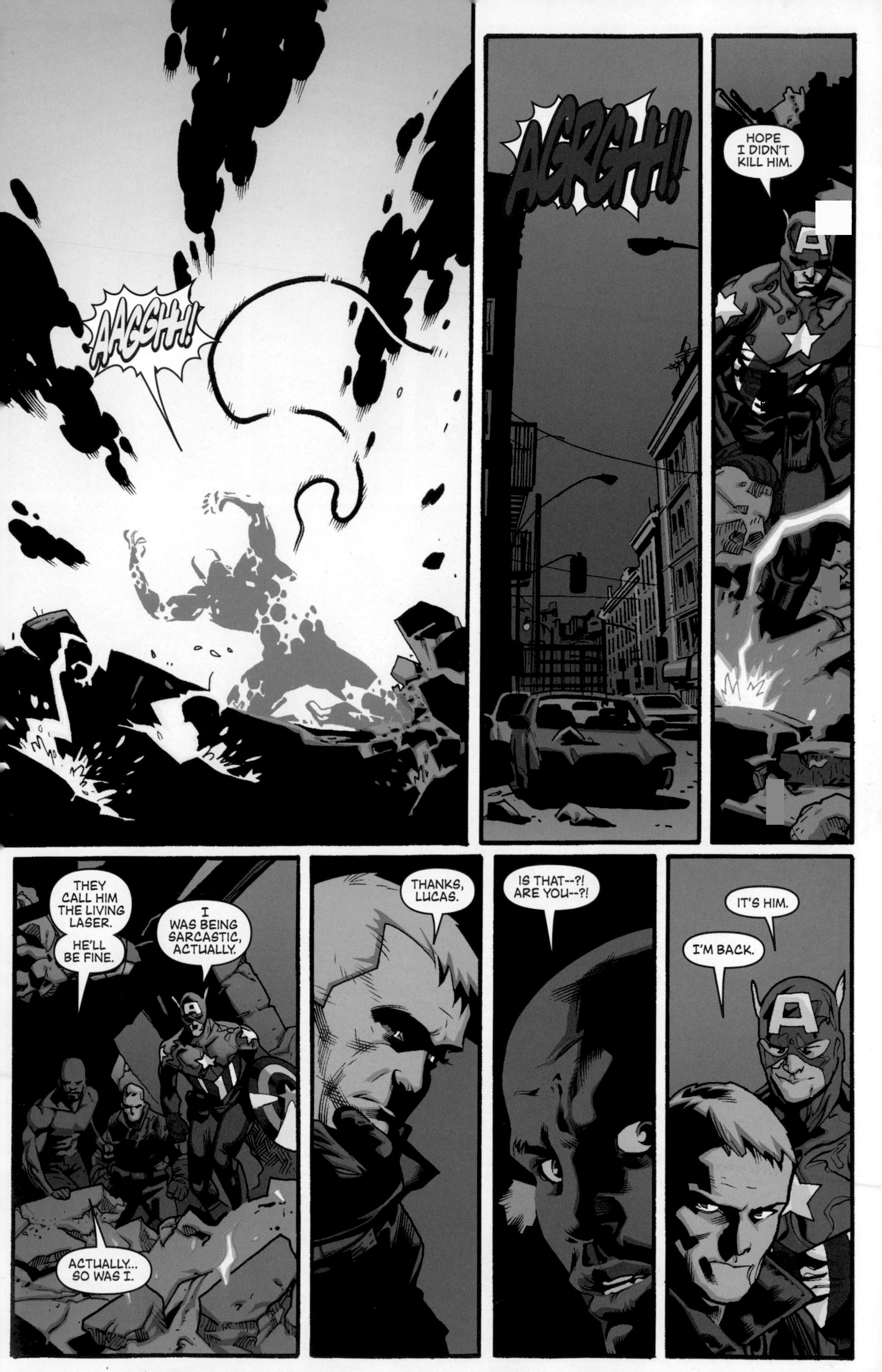
AAGGHH!
AGRGHH!
HOPE I DIDN'T KILL HIM.
THEY CALL HIM THE LIVING LASER.
HE'LL BE FINE.
I WAS BEING SARCASTIC, ACTUALLY.
ACTUALLY... SO WAS I.
THANKS, LUCAS.
IS THAT--?! ARE YOU--?!
IT'S HIM.
I'M BACK.

WHOA!

SORRY.

BUT I MEAN, WHAT *THE HELL?*

IT'S A STORY.

NO @#$%.

WHAT WERE YOU DOING HERE? IT'S NOT SAFE HERE. YOU'RE SUPPOSED TO BE AT THE SAFEHOUSE WITH JESSICA.

I CAME BACK FOR SOME-THIN'.

THERE.

WHAT IS THAT?

BABY BINKY.

YOU CAN'T BUY THAT IN A STORE? ANY STORE IN THE WORLD?

IT'S HER FAVORITE.

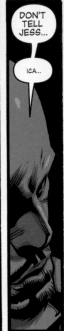

DON'T TELL JESS...

ICA...

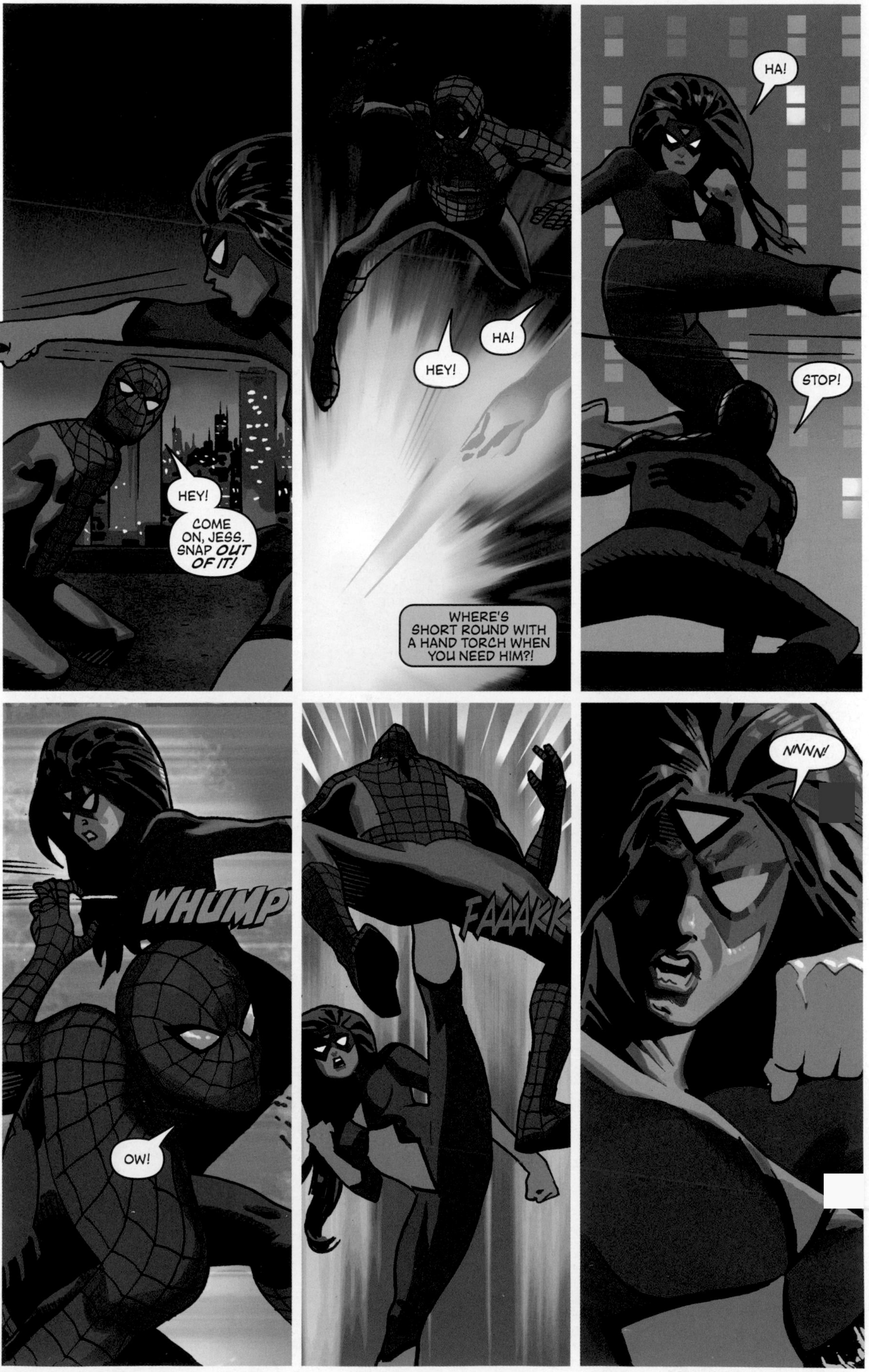
HEY!
COME ON, JESS. SNAP OUT OF IT!
HEY!
HA!
WHERE'S SHORT ROUND WITH A HAND TORCH WHEN YOU NEED HIM?!
HA!
STOP!
WHUMP
OW!
FAAAKK
NNNN!

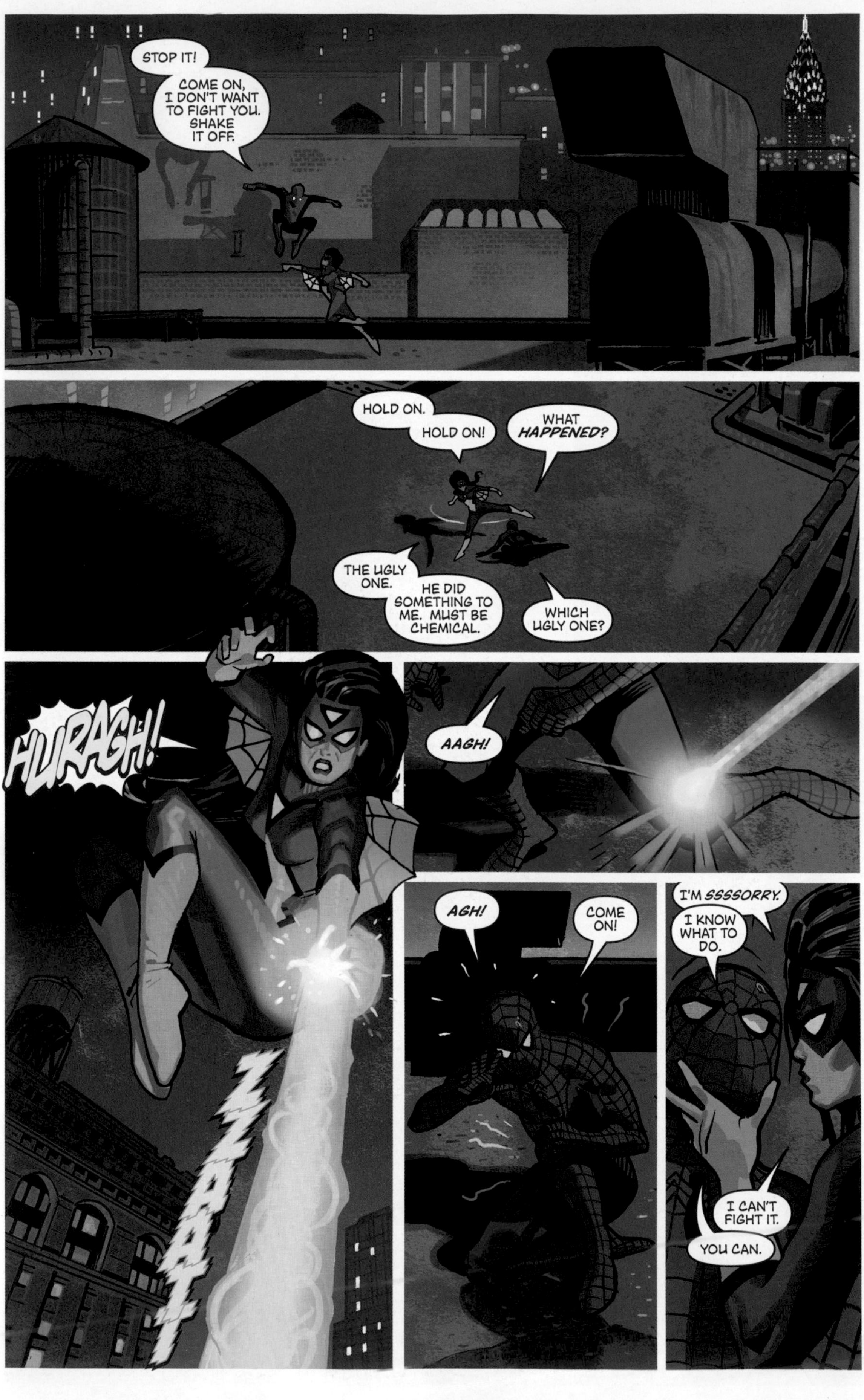
STOP IT!
COME ON, I DON'T WANT TO FIGHT YOU. SHAKE IT OFF.
HOLD ON.
HOLD ON!
WHAT *HAPPENED?*
THE UGLY ONE.
HE DID SOMETHING TO ME. MUST BE CHEMICAL.
WHICH UGLY ONE?
HURAGH!
ZZAPT
AAGH!
AGH!
COME ON!
I'M *SSSSORRY.*
I KNOW WHAT TO DO.
I CAN'T FIGHT IT.
YOU CAN.

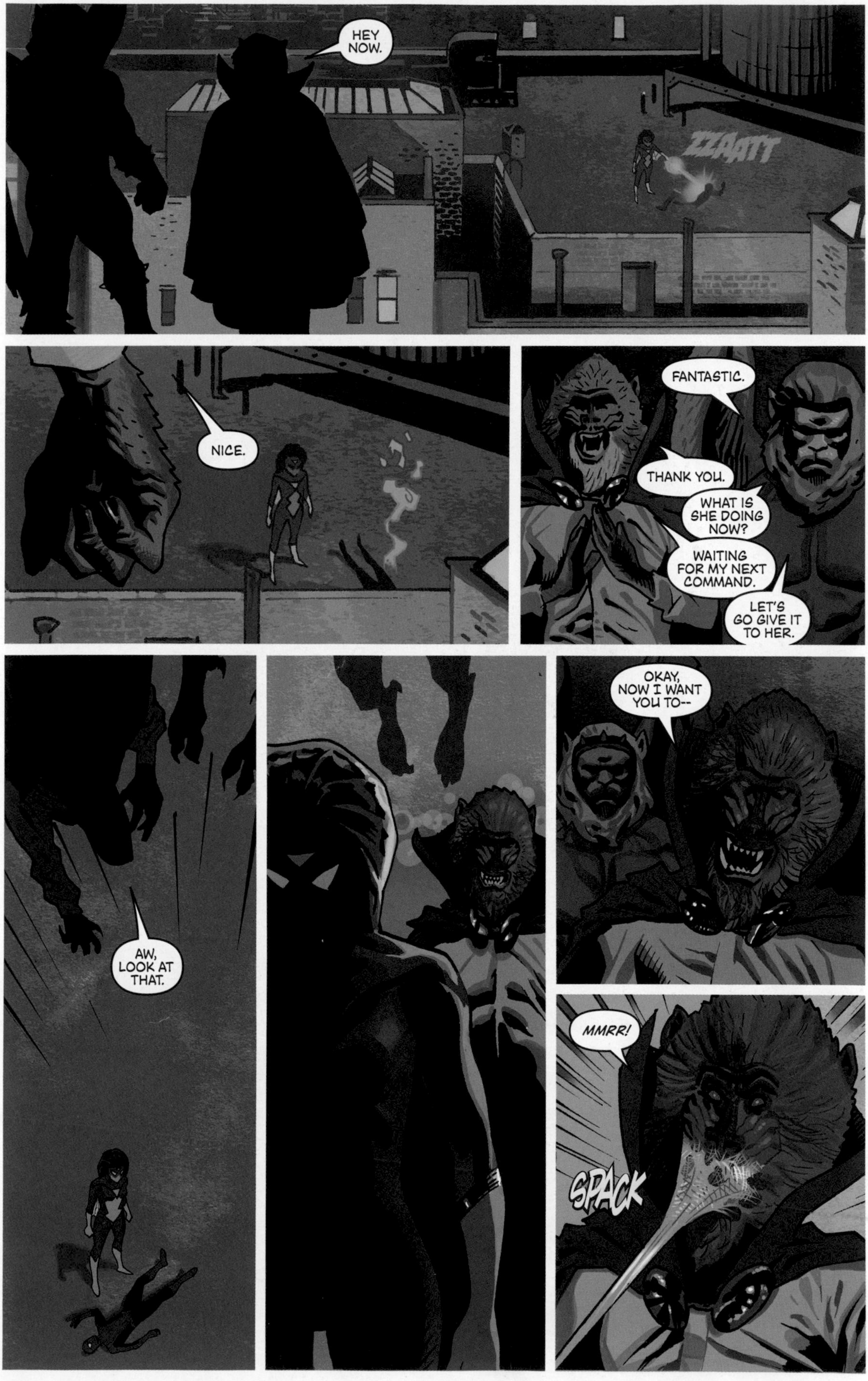
HEY NOW.
ZZAATT
NICE.
FANTASTIC.
THANK YOU.
WHAT IS SHE DOING NOW?
WAITING FOR MY NEXT COMMAND.
LET'S GO GIVE IT TO HER.
AW, LOOK AT THAT.
OKAY, NOW I WANT YOU TO--
MMRR!
SPACK

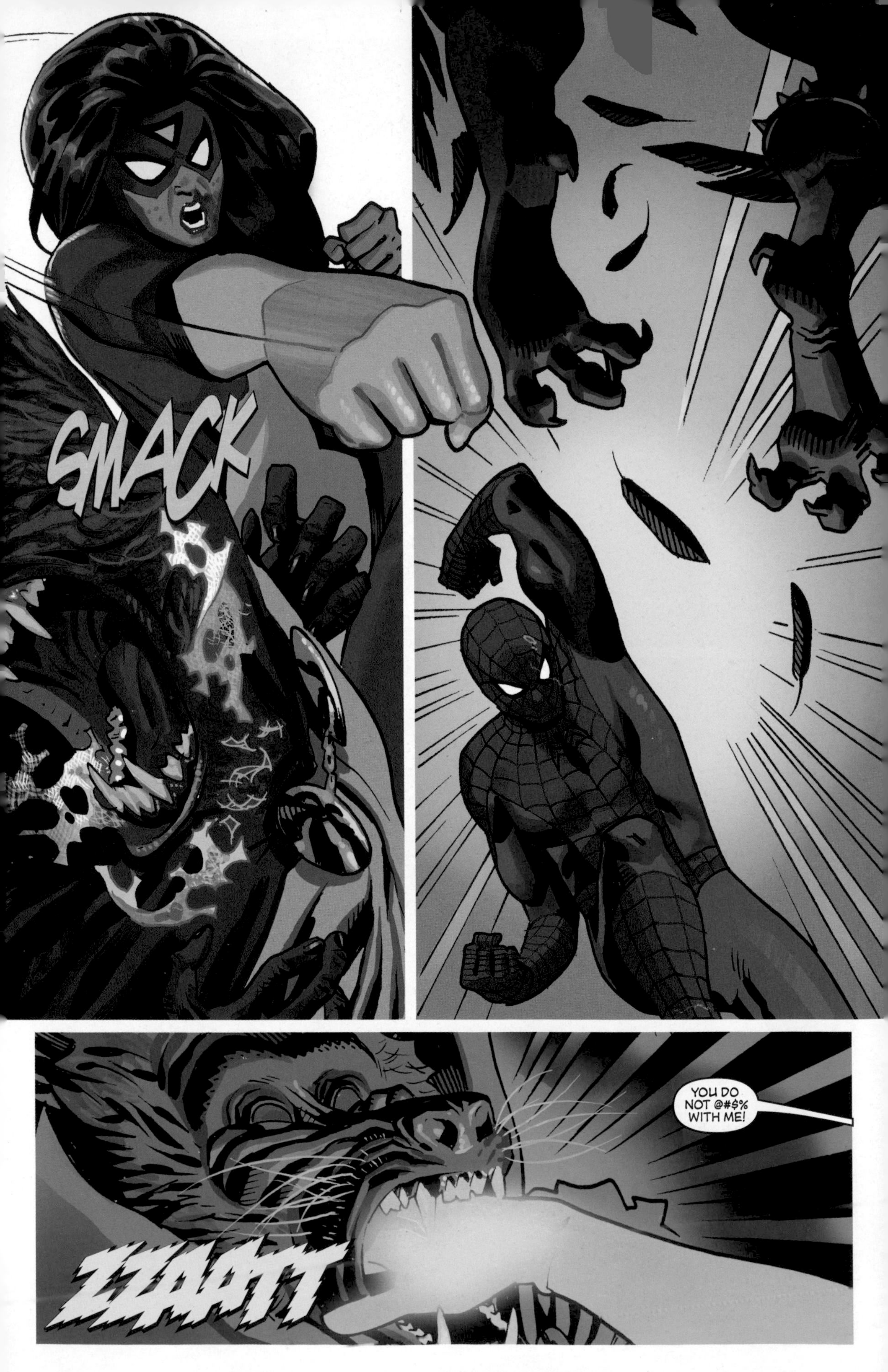
SMACK
YOU DO NOT @#$% WITH ME!
ZZAATT

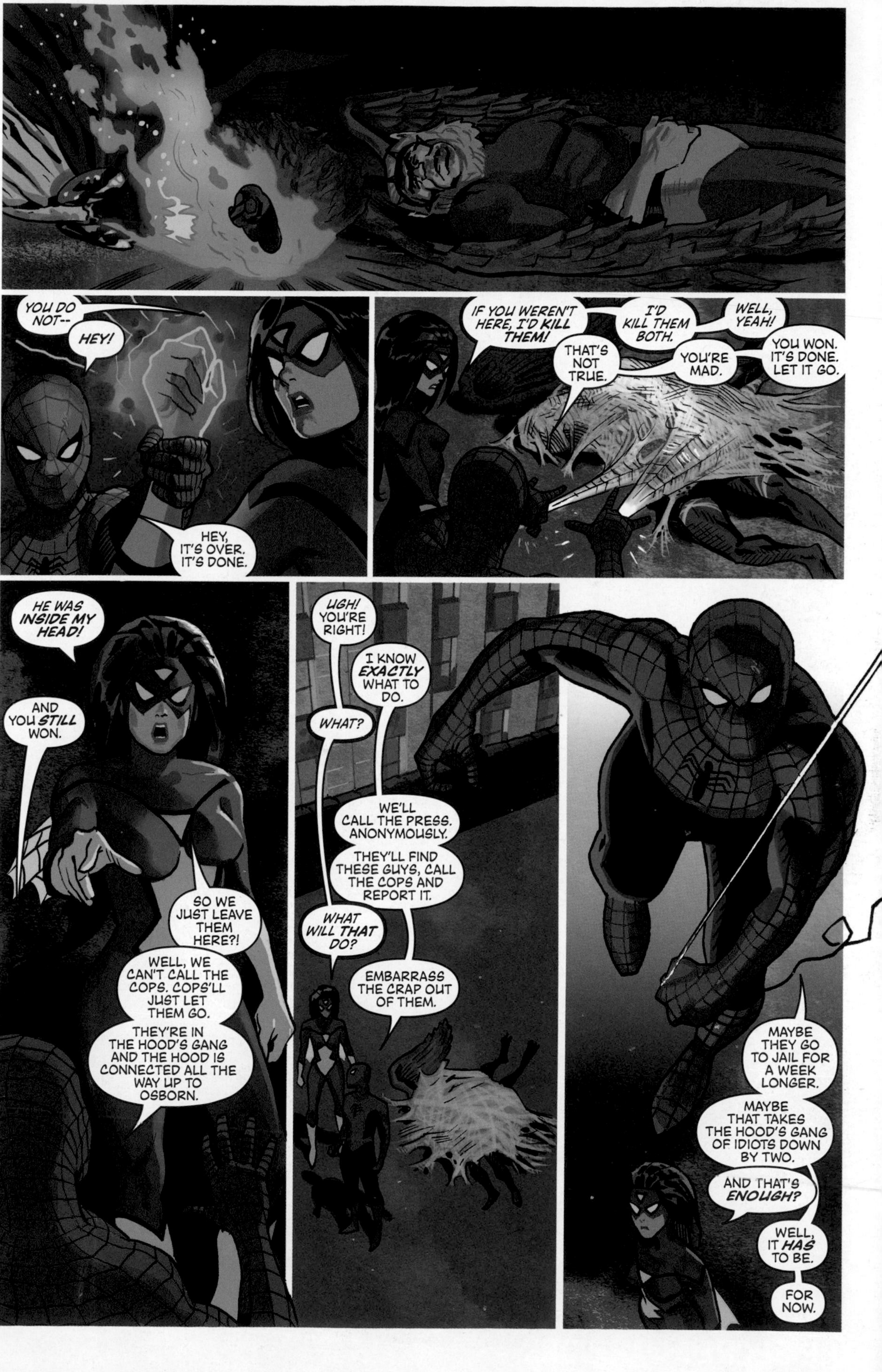
YOU DO NOT--
HEY!
HEY, IT'S OVER. IT'S DONE.
IF YOU WEREN'T HERE, I'D KILL THEM!
I'D KILL THEM BOTH.
WELL, YEAH!
THAT'S NOT TRUE.
YOU'RE MAD.
YOU WON. IT'S DONE. LET IT GO.
HE WAS INSIDE MY HEAD!
AND YOU STILL WON.
SO WE JUST LEAVE THEM HERE?!
WELL, WE CAN'T CALL THE COPS. COPS'LL JUST LET THEM GO.
THEY'RE IN THE HOOD'S GANG AND THE HOOD IS CONNECTED ALL THE WAY UP TO OSBORN.
UGH! YOU'RE RIGHT!
I KNOW EXACTLY WHAT TO DO.
WHAT?
WE'LL CALL THE PRESS. ANONYMOUSLY.
THEY'LL FIND THESE GUYS, CALL THE COPS AND REPORT IT.
WHAT WILL THAT DO?
EMBARRASS THE CRAP OUT OF THEM.
MAYBE THEY GO TO JAIL FOR A WEEK LONGER.
MAYBE THAT TAKES THE HOOD'S GANG OF IDIOTS DOWN BY TWO.
AND THAT'S ENOUGH?
WELL, IT HAS TO BE.
FOR NOW.

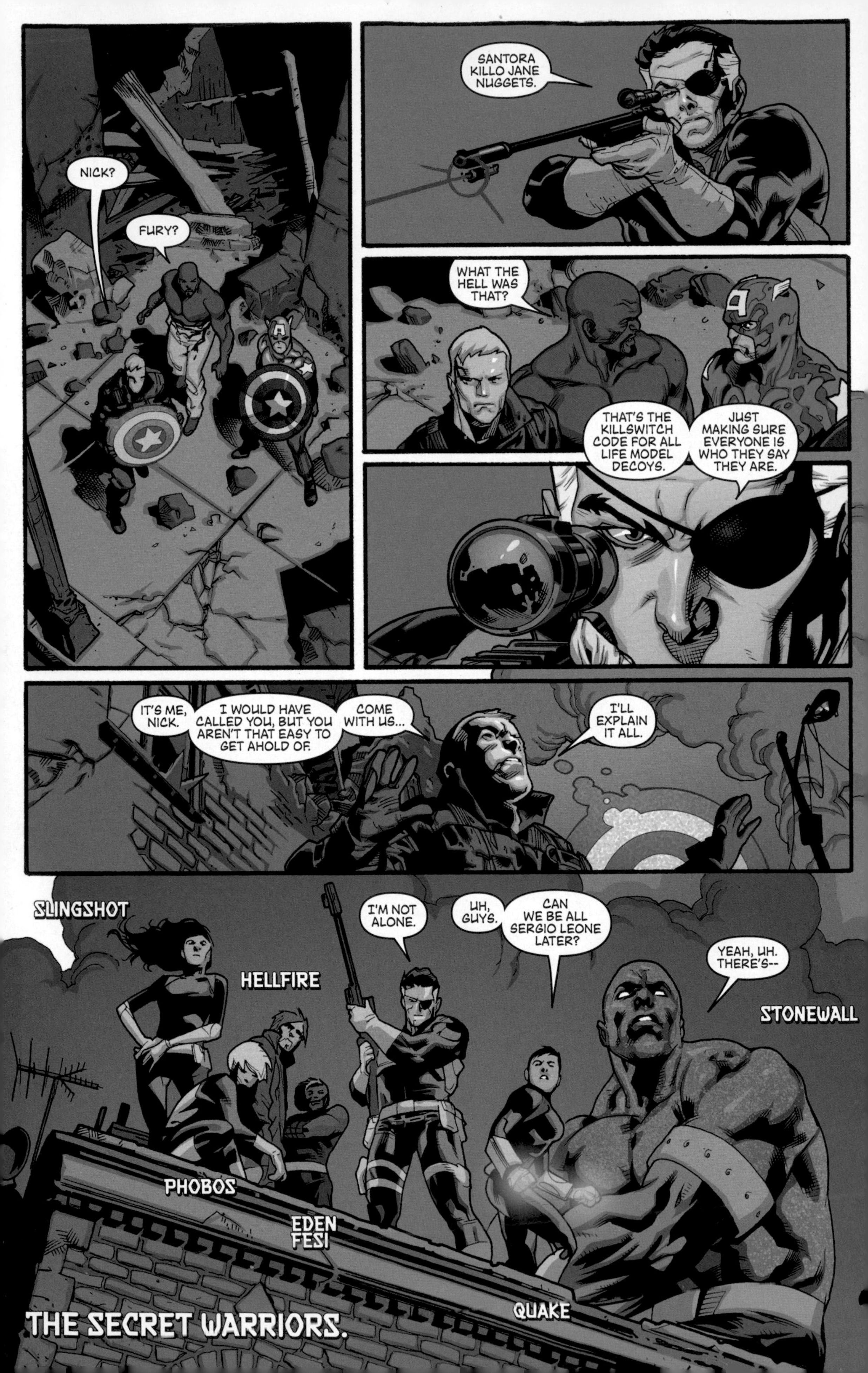
NICK?
FURY?
SANTORA KILLO JANE NUGGETS.
WHAT THE HELL WAS THAT?
THAT'S THE KILLSWITCH CODE FOR ALL LIFE MODEL DECOYS.
JUST MAKING SURE EVERYONE IS WHO THEY SAY THEY ARE.
IT'S ME, NICK.
I WOULD HAVE CALLED YOU, BUT YOU AREN'T THAT EASY TO GET AHOLD OF.
COME WITH US...
I'LL EXPLAIN IT ALL.
SLINGSHOT
I'M NOT ALONE.
UH, GUYS.
CAN WE BE ALL SERGIO LEONE LATER?
YEAH, UH. THERE'S--
HELLFIRE
STONEWALL
PHOBOS
EDEN FESI
QUAKE
THE SECRET WARRIORS.

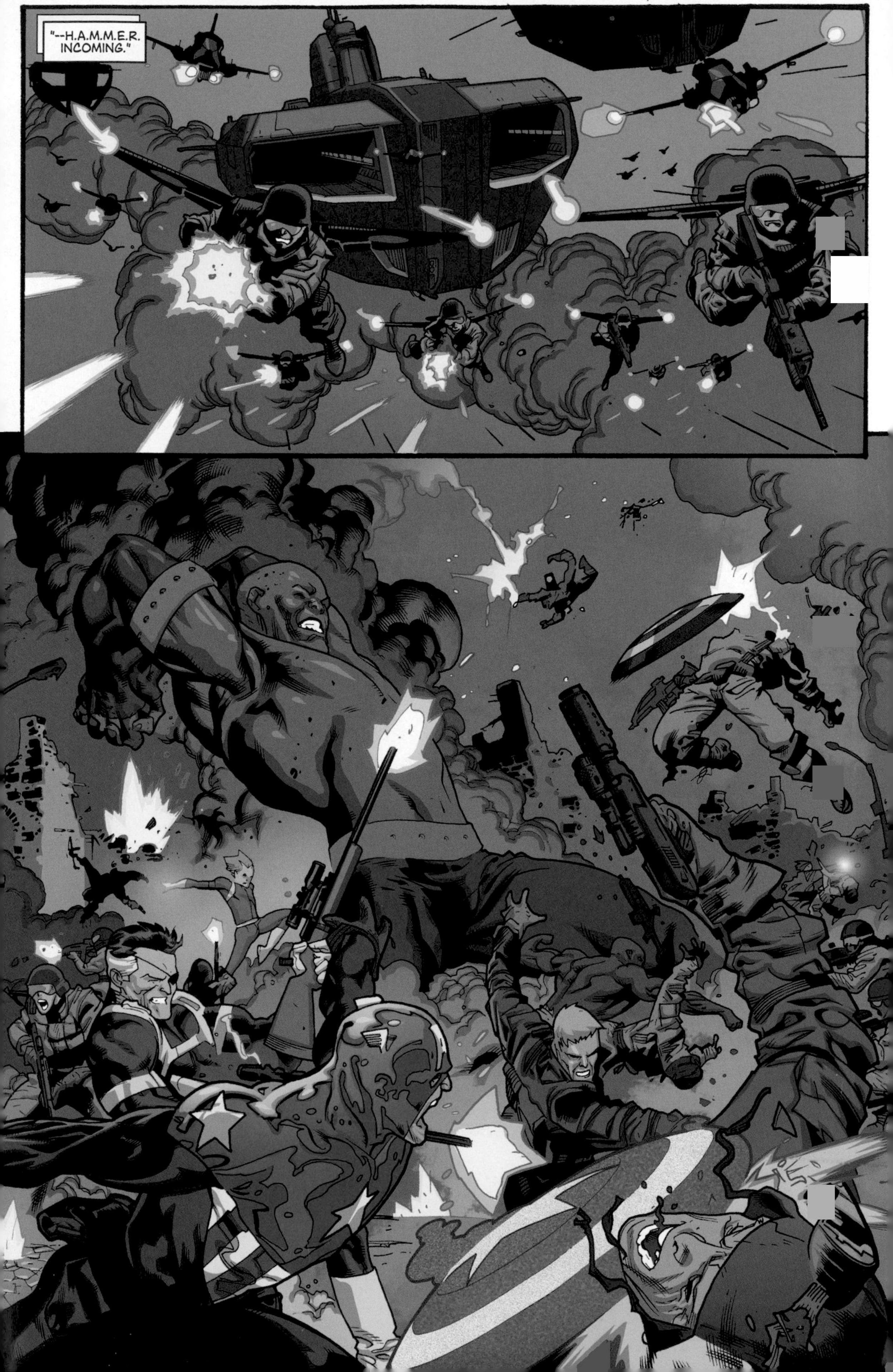
"--H.A.M.M.E.R. INCOMING."

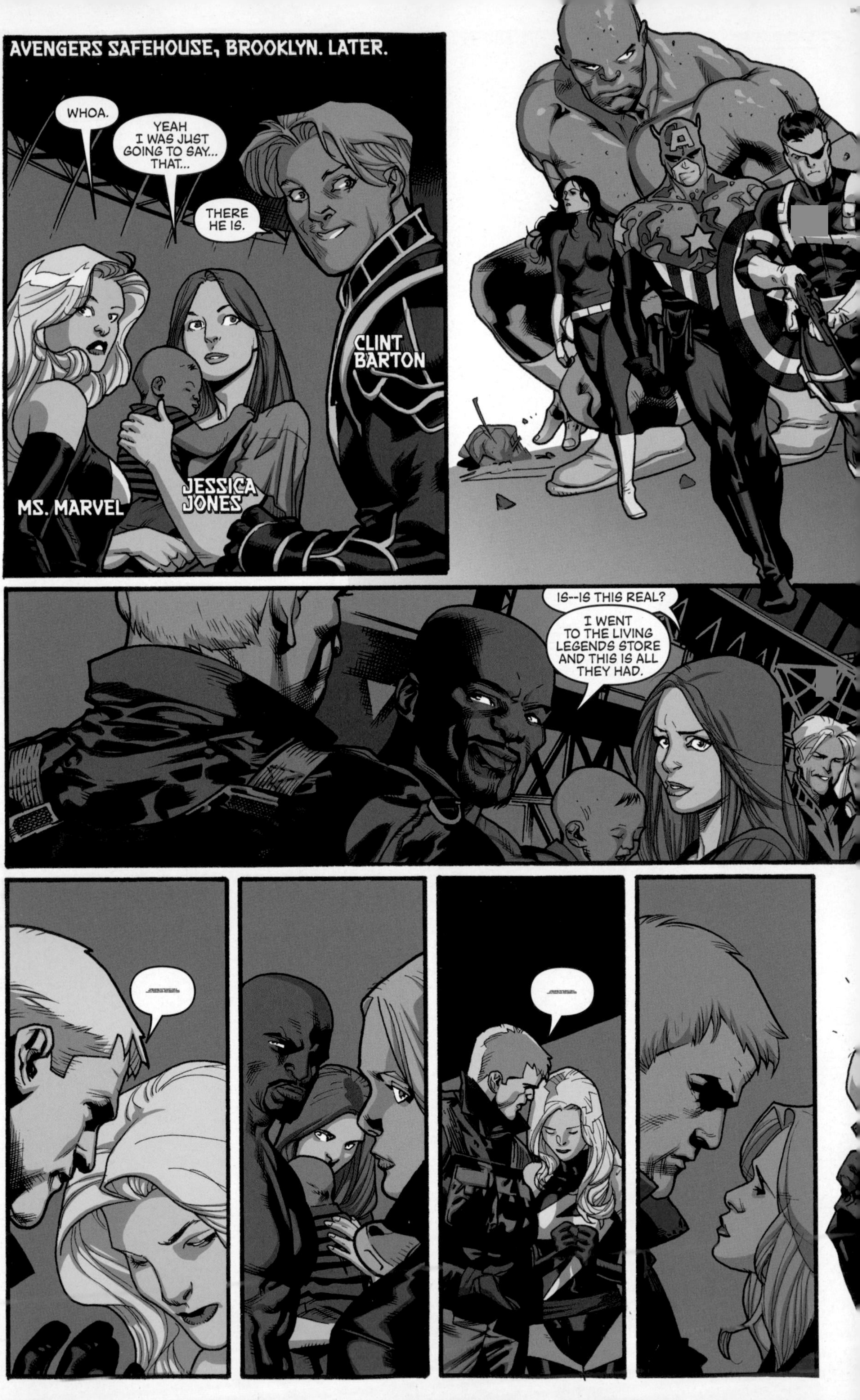
AVENGERS SAFEHOUSE, BROOKLYN. LATER.
WHOA.
YEAH I WAS JUST GOING TO SAY... THAT...
THERE HE IS.
MS. MARVEL
JESSICA JONES
CLINT BARTON
IS--IS THIS REAL?
I WENT TO THE LIVING LEGENDS STORE AND THIS IS ALL THEY HAD.

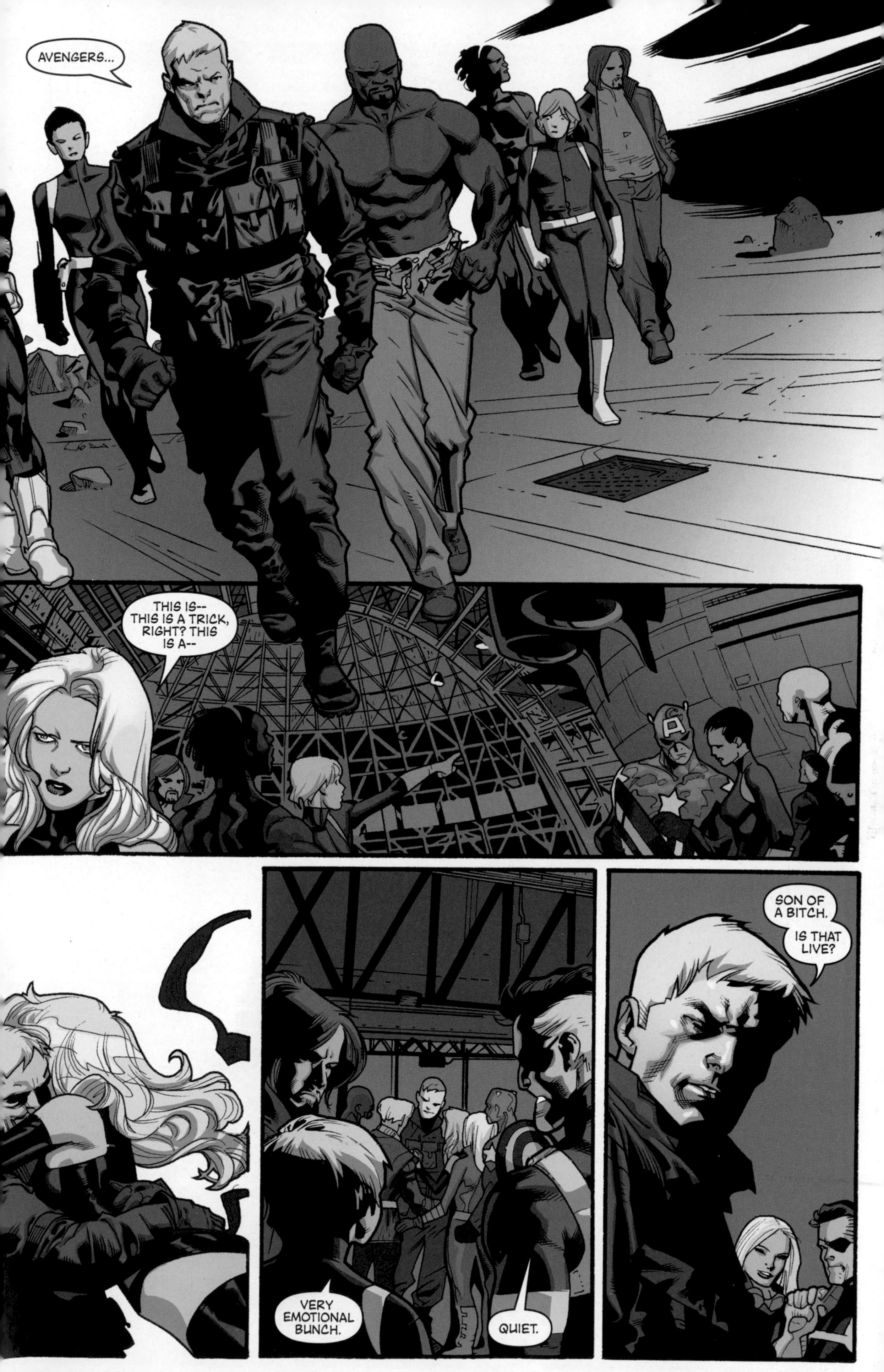

AVENGERS...
THIS IS-- THIS IS A TRICK, RIGHT? THIS IS A--
VERY EMOTIONAL BUNCH.
QUIET.
SON OF A BITCH.
IS THAT LIVE?

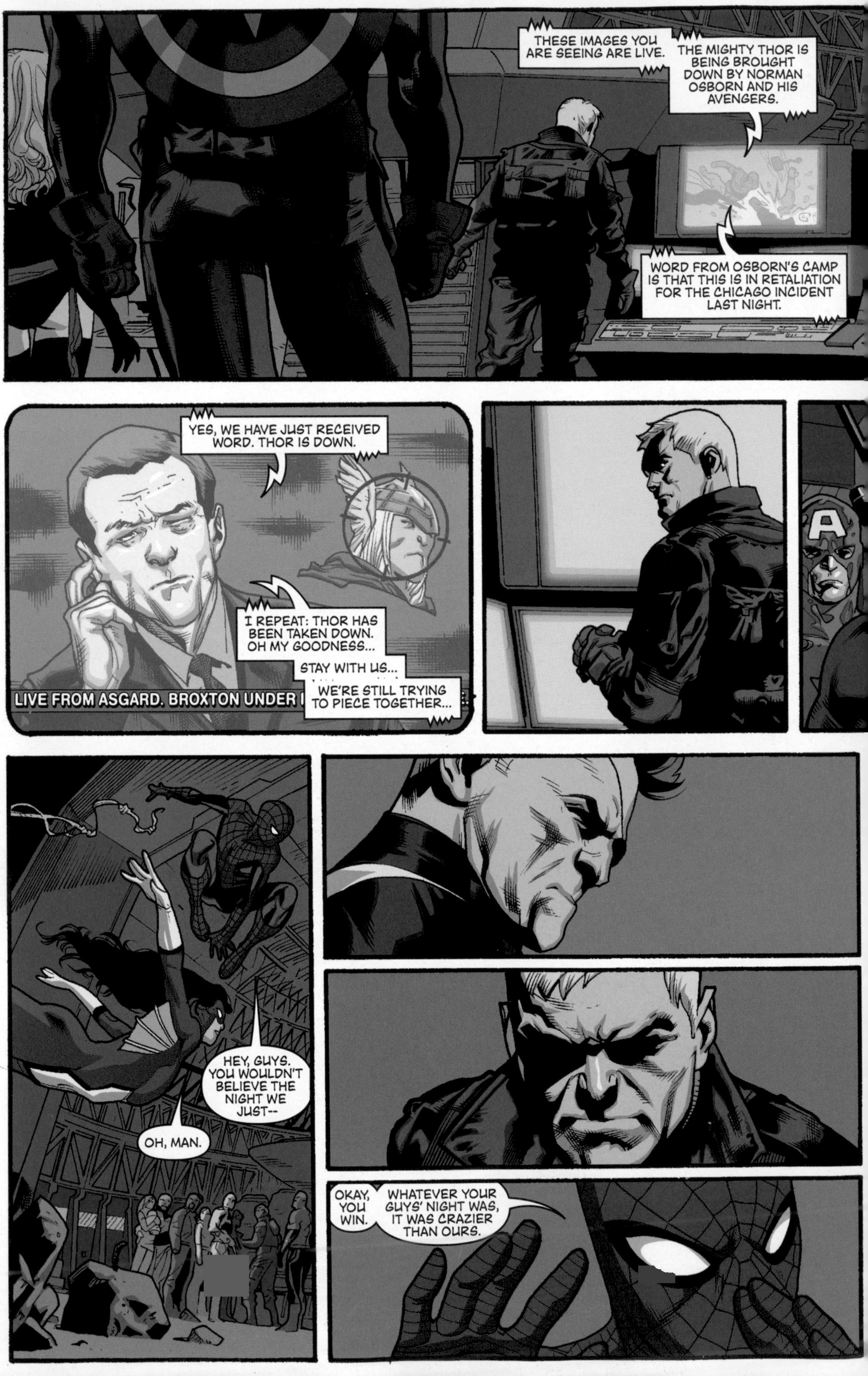
THESE IMAGES YOU ARE SEEING ARE LIVE.
THE MIGHTY THOR IS BEING BROUGHT DOWN BY NORMAN OSBORN AND HIS AVENGERS.
WORD FROM OSBORN'S CAMP IS THAT THIS IS IN RETALIATION FOR THE CHICAGO INCIDENT LAST NIGHT.
YES, WE HAVE JUST RECEIVED WORD. THOR IS DOWN.
I REPEAT: THOR HAS BEEN TAKEN DOWN. OH MY GOODNESS...
STAY WITH US...
WE'RE STILL TRYING TO PIECE TOGETHER...
LIVE FROM ASGARD. BROXTON UNDER
HEY, GUYS. YOU WOULDN'T BELIEVE THE NIGHT WE JUST--
OH, MAN.
OKAY, YOU WIN.
WHATEVER YOUR GUYS' NIGHT WAS, IT WAS CRAZIER THAN OURS.

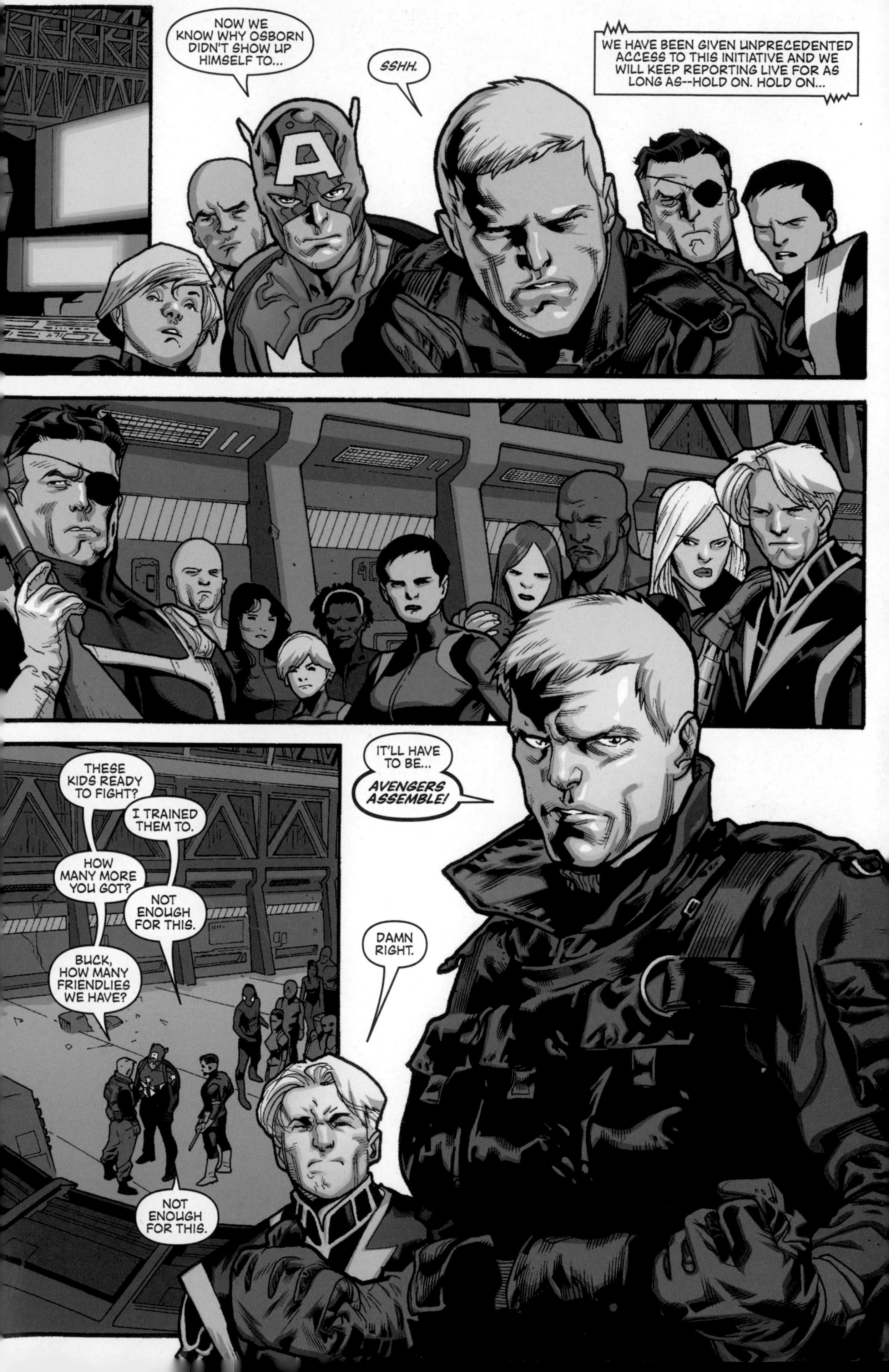
NOW WE KNOW WHY OSBORN DIDN'T SHOW UP HIMSELF TO...
SSHH.
WE HAVE BEEN GIVEN UNPRECEDENTED ACCESS TO THIS INITIATIVE AND WE WILL KEEP REPORTING LIVE FOR AS LONG AS--HOLD ON. HOLD ON...
THESE KIDS READY TO FIGHT?
I TRAINED THEM TO.
HOW MANY MORE YOU GOT?
NOT ENOUGH FOR THIS.
BUCK, HOW MANY FRIENDLIES WE HAVE?
NOT ENOUGH FOR THIS.
DAMN RIGHT.
IT'LL HAVE TO BE... AVENGERS ASSEMBLE!

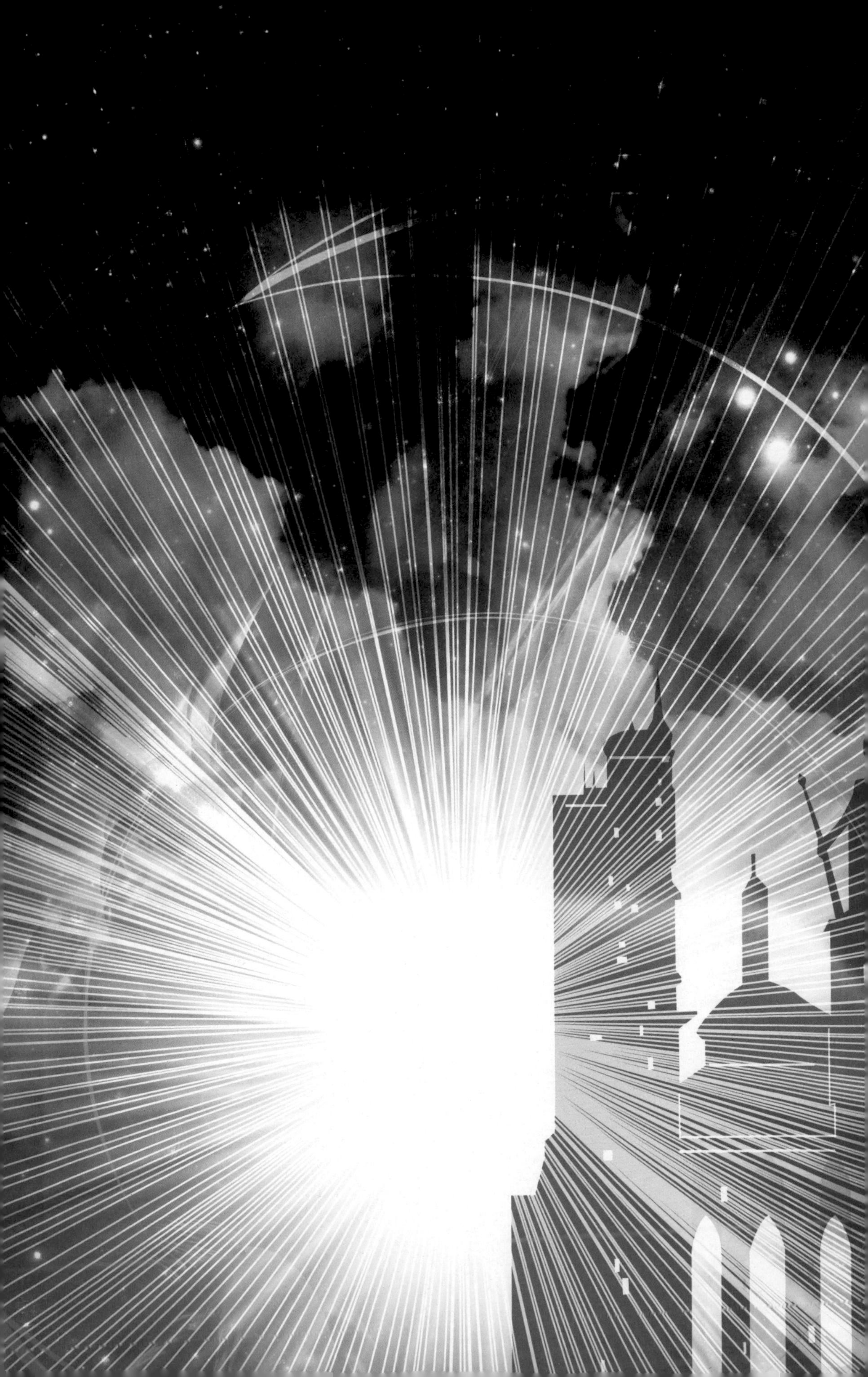

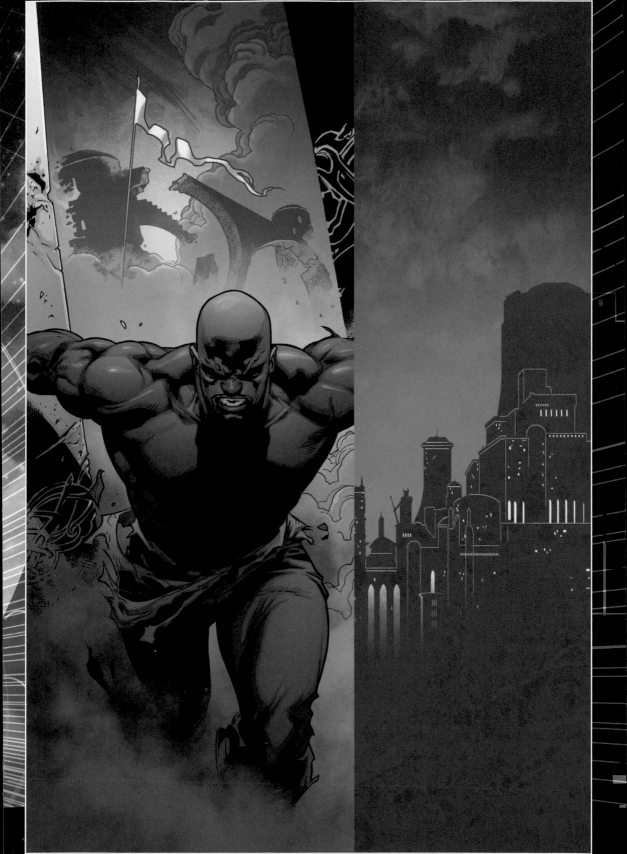

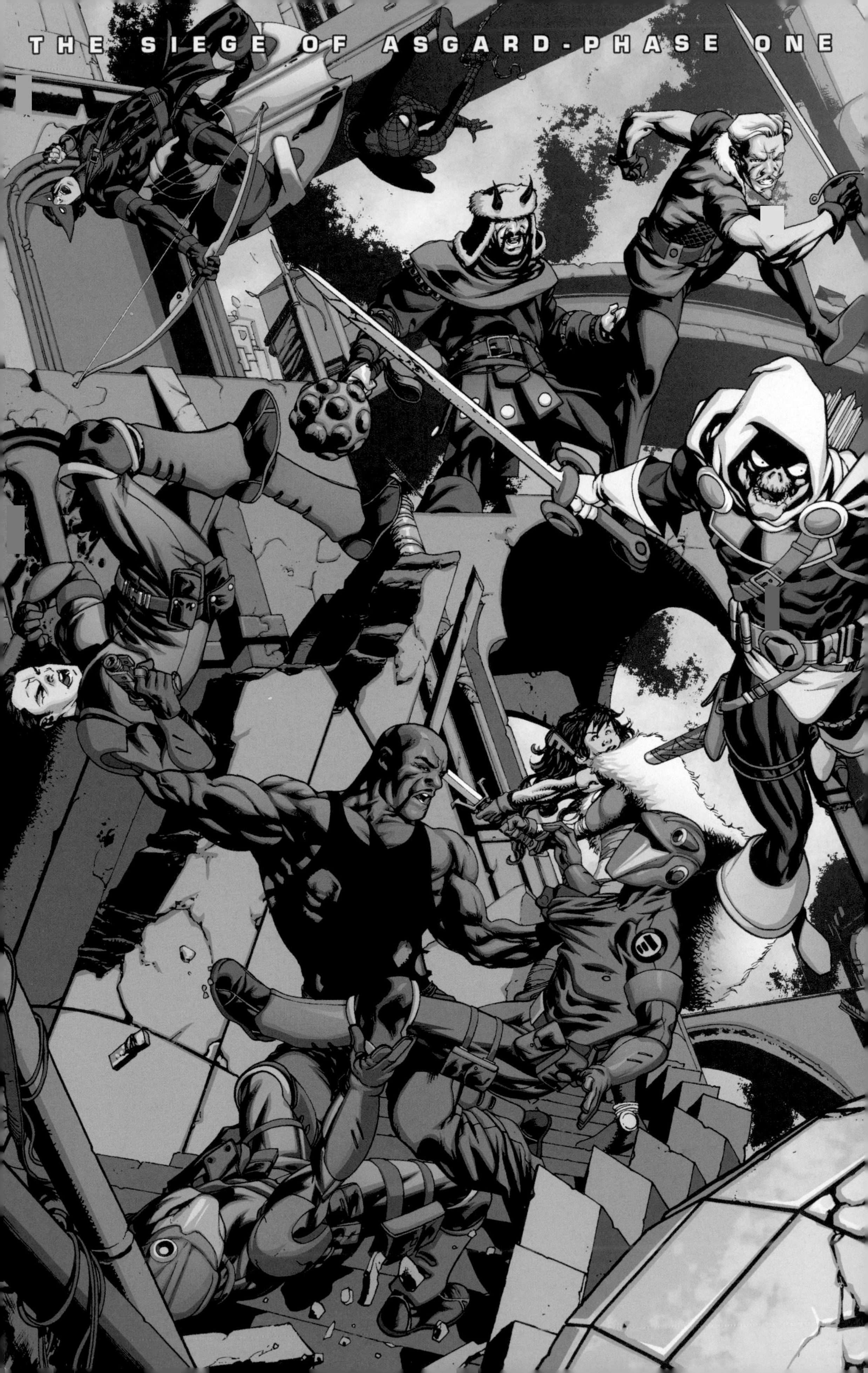
THE SIEGE OF ASGARD-PHASE ONE

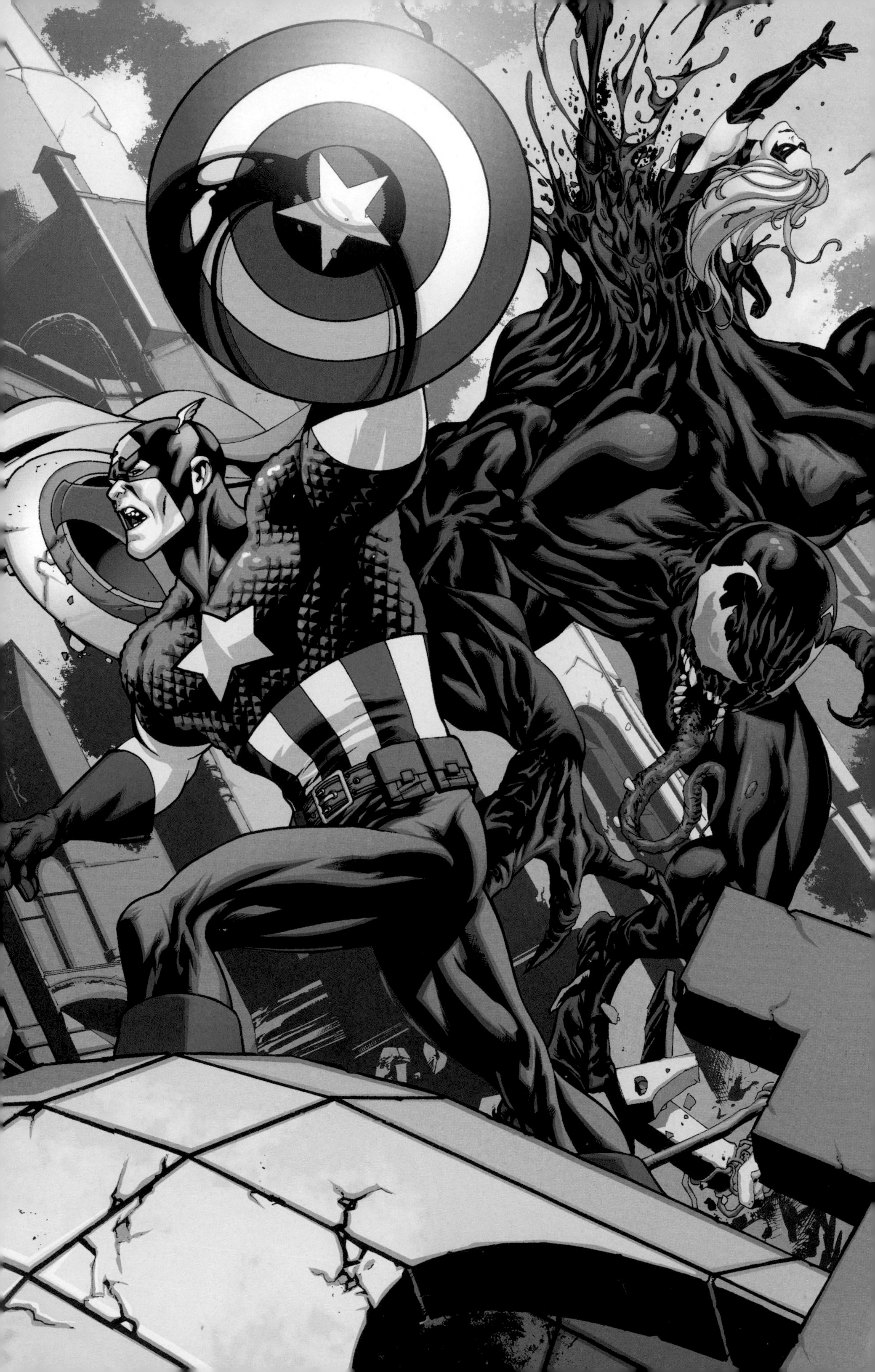

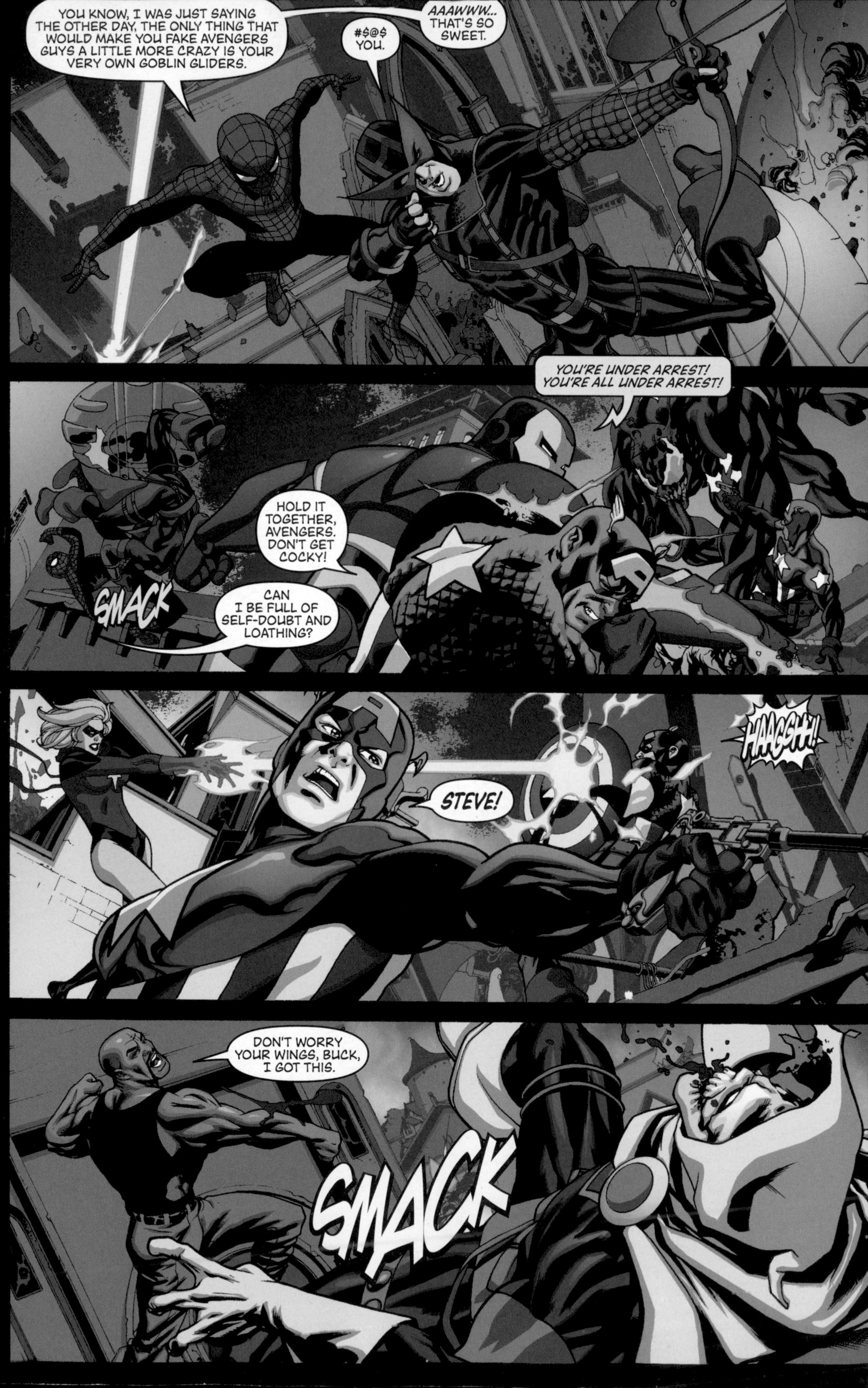
YOU KNOW, I WAS JUST SAYING THE OTHER DAY, THE ONLY THING THAT WOULD MAKE YOU FAKE AVENGERS GUYS A LITTLE MORE CRAZY IS YOUR VERY OWN GOBLIN GLIDERS.
#$@$ YOU.
AAAWWW... THAT'S SO SWEET.
YOU'RE UNDER ARREST! YOU'RE ALL UNDER ARREST!
HOLD IT TOGETHER, AVENGERS. DON'T GET COCKY!
SMACK
CAN I BE FULL OF SELF-DOUBT AND LOATHING?
HAAGGHH!
STEVE!
DON'T WORRY YOUR WINGS, BUCK, I GOT THIS.
SMACK

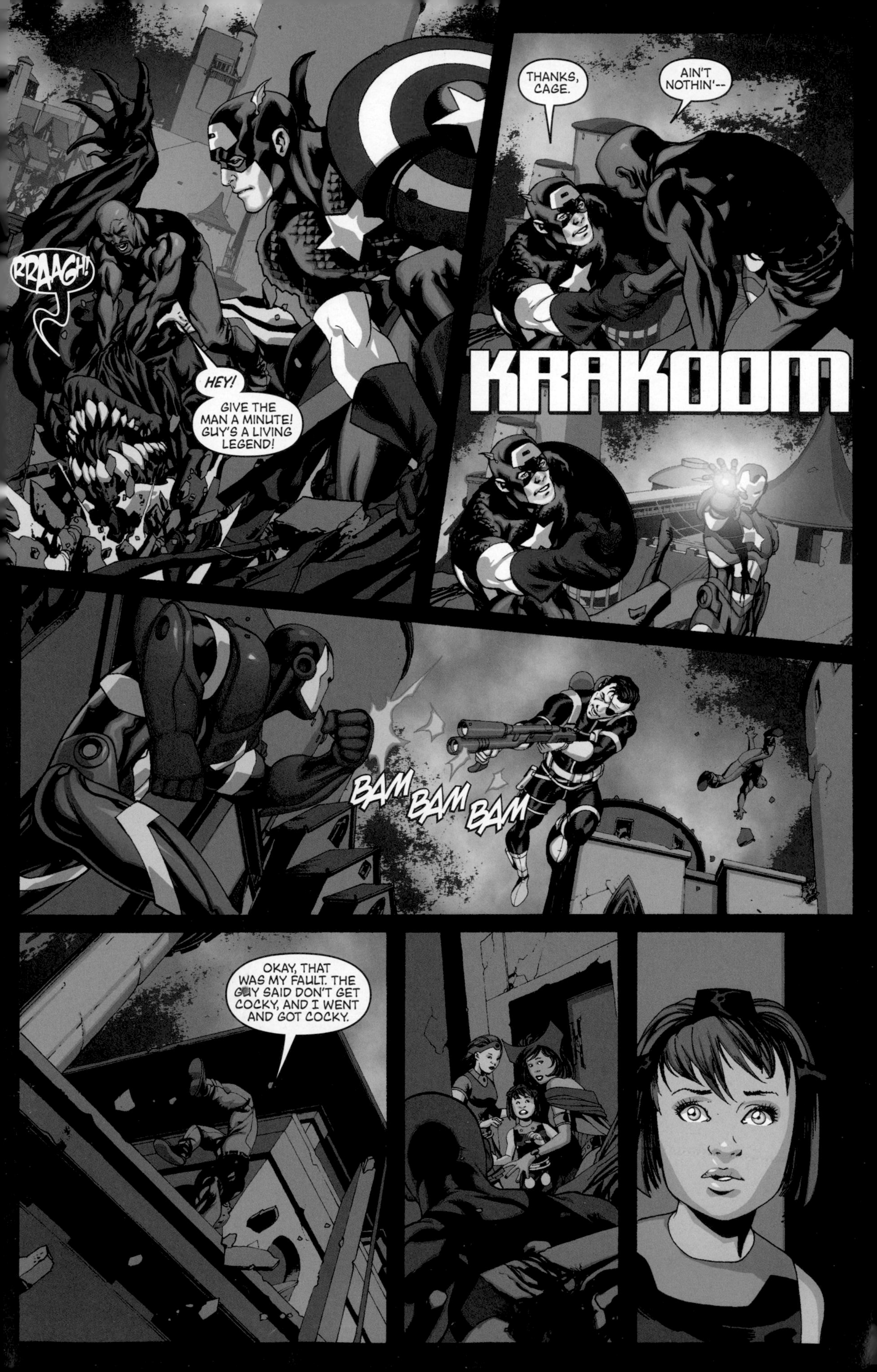
RRAAGH!
HEY!
GIVE THE MAN A MINUTE! GUY'S A LIVING LEGEND!
THANKS, CAGE.
AIN'T NOTHIN'--
KRAKOOM
BAM BAM BAM
OKAY, THAT WAS MY FAULT. THE GUY SAID DON'T GET COCKY, AND I WENT AND GOT COCKY.

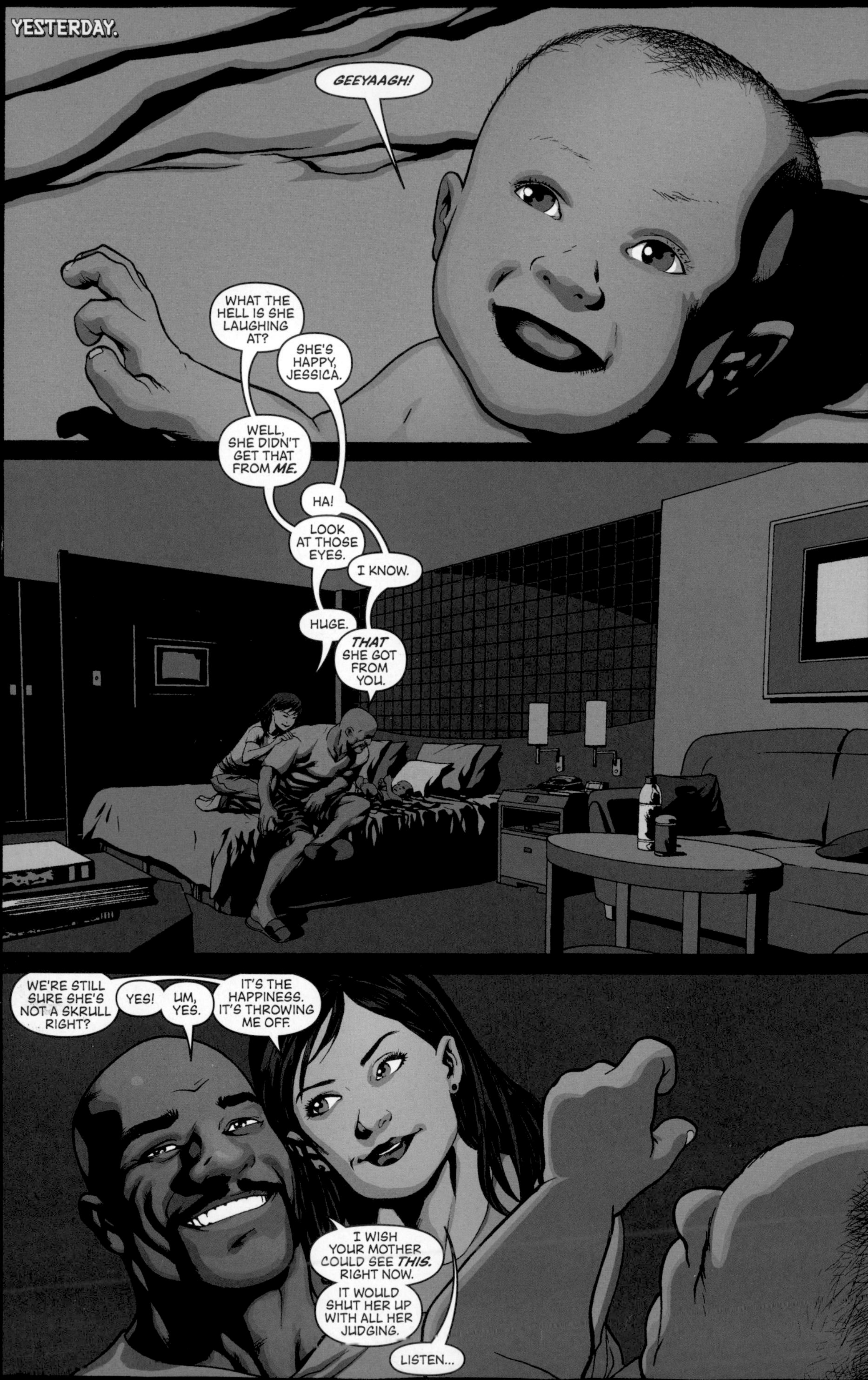
YESTERDAY.
GEEYAAGH!
WHAT THE HELL IS SHE LAUGHING AT?
SHE'S HAPPY, JESSICA.
WELL, SHE DIDN'T GET THAT FROM *ME.*
HA!
LOOK AT THOSE EYES.
I KNOW.
HUGE.
THAT SHE GOT FROM YOU.
WE'RE STILL SURE SHE'S NOT A SKRULL RIGHT?
YES!
UM, YES.
IT'S THE HAPPINESS. IT'S THROWING ME OFF.
I WISH YOUR MOTHER COULD SEE *THIS.* RIGHT NOW.
IT WOULD SHUT HER UP WITH ALL HER JUDGING.
LISTEN...

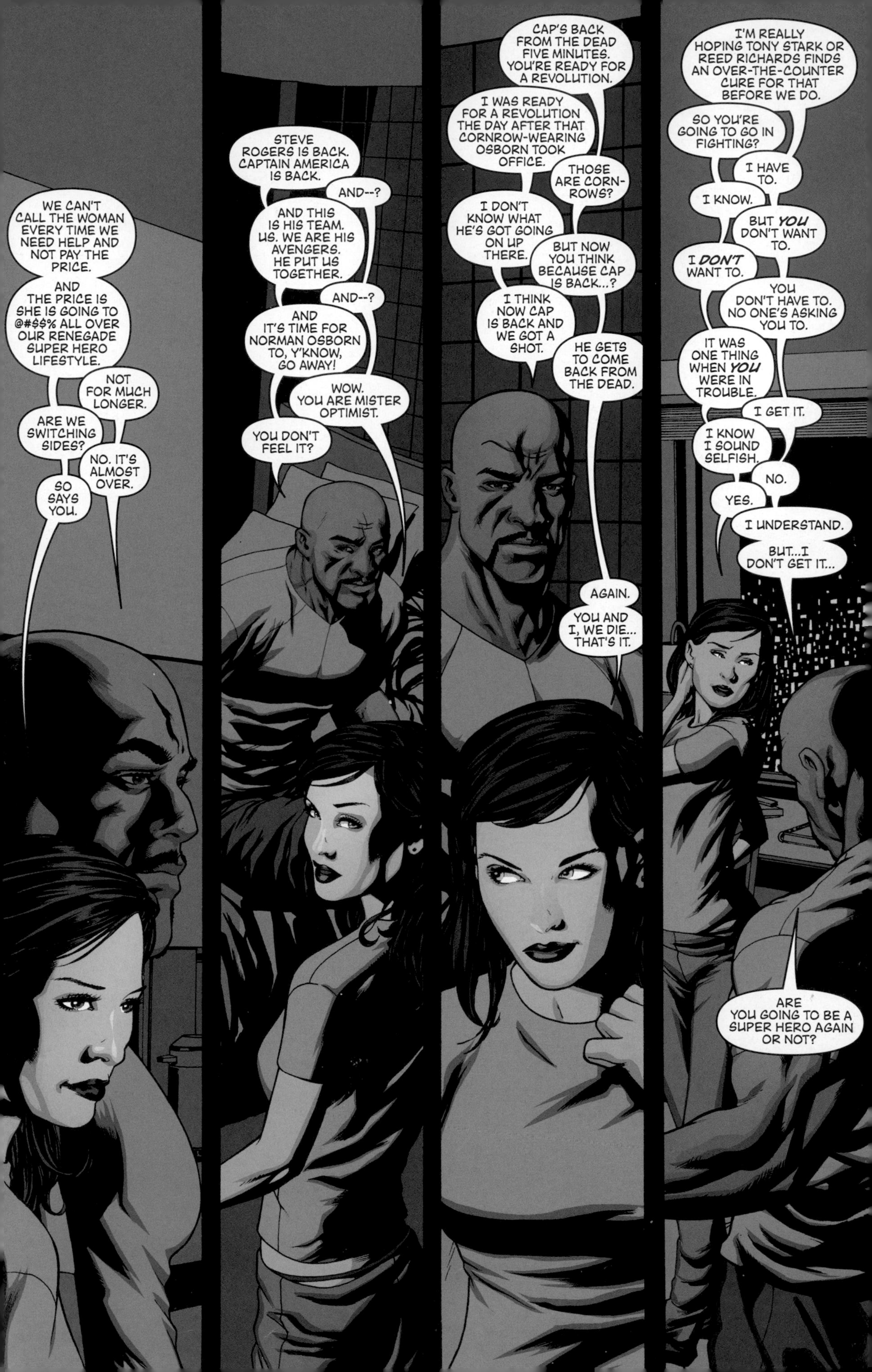
WE CAN'T CALL THE WOMAN EVERY TIME WE NEED HELP AND NOT PAY THE PRICE.
AND THE PRICE IS SHE IS GOING TO @#$$% ALL OVER OUR RENEGADE SUPER HERO LIFESTYLE.
NOT FOR MUCH LONGER.
ARE WE SWITCHING SIDES?
NO. IT'S ALMOST OVER.
SO SAYS YOU.
STEVE ROGERS IS BACK. CAPTAIN AMERICA IS BACK.
AND--?
AND THIS IS HIS TEAM. US. WE ARE HIS AVENGERS. HE PUT US TOGETHER.
AND--?
AND IT'S TIME FOR NORMAN OSBORN TO, Y'KNOW, GO AWAY!
WOW. YOU ARE MISTER OPTIMIST.
YOU DON'T FEEL IT?
CAP'S BACK FROM THE DEAD FIVE MINUTES. YOU'RE READY FOR A REVOLUTION.
I WAS READY FOR A REVOLUTION THE DAY AFTER THAT CORNROW-WEARING OSBORN TOOK OFFICE.
THOSE ARE CORN-ROWS?
I DON'T KNOW WHAT HE'S GOT GOING ON UP THERE.
BUT NOW YOU THINK BECAUSE CAP IS BACK...?
I THINK NOW CAP IS BACK AND WE GOT A SHOT.
HE GETS TO COME BACK FROM THE DEAD.
AGAIN.
YOU AND I, WE DIE... THAT'S IT.
I'M REALLY HOPING TONY STARK OR REED RICHARDS FINDS AN OVER-THE-COUNTER CURE FOR THAT BEFORE WE DO.
SO YOU'RE GOING TO GO IN FIGHTING?
I HAVE TO.
I KNOW.
BUT *YOU* DON'T WANT TO.
I *DON'T* WANT TO.
YOU DON'T HAVE TO. NO ONE'S ASKING YOU TO.
IT WAS ONE THING WHEN *YOU* WERE IN TROUBLE.
I GET IT.
I KNOW I SOUND SELFISH.
NO.
YES.
I UNDERSTAND.
BUT...I DON'T GET IT...
ARE YOU GOING TO BE A SUPER HERO AGAIN OR NOT?

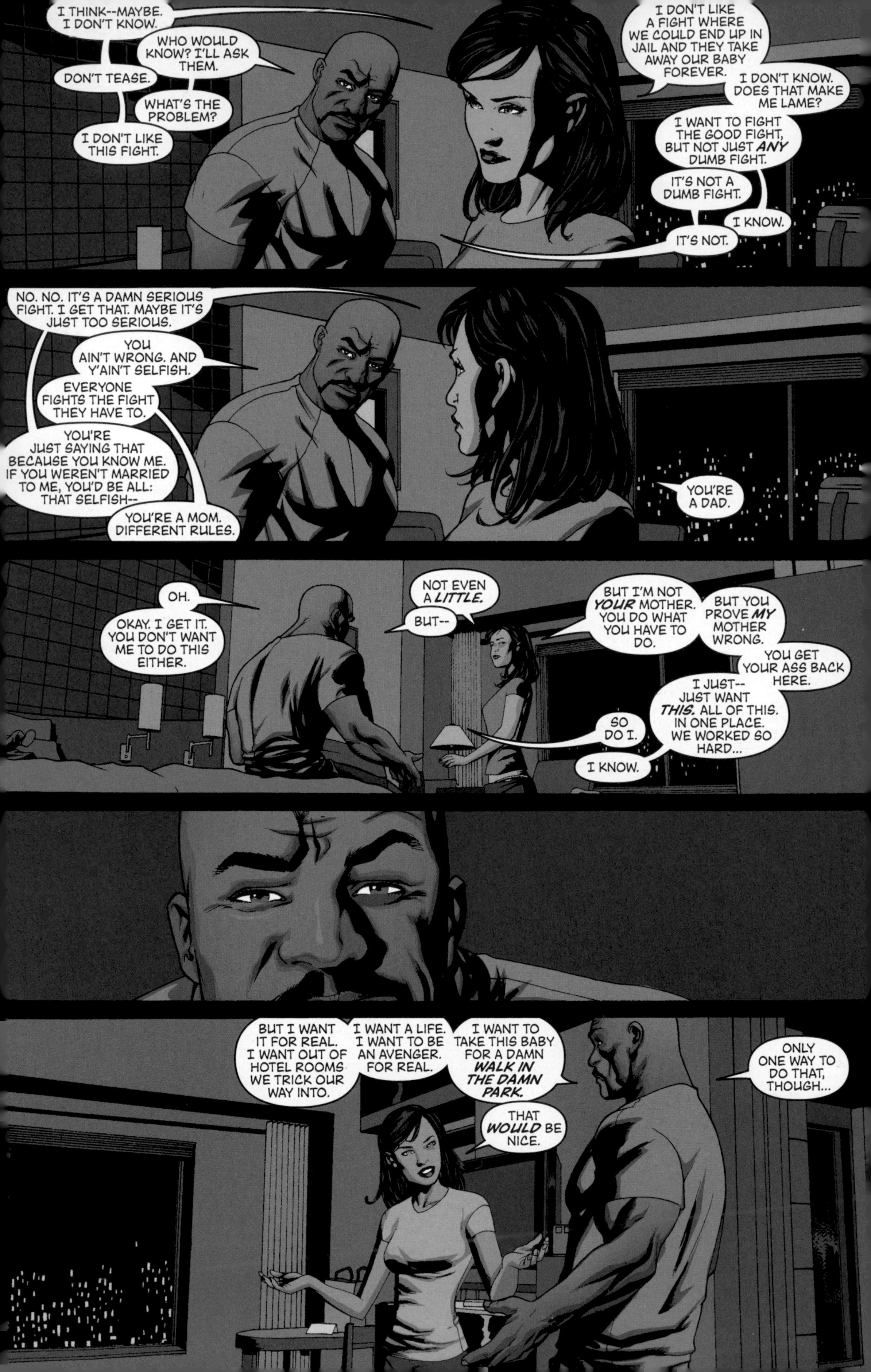
I THINK--MAYBE. I DON'T KNOW.
WHO WOULD KNOW? I'LL ASK THEM.
DON'T TEASE.
WHAT'S THE PROBLEM?
I DON'T LIKE THIS FIGHT.
I DON'T LIKE A FIGHT WHERE WE COULD END UP IN JAIL AND THEY TAKE AWAY OUR BABY FOREVER.
I DON'T KNOW. DOES THAT MAKE ME LAME?
I WANT TO FIGHT THE GOOD FIGHT, BUT NOT JUST ANY DUMB FIGHT.
IT'S NOT A DUMB FIGHT.
I KNOW.
IT'S NOT.
NO. NO. IT'S A DAMN SERIOUS FIGHT. I GET THAT. MAYBE IT'S JUST TOO SERIOUS.
YOU AIN'T WRONG. AND Y'AIN'T SELFISH.
EVERYONE FIGHTS THE FIGHT THEY HAVE TO.
YOU'RE JUST SAYING THAT BECAUSE YOU KNOW ME. IF YOU WEREN'T MARRIED TO ME, YOU'D BE ALL: THAT SELFISH--
YOU'RE A MOM. DIFFERENT RULES.
YOU'RE A DAD.
OH.
OKAY. I GET IT. YOU DON'T WANT ME TO DO THIS EITHER.
NOT EVEN A LITTLE.
BUT--
BUT I'M NOT YOUR MOTHER. YOU DO WHAT YOU HAVE TO DO.
BUT YOU PROVE MY MOTHER WRONG.
YOU GET YOUR ASS BACK HERE.
I JUST-- JUST WANT THIS. ALL OF THIS. IN ONE PLACE. WE WORKED SO HARD...
SO DO I.
I KNOW.
BUT I WANT IT FOR REAL. I WANT OUT OF HOTEL ROOMS WE TRICK OUR WAY INTO.
I WANT A LIFE. I WANT TO BE AN AVENGER. FOR REAL.
I WANT TO TAKE THIS BABY FOR A DAMN WALK IN THE DAMN PARK.
THAT WOULD BE NICE.
ONLY ONE WAY TO DO THAT, THOUGH...

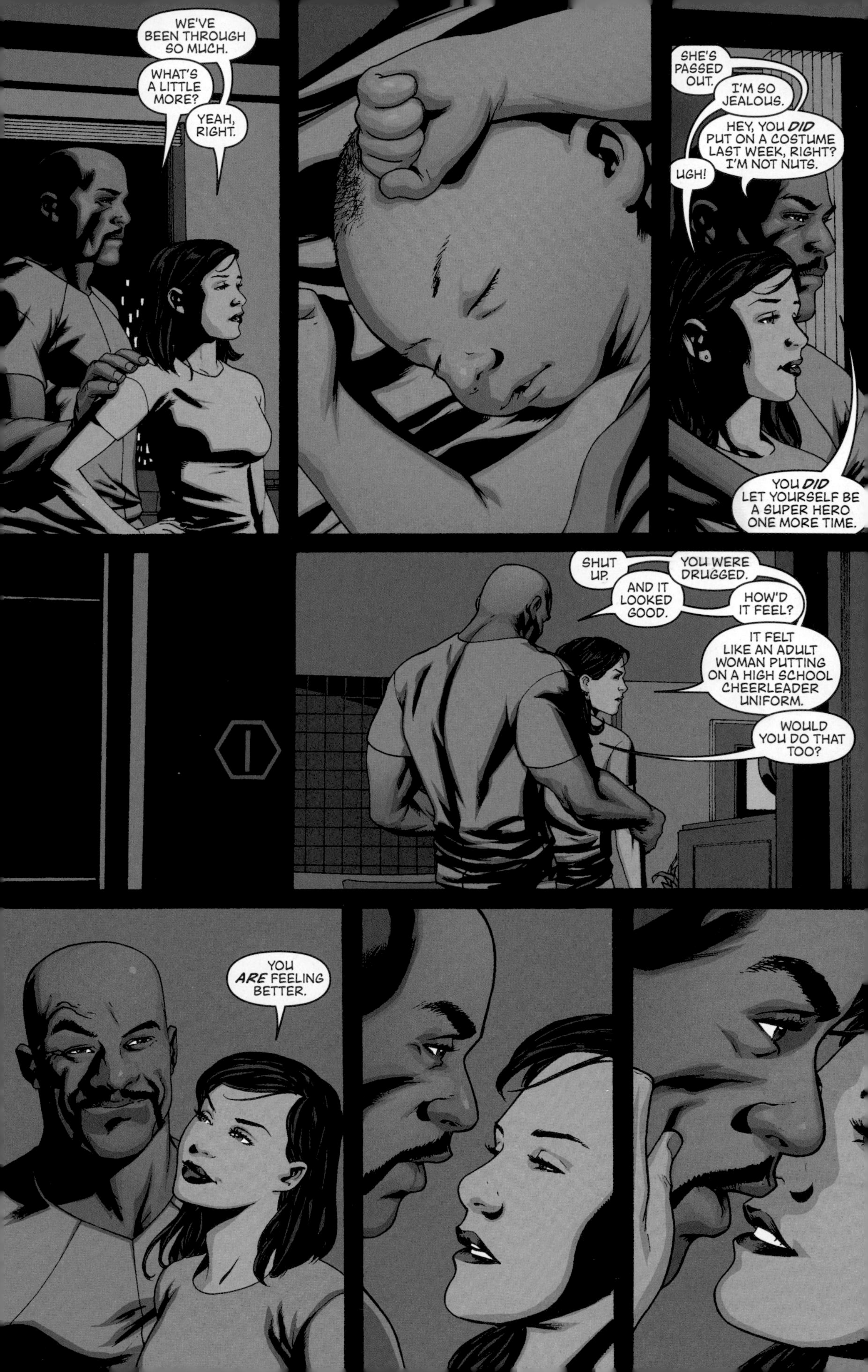
WE'VE BEEN THROUGH SO MUCH.
WHAT'S A LITTLE MORE?
YEAH, RIGHT.
SHE'S PASSED OUT.
I'M SO JEALOUS.
HEY, YOU *DID* PUT ON A COSTUME LAST WEEK, RIGHT? I'M NOT NUTS.
UGH!
YOU *DID* LET YOURSELF BE A SUPER HERO ONE MORE TIME.
SHUT UP.
YOU WERE DRUGGED.
AND IT LOOKED GOOD.
HOW'D IT FEEL?
IT FELT LIKE AN ADULT WOMAN PUTTING ON A HIGH SCHOOL CHEERLEADER UNIFORM.
WOULD YOU DO THAT TOO?
YOU *ARE* FEELING BETTER.

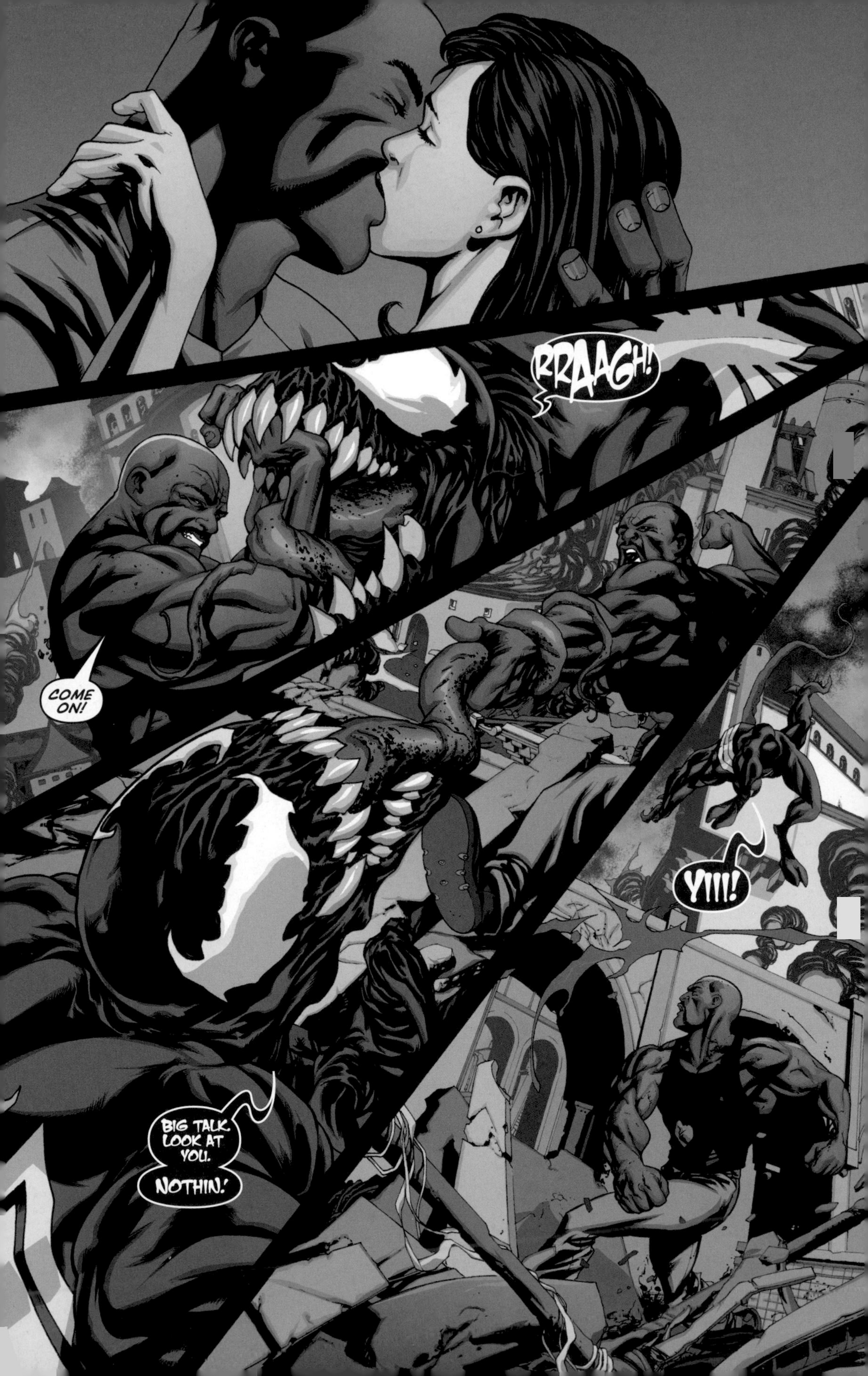
RRAAGH!
COME ON!
YIII!
BIG TALK. LOOK AT YOU.
NOTHIN'!

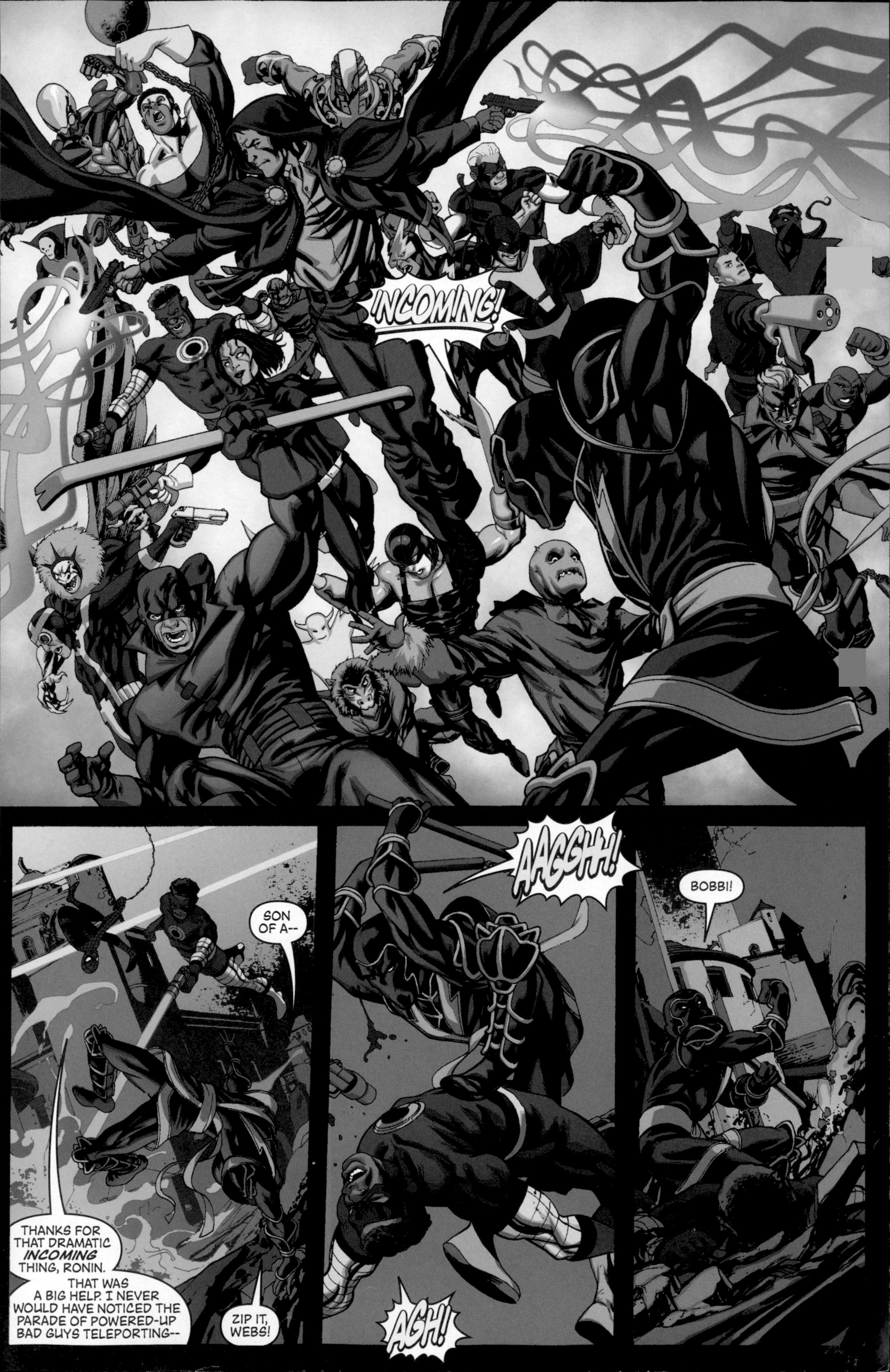

INCOMING!
SON OF A--
AAGGHH!
BOBBI!
THANKS FOR THAT DRAMATIC INCOMING THING, RONIN.
THAT WAS A BIG HELP. I NEVER WOULD HAVE NOTICED THE PARADE OF POWERED-UP BAD GUYS TELEPORTING--
ZIP IT, WEBS!
AGH!

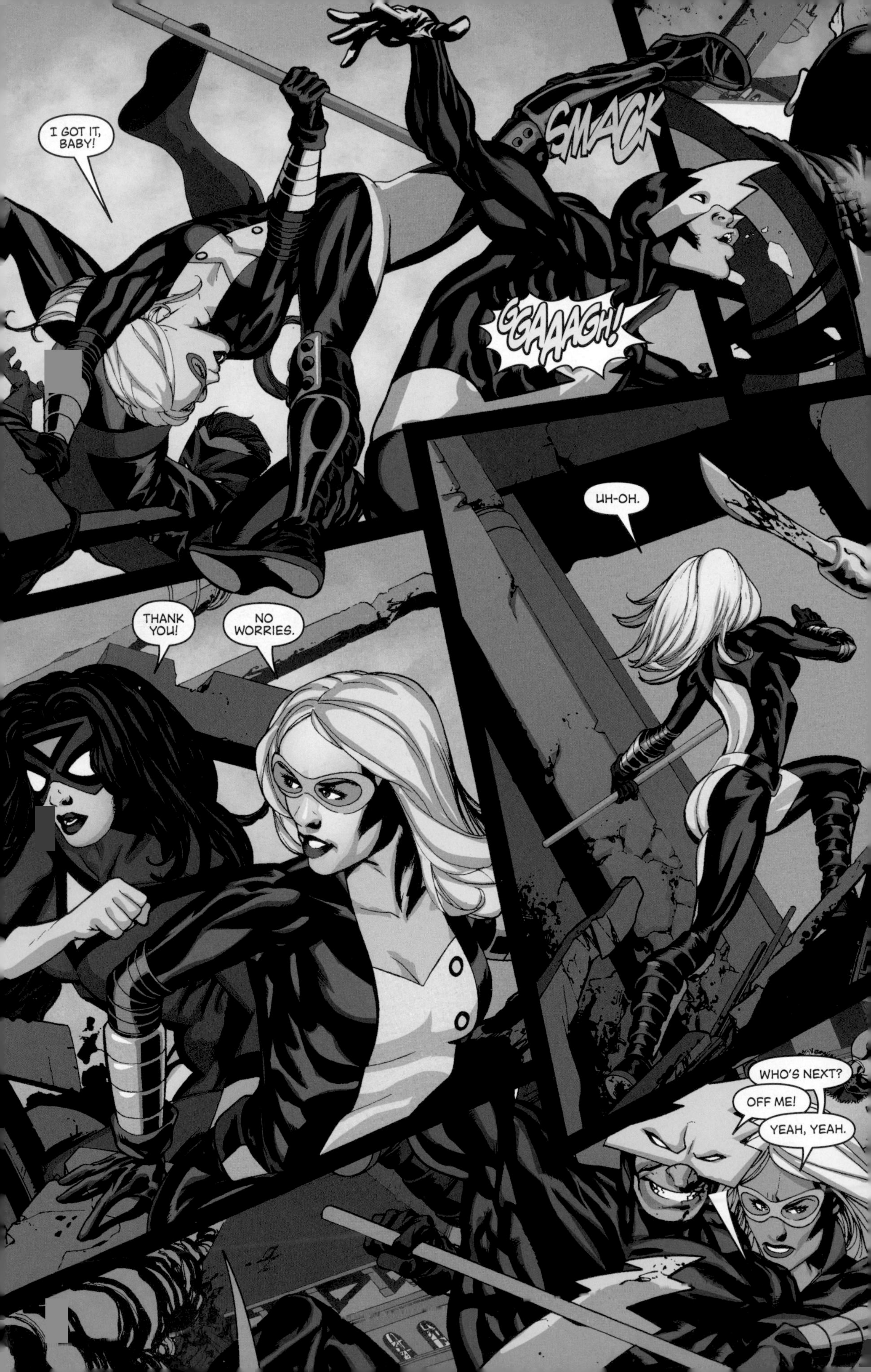
I GOT IT, BABY!
SMACK
GGAAAGH!
UH-OH.
THANK YOU!
NO WORRIES.
WHO'S NEXT?
OFF ME!
YEAH, YEAH.

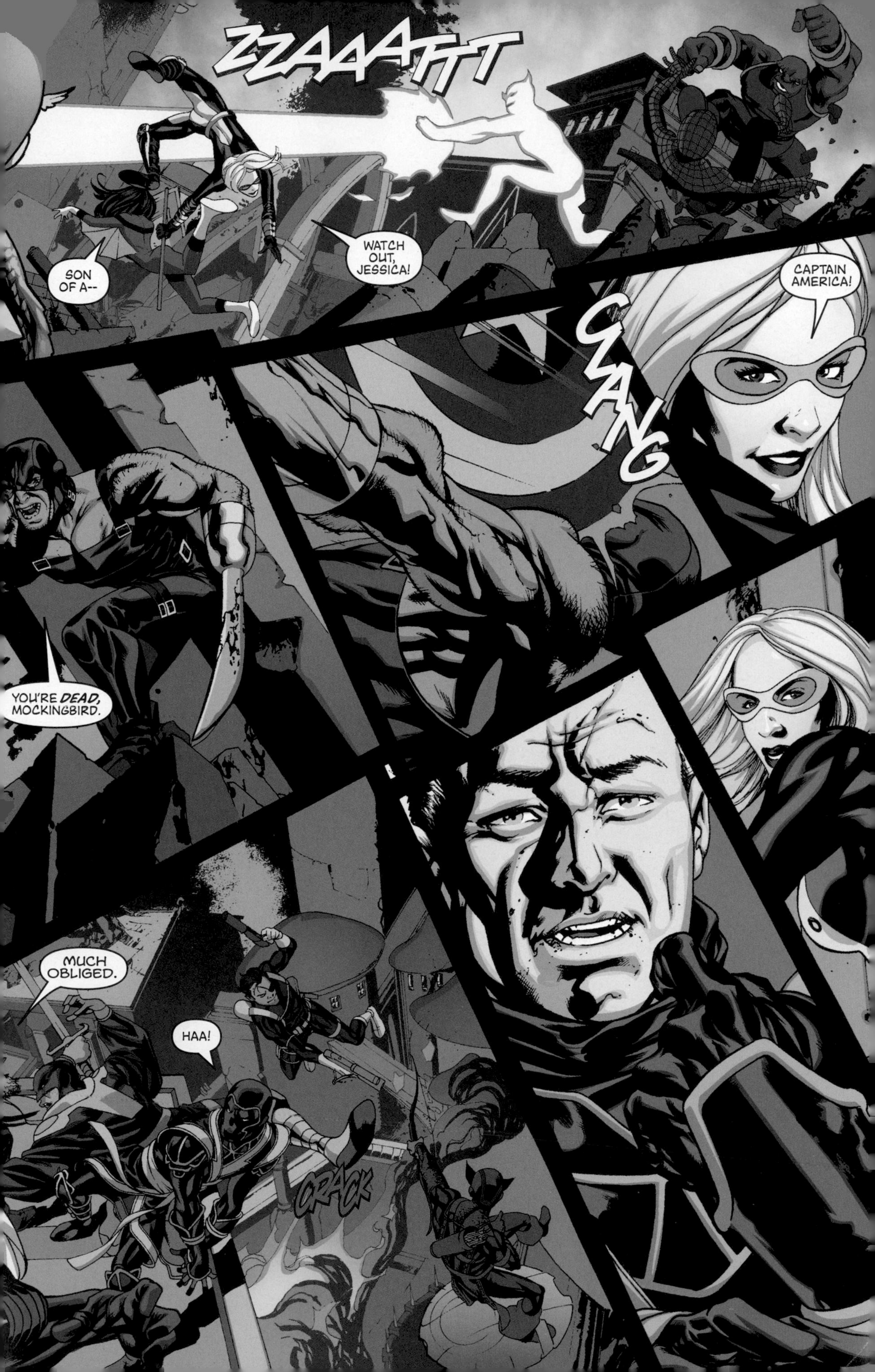

ZZAAAATTT
SON OF A--
WATCH OUT, JESSICA!
CAPTAIN AMERICA!
CLANG
YOU'RE *DEAD*, MOCKINGBIRD.
MUCH OBLIGED.
HAA!
CRACK

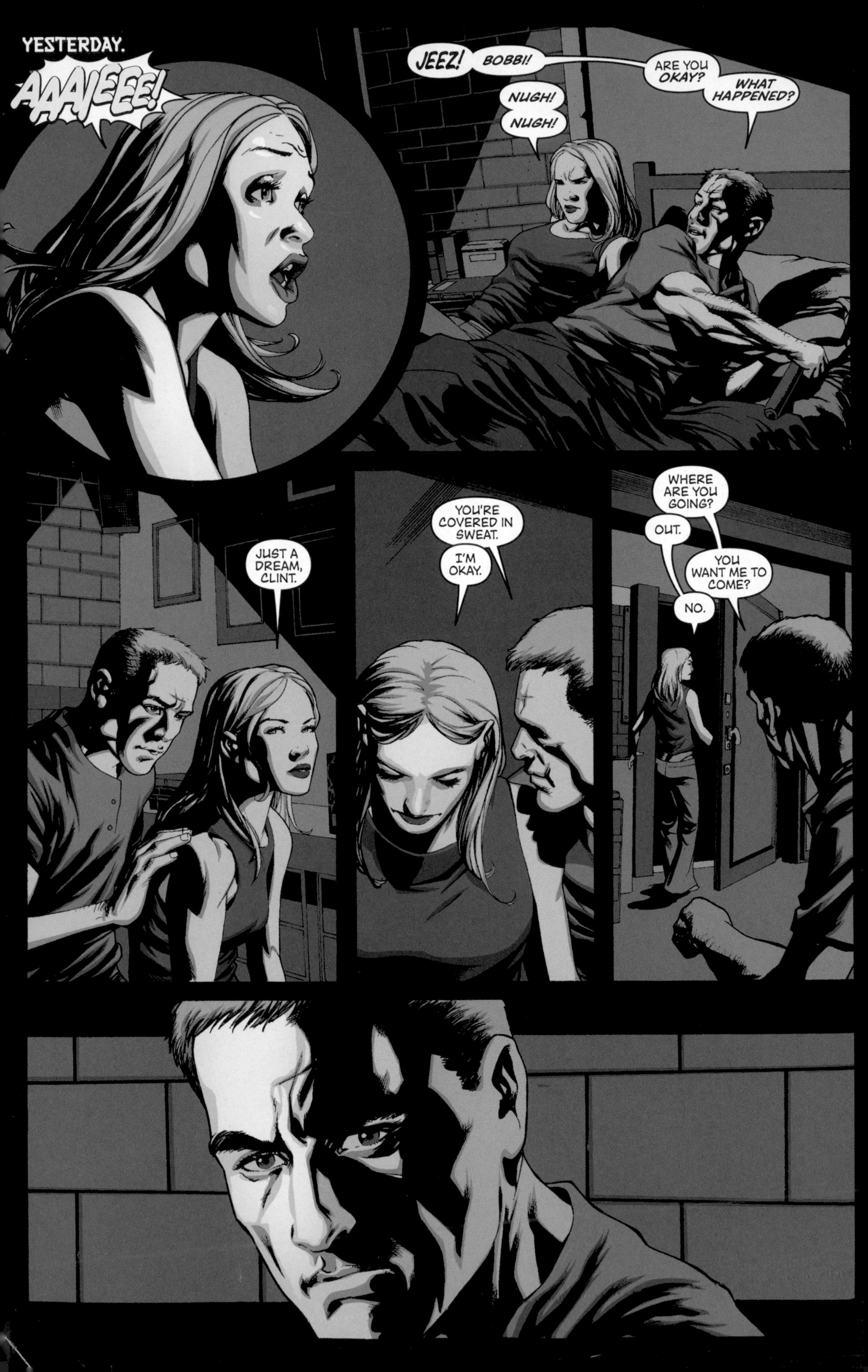
YESTERDAY.
AAAIEEE!
JEEZ! BOBBI!
NUGH!
NUGH!
ARE YOU OKAY?
WHAT HAPPENED?
JUST A DREAM, CLINT.
YOU'RE COVERED IN SWEAT.
I'M OKAY.
WHERE ARE YOU GOING?
OUT.
YOU WANT ME TO COME?
NO.

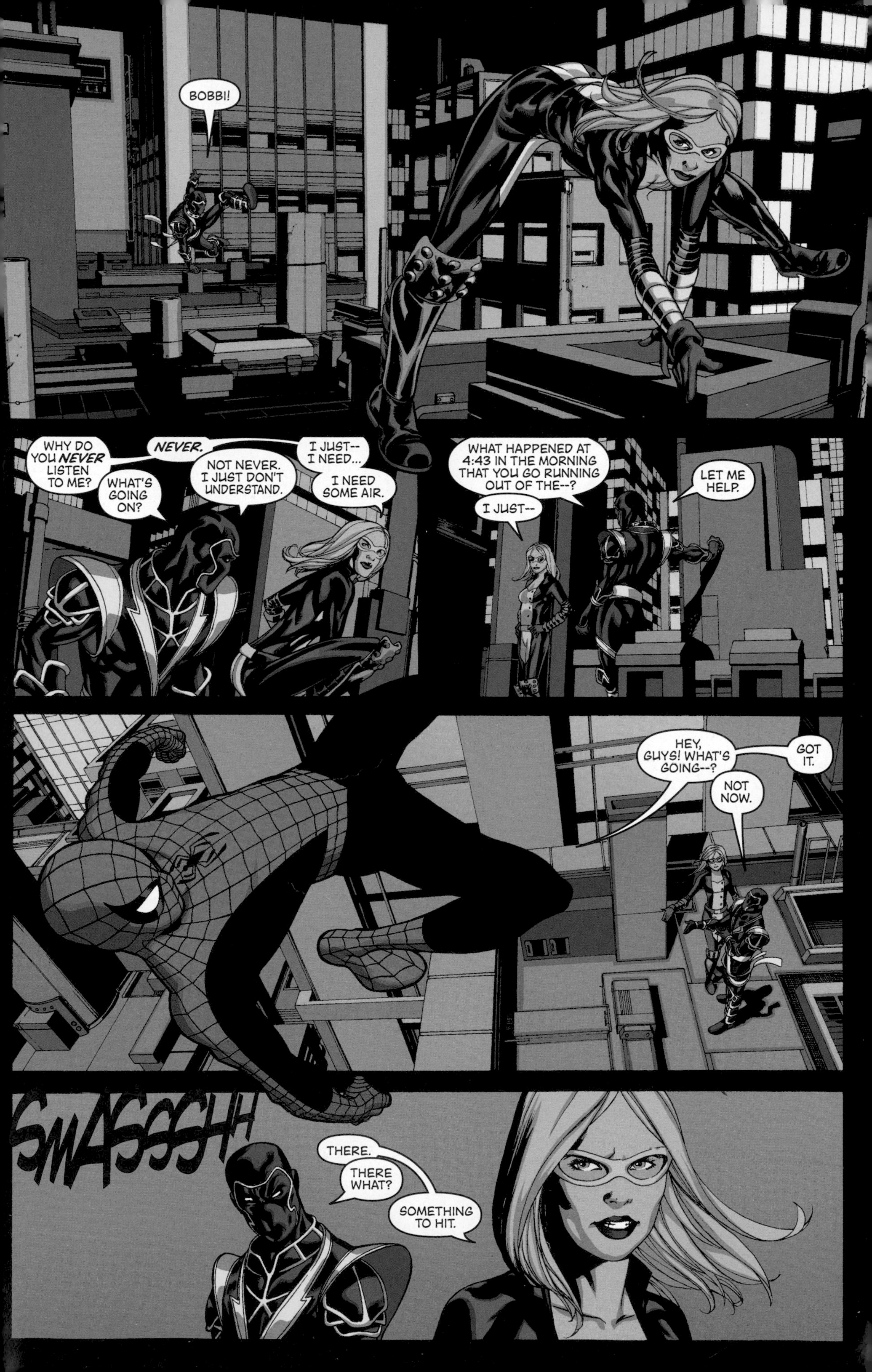
BOBBI!
WHY DO YOU NEVER LISTEN TO ME?
NEVER.
WHAT'S GOING ON?
NOT NEVER. I JUST DON'T UNDERSTAND.
I JUST-- I NEED...
I NEED SOME AIR.
WHAT HAPPENED AT 4:43 IN THE MORNING THAT YOU GO RUNNING OUT OF THE--?
I JUST--
LET ME HELP.
HEY, GUYS! WHAT'S GOING--?
GOT IT.
NOT NOW.
SWASSSHH
THERE.
THERE WHAT?
SOMETHING TO HIT.

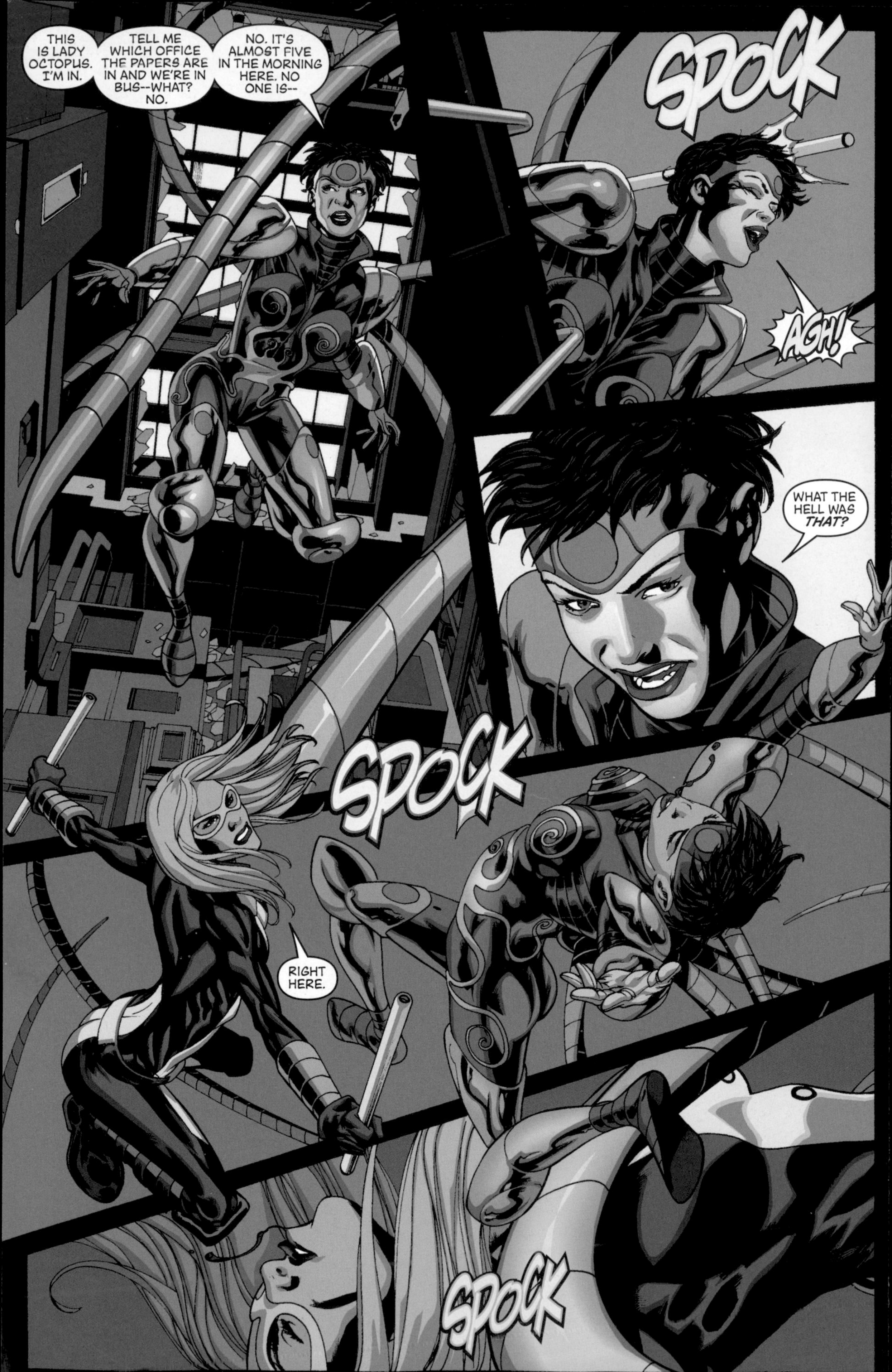
THIS IS LADY OCTOPUS. I'M IN.
TELL ME WHICH OFFICE THE PAPERS ARE IN AND WE'RE IN BUS--WHAT? NO.
NO. IT'S ALMOST FIVE IN THE MORNING HERE. NO ONE IS--
SPOCK
AGH!
WHAT THE HELL WAS *THAT?*
SPOCK
RIGHT HERE.
SPOCK

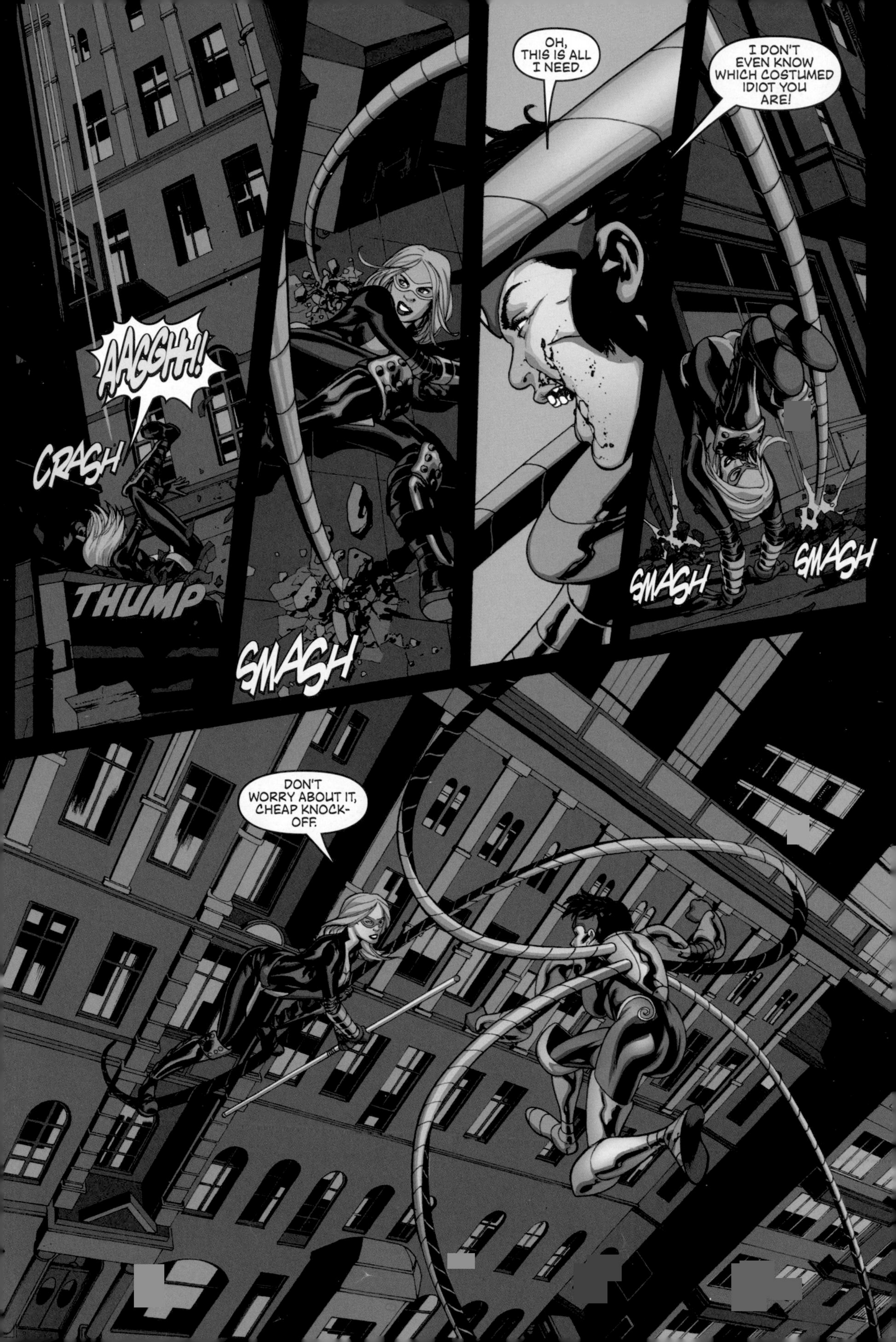
AAGGHH!
CRASH
THUMP
SMASH
OH, THIS IS ALL I NEED.
I DON'T EVEN KNOW WHICH COSTUMED IDIOT YOU ARE!
SMASH
SMASH
DON'T WORRY ABOUT IT, CHEAP KNOCK-OFF.

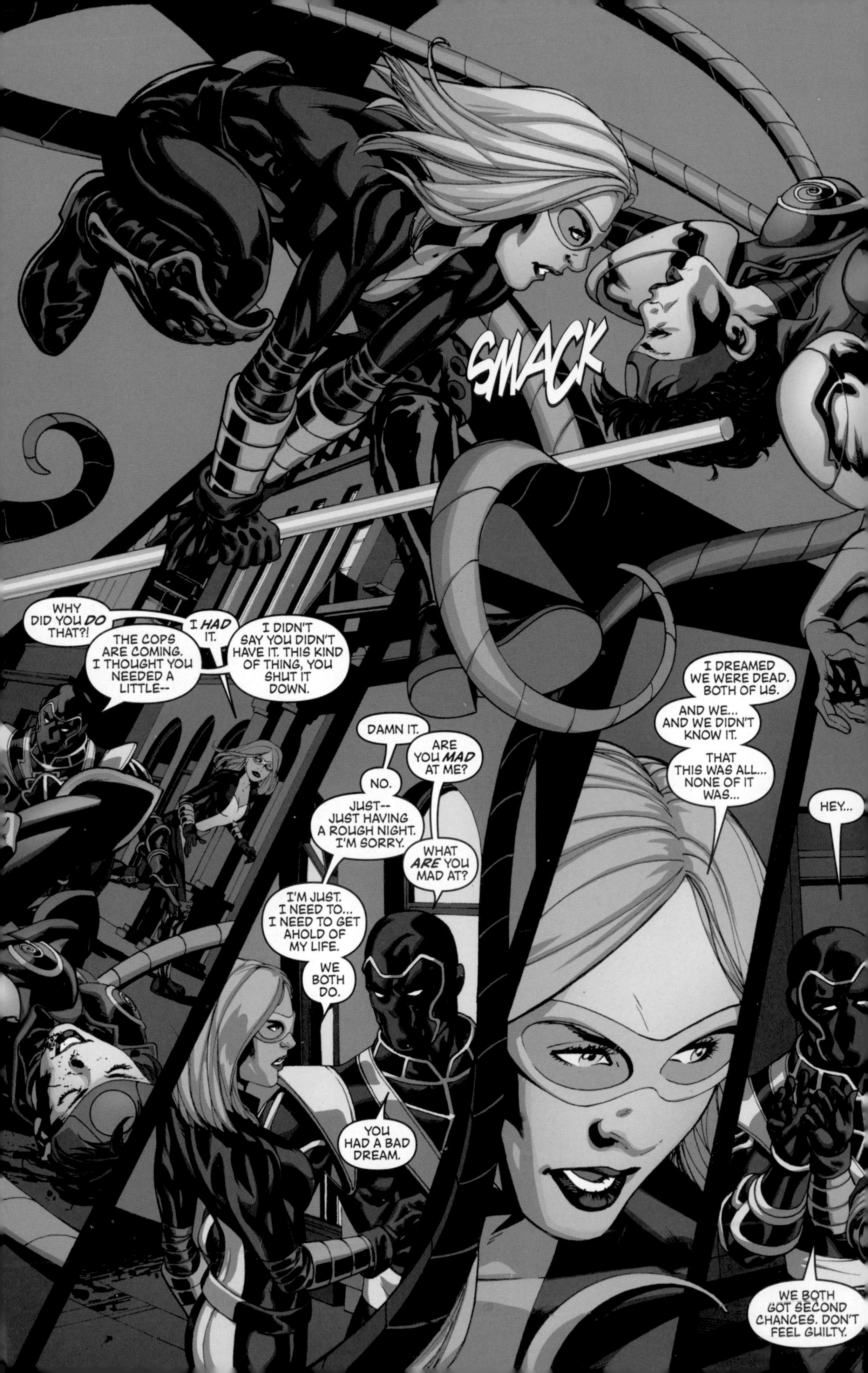

SMACK
WHY DID YOU DO THAT?!
THE COPS ARE COMING. I THOUGHT YOU NEEDED A LITTLE--
I HAD IT.
I DIDN'T SAY YOU DIDN'T HAVE IT. THIS KIND OF THING, YOU SHUT IT DOWN.
DAMN IT.
ARE YOU MAD AT ME?
NO.
JUST-- JUST HAVING A ROUGH NIGHT. I'M SORRY.
WHAT ARE YOU MAD AT?
I'M JUST. I NEED TO... I NEED TO GET AHOLD OF MY LIFE.
WE BOTH DO.
YOU HAD A BAD DREAM.
I DREAMED WE WERE DEAD. BOTH OF US.
AND WE... AND WE DIDN'T KNOW IT.
THAT THIS WAS ALL... NONE OF IT WAS...
HEY...
WE BOTH GOT SECOND CHANCES. DON'T FEEL GUILTY.

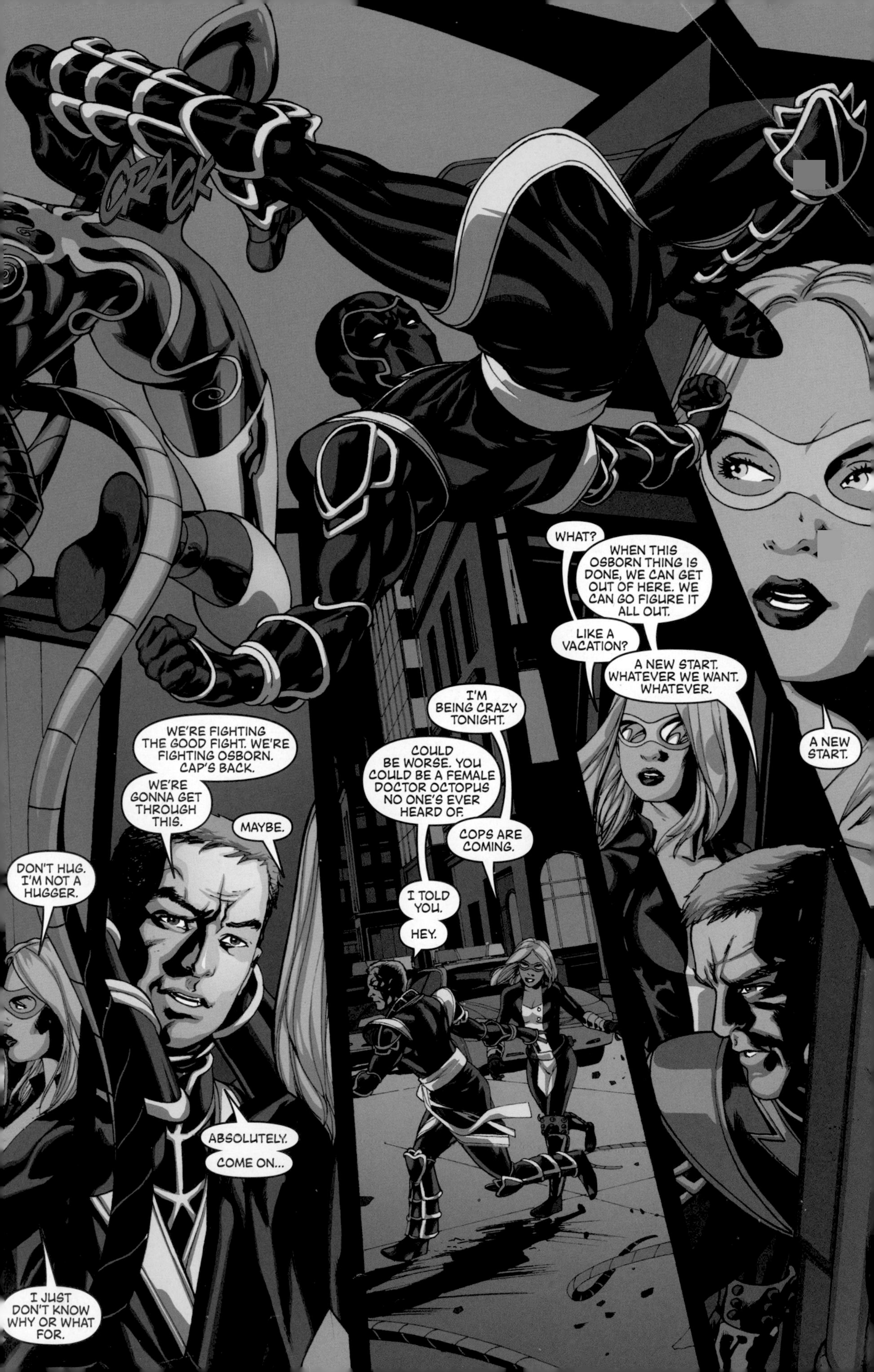
CRACK
WHAT?
WHEN THIS OSBORN THING IS DONE, WE CAN GET OUT OF HERE. WE CAN GO FIGURE IT ALL OUT.
LIKE A VACATION?
A NEW START. WHATEVER WE WANT. WHATEVER.
A NEW START.
WE'RE FIGHTING THE GOOD FIGHT. WE'RE FIGHTING OSBORN. CAP'S BACK.
WE'RE GONNA GET THROUGH THIS.
MAYBE.
DON'T HUG. I'M NOT A HUGGER.
ABSOLUTELY.
COME ON...
I JUST DON'T KNOW WHY OR WHAT FOR.
I'M BEING CRAZY TONIGHT.
COULD BE WORSE. YOU COULD BE A FEMALE DOCTOR OCTOPUS NO ONE'S EVER HEARD OF.
COPS ARE COMING.
I TOLD YOU.
HEY.

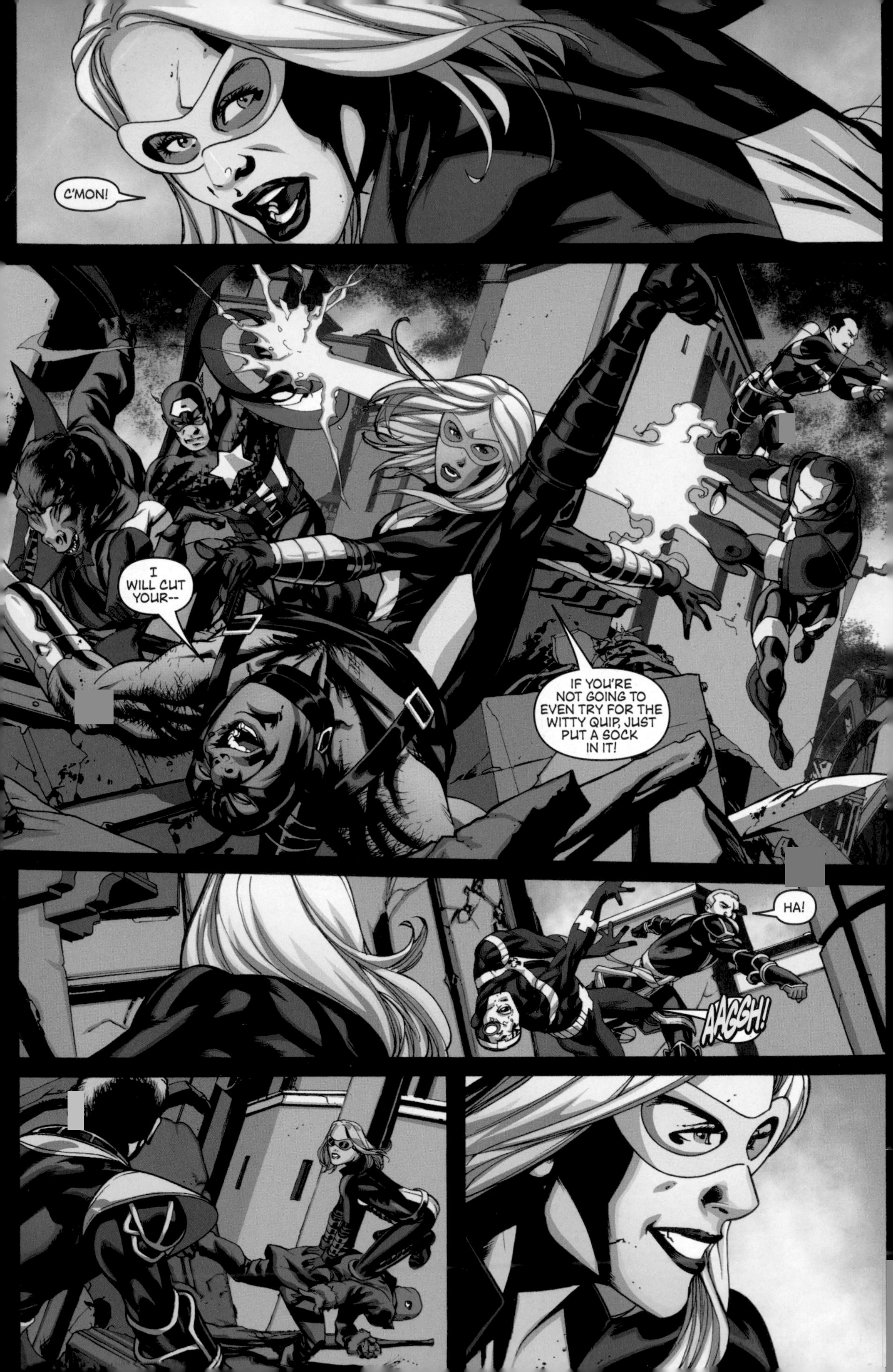
C'MON!
I WILL CUT YOUR--
IF YOU'RE NOT GOING TO EVEN TRY FOR THE WITTY QUIP, JUST PUT A SOCK IN IT!
HA!
AAGGH!

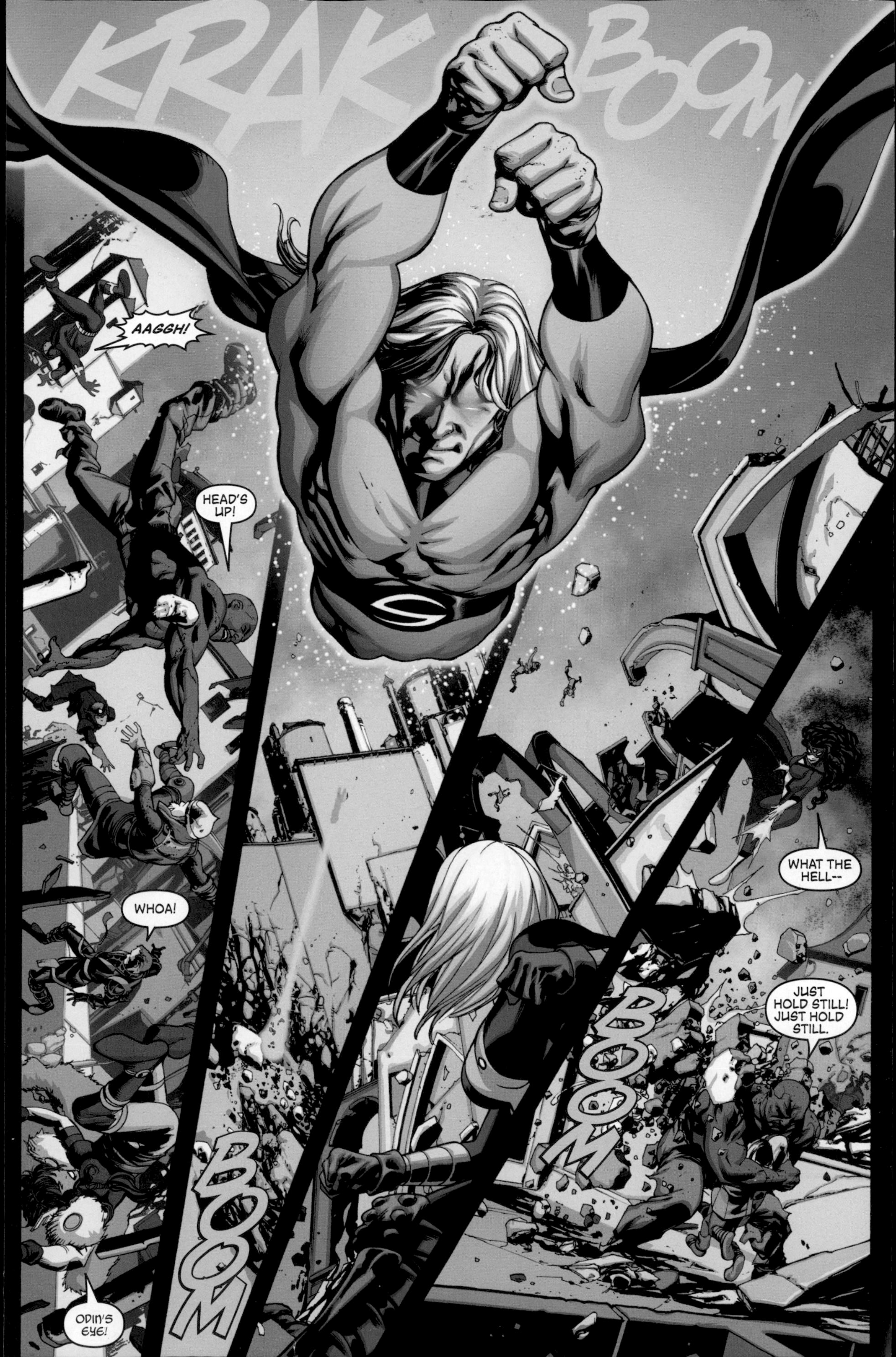
KRAK
BOOM
AAGGH!
HEAD'S UP!
WHAT THE HELL--
WHOA!
JUST HOLD STILL! JUST HOLD STILL.
BOOM
BOOM
ODIN'S EYE!

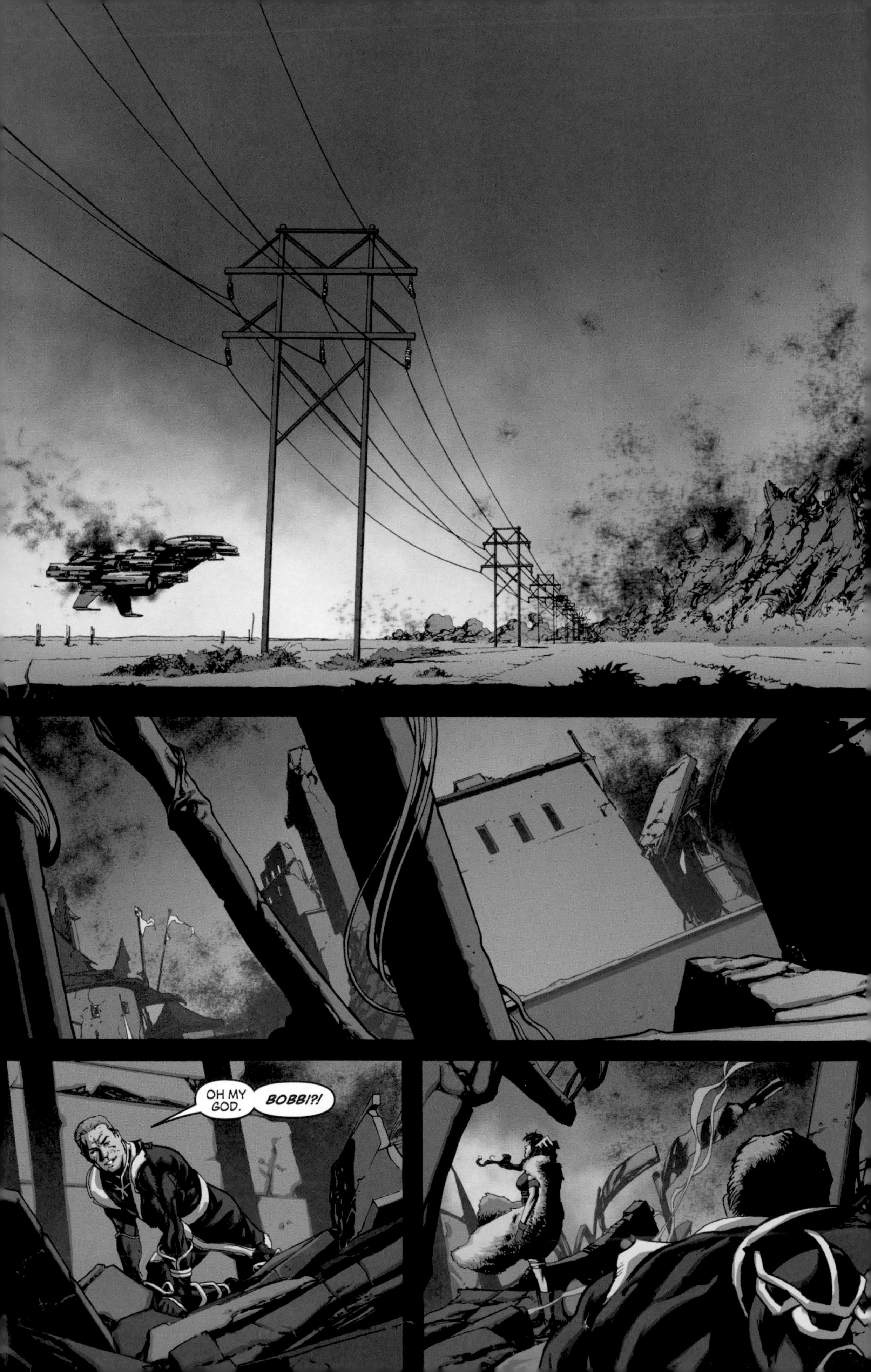
OH MY GOD. BOBBI?!

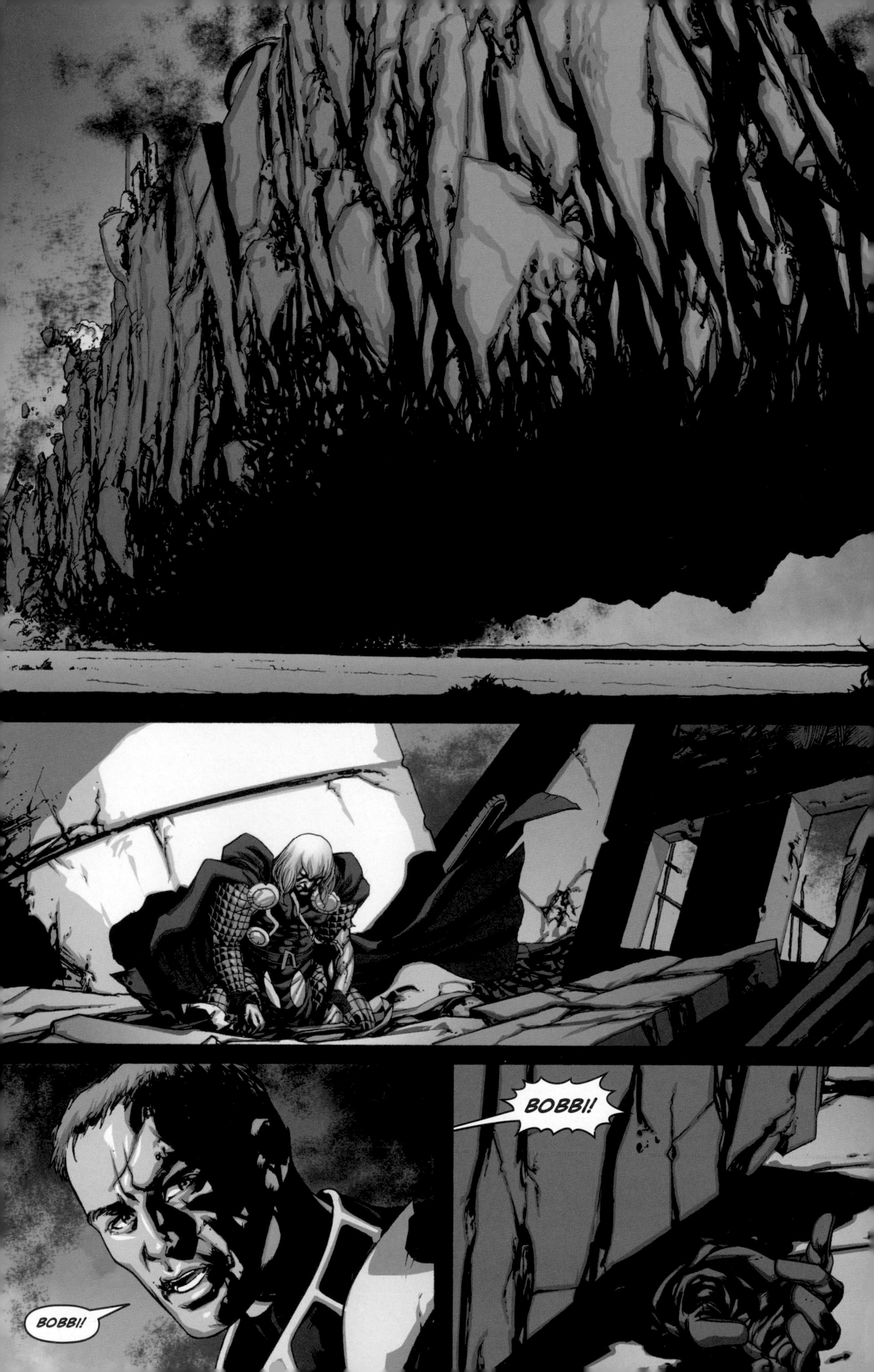
BOBBI!
BOBBI!

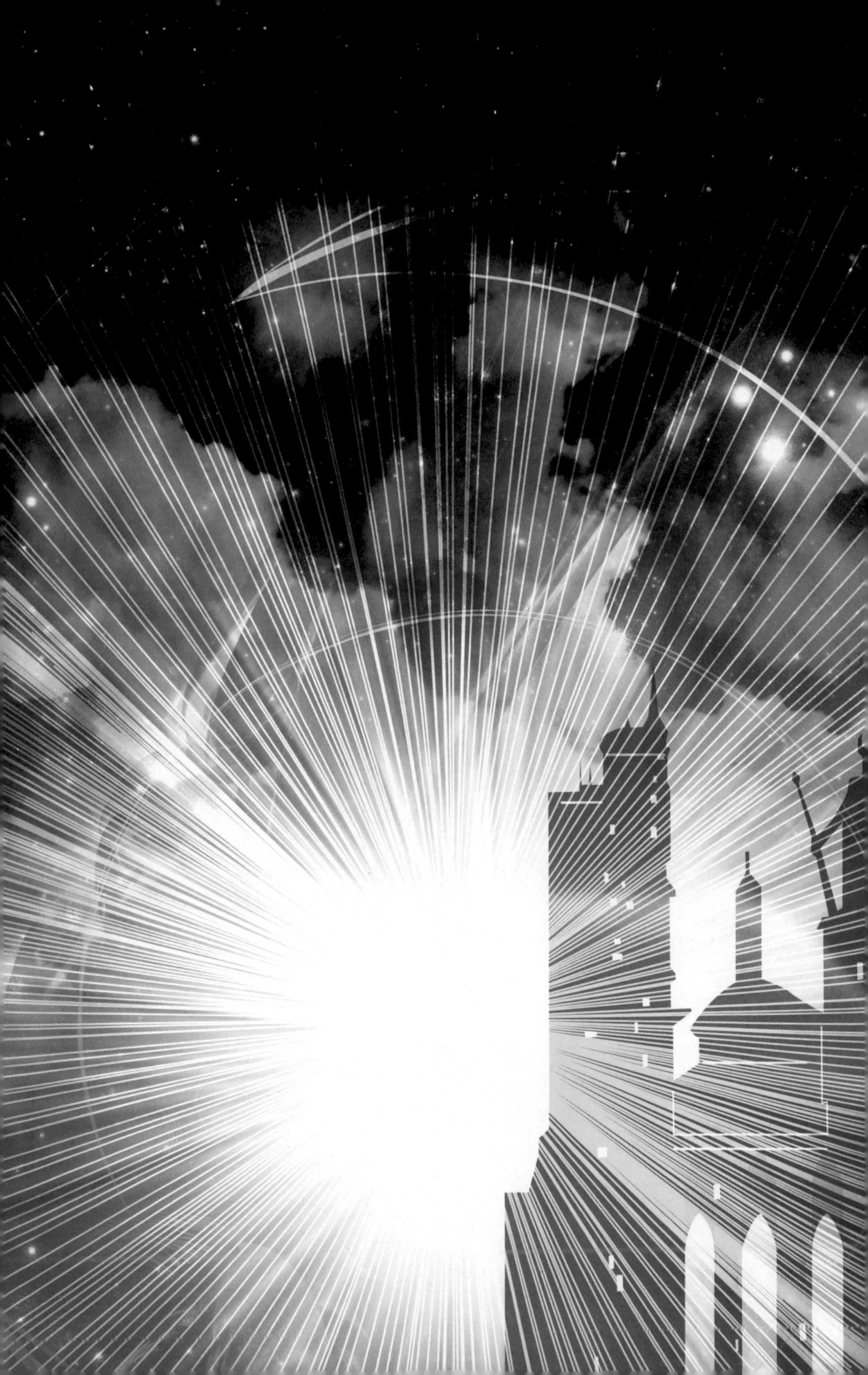

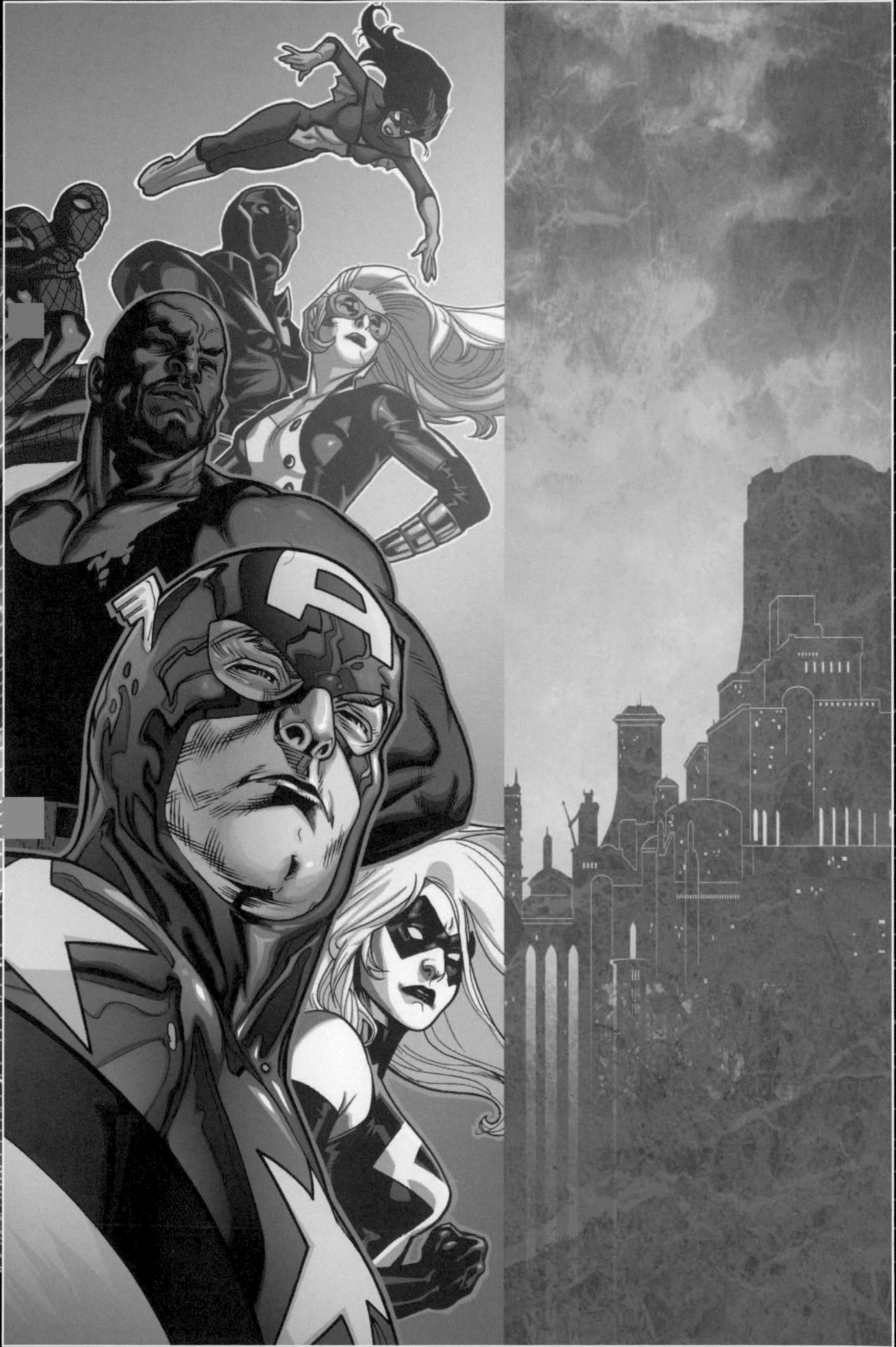

NEW AVENGERS #64

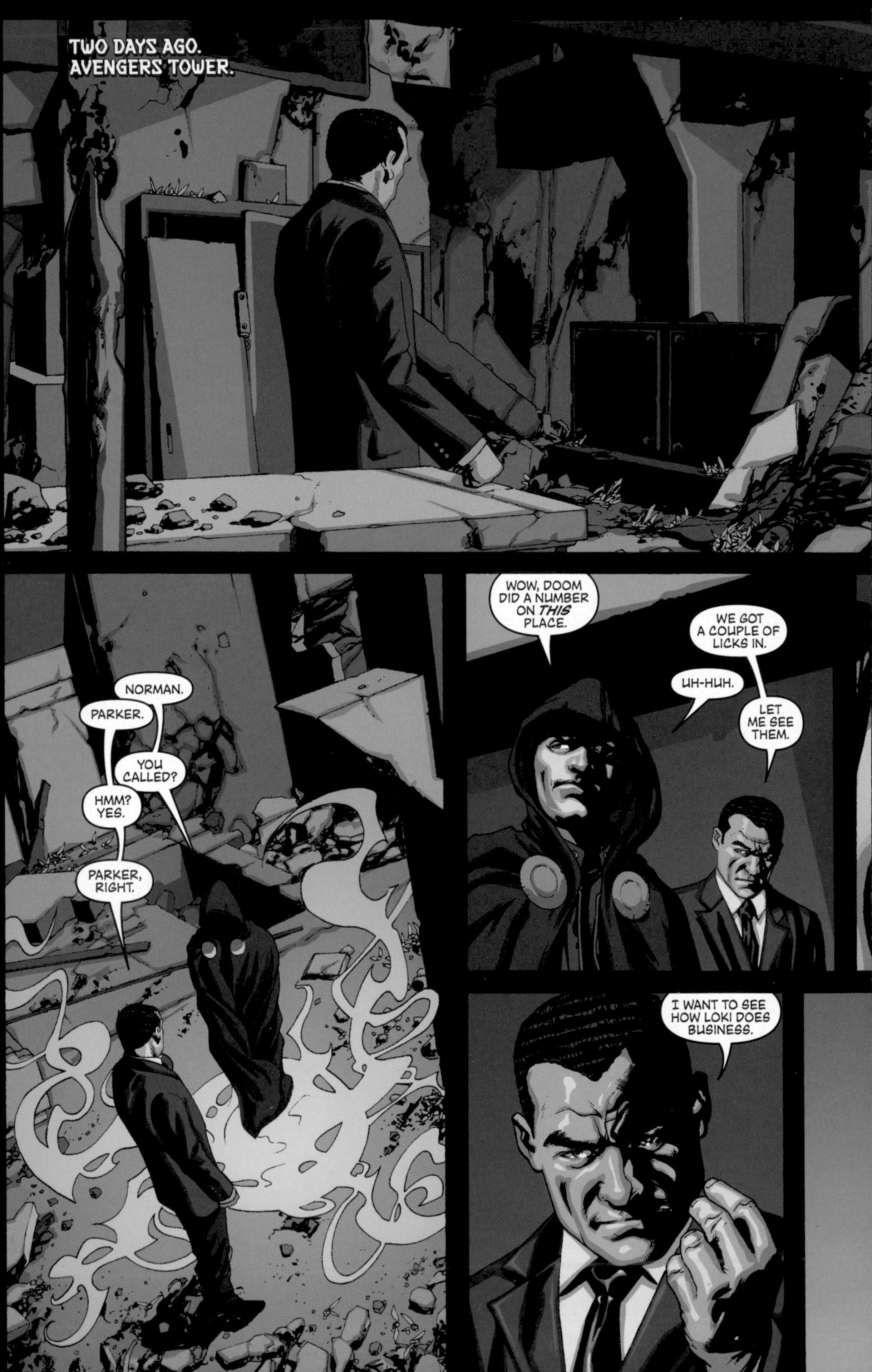
TWO DAYS AGO.
AVENGERS TOWER.
NORMAN.
PARKER.
YOU CALLED?
HMM? YES.
PARKER, RIGHT.
WOW, DOOM DID A NUMBER ON THIS PLACE.
WE GOT A COUPLE OF LICKS IN.
UH-HUH.
LET ME SEE THEM.
I WANT TO SEE HOW LOKI DOES BUSINESS.

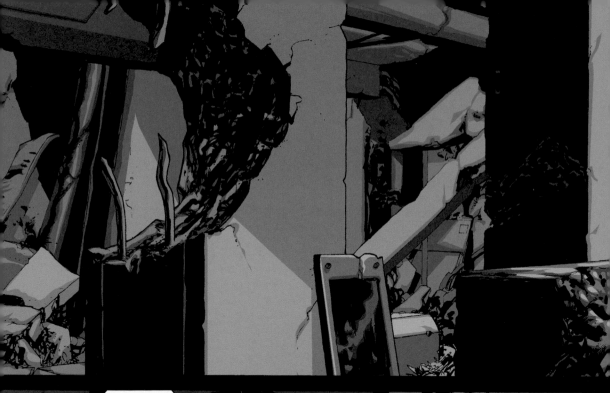

EXCUSE ME?

THE SOURCE OF YOUR NEW POWERS.

LET ME SEE.

WHY?

HMM. ALL RIGHT. SURE.

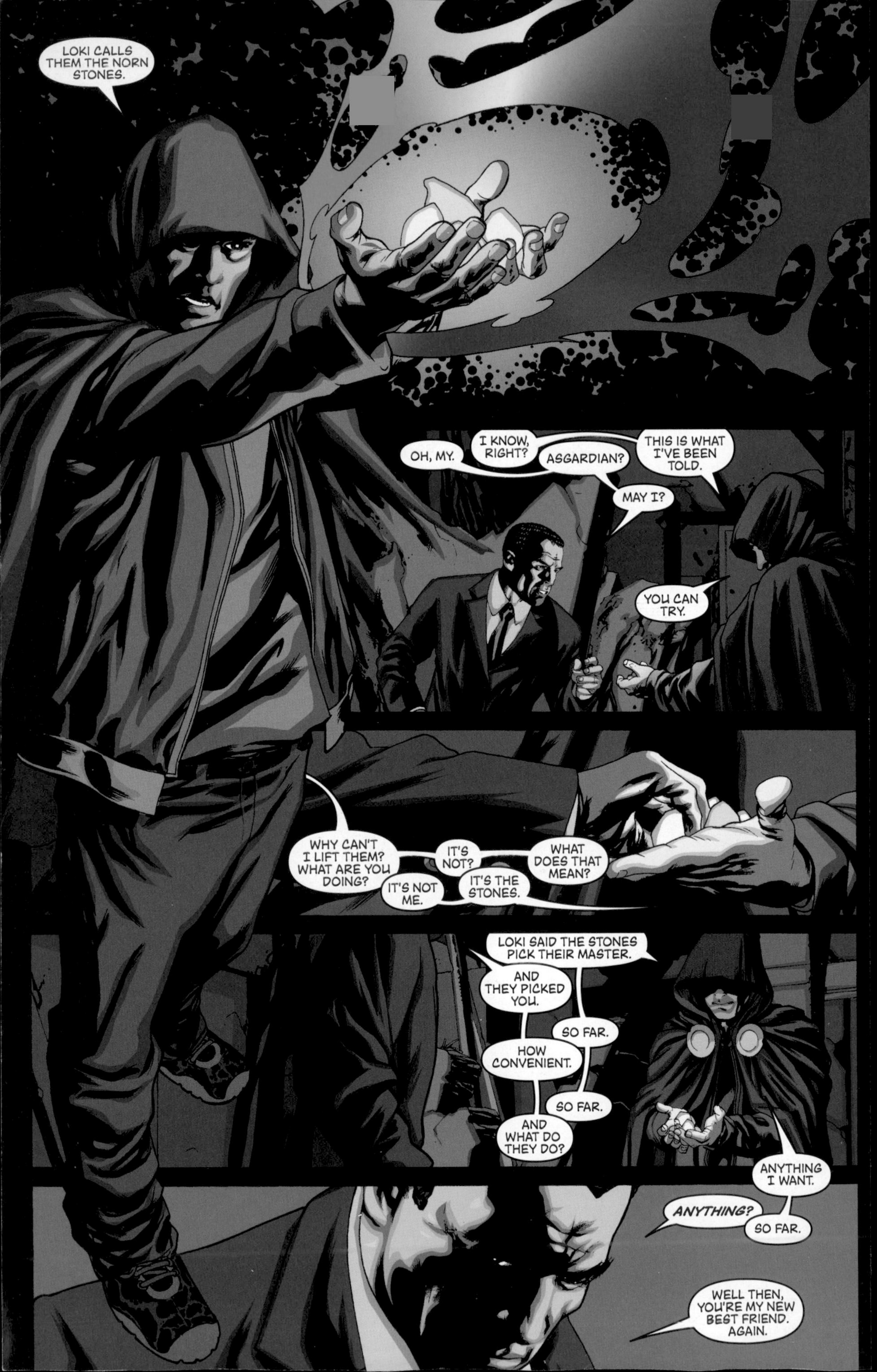
LOKI CALLS THEM THE NORN STONES.
OH, MY.
I KNOW, RIGHT?
ASGARDIAN?
THIS IS WHAT I'VE BEEN TOLD.
MAY I?
YOU CAN TRY.
WHY CAN'T I LIFT THEM? WHAT ARE YOU DOING?
IT'S NOT ME.
IT'S NOT?
IT'S THE STONES.
WHAT DOES THAT MEAN?
LOKI SAID THE STONES PICK THEIR MASTER.
AND THEY PICKED YOU.
SO FAR.
HOW CONVENIENT.
SO FAR.
AND WHAT DO THEY DO?
ANYTHING I WANT.
ANYTHING?
SO FAR.
WELL THEN, YOU'RE MY NEW BEST FRIEND. AGAIN.

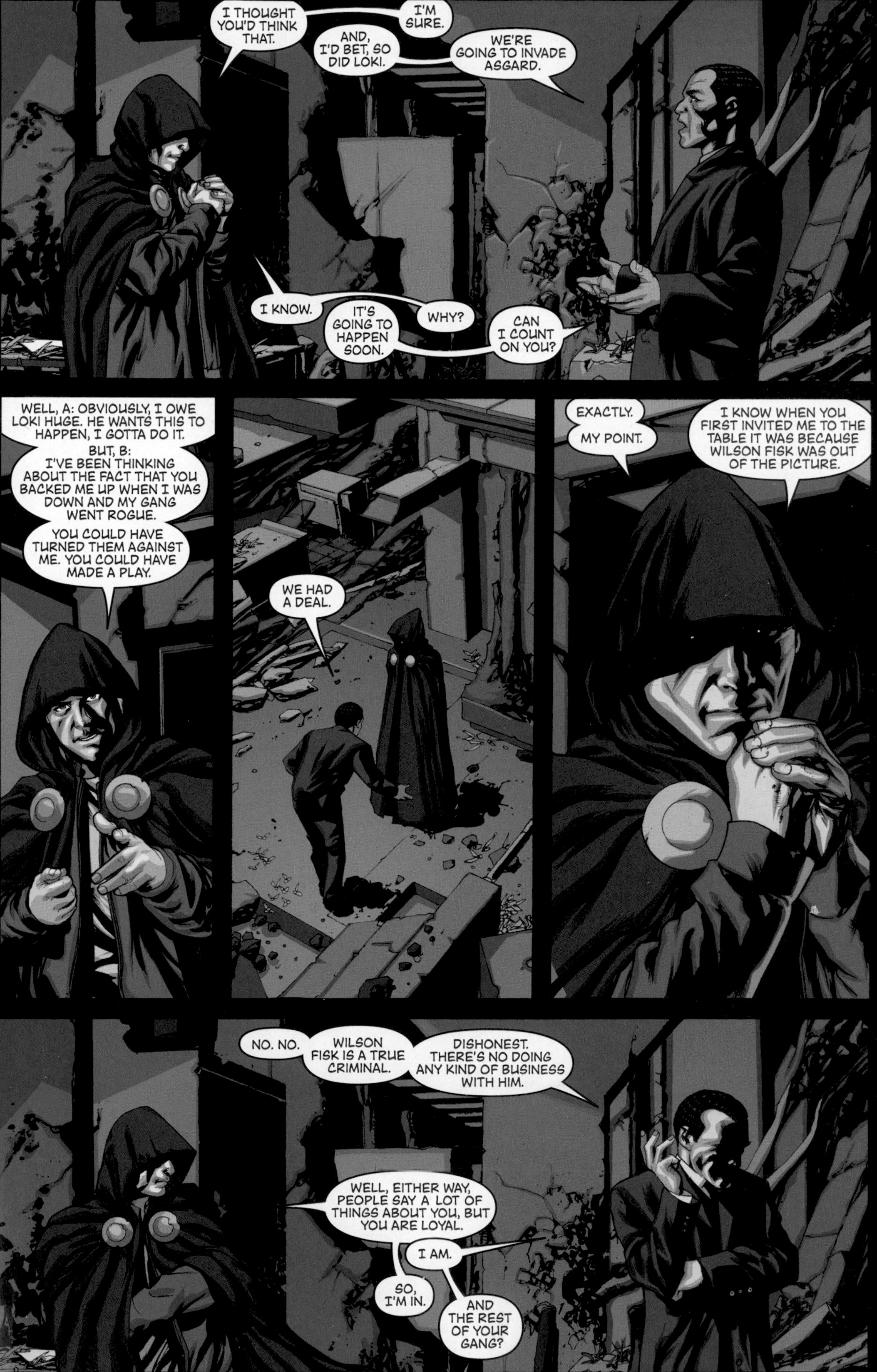
I THOUGHT YOU'D THINK THAT.
I'M SURE.
AND, I'D BET, SO DID LOKI.
WE'RE GOING TO INVADE ASGARD.
I KNOW.
WHY?
IT'S GOING TO HAPPEN SOON.
CAN I COUNT ON YOU?
WELL, A: OBVIOUSLY, I OWE LOKI HUGE. HE WANTS THIS TO HAPPEN, I GOTTA DO IT.
BUT, B: I'VE BEEN THINKING ABOUT THE FACT THAT YOU BACKED ME UP WHEN I WAS DOWN AND MY GANG WENT ROGUE.
YOU COULD HAVE TURNED THEM AGAINST ME. YOU COULD HAVE MADE A PLAY.
WE HAD A DEAL.
EXACTLY.
MY POINT.
I KNOW WHEN YOU FIRST INVITED ME TO THE TABLE IT WAS BECAUSE WILSON FISK WAS OUT OF THE PICTURE.
NO. NO.
WILSON FISK IS A TRUE CRIMINAL.
DISHONEST. THERE'S NO DOING ANY KIND OF BUSINESS WITH HIM.
WELL, EITHER WAY, PEOPLE SAY A LOT OF THINGS ABOUT YOU, BUT YOU ARE LOYAL.
I AM.
SO, I'M IN.
AND THE REST OF YOUR GANG?

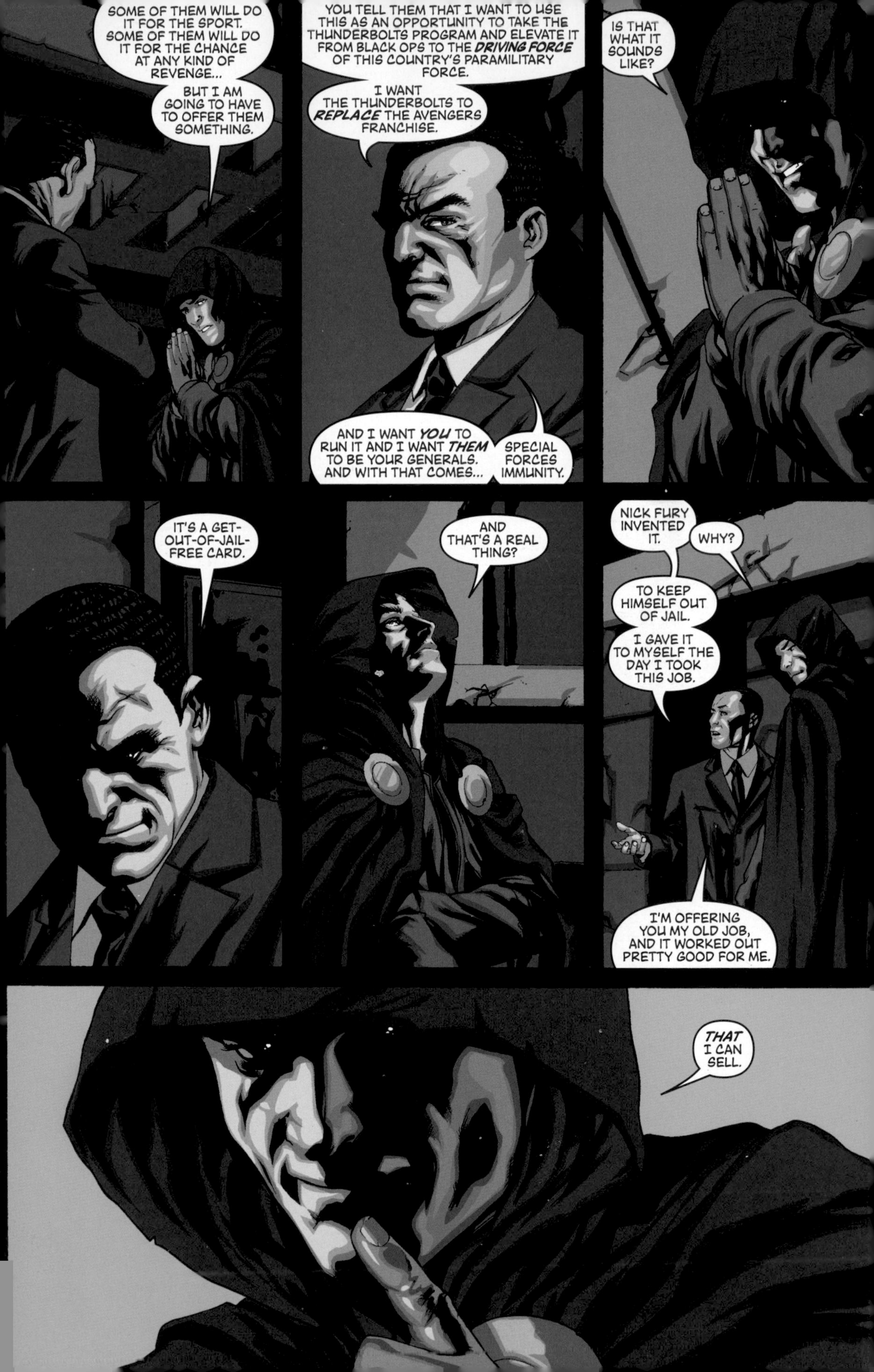
SOME OF THEM WILL DO IT FOR THE SPORT. SOME OF THEM WILL DO IT FOR THE CHANCE AT ANY KIND OF REVENGE...
BUT I AM GOING TO HAVE TO OFFER THEM SOMETHING.
YOU TELL THEM THAT I WANT TO USE THIS AS AN OPPORTUNITY TO TAKE THE THUNDERBOLTS PROGRAM AND ELEVATE IT FROM BLACK OPS TO THE DRIVING FORCE OF THIS COUNTRY'S PARAMILITARY FORCE.
I WANT THE THUNDERBOLTS TO REPLACE THE AVENGERS FRANCHISE.
AND I WANT YOU TO RUN IT AND I WANT THEM TO BE YOUR GENERALS. AND WITH THAT COMES...
SPECIAL FORCES IMMUNITY.
IS THAT WHAT IT SOUNDS LIKE?
IT'S A GET-OUT-OF-JAIL-FREE CARD.
AND THAT'S A REAL THING?
NICK FURY INVENTED IT.
WHY?
TO KEEP HIMSELF OUT OF JAIL.
I GAVE IT TO MYSELF THE DAY I TOOK THIS JOB.
I'M OFFERING YOU MY OLD JOB, AND IT WORKED OUT PRETTY GOOD FOR ME.
THAT I CAN SELL.

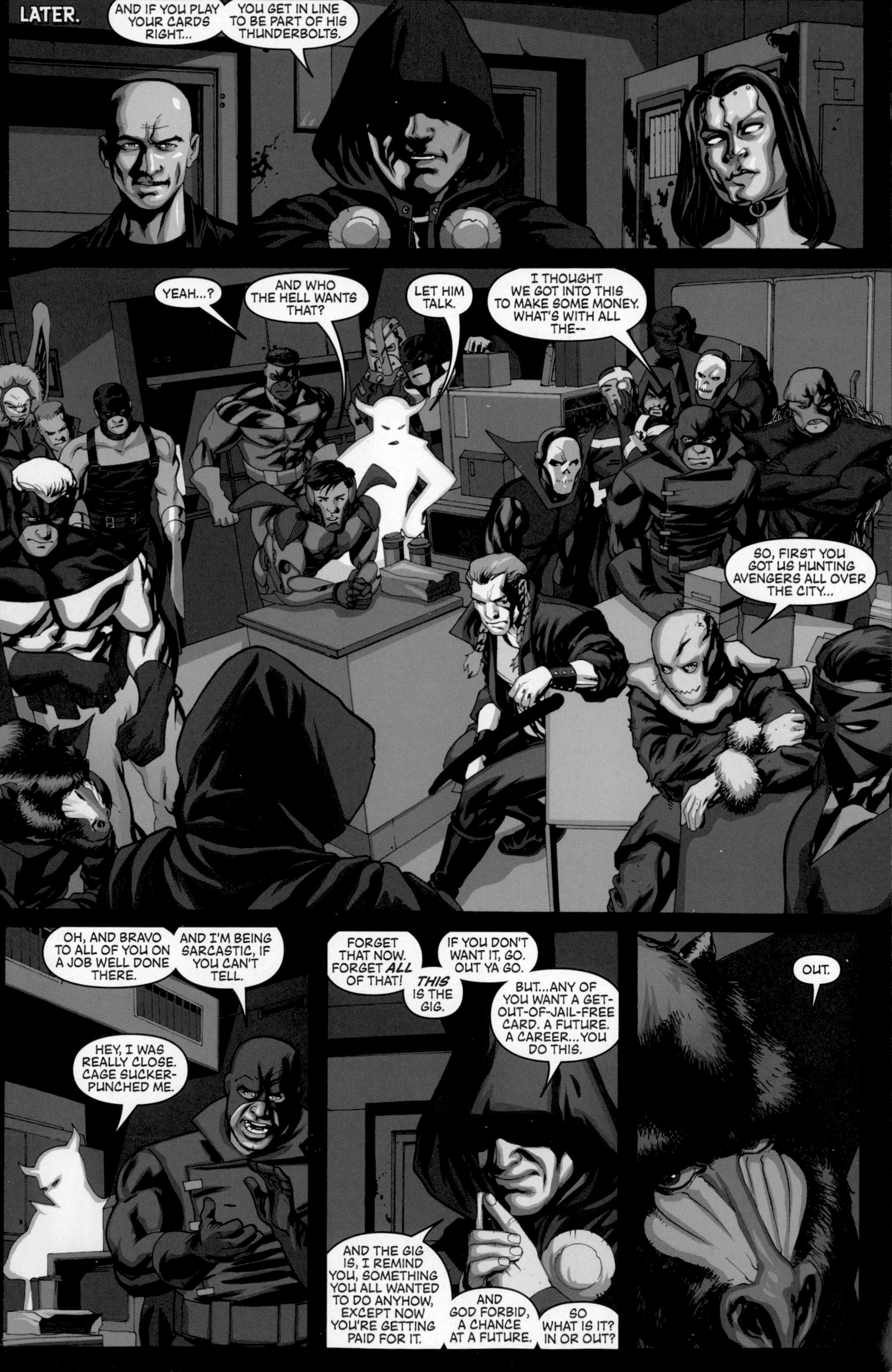

LATER.
AND IF YOU PLAY YOUR CARDS RIGHT...
YOU GET IN LINE TO BE PART OF HIS THUNDERBOLTS.
YEAH...?
AND WHO THE HELL WANTS THAT?
LET HIM TALK.
I THOUGHT WE GOT INTO THIS TO MAKE SOME MONEY. WHAT'S WITH ALL THE--
SO, FIRST YOU GOT US HUNTING AVENGERS ALL OVER THE CITY...
OH, AND BRAVO TO ALL OF YOU ON A JOB WELL DONE THERE.
AND I'M BEING SARCASTIC, IF YOU CAN'T TELL.
HEY, I WAS REALLY CLOSE. CAGE SUCKER-PUNCHED ME.
FORGET THAT NOW. FORGET ALL OF THAT!
THIS IS THE GIG.
IF YOU DON'T WANT IT, GO. OUT YA GO.
BUT...ANY OF YOU WANT A GET-OUT-OF-JAIL-FREE CARD. A FUTURE. A CAREER...YOU DO THIS.
AND THE GIG IS, I REMIND YOU, SOMETHING YOU ALL WANTED TO DO ANYHOW, EXCEPT NOW YOU'RE GETTING PAID FOR IT.
AND GOD FORBID, A CHANCE AT A FUTURE.
SO WHAT IS IT? IN OR OUT?
OUT.

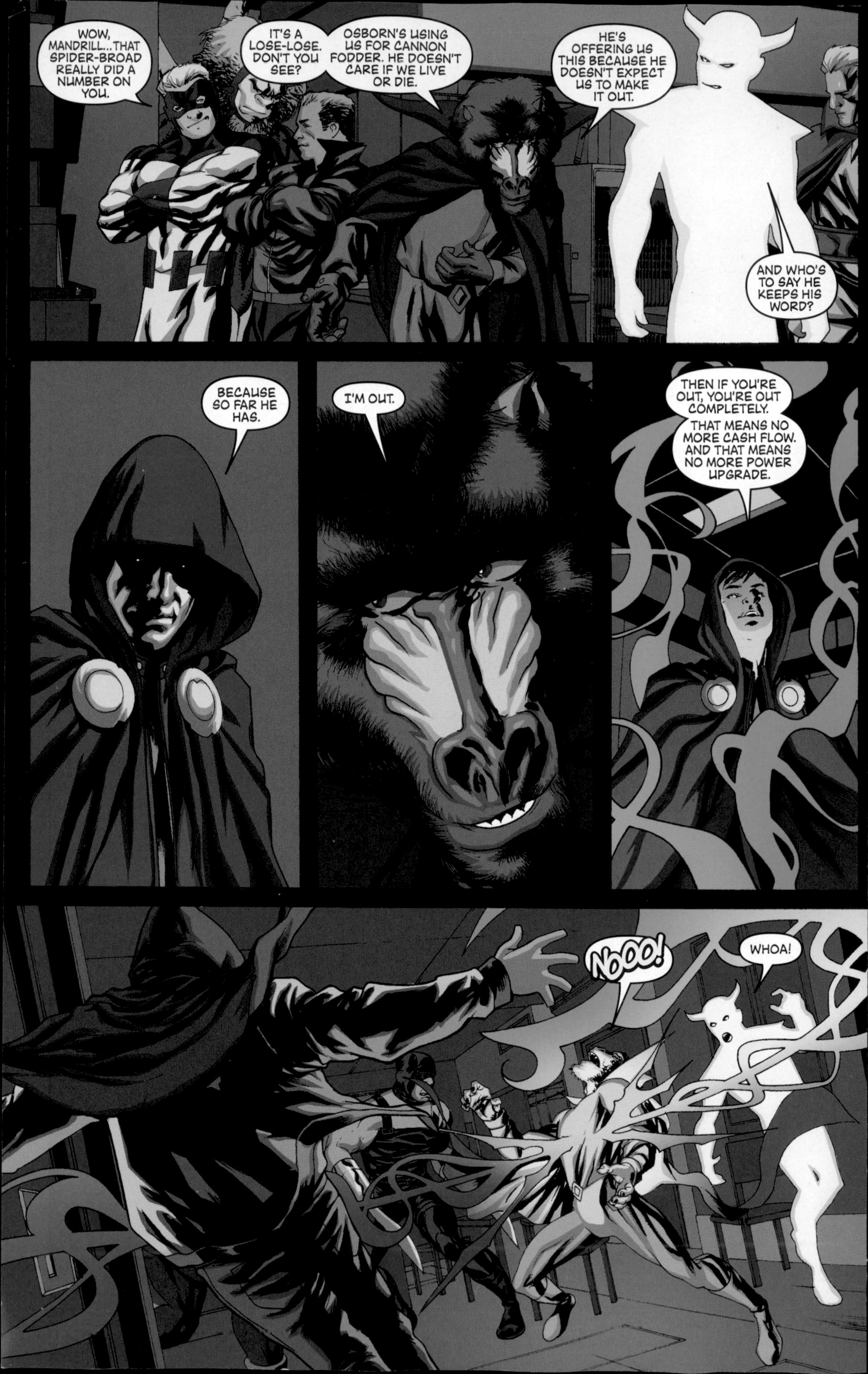
WOW, MANDRILL...THAT SPIDER-BROAD REALLY DID A NUMBER ON YOU.
IT'S A LOSE-LOSE. DON'T YOU SEE?
OSBORN'S USING US FOR CANNON FODDER. HE DOESN'T CARE IF WE LIVE OR DIE.
HE'S OFFERING US THIS BECAUSE HE DOESN'T EXPECT US TO MAKE IT OUT.
AND WHO'S TO SAY HE KEEPS HIS WORD?
BECAUSE SO FAR HE HAS.
I'M OUT.
THEN IF YOU'RE OUT, YOU'RE OUT COMPLETELY.
THAT MEANS NO MORE CASH FLOW. AND THAT MEANS NO MORE POWER UPGRADE.
NOOO!
WHOA!

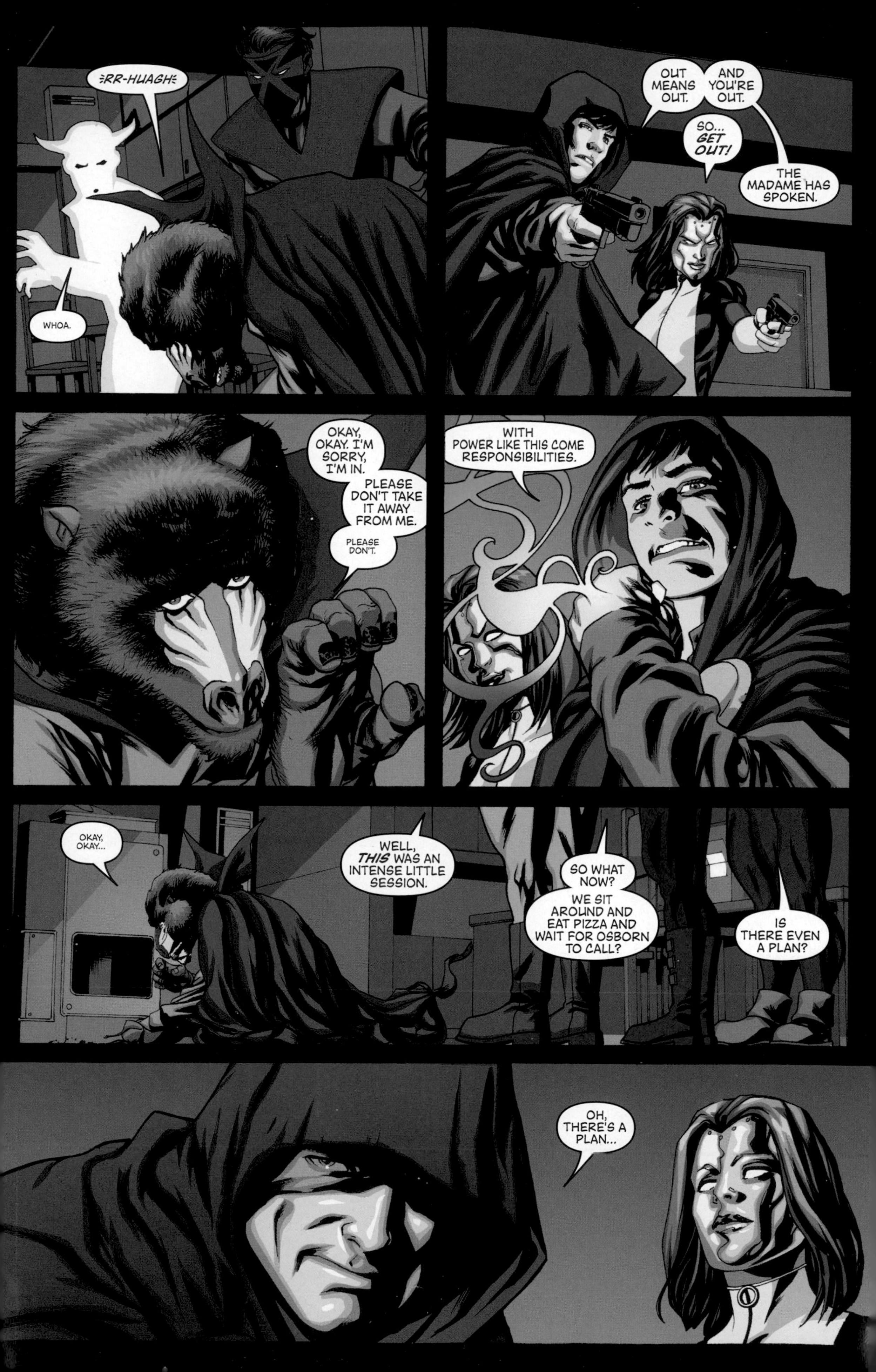
RR-HUAGH
WHOA.
OUT MEANS OUT.
AND YOU'RE OUT.
SO... GET OUT!
THE MADAME HAS SPOKEN.
OKAY, OKAY. I'M SORRY, I'M IN.
PLEASE DON'T TAKE IT AWAY FROM ME.
PLEASE DON'T.
WITH POWER LIKE THIS COME RESPONSIBILITIES.
OKAY, OKAY...
WELL, THIS WAS AN INTENSE LITTLE SESSION.
SO WHAT NOW?
WE SIT AROUND AND EAT PIZZA AND WAIT FOR OSBORN TO CALL?
IS THERE EVEN A PLAN?
OH, THERE'S A PLAN...

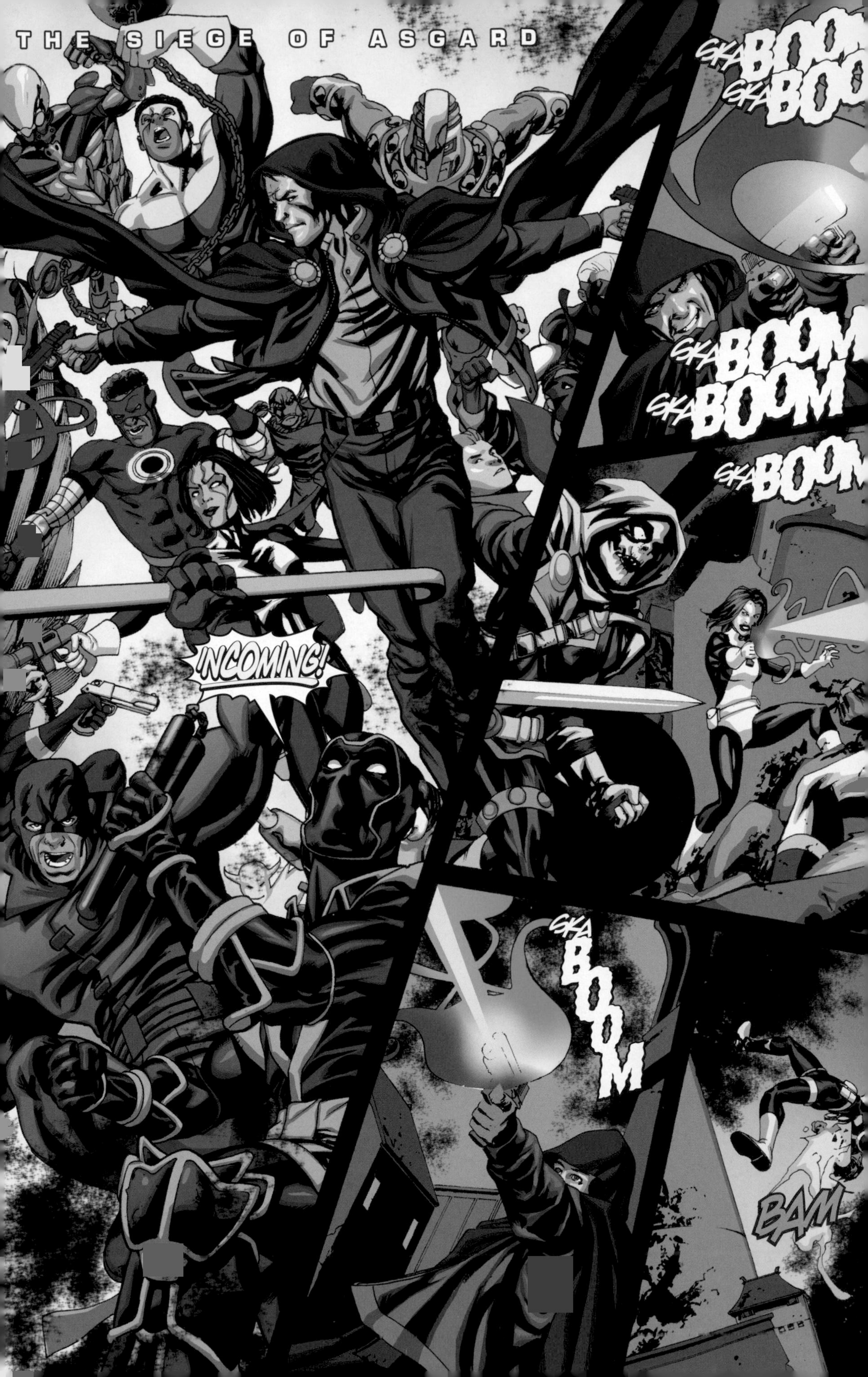
THE SIEGE OF ASGARD
SKABOOM
SKABOOM
SKABOOM
SKABOOM
SKABOOM
INCOMING!
SKABOOM
BAM

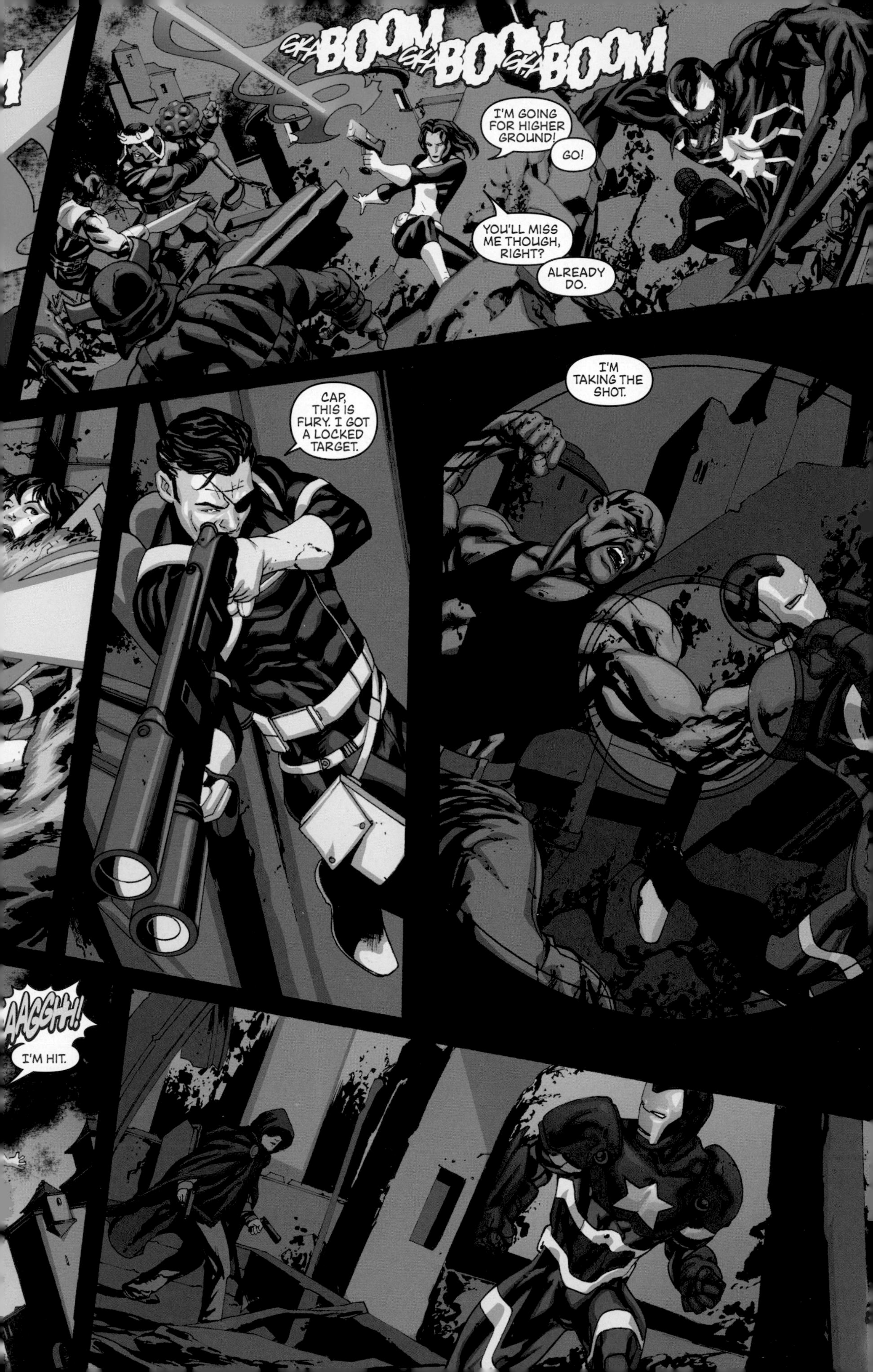

GKA BOOM GKA BOOM GKA BOOM
I'M GOING FOR HIGHER GROUND!
GO!
YOU'LL MISS ME THOUGH, RIGHT?
ALREADY DO.
CAP, THIS IS FURY. I GOT A LOCKED TARGET.
I'M TAKING THE SHOT.
AAGGHH!
I'M HIT.

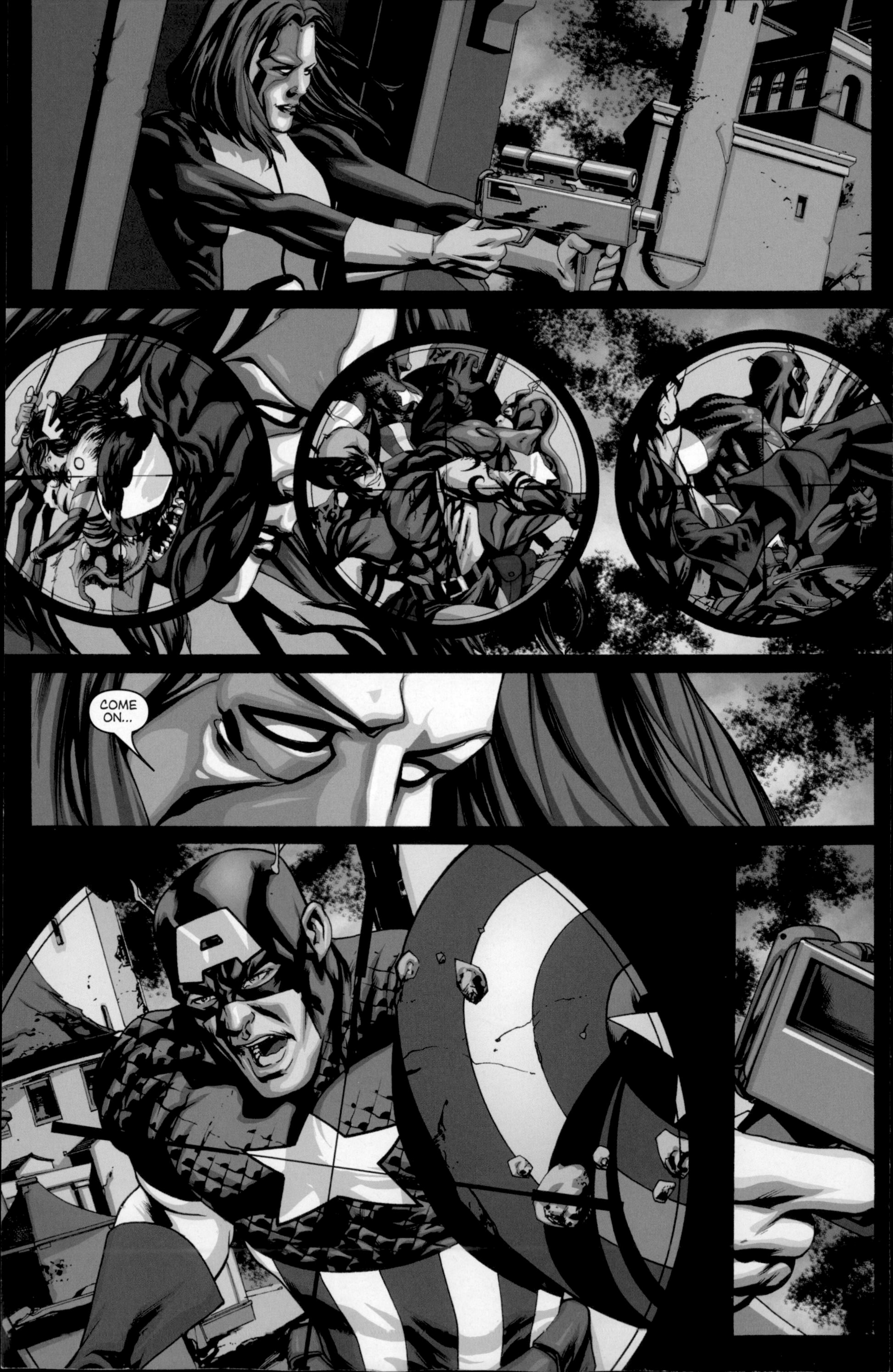
COME ON...

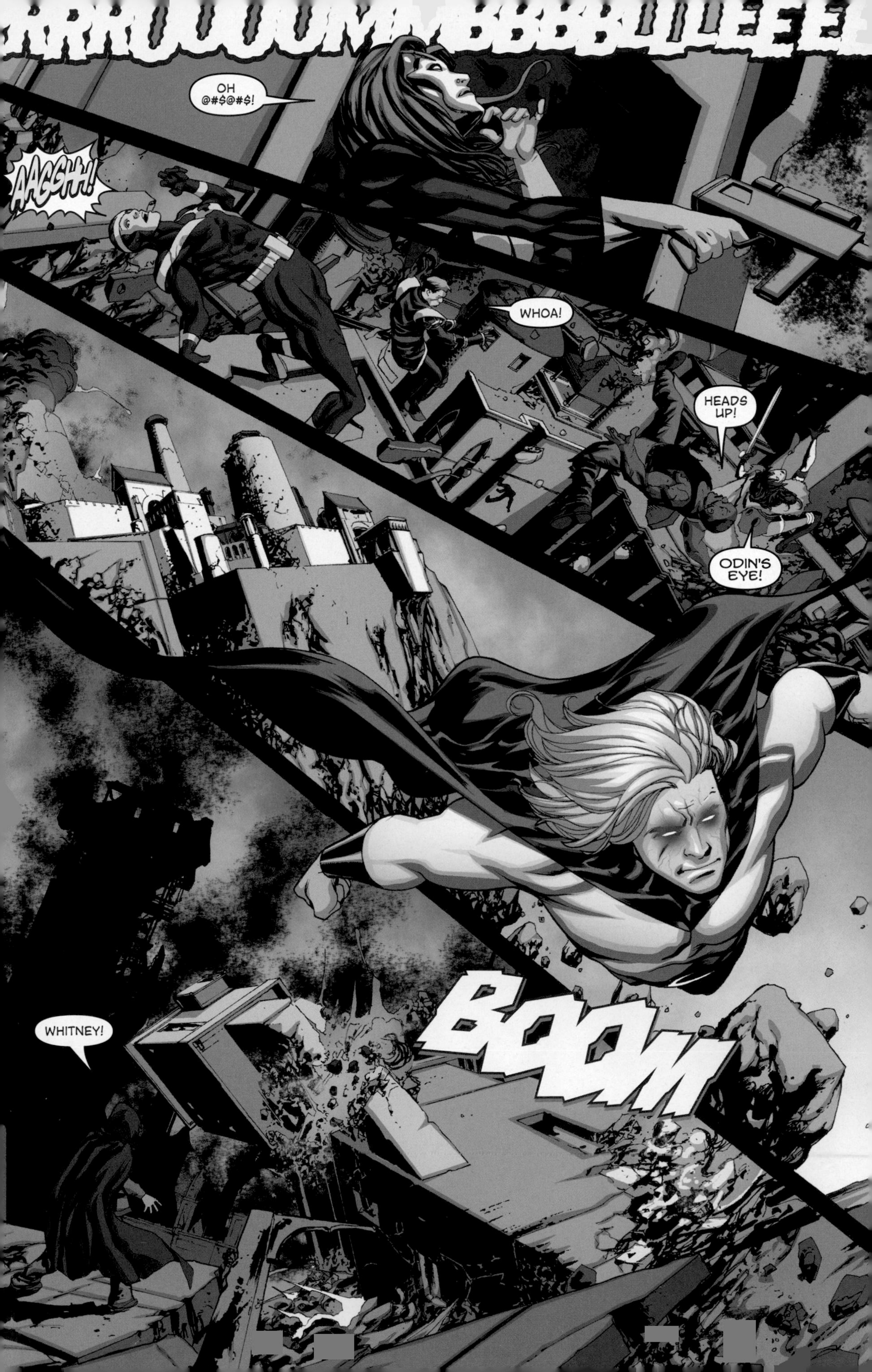
RRRUUUUMMBBBBULEEE
OH @#$@#$!
AAGGHH!
WHOA!
HEADS UP!
ODIN'S EYE!
WHITNEY!
BOOM

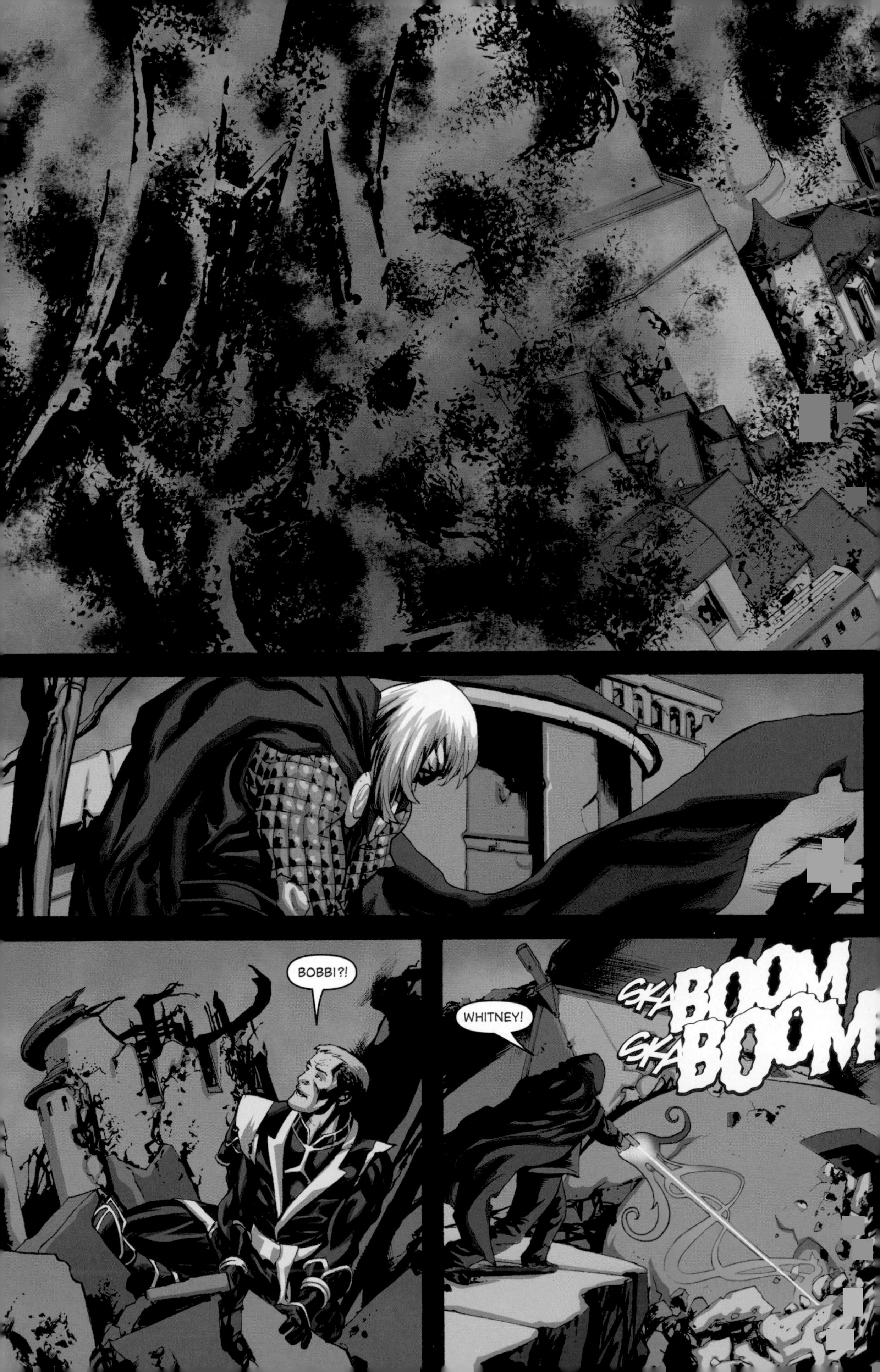
BOBBI?!
WHITNEY!
SKABOOM
SKABOOM

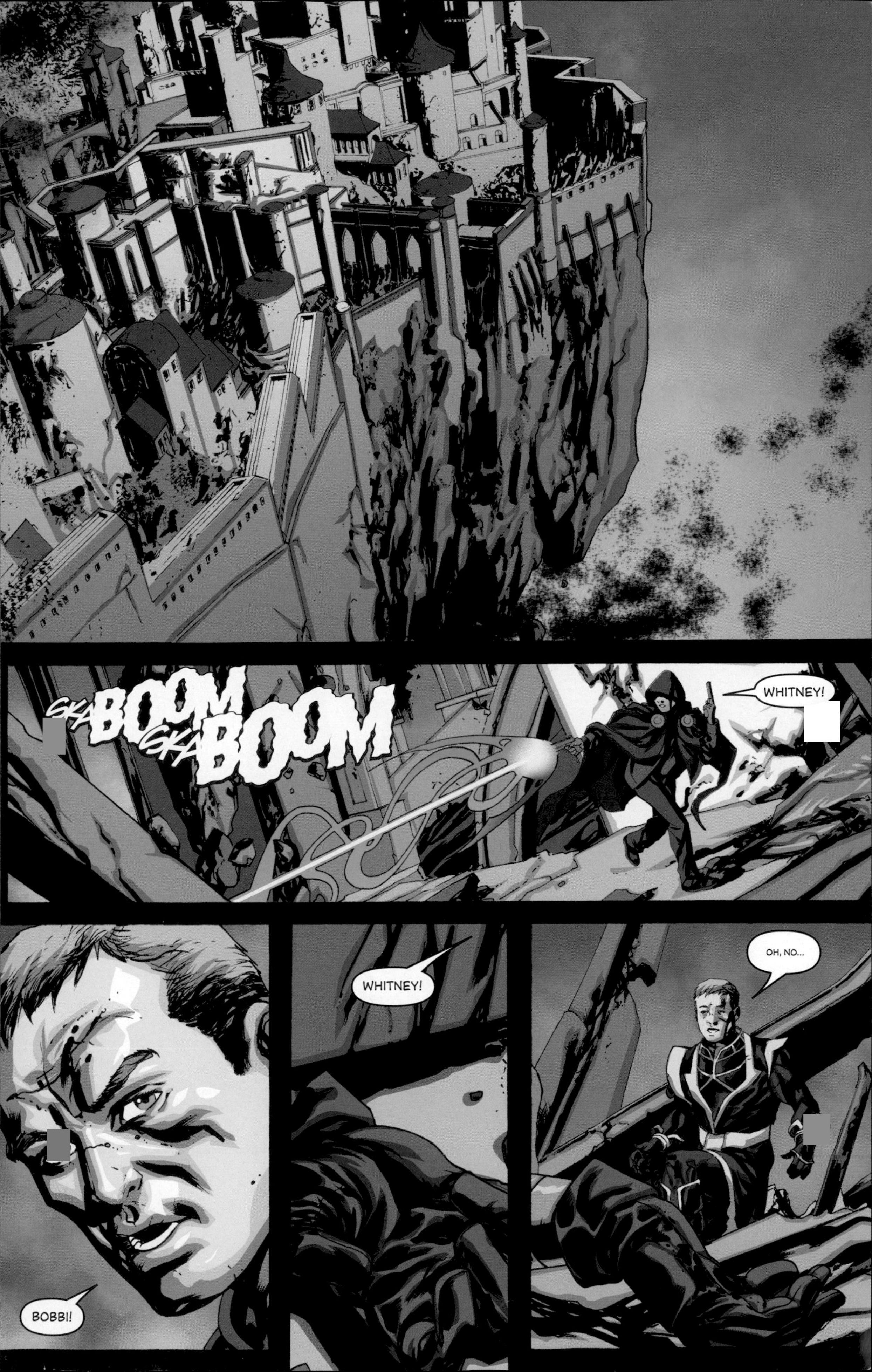
SKA BOOM
SKA BOOM
WHITNEY!
WHITNEY!
OH, NO...
BOBBI!

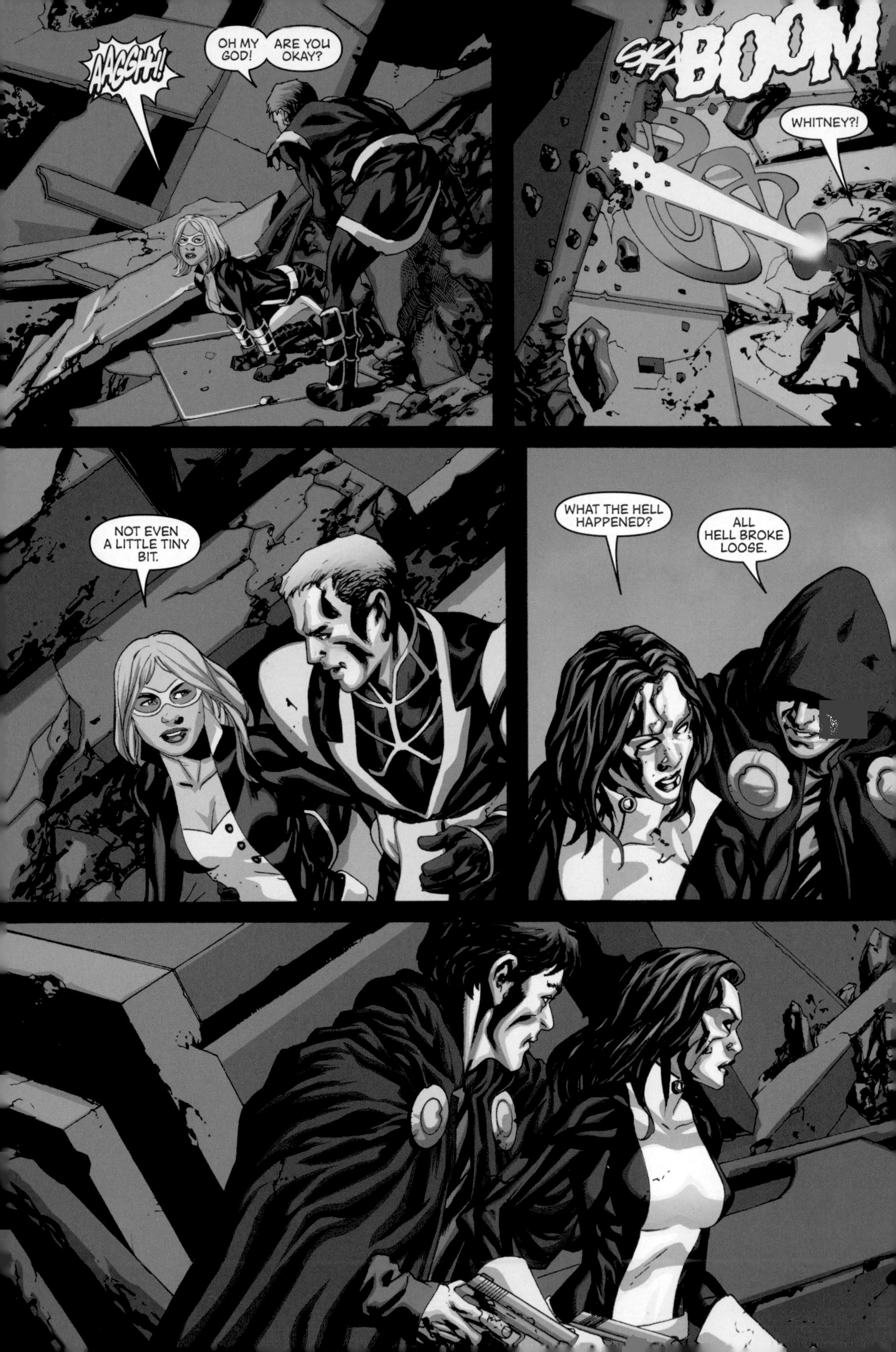

AAGGHH!
OH MY GOD!
ARE YOU OKAY?
SKA BOOM
WHITNEY?!
NOT EVEN A LITTLE TINY BIT.
WHAT THE HELL HAPPENED?
ALL HELL BROKE LOOSE.

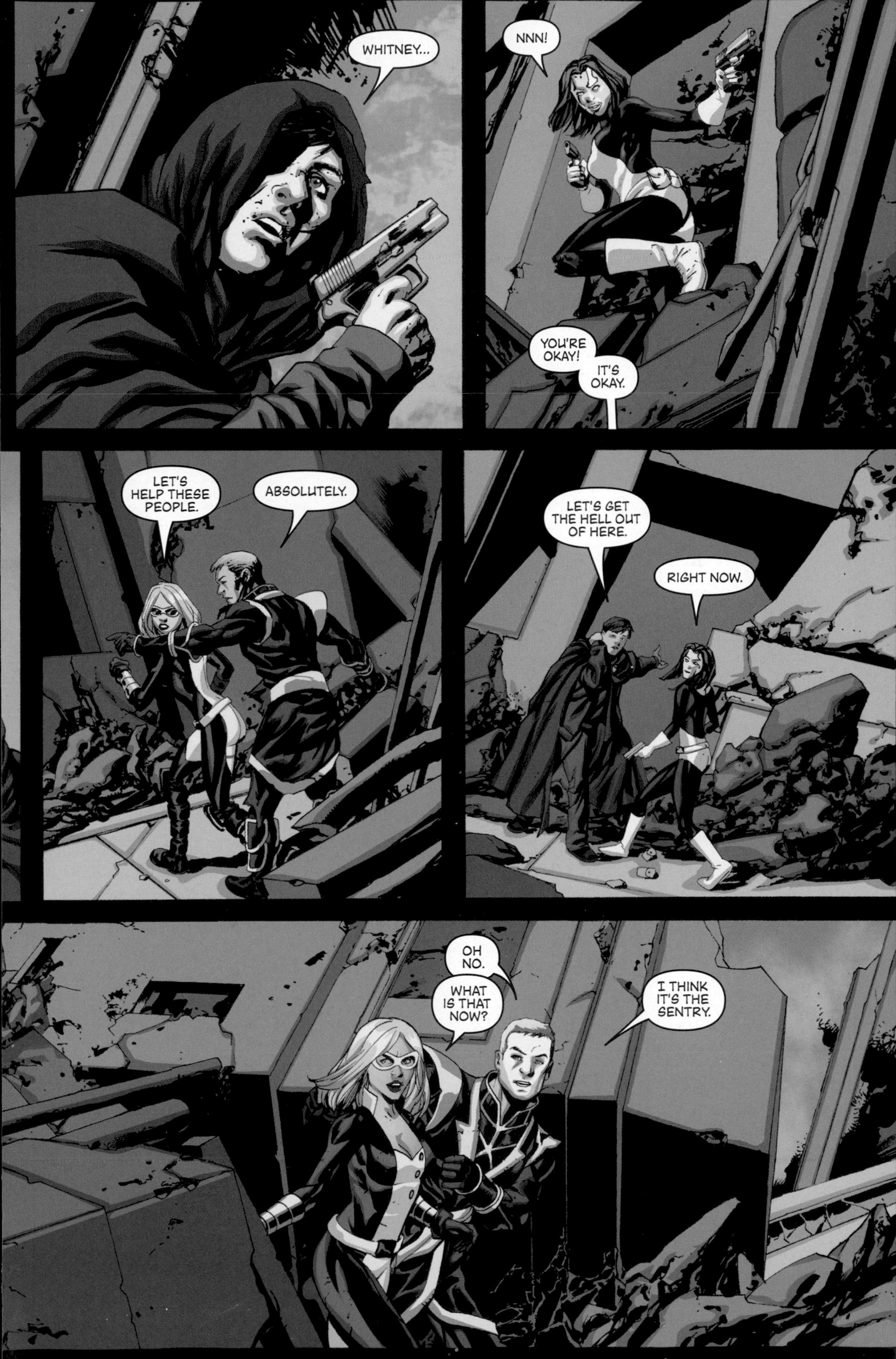
WHITNEY...
NNN!
YOU'RE OKAY!
IT'S OKAY.
LET'S HELP THESE PEOPLE.
ABSOLUTELY.
LET'S GET THE HELL OUT OF HERE.
RIGHT NOW.
OH NO.
WHAT IS THAT NOW?
I THINK IT'S THE SENTRY.

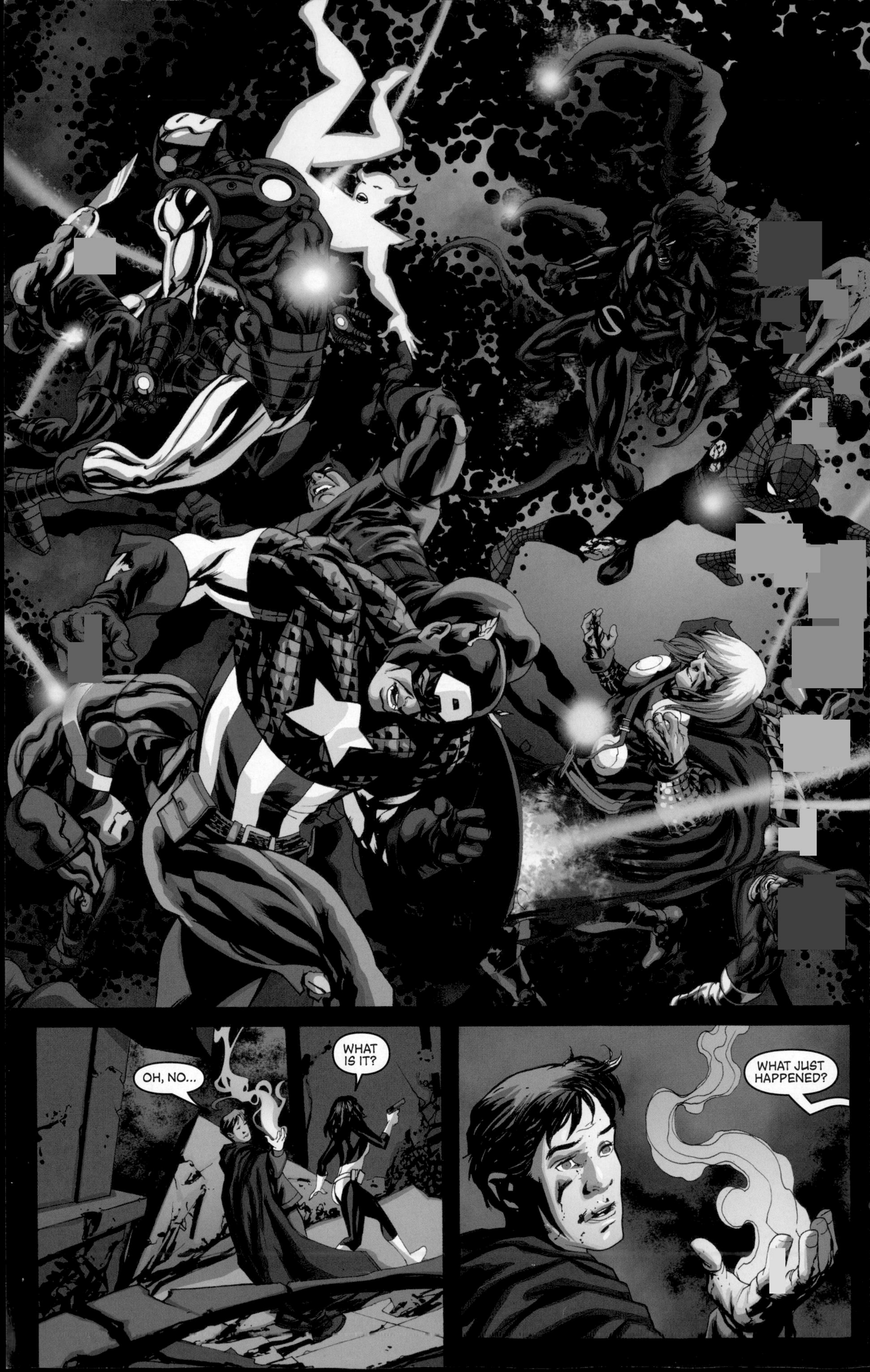
OH, NO...
WHAT IS IT?
WHAT JUST HAPPENED?

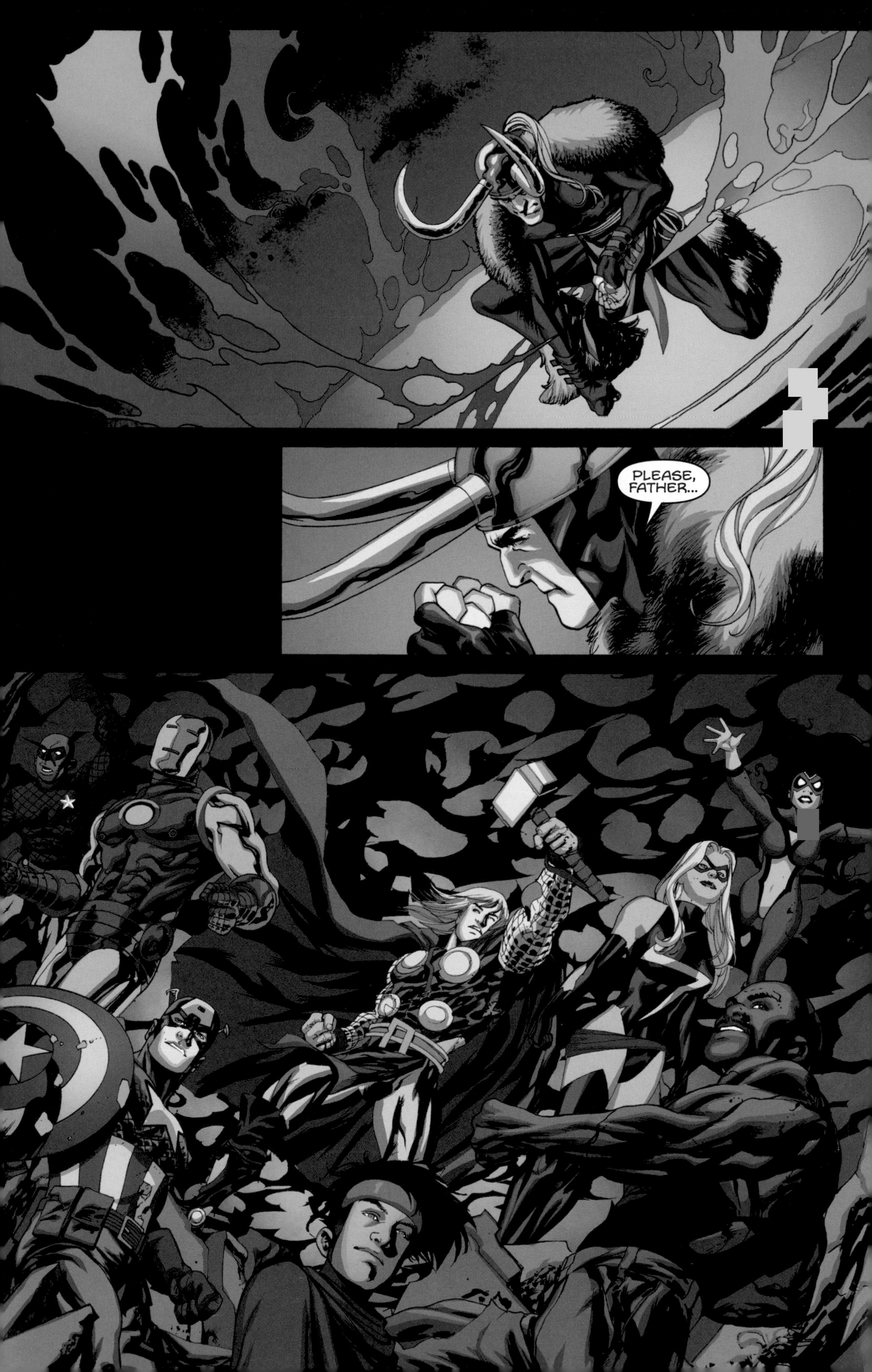
PLEASE, FATHER...

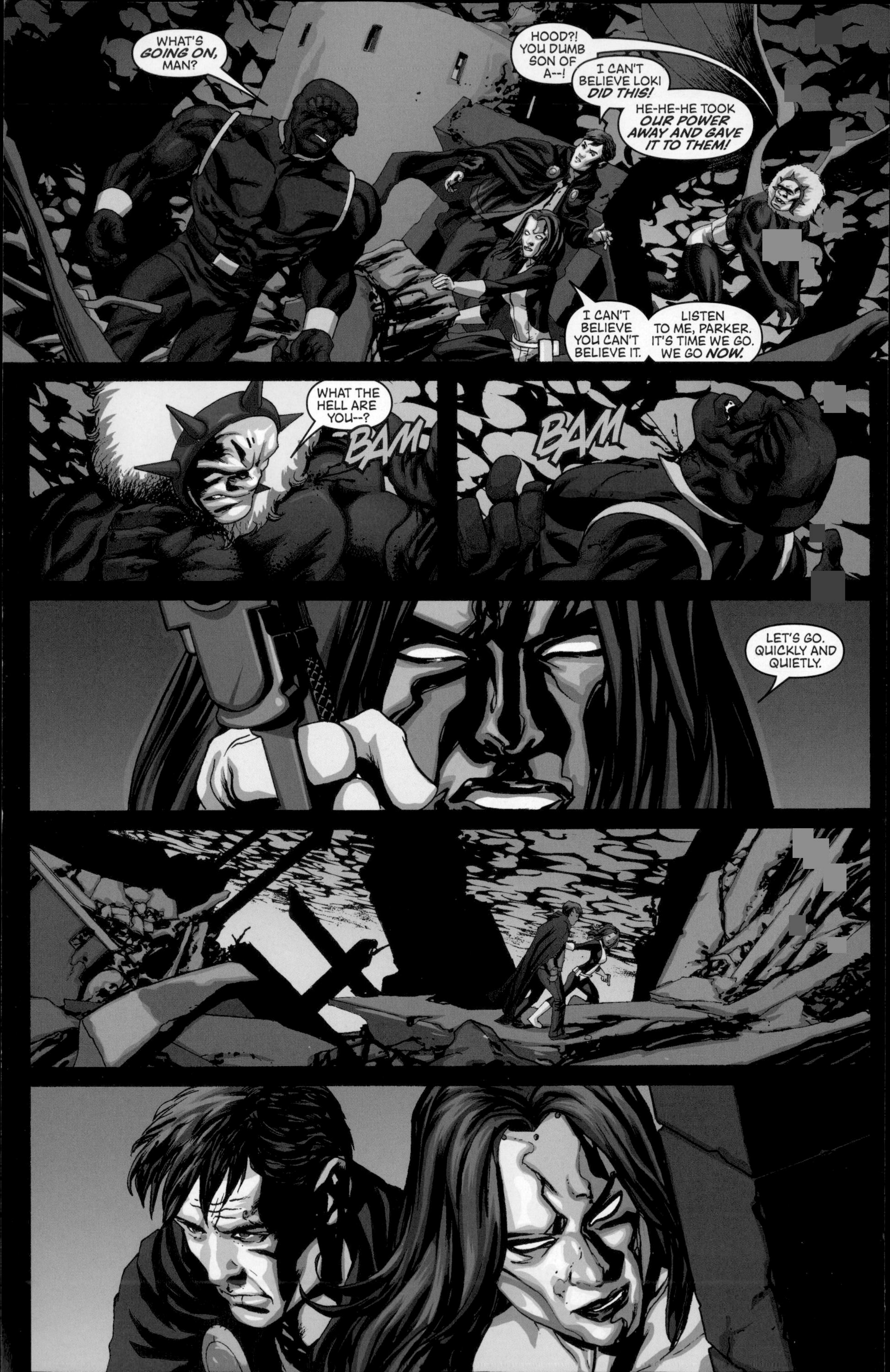
WHAT'S GOING ON, MAN?
HOOD?! YOU DUMB SON OF A--!
I CAN'T BELIEVE LOKI DID THIS!
HE-HE-HE TOOK OUR POWER AWAY AND GAVE IT TO THEM!
I CAN'T BELIEVE YOU CAN'T BELIEVE IT.
LISTEN TO ME, PARKER. IT'S TIME WE GO. WE GO NOW.
WHAT THE HELL ARE YOU--?
BAM
BAM
LET'S GO. QUICKLY AND QUIETLY.

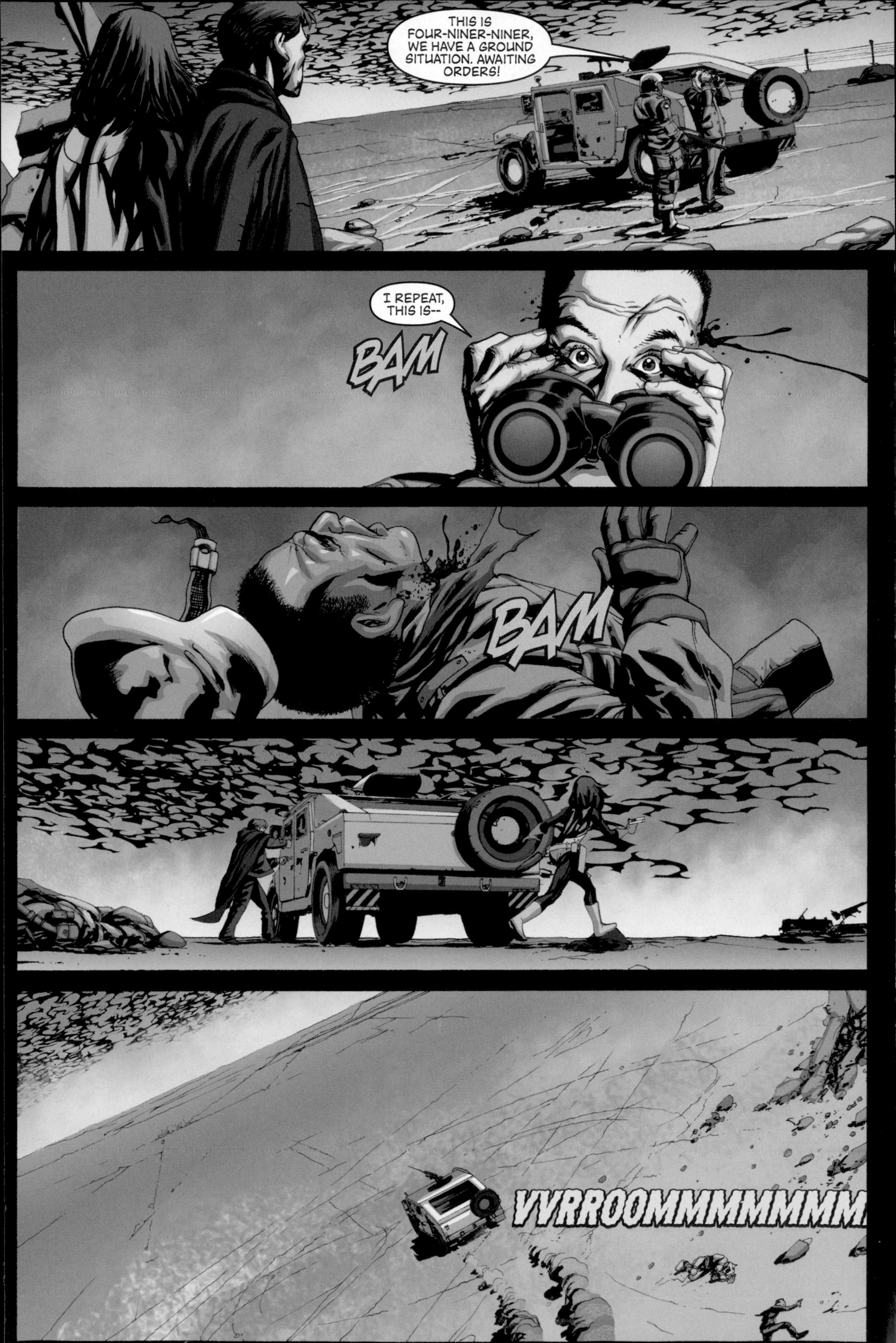
THIS IS FOUR-NINER-NINER, WE HAVE A GROUND SITUATION. AWAITING ORDERS!
I REPEAT, THIS IS--
BAM
BAM
VVRROOMMMMMMMMM

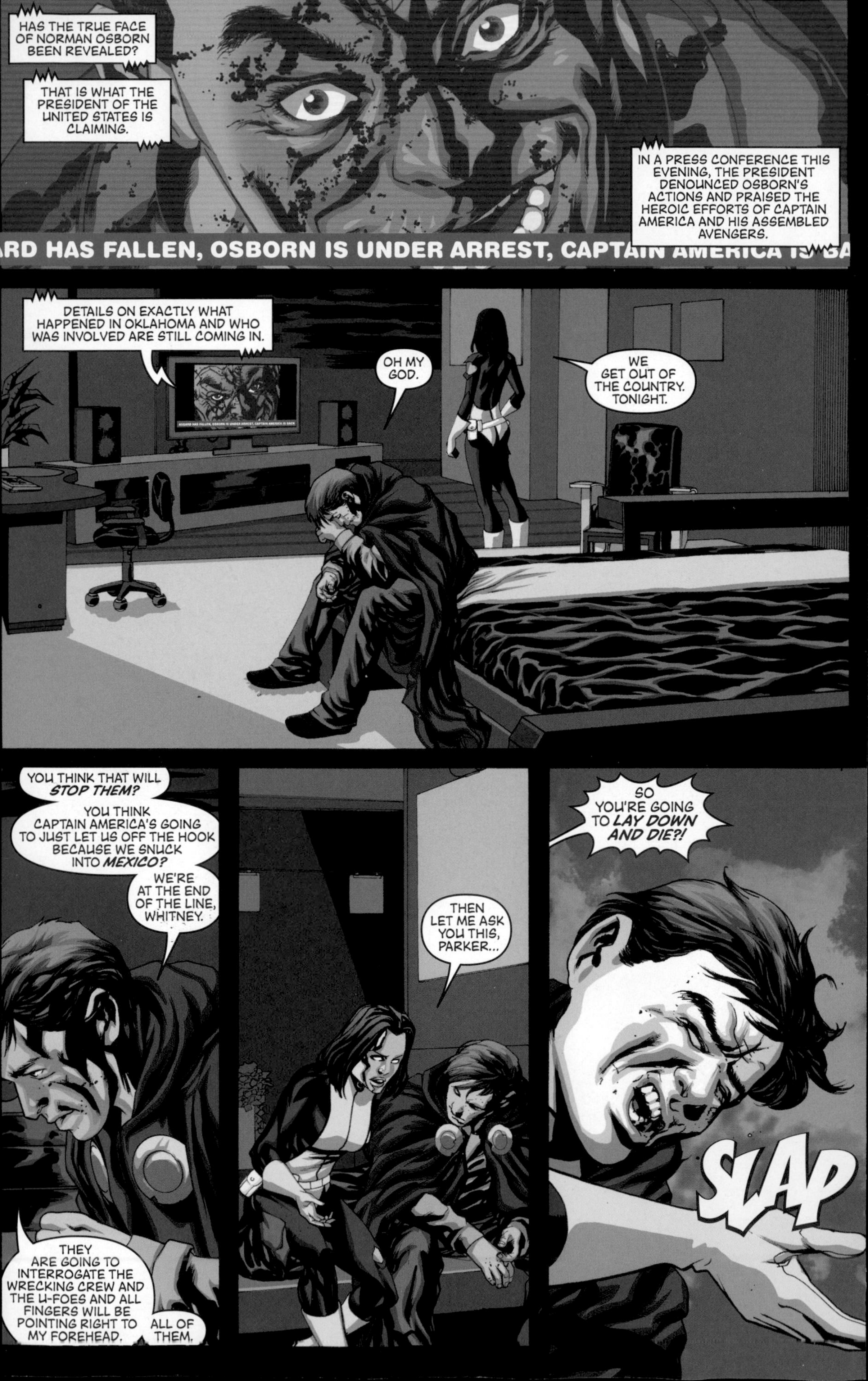
HAS THE TRUE FACE OF NORMAN OSBORN BEEN REVEALED?
THAT IS WHAT THE PRESIDENT OF THE UNITED STATES IS CLAIMING.
IN A PRESS CONFERENCE THIS EVENING, THE PRESIDENT DENOUNCED OSBORN'S ACTIONS AND PRAISED THE HEROIC EFFORTS OF CAPTAIN AMERICA AND HIS ASSEMBLED AVENGERS.
ARD HAS FALLEN, OSBORN IS UNDER ARREST, CAPTAIN AMERICA IS BA
DETAILS ON EXACTLY WHAT HAPPENED IN OKLAHOMA AND WHO WAS INVOLVED ARE STILL COMING IN.
OH MY GOD.
WE GET OUT OF THE COUNTRY. TONIGHT.
YOU THINK THAT WILL *STOP THEM?*
YOU THINK CAPTAIN AMERICA'S GOING TO JUST LET US OFF THE HOOK BECAUSE WE SNUCK INTO *MEXICO?*
WE'RE AT THE END OF THE LINE, WHITNEY.
THEY ARE GOING TO INTERROGATE THE WRECKING CREW AND THE U-FOES AND ALL FINGERS WILL BE POINTING RIGHT TO MY FOREHEAD.
ALL OF THEM.
THEN LET ME ASK YOU THIS, PARKER...
SO YOU'RE GOING TO *LAY DOWN AND DIE?!*
SLAP

IT IS WHAT IT IS.

YOU DON'T LIKE THE ODDS? YOU *CHANGE THEM!*

YOU'RE RIGHT. THE AVENGERS *ARE* COMING FOR YOU.

AND I DON'T HAVE *ANY* POWERS!

SO WHEN THEY COME FOR US... YOU MAKE *SURE YOU'RE READY.*

YOU MAKE SURE YOU HAVE SOMETHING THEY WOULD NEVER SEE COMING.

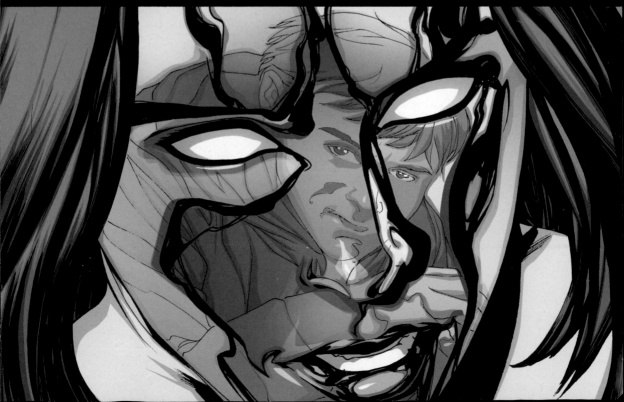

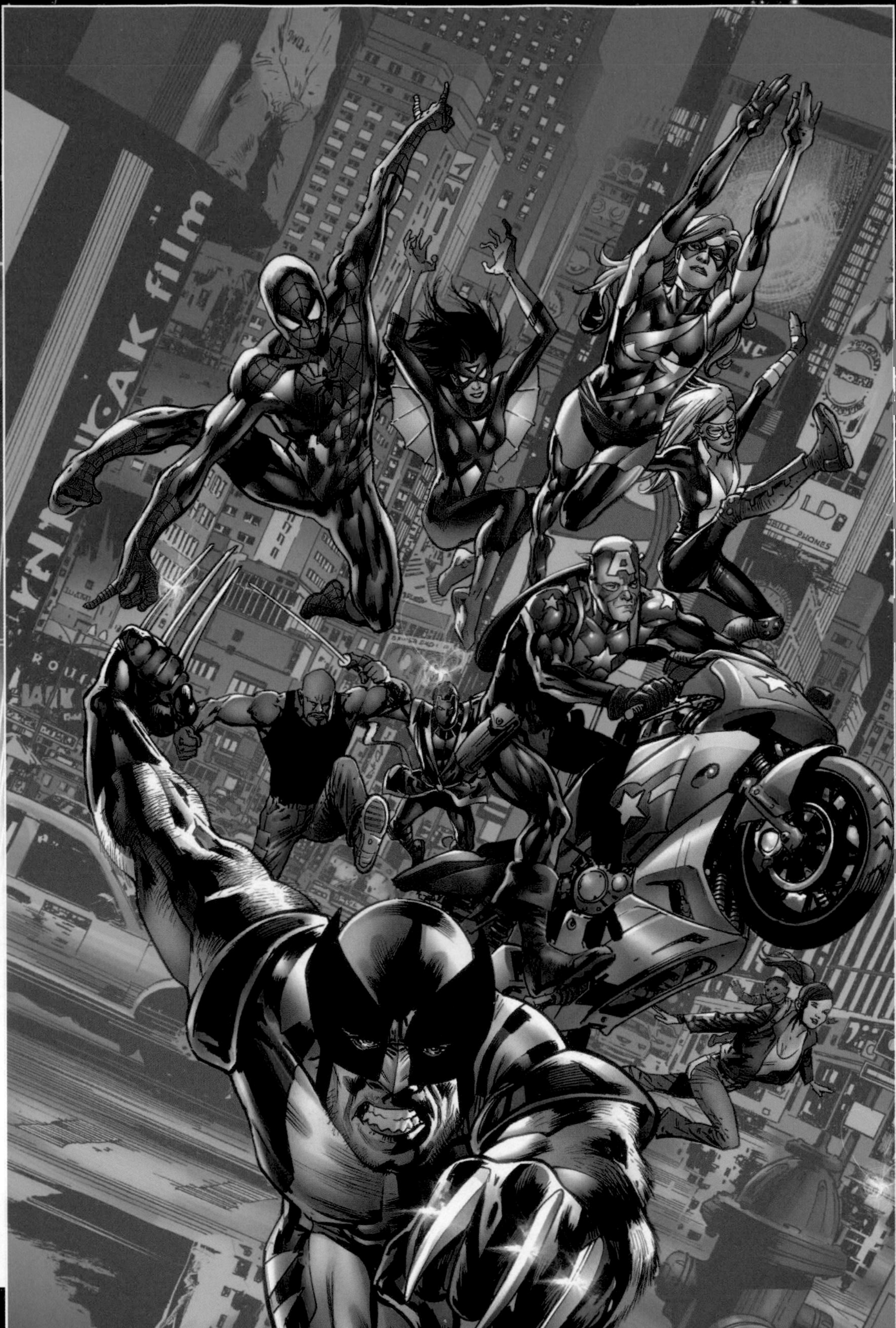
film
AK

NEW AVENGERS FINALE

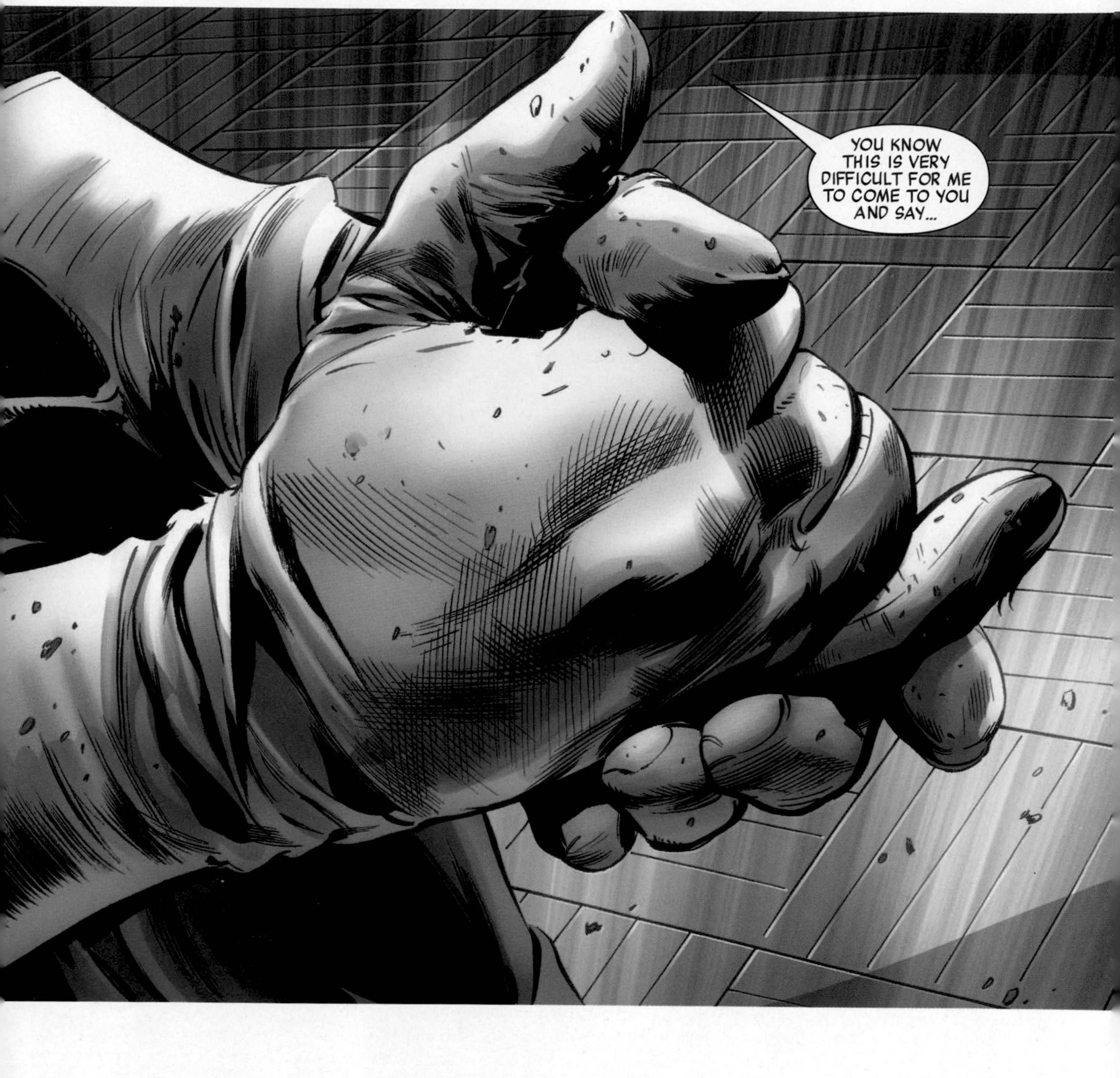
YOU KNOW THIS IS VERY DIFFICULT FOR ME TO COME TO YOU AND SAY...

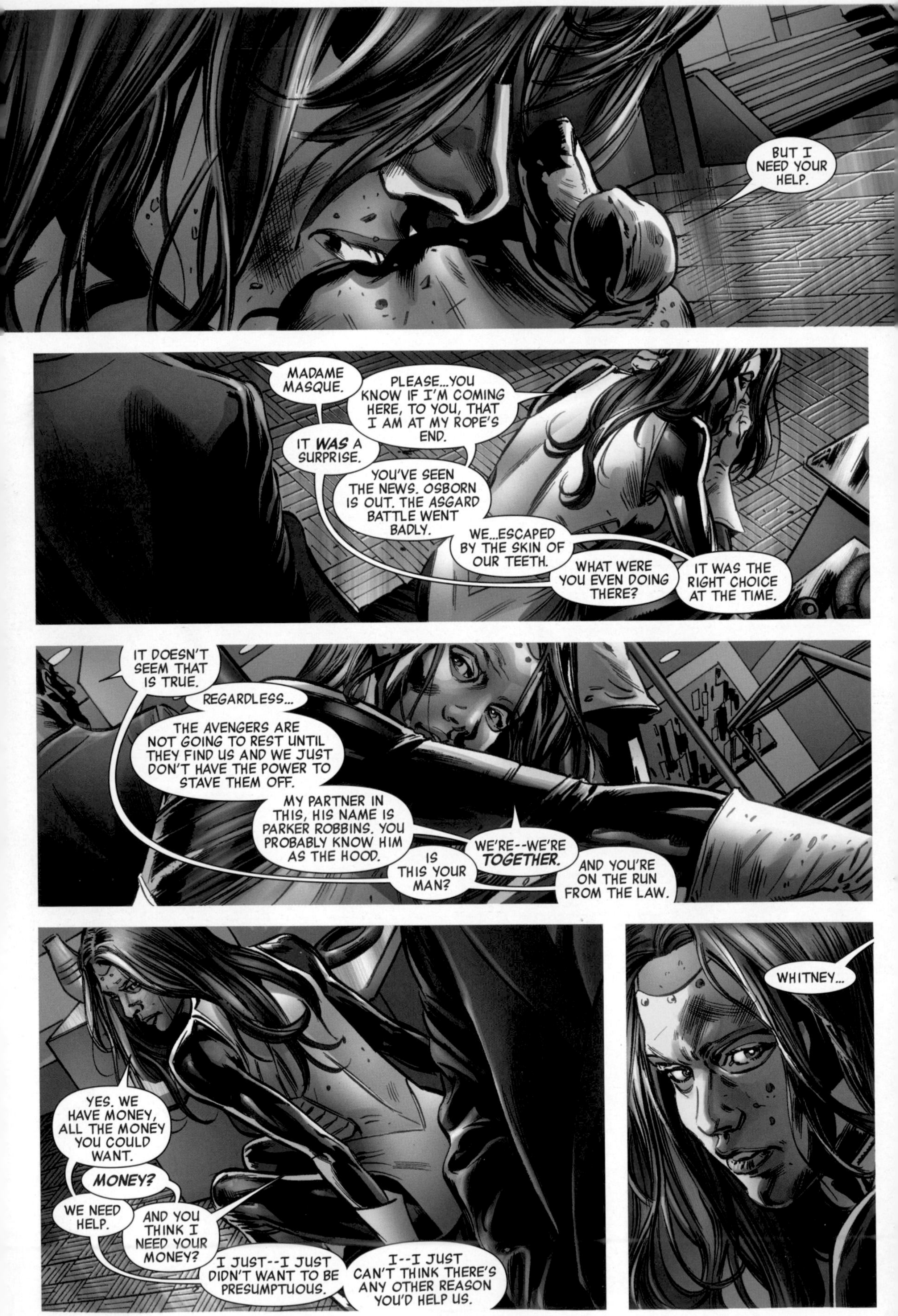
BUT I NEED YOUR HELP.
MADAME MASQUE.
PLEASE...YOU KNOW IF I'M COMING HERE, TO YOU, THAT I AM AT MY ROPE'S END.
IT WAS A SURPRISE.
YOU'VE SEEN THE NEWS. OSBORN IS OUT. THE ASGARD BATTLE WENT BADLY.
WE...ESCAPED BY THE SKIN OF OUR TEETH.
WHAT WERE YOU EVEN DOING THERE?
IT WAS THE RIGHT CHOICE AT THE TIME.
IT DOESN'T SEEM THAT IS TRUE.
REGARDLESS...
THE AVENGERS ARE NOT GOING TO REST UNTIL THEY FIND US AND WE JUST DON'T HAVE THE POWER TO STAVE THEM OFF.
MY PARTNER IN THIS, HIS NAME IS PARKER ROBBINS. YOU PROBABLY KNOW HIM AS THE HOOD.
IS THIS YOUR MAN?
WE'RE--WE'RE TOGETHER.
AND YOU'RE ON THE RUN FROM THE LAW.
YES. WE HAVE MONEY, ALL THE MONEY YOU COULD WANT.
MONEY?
WE NEED HELP.
AND YOU THINK I NEED YOUR MONEY?
I JUST--I JUST DIDN'T WANT TO BE PRESUMPTUOUS.
I--I JUST CAN'T THINK THERE'S ANY OTHER REASON YOU'D HELP US.
WHITNEY...

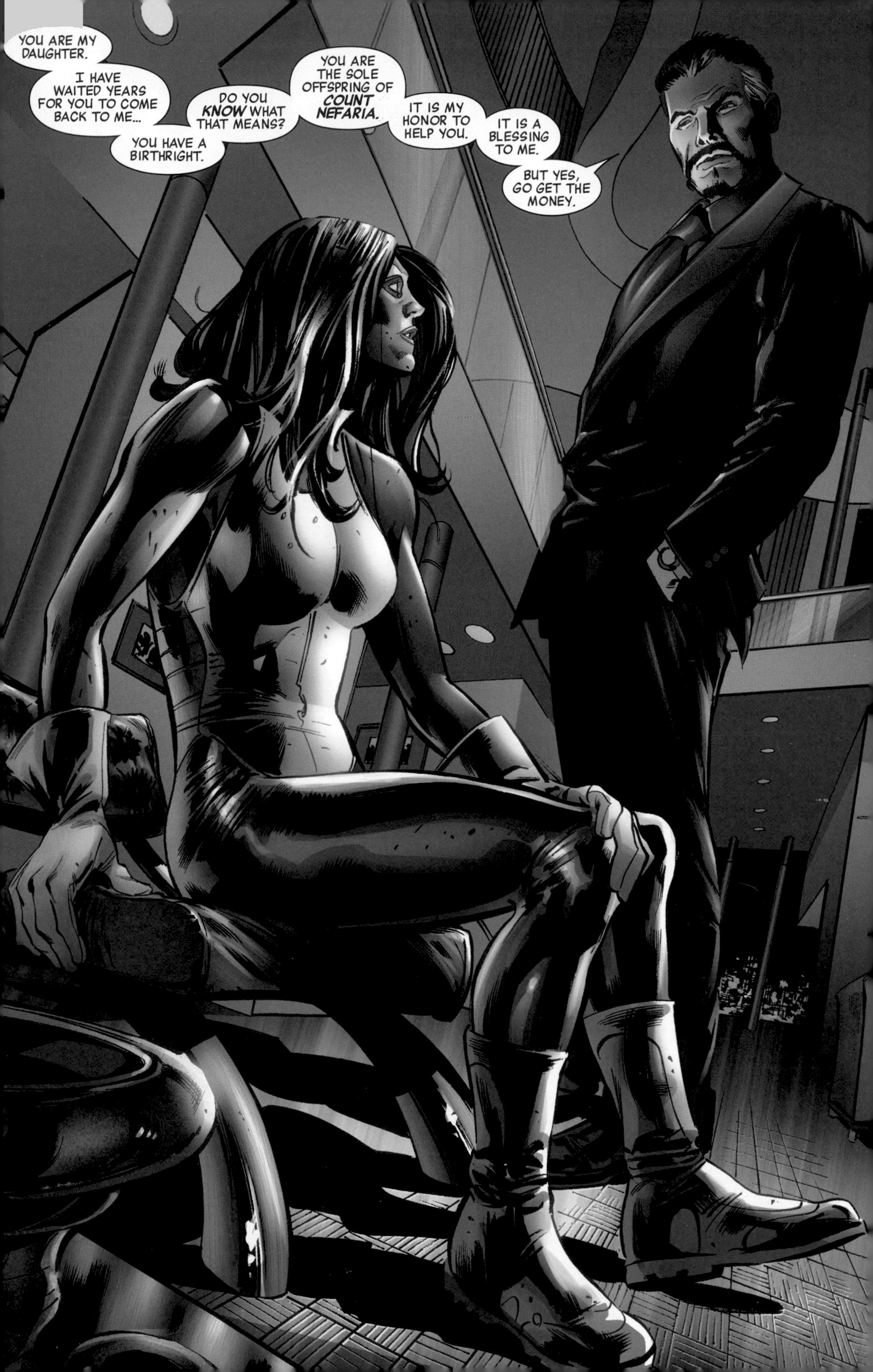
YOU ARE MY DAUGHTER.
I HAVE WAITED YEARS FOR YOU TO COME BACK TO ME...
YOU HAVE A BIRTHRIGHT.
DO YOU KNOW WHAT THAT MEANS?
YOU ARE THE SOLE OFFSPRING OF COUNT NEFARIA.
IT IS MY HONOR TO HELP YOU.
IT IS A BLESSING TO ME.
BUT YES, GO GET THE MONEY.

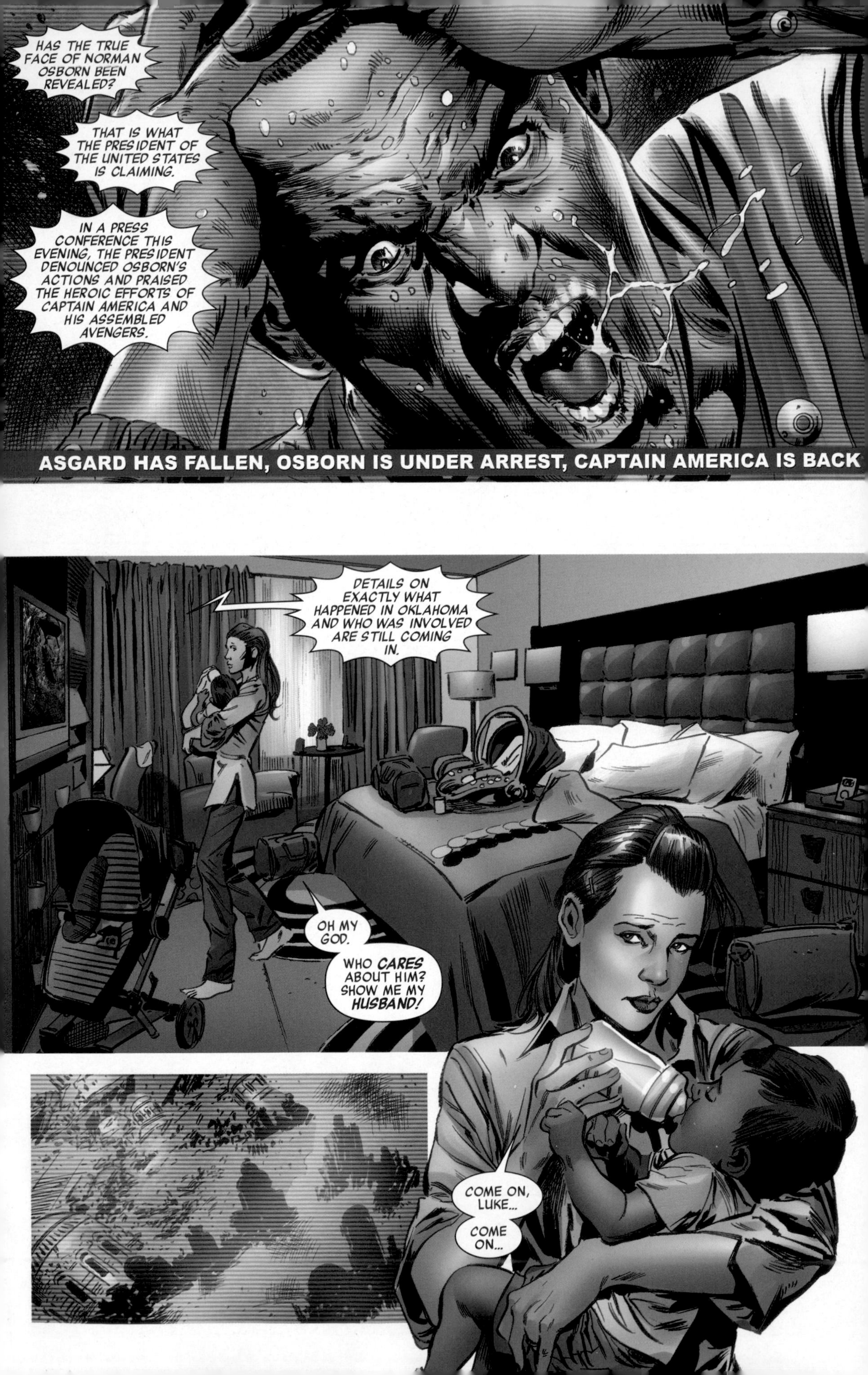
HAS THE TRUE FACE OF NORMAN OSBORN BEEN REVEALED?
THAT IS WHAT THE PRESIDENT OF THE UNITED STATES IS CLAIMING.
IN A PRESS CONFERENCE THIS EVENING, THE PRESIDENT DENOUNCED OSBORN'S ACTIONS AND PRAISED THE HEROIC EFFORTS OF CAPTAIN AMERICA AND HIS ASSEMBLED AVENGERS.
ASGARD HAS FALLEN, OSBORN IS UNDER ARREST, CAPTAIN AMERICA IS BACK
DETAILS ON EXACTLY WHAT HAPPENED IN OKLAHOMA AND WHO WAS INVOLVED ARE STILL COMING IN.
OH MY GOD.
WHO CARES ABOUT HIM? SHOW ME MY HUSBAND!
COME ON, LUKE...
COME ON...

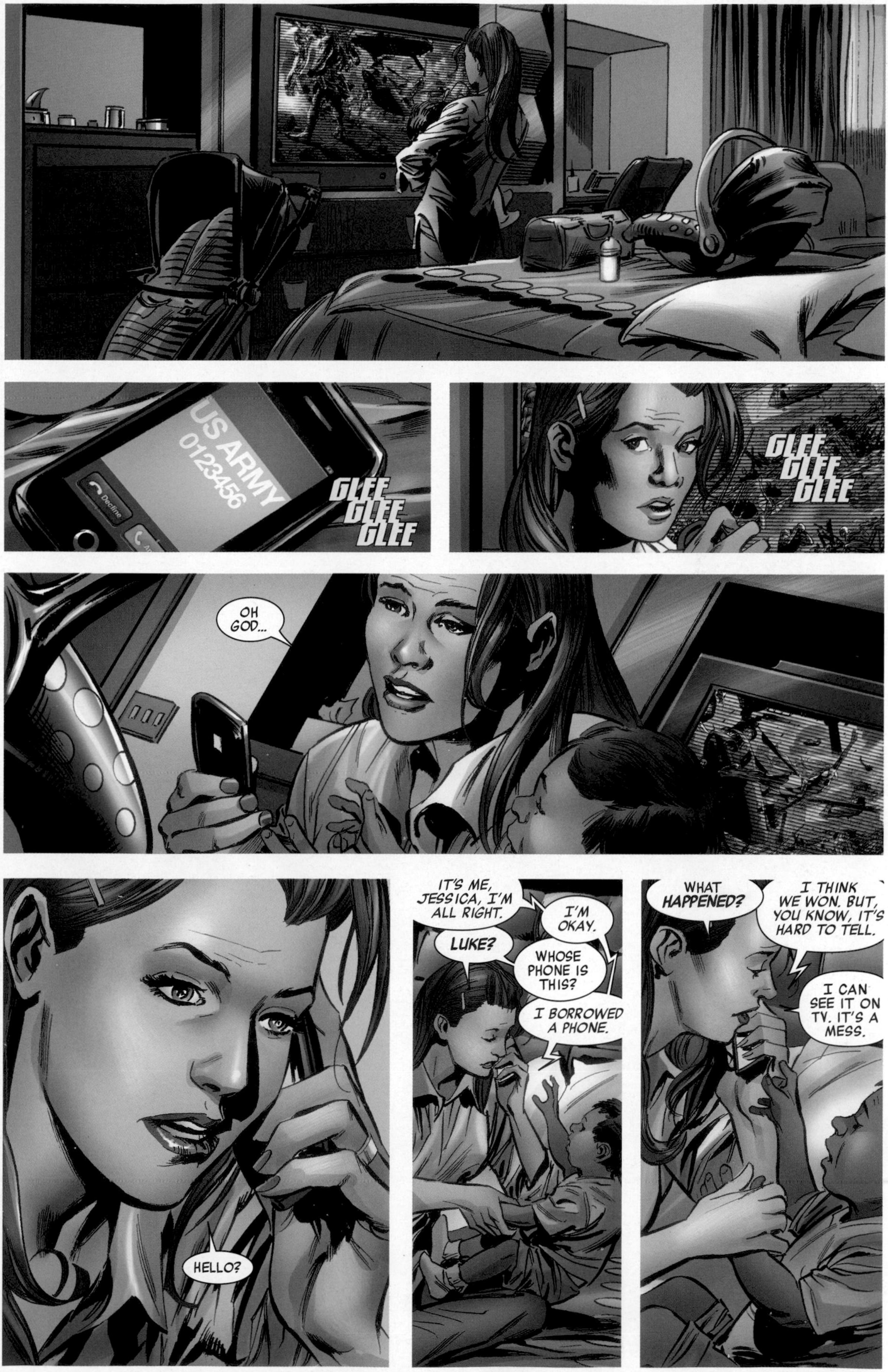
US ARMY
0123456
Decline
GLEE GLEE GLEE
GLEE GLEE GLEE
OH GOD...
HELLO?
LUKE?
IT'S ME, JESSICA, I'M ALL RIGHT.
I'M OKAY.
WHOSE PHONE IS THIS?
I BORROWED A PHONE.
WHAT HAPPENED?
I THINK WE WON. BUT, YOU KNOW, IT'S HARD TO TELL.
I CAN SEE IT ON TV. IT'S A MESS.

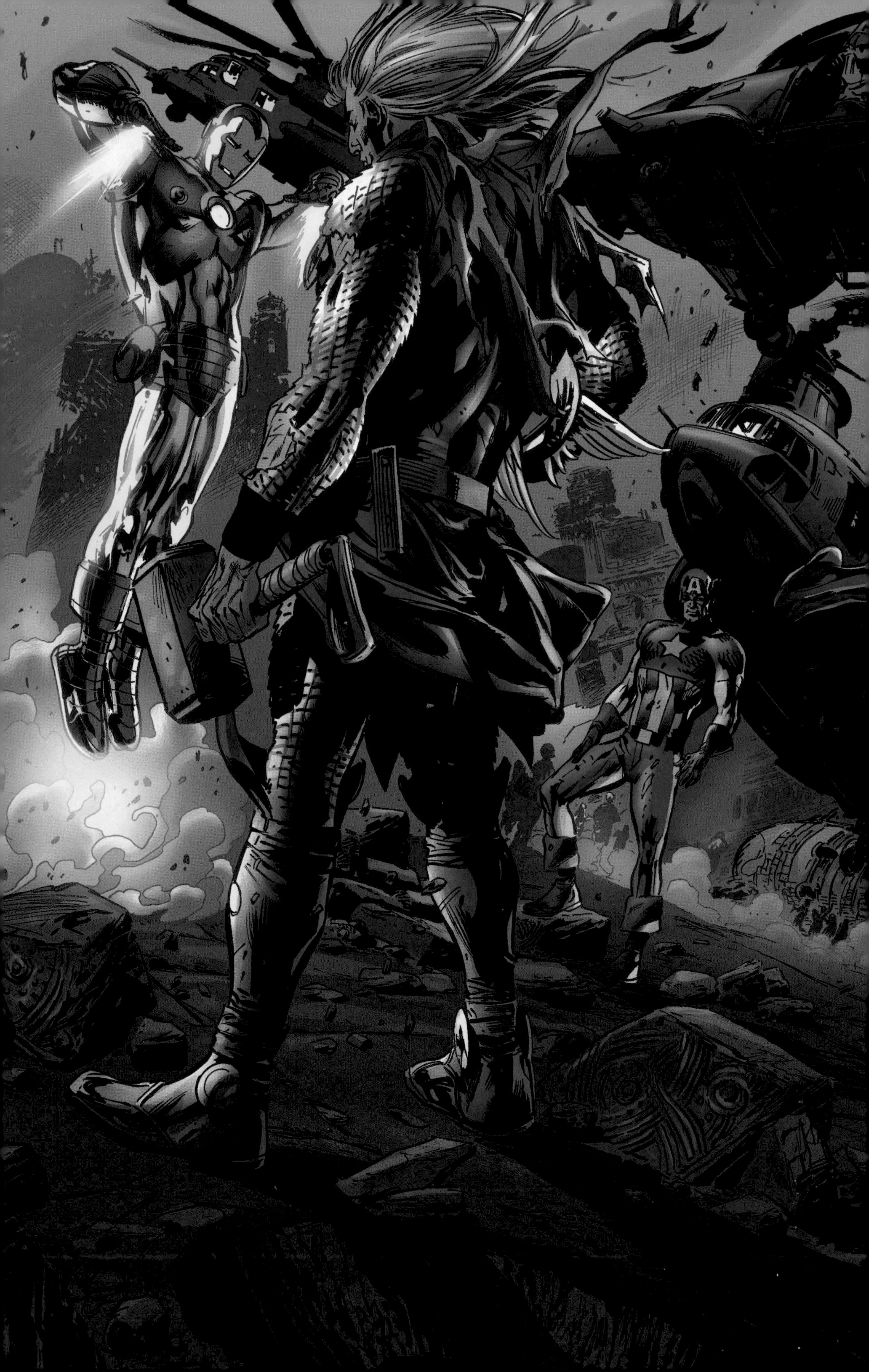

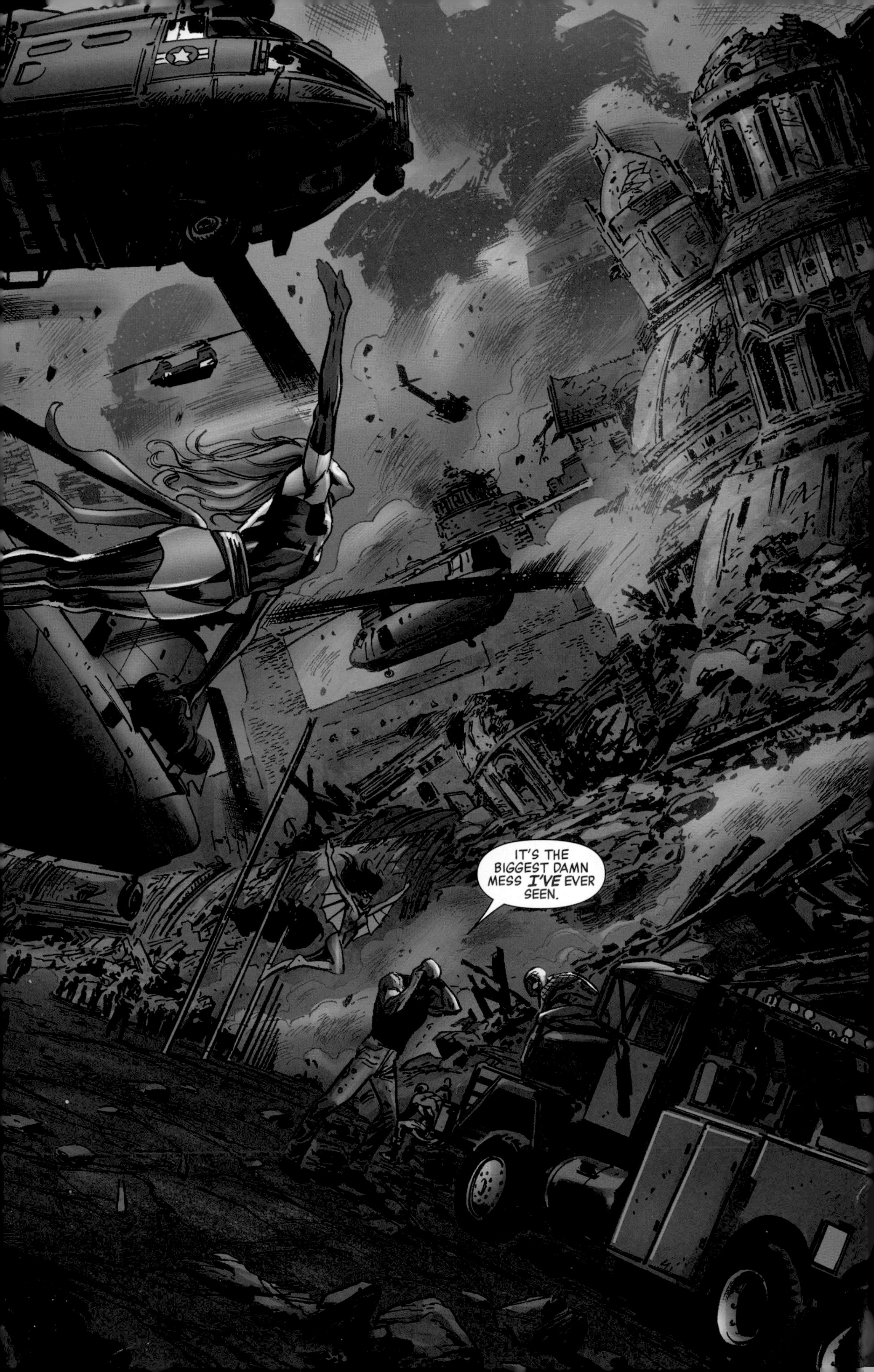
IT'S THE BIGGEST DAMN MESS I'VE EVER SEEN.

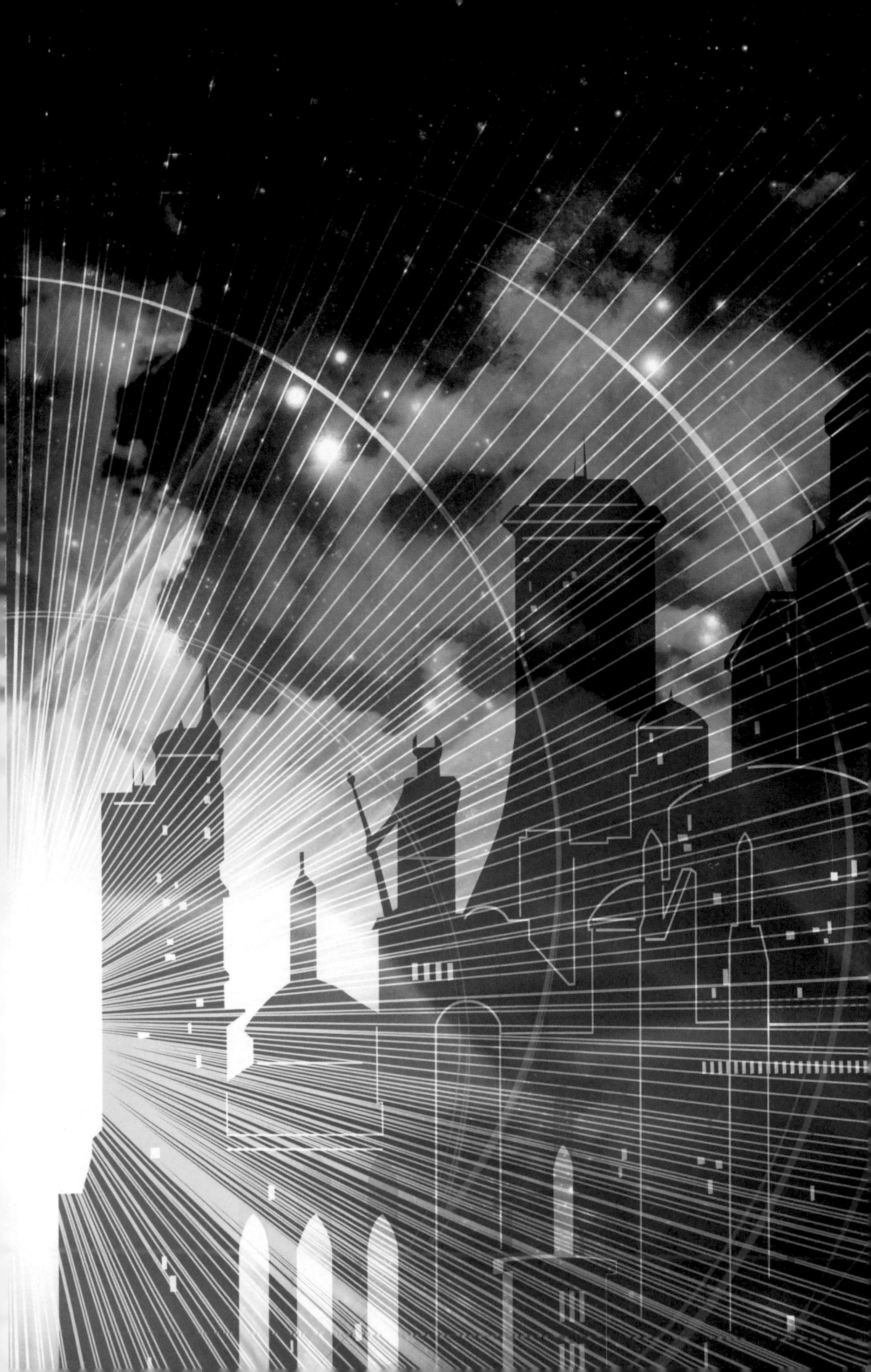

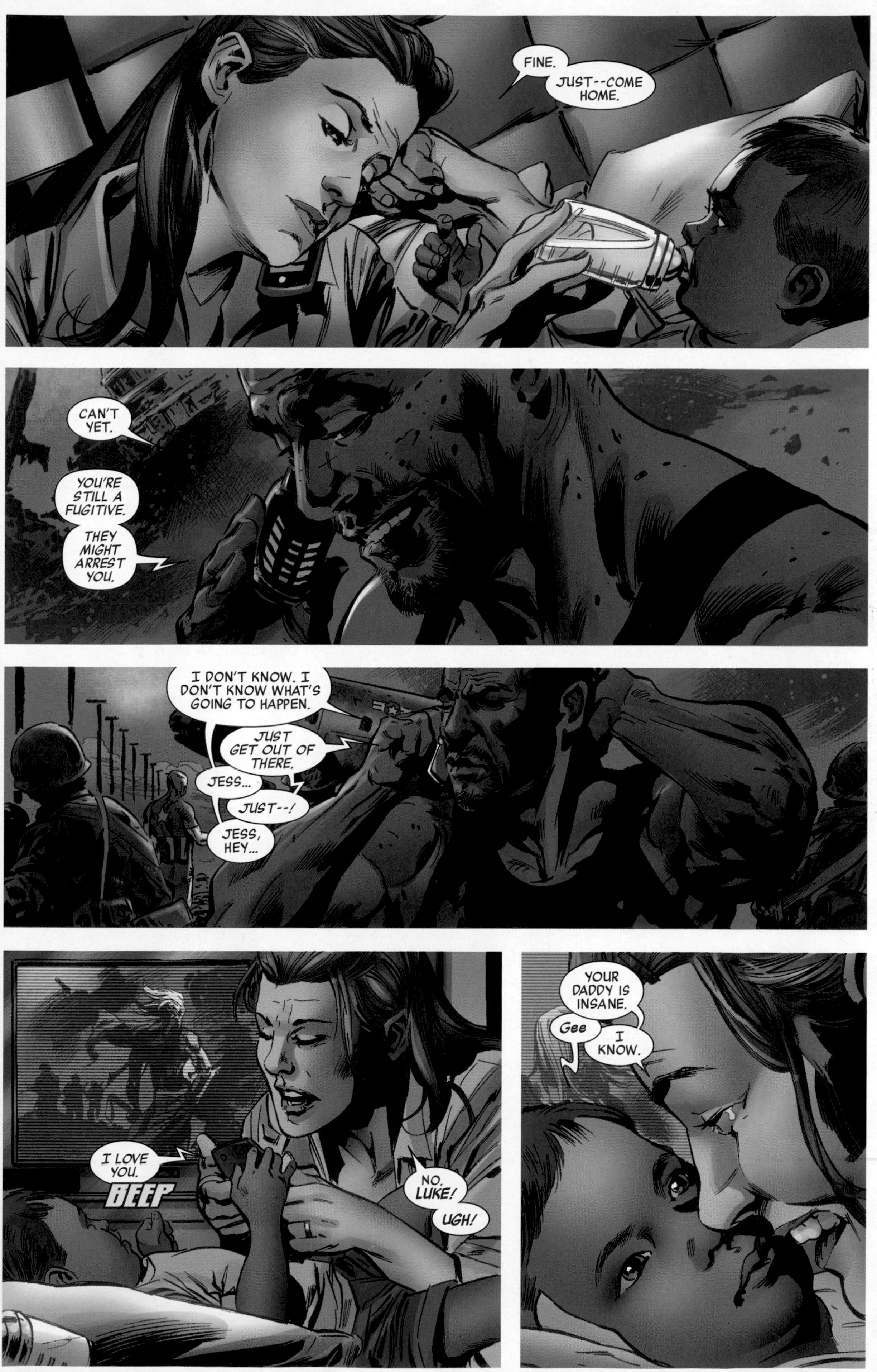
FINE.
JUST--COME HOME.
CAN'T YET.
YOU'RE STILL A FUGITIVE.
THEY MIGHT ARREST YOU.
I DON'T KNOW. I DON'T KNOW WHAT'S GOING TO HAPPEN.
JUST GET OUT OF THERE.
JESS...
JUST--!
JESS, HEY...
I LOVE YOU.
BEEP
NO. LUKE!
UGH!
YOUR DADDY IS INSANE.
Gee
I KNOW.

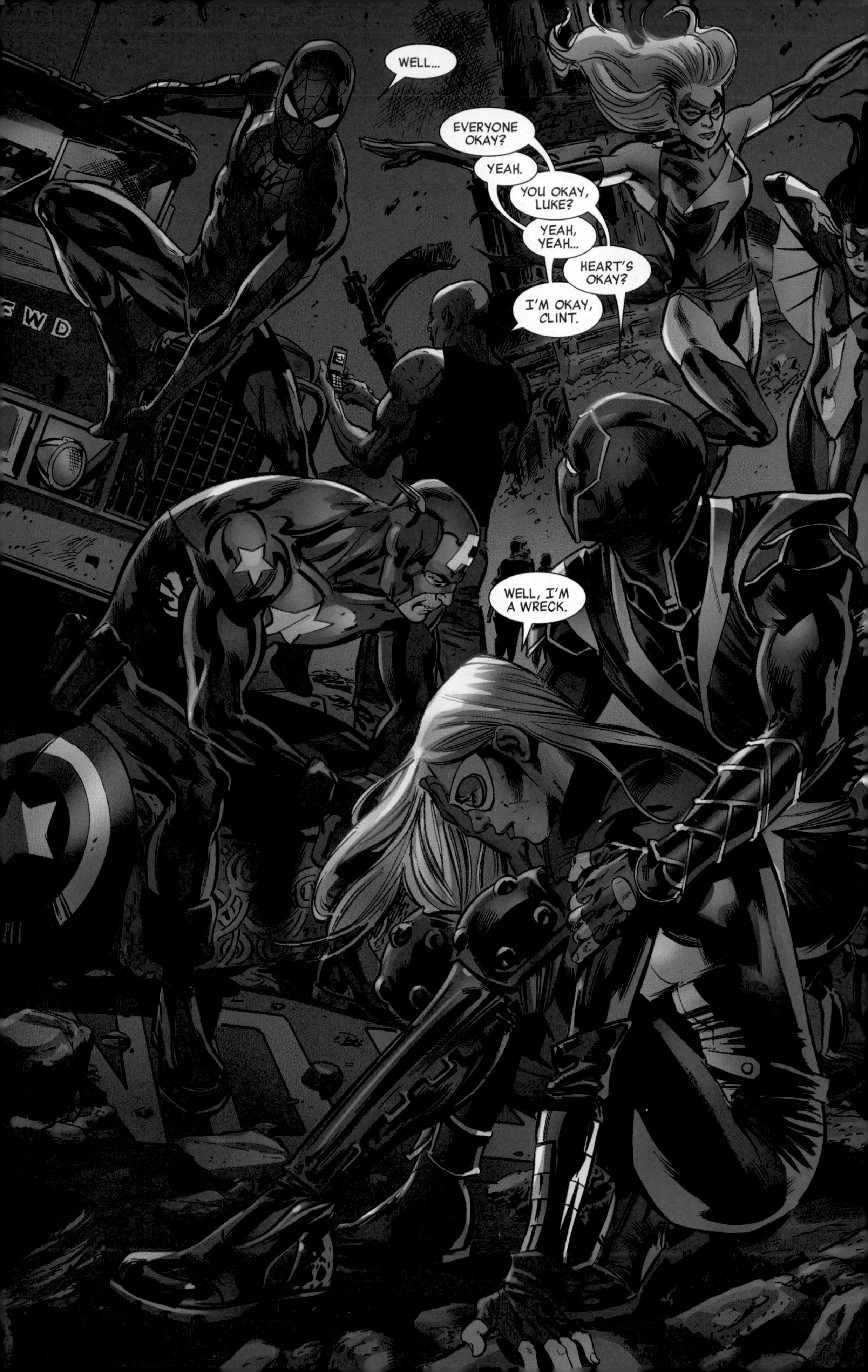
WELL...
EVERYONE OKAY?
YEAH.
YOU OKAY, LUKE?
YEAH, YEAH...
HEART'S OKAY?
I'M OKAY, CLINT.
WELL, I'M A WRECK.

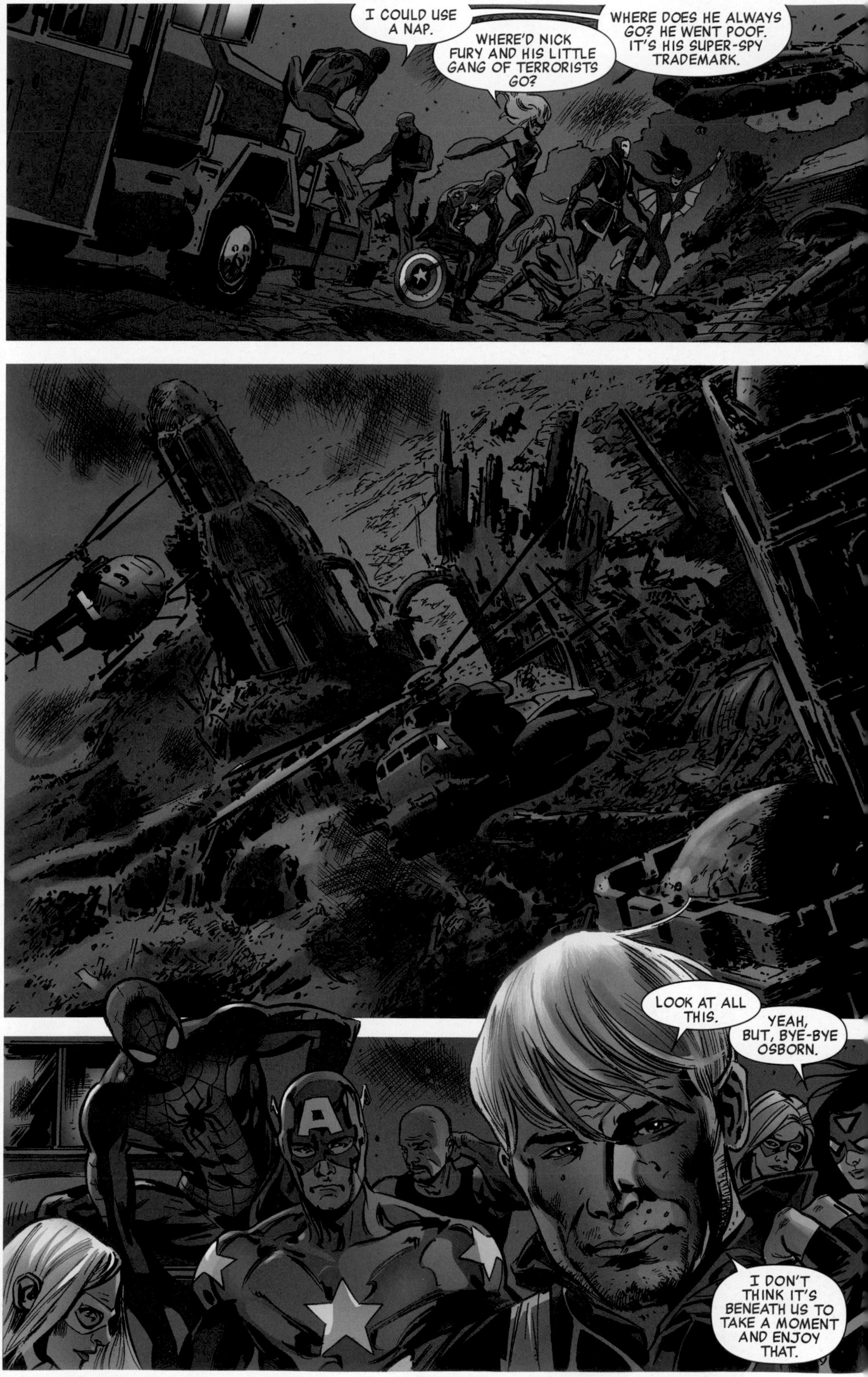
I COULD USE A NAP.
WHERE'D NICK FURY AND HIS LITTLE GANG OF TERRORISTS GO?
WHERE DOES HE ALWAYS GO? HE WENT POOF. IT'S HIS SUPER-SPY TRADEMARK.
LOOK AT ALL THIS.
YEAH, BUT, BYE-BYE OSBORN.
I DON'T THINK IT'S BENEATH US TO TAKE A MOMENT AND ENJOY THAT.

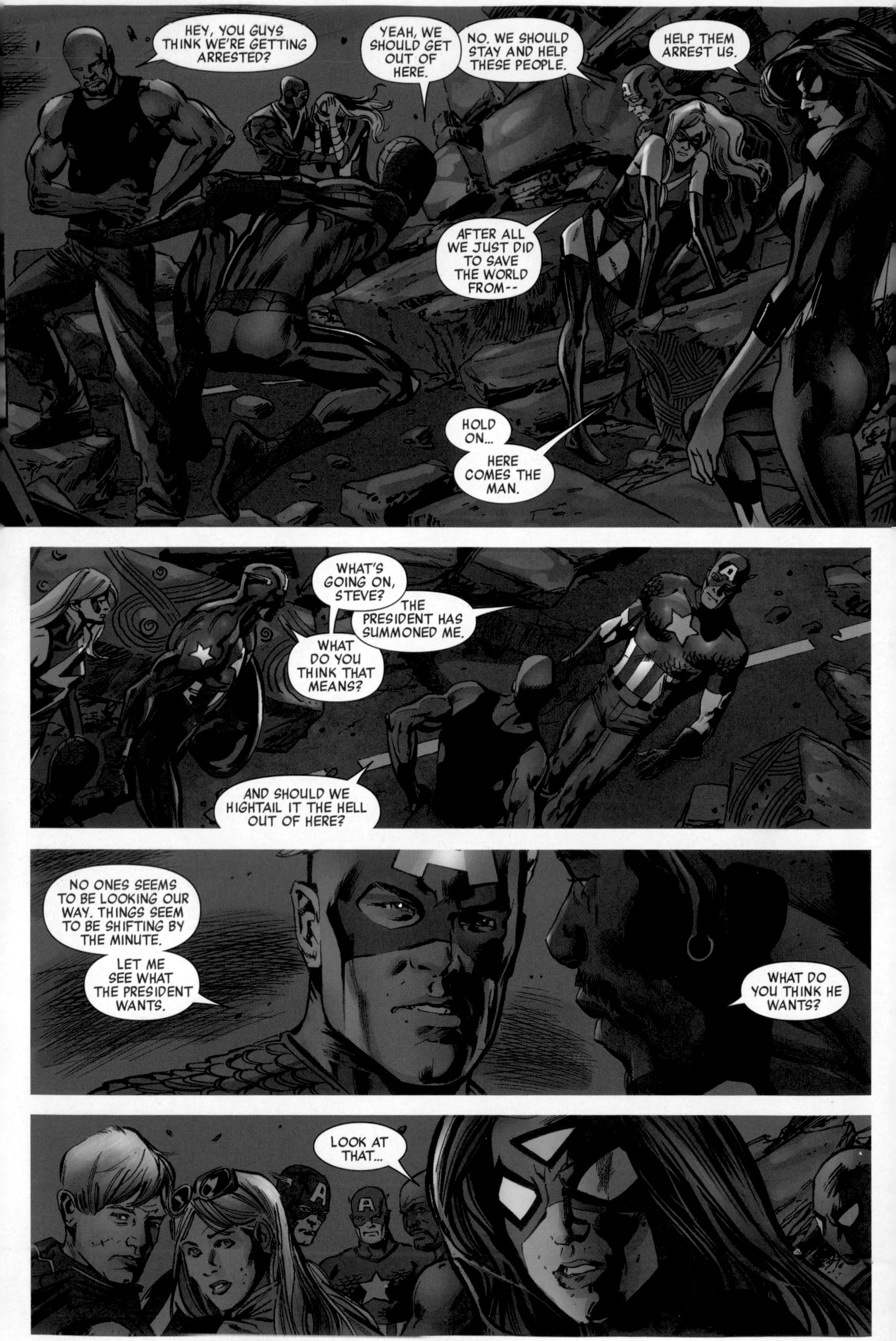
HEY, YOU GUYS THINK WE'RE GETTING ARRESTED?
YEAH, WE SHOULD GET OUT OF HERE.
NO. WE SHOULD STAY AND HELP THESE PEOPLE.
HELP THEM ARREST US.
AFTER ALL WE JUST DID TO SAVE THE WORLD FROM--
HOLD ON...
HERE COMES THE MAN.
WHAT'S GOING ON, STEVE?
THE PRESIDENT HAS SUMMONED ME.
WHAT DO YOU THINK THAT MEANS?
AND SHOULD WE HIGHTAIL IT THE HELL OUT OF HERE?
NO ONES SEEMS TO BE LOOKING OUR WAY. THINGS SEEM TO BE SHIFTING BY THE MINUTE.
LET ME SEE WHAT THE PRESIDENT WANTS.
WHAT DO YOU THINK HE WANTS?
LOOK AT THAT...

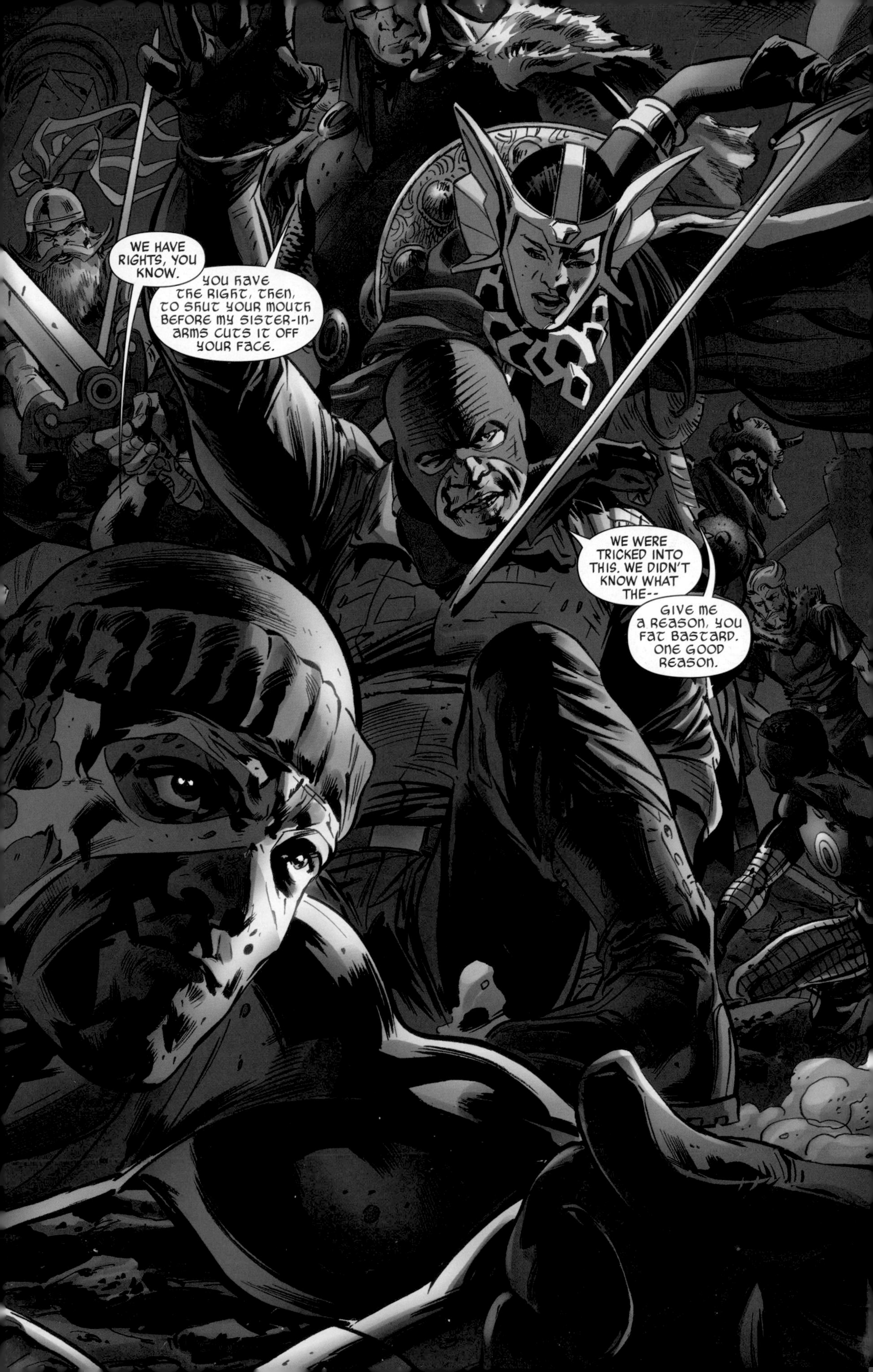
WE HAVE RIGHTS, YOU KNOW.
YOU HAVE THE RIGHT, THEN, TO SHUT YOUR MOUTH BEFORE MY SISTER-IN-ARMS CUTS IT OFF YOUR FACE.
WE WERE TRICKED INTO THIS. WE DIDN'T KNOW WHAT THE--
GIVE ME A REASON, YOU FAT BASTARD. ONE GOOD REASON.

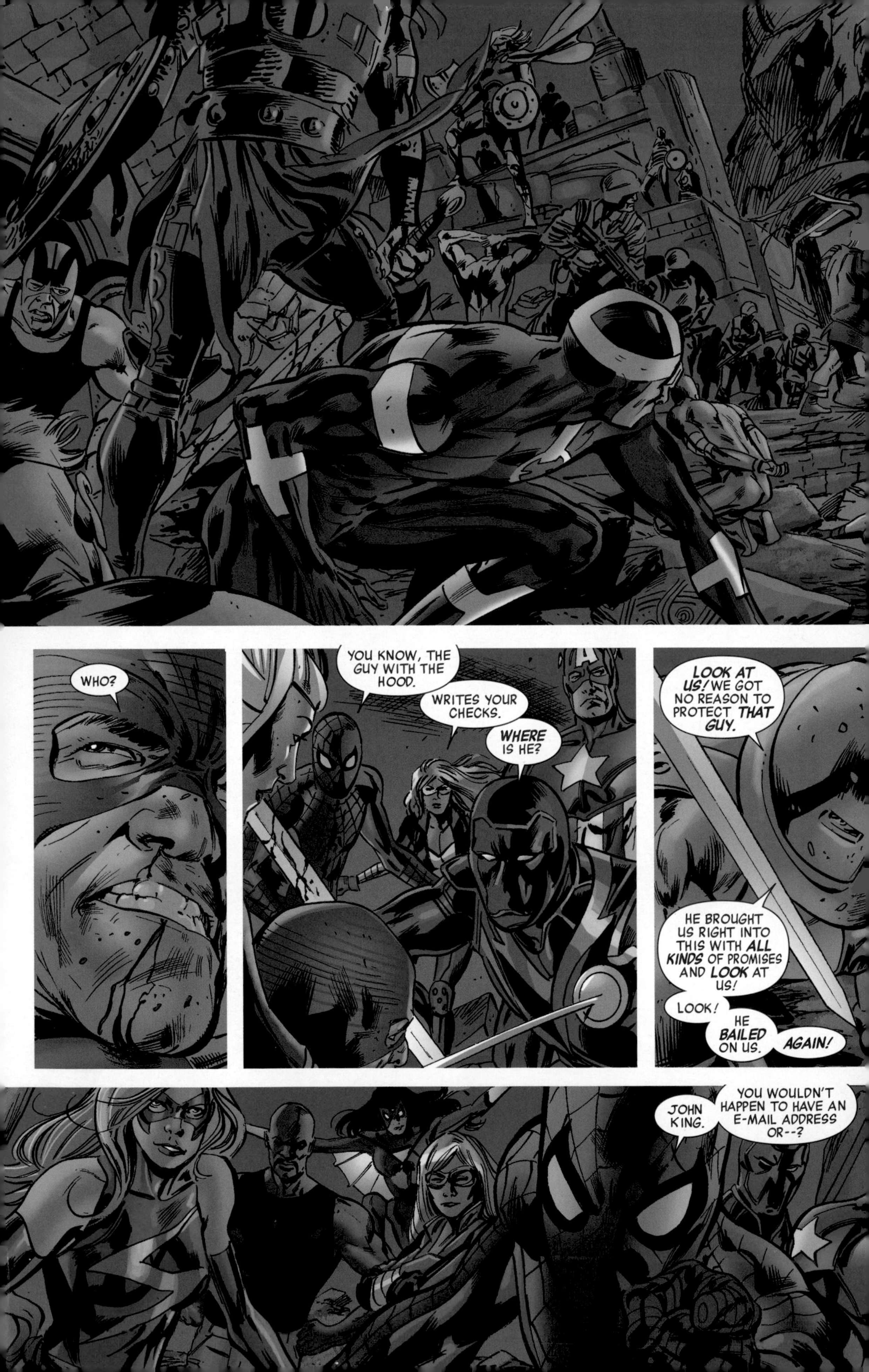
WHO?
YOU KNOW, THE GUY WITH THE HOOD.
WRITES YOUR CHECKS.
WHERE IS HE?
LOOK AT US! WE GOT NO REASON TO PROTECT THAT GUY.
HE BROUGHT US RIGHT INTO THIS WITH ALL KINDS OF PROMISES AND LOOK AT US!
LOOK!
HE BAILED ON US.
AGAIN!
JOHN KING.
YOU WOULDN'T HAPPEN TO HAVE AN E-MAIL ADDRESS OR--?

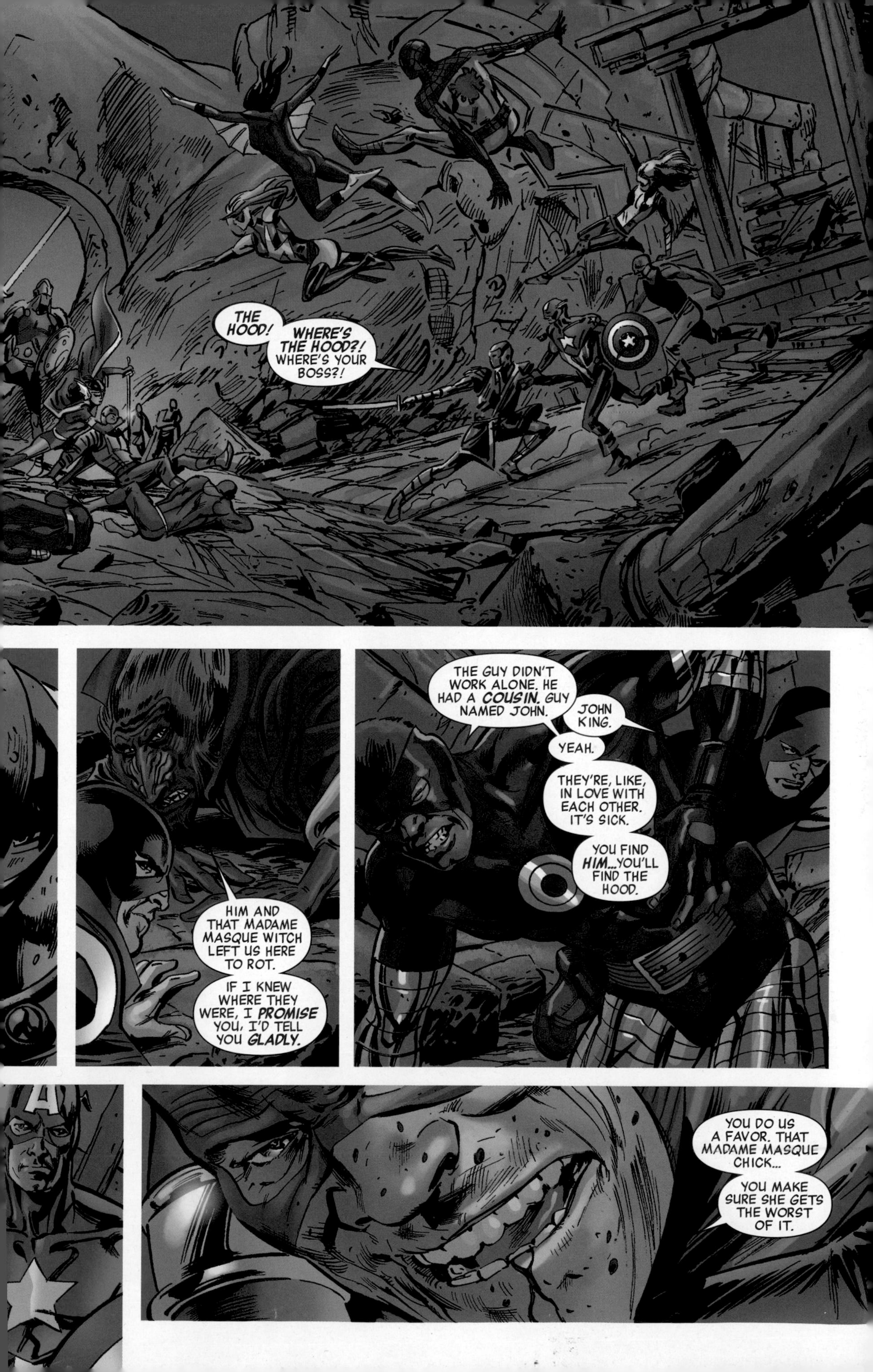
THE HOOD! WHERE'S THE HOOD?! WHERE'S YOUR BOSS?!
HIM AND THAT MADAME MASQUE WITCH LEFT US HERE TO ROT.
IF I KNEW WHERE THEY WERE, I PROMISE YOU, I'D TELL YOU GLADLY.
THE GUY DIDN'T WORK ALONE. HE HAD A COUSIN. GUY NAMED JOHN.
JOHN KING.
YEAH.
THEY'RE, LIKE, IN LOVE WITH EACH OTHER. IT'S SICK.
YOU FIND HIM...YOU'LL FIND THE HOOD.
YOU DO US A FAVOR. THAT MADAME MASQUE CHICK...
YOU MAKE SURE SHE GETS THE WORST OF IT.

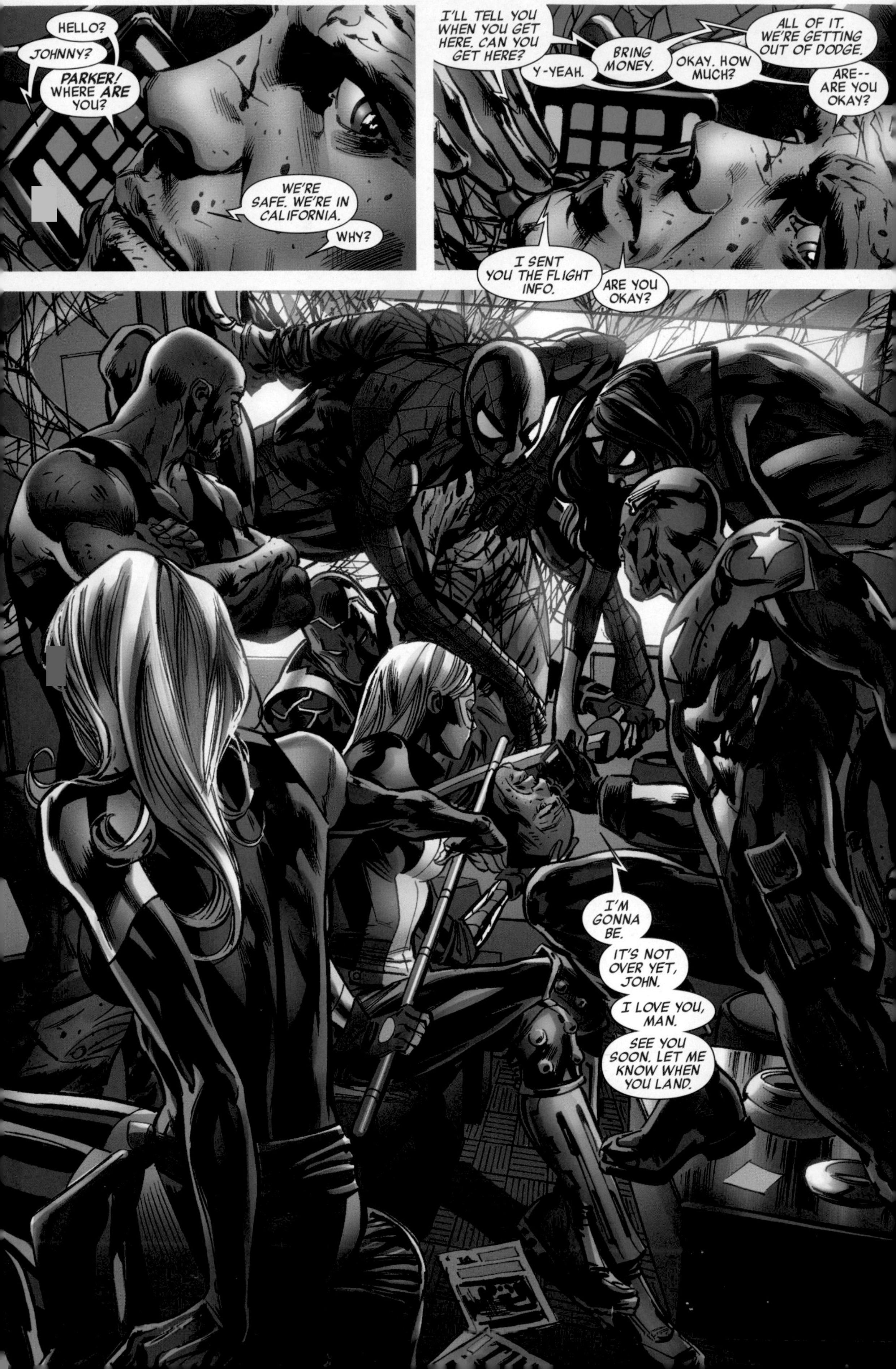
HELLO?
JOHNNY?
PARKER! WHERE ARE YOU?
WE'RE SAFE. WE'RE IN CALIFORNIA.
WHY?
I'LL TELL YOU WHEN YOU GET HERE. CAN YOU GET HERE?
Y-YEAH.
BRING MONEY.
OKAY. HOW MUCH?
ALL OF IT. WE'RE GETTING OUT OF DODGE.
ARE-- ARE YOU OKAY?
I SENT YOU THE FLIGHT INFO.
ARE YOU OKAY?
I'M GONNA BE.
IT'S NOT OVER YET, JOHN.
I LOVE YOU, MAN.
SEE YOU SOON. LET ME KNOW WHEN YOU LAND.

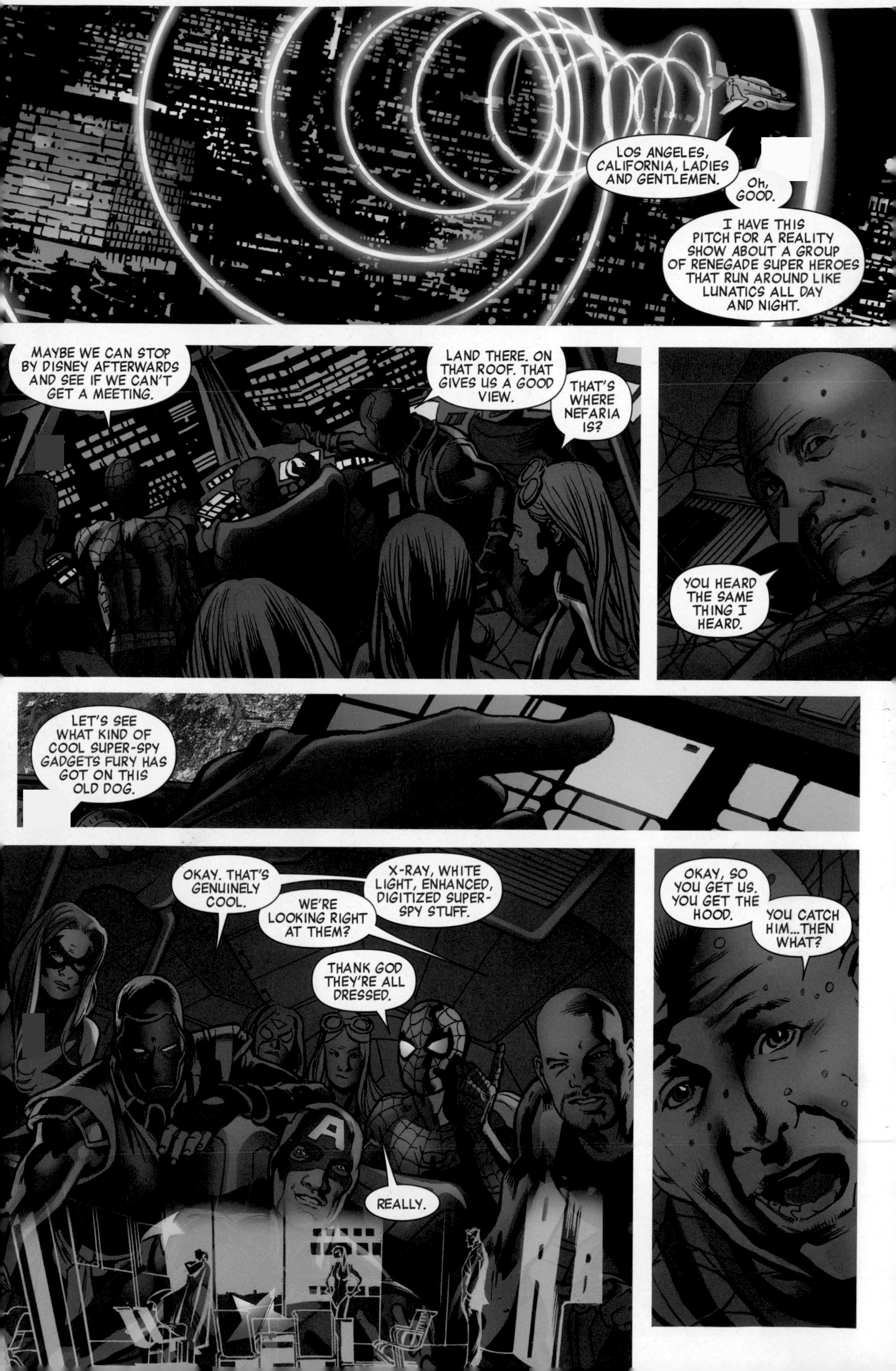
LOS ANGELES, CALIFORNIA, LADIES AND GENTLEMEN.
Oh, GOOD.
I HAVE THIS PITCH FOR A REALITY SHOW ABOUT A GROUP OF RENEGADE SUPER HEROES THAT RUN AROUND LIKE LUNATICS ALL DAY AND NIGHT.
MAYBE WE CAN STOP BY DISNEY AFTERWARDS AND SEE IF WE CAN'T GET A MEETING.
LAND THERE. ON THAT ROOF. THAT GIVES US A GOOD VIEW.
THAT'S WHERE NEFARIA IS?
YOU HEARD THE SAME THING I HEARD.
LET'S SEE WHAT KIND OF COOL SUPER-SPY GADGETS FURY HAS GOT ON THIS OLD DOG.
OKAY. THAT'S GENUINELY COOL.
X-RAY, WHITE LIGHT, ENHANCED, DIGITIZED SUPER-SPY STUFF.
WE'RE LOOKING RIGHT AT THEM?
THANK GOD THEY'RE ALL DRESSED.
REALLY.
OKAY, SO YOU GET US. YOU GET THE HOOD.
YOU CATCH HIM...THEN WHAT?

NOTHING WILL CHANGE. IT WON'T STOP ANYTHING.

HOW DO YOU THINK WE CARVED OUT OUR NICHE IN THE FIRST PLACE?

BECAUSE OF YOU. GUYS LIKE YOU TOOK DOWN THE KINGPIN.

YOU MADE A HOLE IN THE WAY OF THE WORLD.

YOU CREATED THE NEED FOR US.

AND NOW--YOU GET RID OF US...SOMEONE ELSE WILL POP RIGHT IN AND START THE WHEELS TURNING ALL OVER AGAIN.

THIS IS THE WAY THE WORLD IS.

YOU ARE ABSOLUTELY RIGHT. IT *IS* OUR FAULT.

SO WE'RE GOING TO FIX IT.

YOU THINK HE CAN'T BUY HIS WAY OUT OF *WHATEVER* YOU DO TO US?

WE HAVE MORE MONEY SACKED AWAY THAN YOU COULD EVEN IMAGINE.

WE HAVE FRIENDS EVERYWHERE.

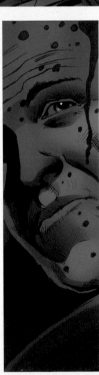

REALLY?

YOU'RE SWEATING.

THERE'S A LITTLE TRUTH THERE.

LITTLE BIT.

WHY ARE WE DOING THIS? REALLY.

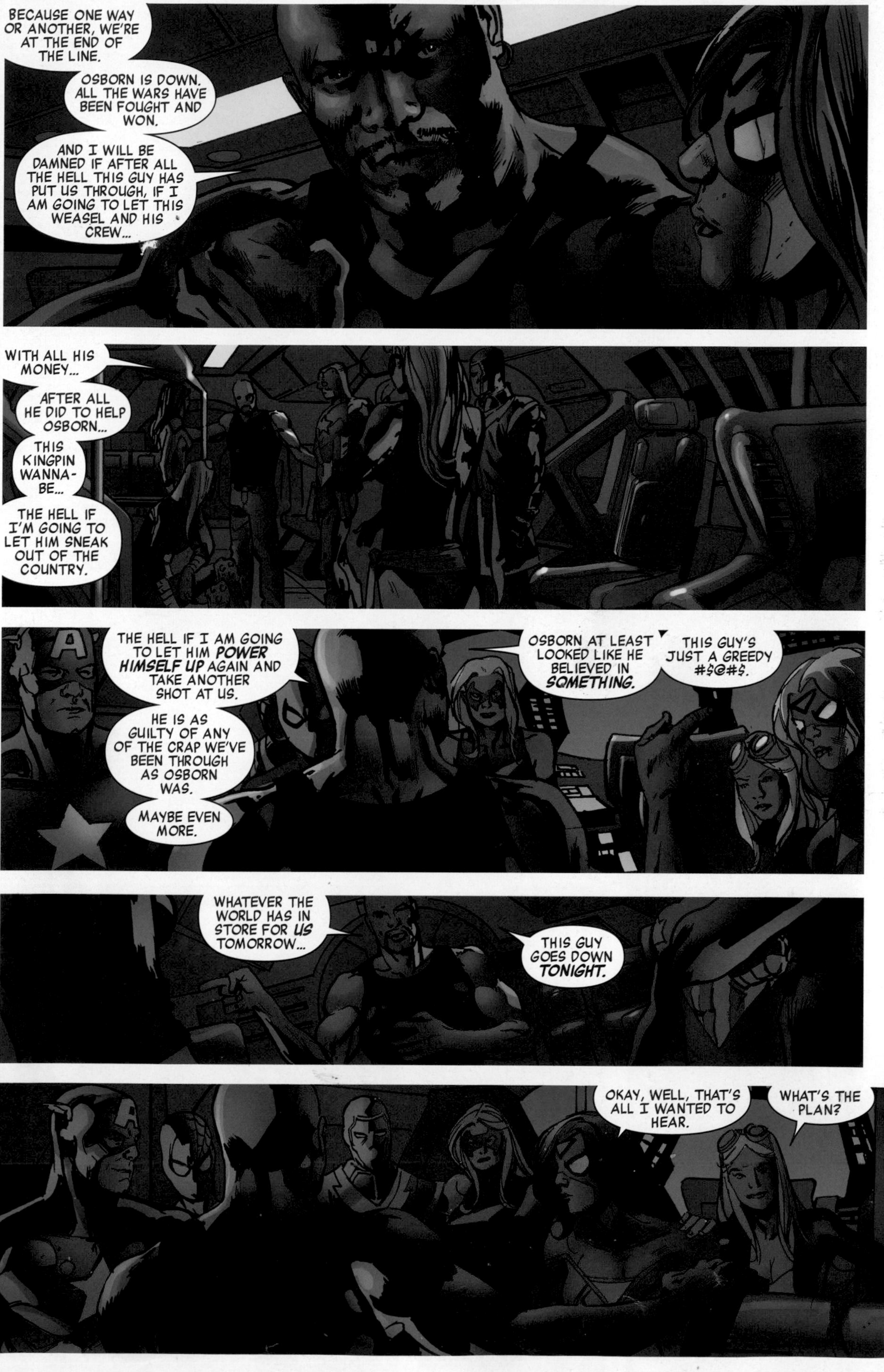
BECAUSE ONE WAY OR ANOTHER, WE'RE AT THE END OF THE LINE.
OSBORN IS DOWN. ALL THE WARS HAVE BEEN FOUGHT AND WON.
AND I WILL BE DAMNED IF AFTER ALL THE HELL THIS GUY HAS PUT US THROUGH, IF I AM GOING TO LET THIS WEASEL AND HIS CREW...
WITH ALL HIS MONEY...
AFTER ALL HE DID TO HELP OSBORN...
THIS KINGPIN WANNA-BE...
THE HELL IF I'M GOING TO LET HIM SNEAK OUT OF THE COUNTRY.
THE HELL IF I AM GOING TO LET HIM POWER HIMSELF UP AGAIN AND TAKE ANOTHER SHOT AT US.
HE IS AS GUILTY OF ANY OF THE CRAP WE'VE BEEN THROUGH AS OSBORN WAS.
MAYBE EVEN MORE.
OSBORN AT LEAST LOOKED LIKE HE BELIEVED IN SOMETHING.
THIS GUY'S JUST A GREEDY #$@#$.
WHATEVER THE WORLD HAS IN STORE FOR US TOMORROW...
THIS GUY GOES DOWN TONIGHT.
OKAY, WELL, THAT'S ALL I WANTED TO HEAR.
WHAT'S THE PLAN?

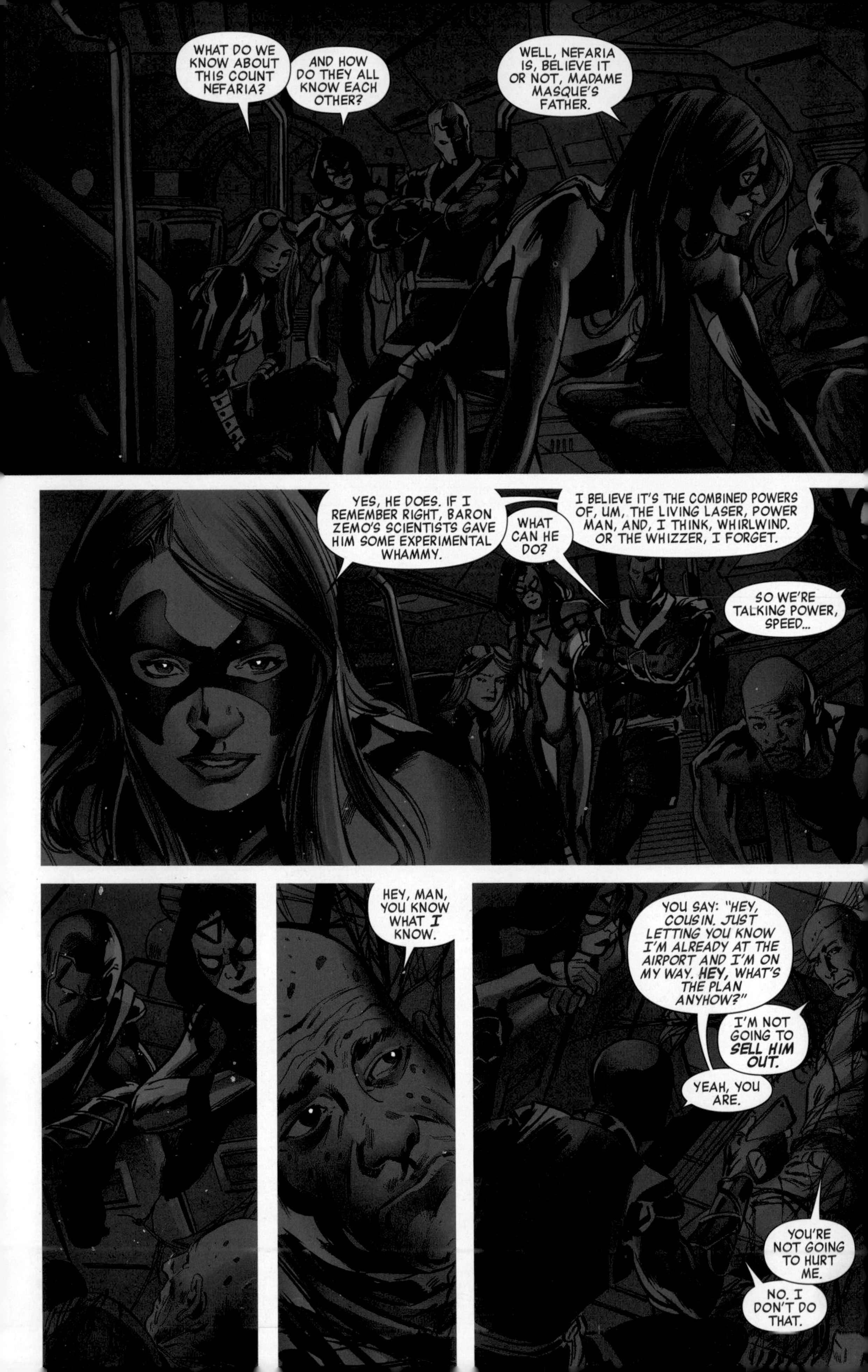
WHAT DO WE KNOW ABOUT THIS COUNT NEFARIA?
AND HOW DO THEY ALL KNOW EACH OTHER?
WELL, NEFARIA IS, BELIEVE IT OR NOT, MADAME MASQUE'S FATHER.
YES, HE DOES. IF I REMEMBER RIGHT, BARON ZEMO'S SCIENTISTS GAVE HIM SOME EXPERIMENTAL WHAMMY.
WHAT CAN HE DO?
I BELIEVE IT'S THE COMBINED POWERS OF, UM, THE LIVING LASER, POWER MAN, AND, I THINK, WHIRLWIND. OR THE WHIZZER, I FORGET.
SO WE'RE TALKING POWER, SPEED...
HEY, MAN, YOU KNOW WHAT I KNOW.
YOU SAY: "HEY, COUSIN. JUST LETTING YOU KNOW I'M ALREADY AT THE AIRPORT AND I'M ON MY WAY. HEY, WHAT'S THE PLAN ANYHOW?"
I'M NOT GOING TO SELL HIM OUT.
YEAH, YOU ARE.
YOU'RE NOT GOING TO HURT ME.
NO. I DON'T DO THAT.

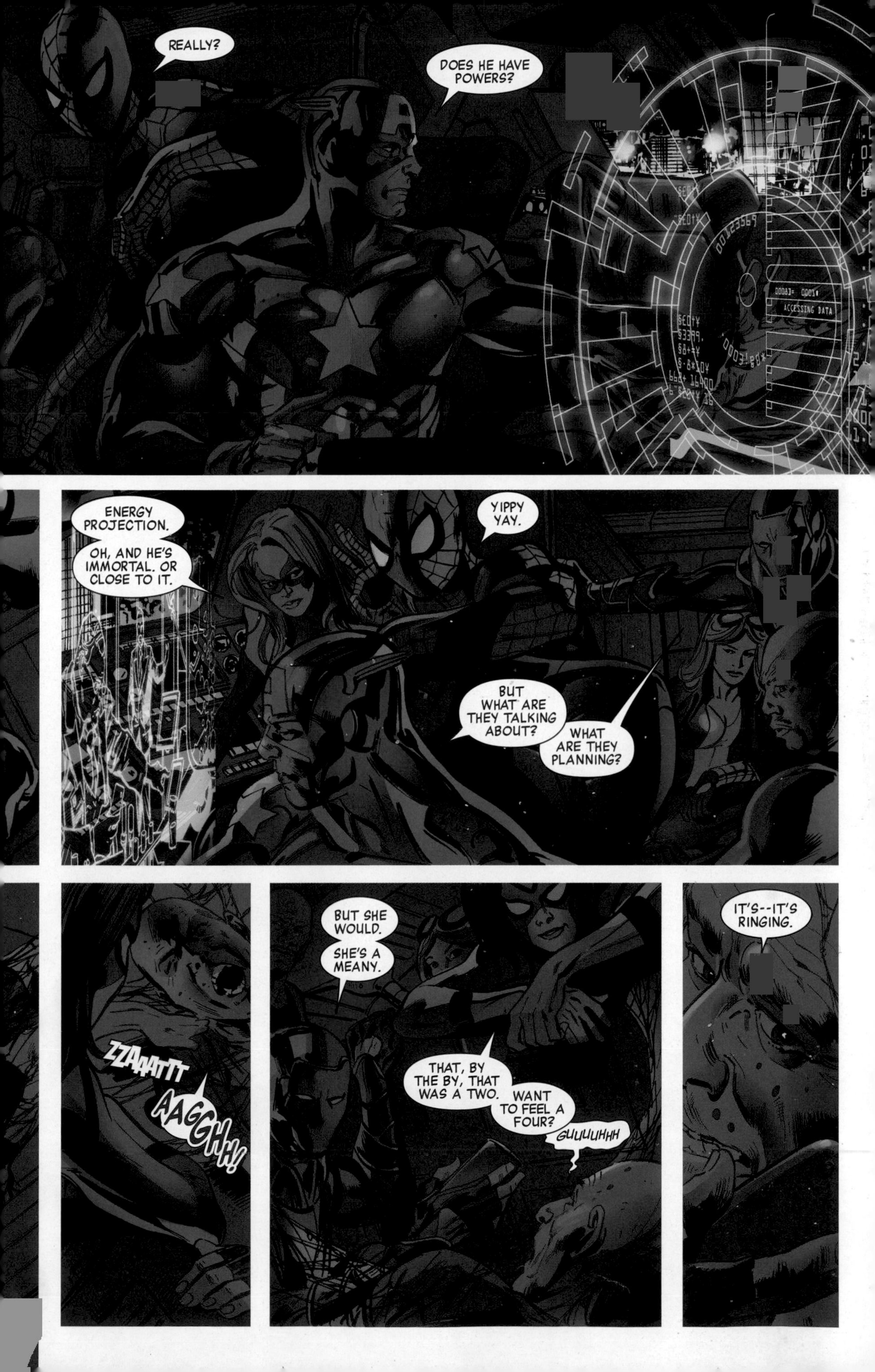
REALLY?
DOES HE HAVE POWERS?
ACCESSING DATA
ENERGY PROJECTION.
OH, AND HE'S IMMORTAL. OR CLOSE TO IT.
YIPPY YAY.
BUT WHAT ARE THEY TALKING ABOUT?
WHAT ARE THEY PLANNING?
ZZAAAATTT
AAGGHH!
BUT SHE WOULD.
SHE'S A MEANY.
THAT, BY THE BY, THAT WAS A TWO.
WANT TO FEEL A FOUR?
GUUUUHHH
IT'S--IT'S RINGING.

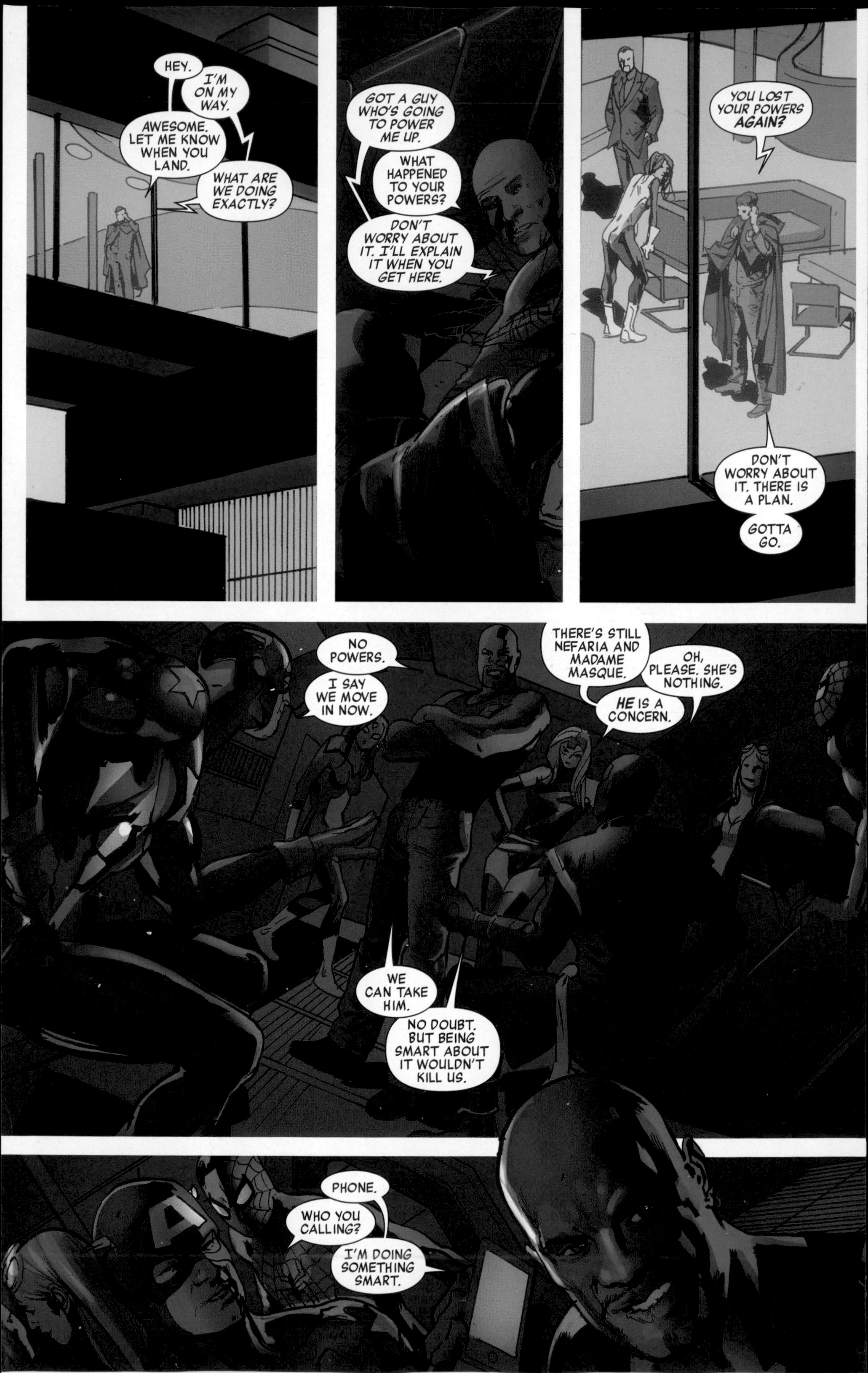
HEY.
I'M ON MY WAY.
AWESOME. LET ME KNOW WHEN YOU LAND.
WHAT ARE WE DOING EXACTLY?
GOT A GUY WHO'S GOING TO POWER ME UP.
WHAT HAPPENED TO YOUR POWERS?
DON'T WORRY ABOUT IT. I'LL EXPLAIN IT WHEN YOU GET HERE.
YOU LOST YOUR POWERS AGAIN?
DON'T WORRY ABOUT IT. THERE IS A PLAN.
GOTTA GO.
NO POWERS.
I SAY WE MOVE IN NOW.
THERE'S STILL NEFARIA AND MADAME MASQUE.
OH, PLEASE. SHE'S NOTHING.
HE IS A CONCERN.
WE CAN TAKE HIM.
NO DOUBT. BUT BEING SMART ABOUT IT WOULDN'T KILL US.
PHONE.
WHO YOU CALLING?
I'M DOING SOMETHING SMART.

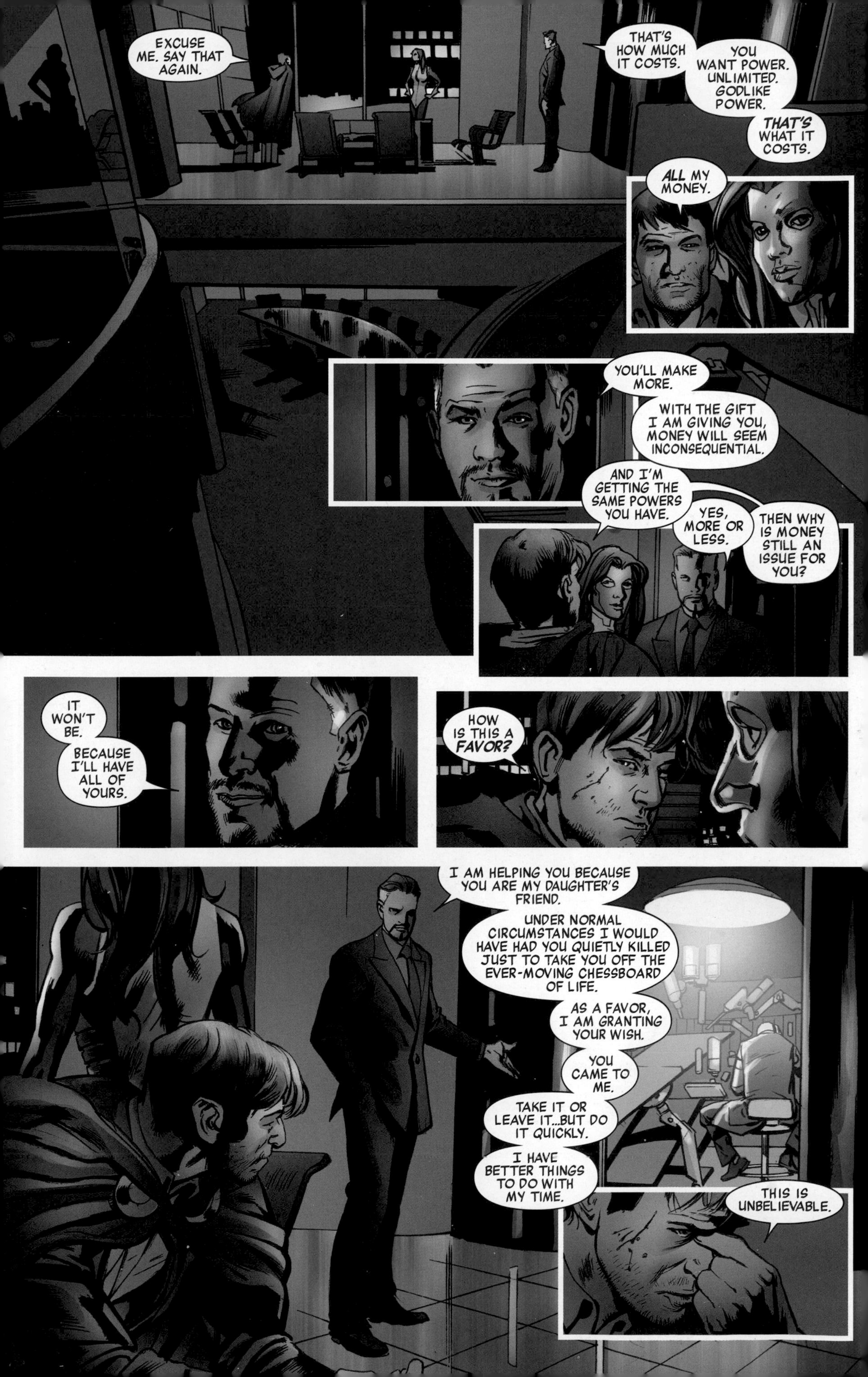
EXCUSE ME. SAY THAT AGAIN.
THAT'S HOW MUCH IT COSTS.
YOU WANT POWER. UNLIMITED. GODLIKE POWER.
THAT'S WHAT IT COSTS.
ALL MY MONEY.
YOU'LL MAKE MORE.
WITH THE GIFT I AM GIVING YOU, MONEY WILL SEEM INCONSEQUENTIAL.
AND I'M GETTING THE SAME POWERS YOU HAVE.
YES, MORE OR LESS.
THEN WHY IS MONEY STILL AN ISSUE FOR YOU?
IT WON'T BE.
BECAUSE I'LL HAVE ALL OF YOURS.
HOW IS THIS A *FAVOR?*
I AM HELPING YOU BECAUSE YOU ARE MY DAUGHTER'S FRIEND.
UNDER NORMAL CIRCUMSTANCES I WOULD HAVE HAD YOU QUIETLY KILLED JUST TO TAKE YOU OFF THE EVER-MOVING CHESSBOARD OF LIFE.
AS A FAVOR, I AM GRANTING YOUR WISH.
YOU CAME TO ME.
TAKE IT OR LEAVE IT...BUT DO IT QUICKLY.
I HAVE BETTER THINGS TO DO WITH MY TIME.
THIS IS UNBELIEVABLE.

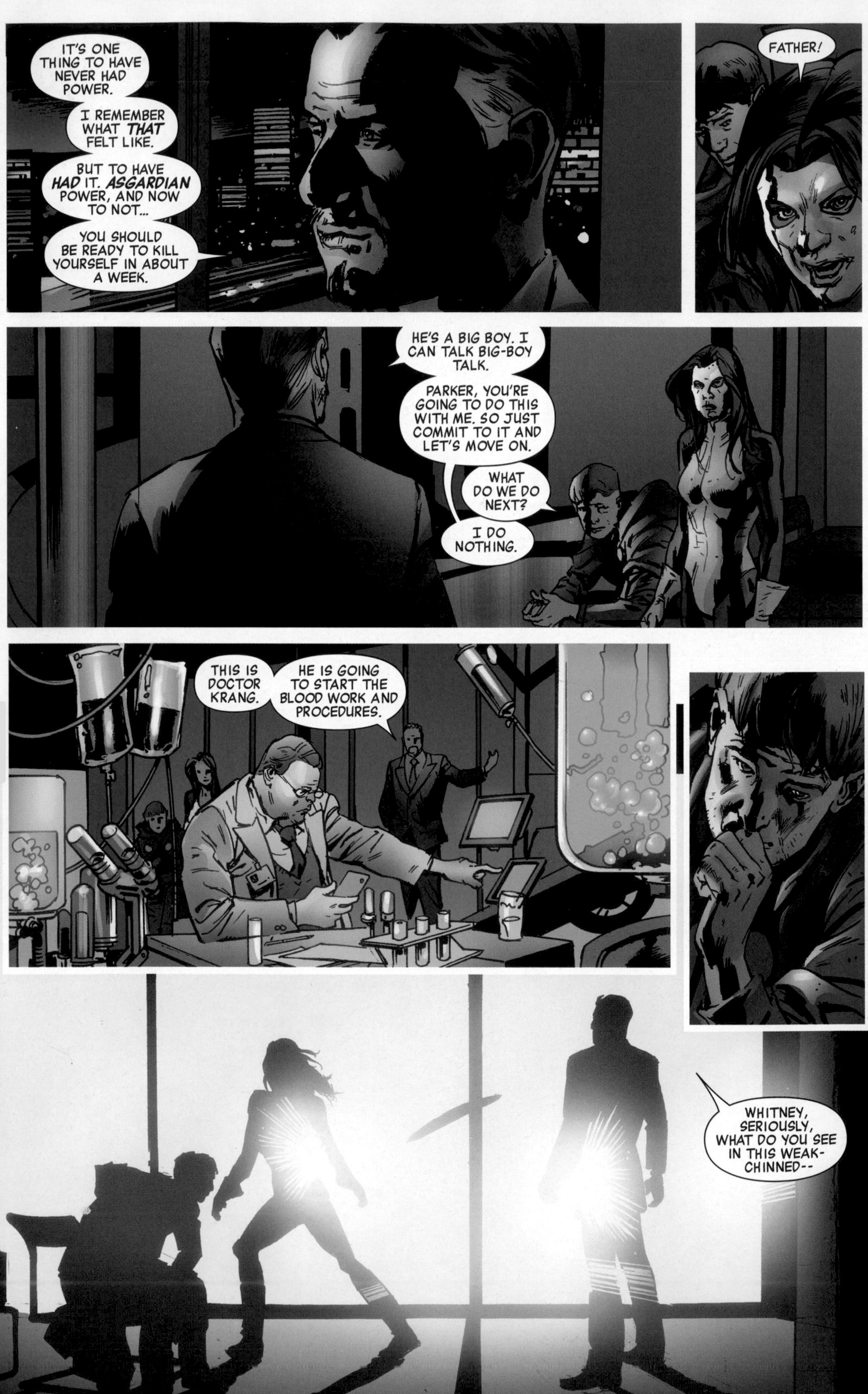
IT'S ONE THING TO HAVE NEVER HAD POWER.
I REMEMBER WHAT THAT FELT LIKE.
BUT TO HAVE HAD IT. ASGARDIAN POWER, AND NOW TO NOT...
YOU SHOULD BE READY TO KILL YOURSELF IN ABOUT A WEEK.
FATHER!
HE'S A BIG BOY. I CAN TALK BIG-BOY TALK.
PARKER, YOU'RE GOING TO DO THIS WITH ME. SO JUST COMMIT TO IT AND LET'S MOVE ON.
WHAT DO WE DO NEXT?
I DO NOTHING.
THIS IS DOCTOR KRANG.
HE IS GOING TO START THE BLOOD WORK AND PROCEDURES.
WHITNEY, SERIOUSLY, WHAT DO YOU SEE IN THIS WEAK-CHINNED--

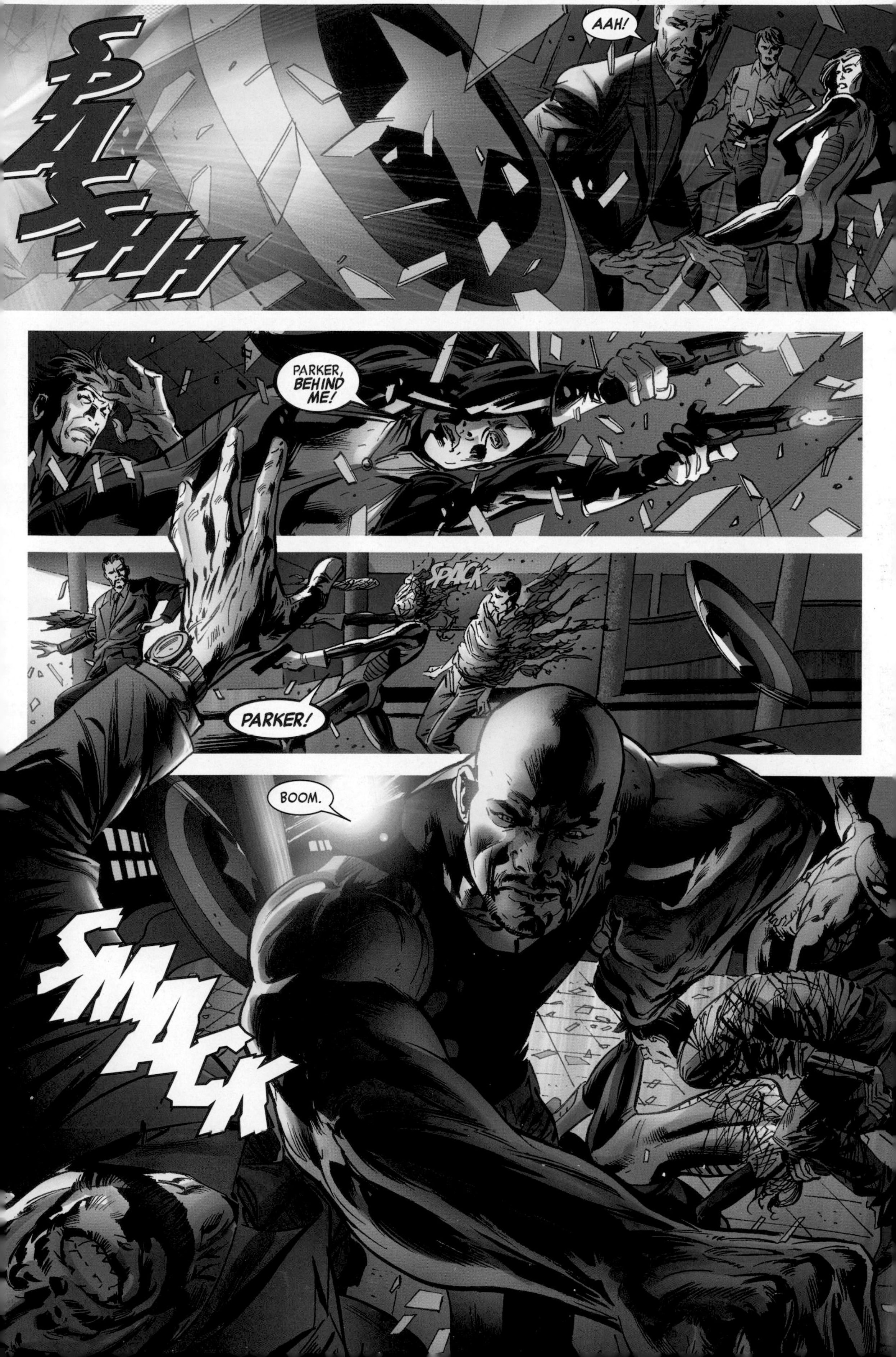
SPLASHH
AAH!
PARKER, BEHIND ME!
SPACK
PARKER!
BOOM.
SMACK

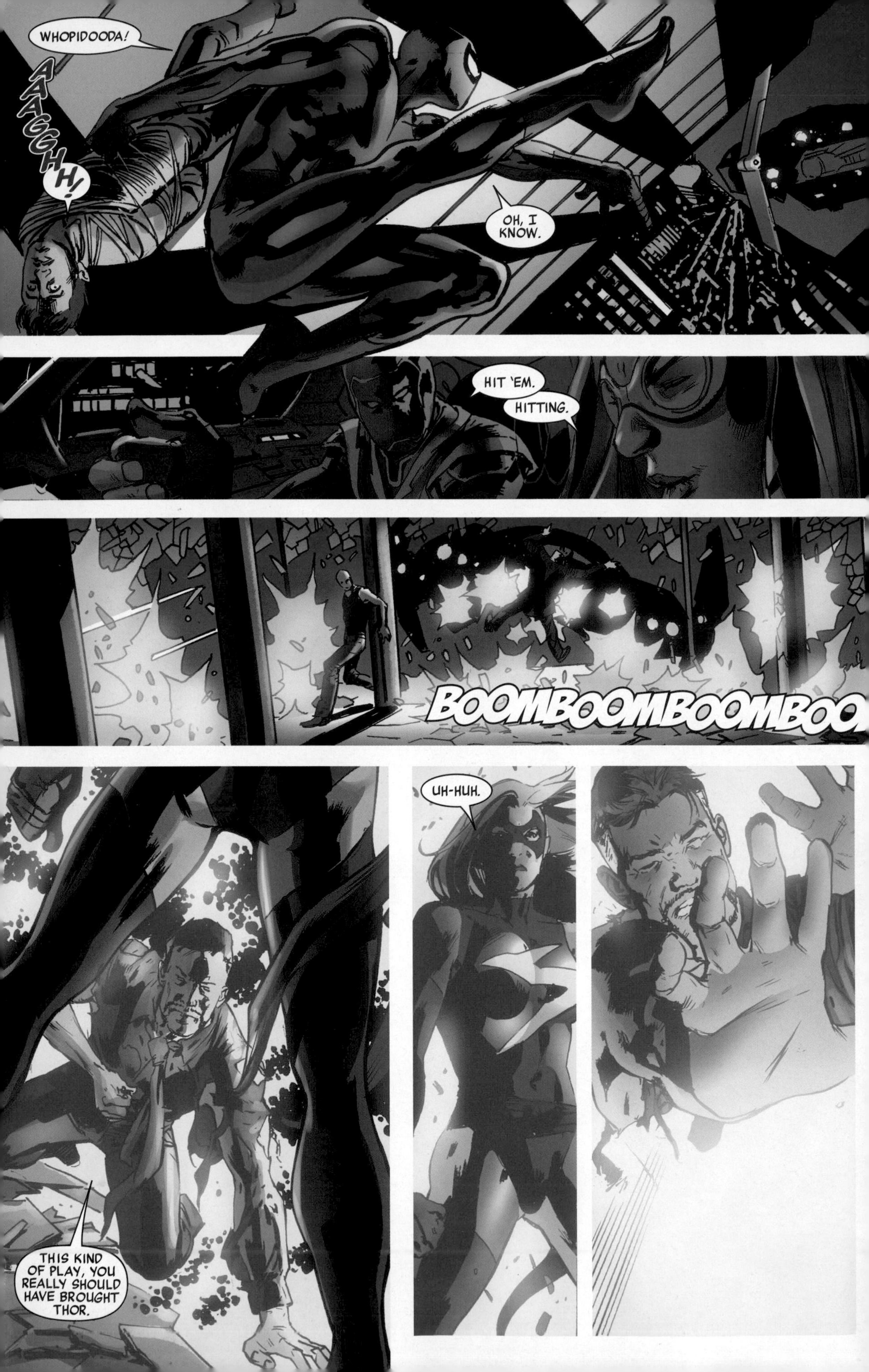

WHOPIDOODA!
AAAGGHH!
OH, I KNOW.
HIT 'EM.
HITTING.
BOOMBOOMBOOMBOO
UH-HUH.
THIS KIND OF PLAY, YOU REALLY SHOULD HAVE BROUGHT THOR.

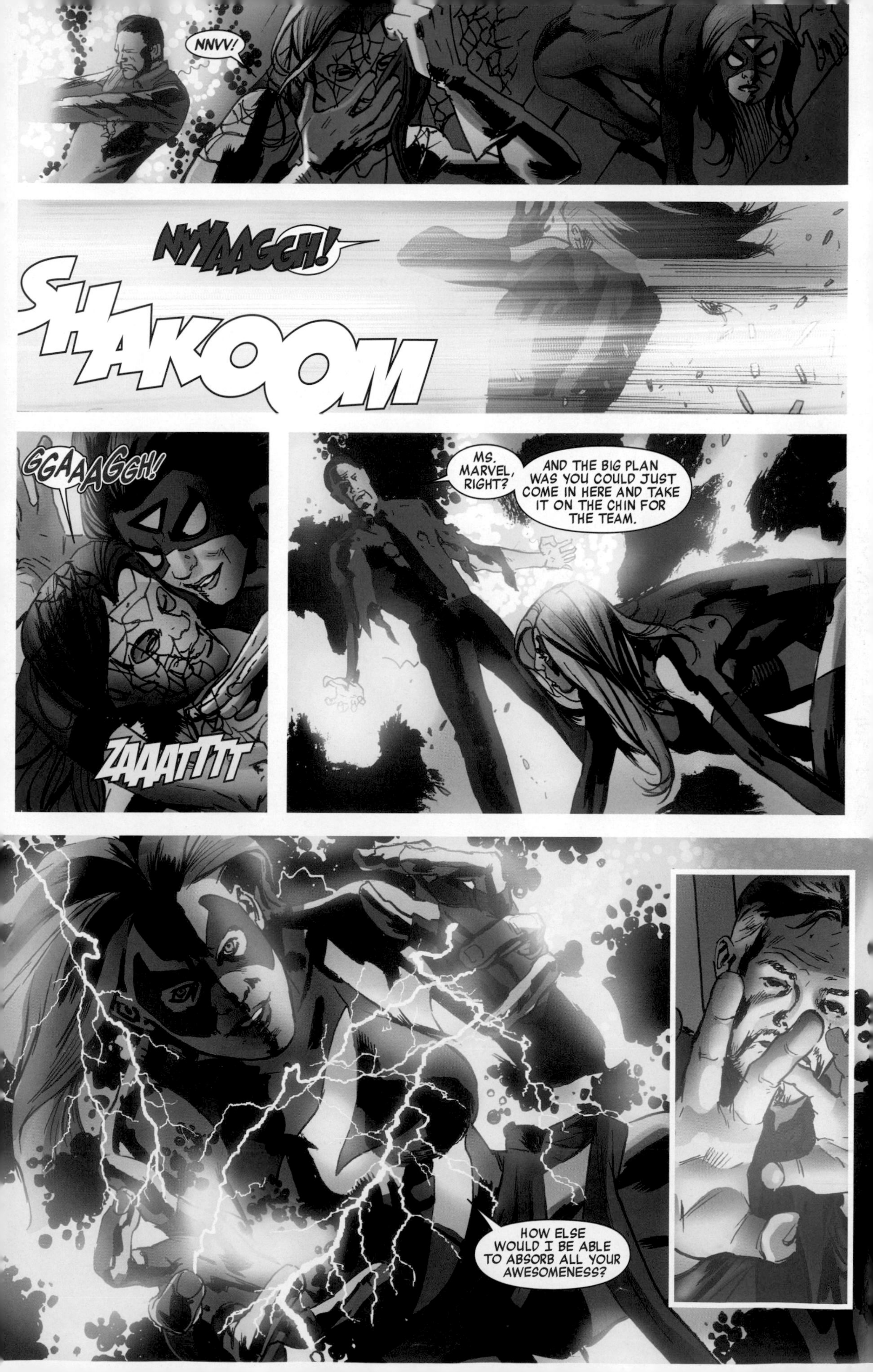
NNVV!
NYYAAGGH!
SHAKOOM
GGAAAAGGH!
ZAAATTTT
MS. MARVEL, RIGHT?
AND THE BIG PLAN WAS YOU COULD JUST COME IN HERE AND TAKE IT ON THE CHIN FOR THE TEAM.
HOW ELSE WOULD I BE ABLE TO ABSORB ALL YOUR AWESOMENESS?

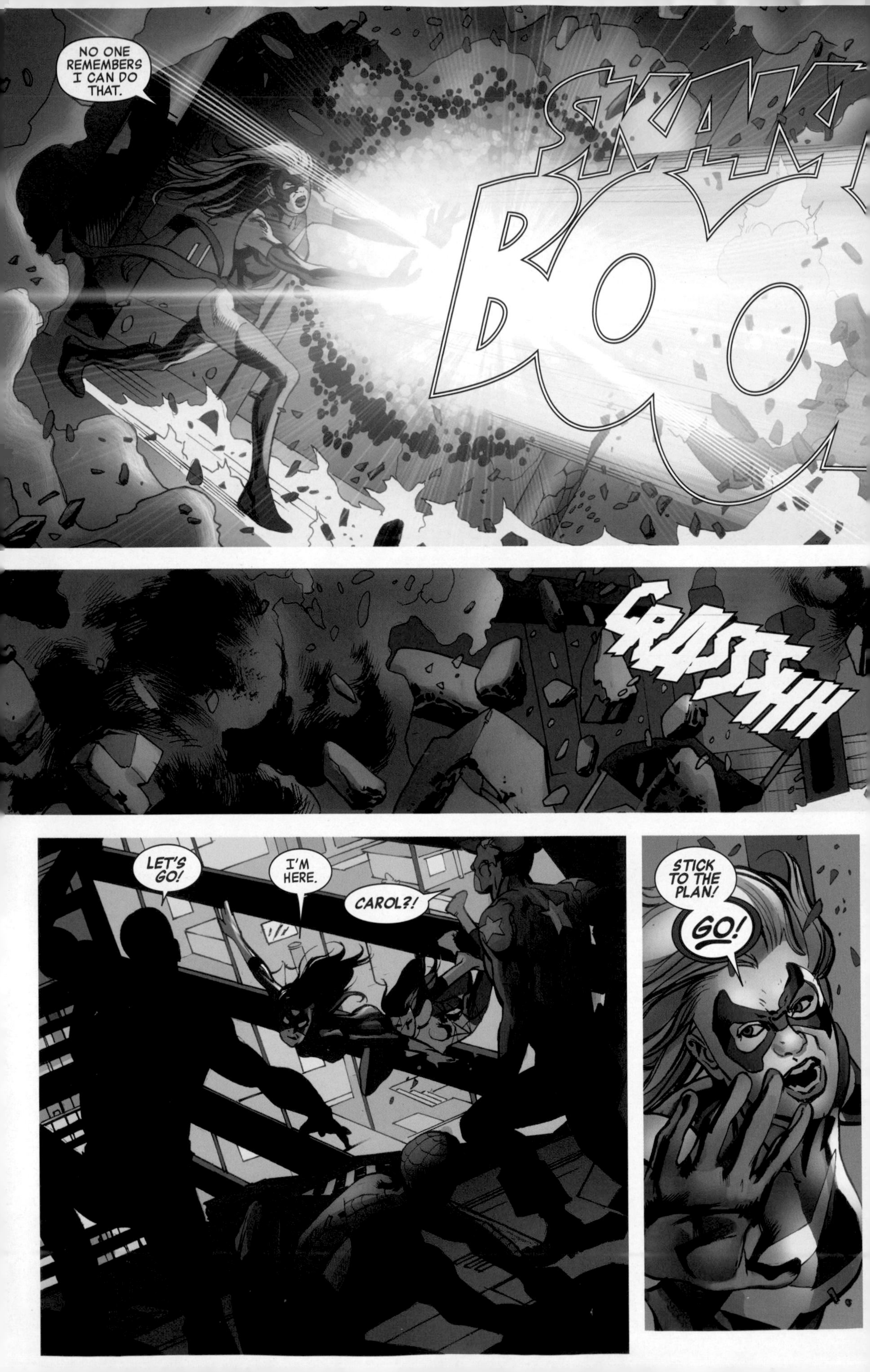
NO ONE REMEMBERS I CAN DO THAT.
LET'S GO!
I'M HERE.
CAROL?!
STICK TO THE PLAN!
GO!

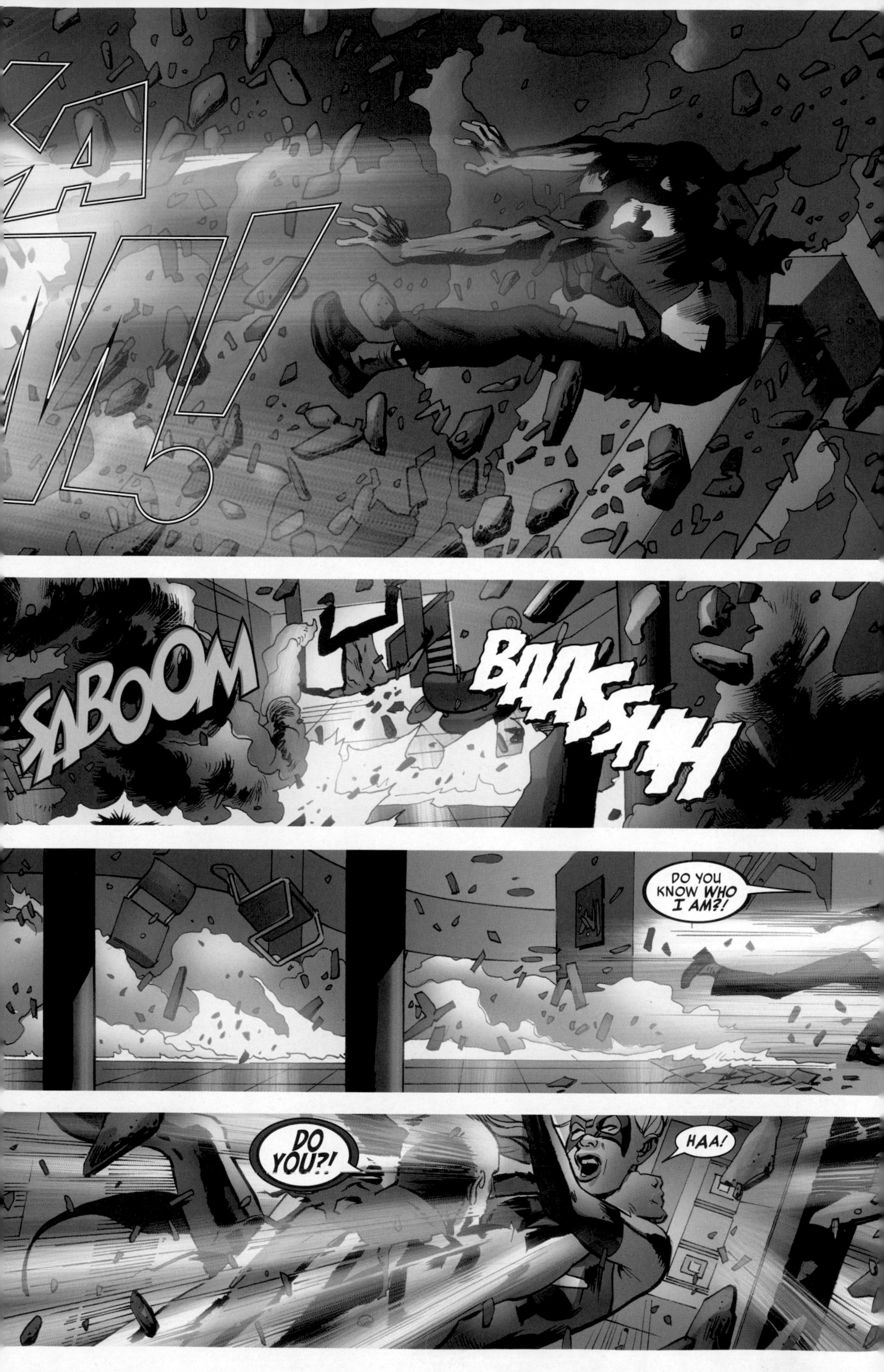
SABOOM
BAASHHH
DO YOU KNOW WHO I AM?!
DO YOU?!
HAA!

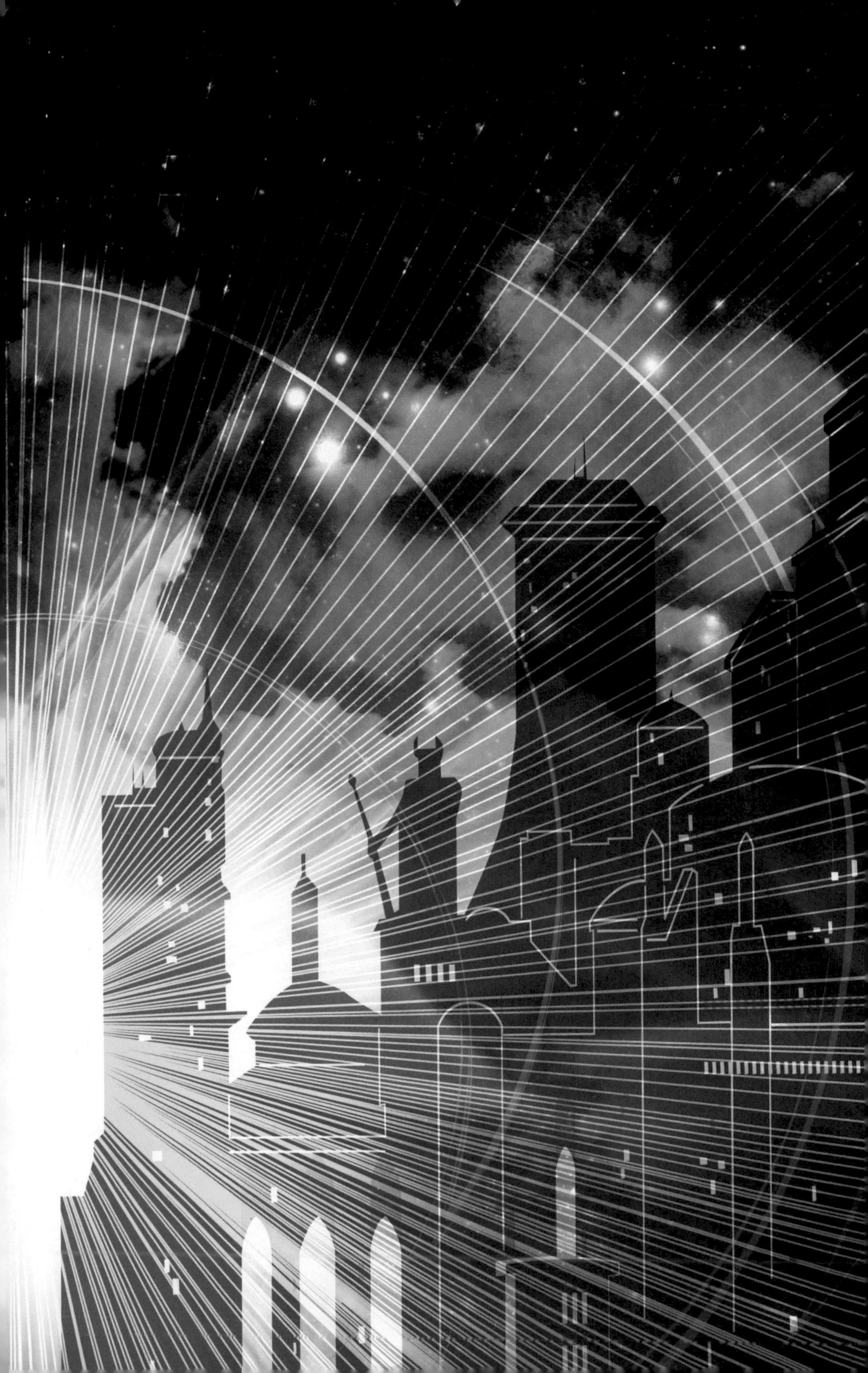

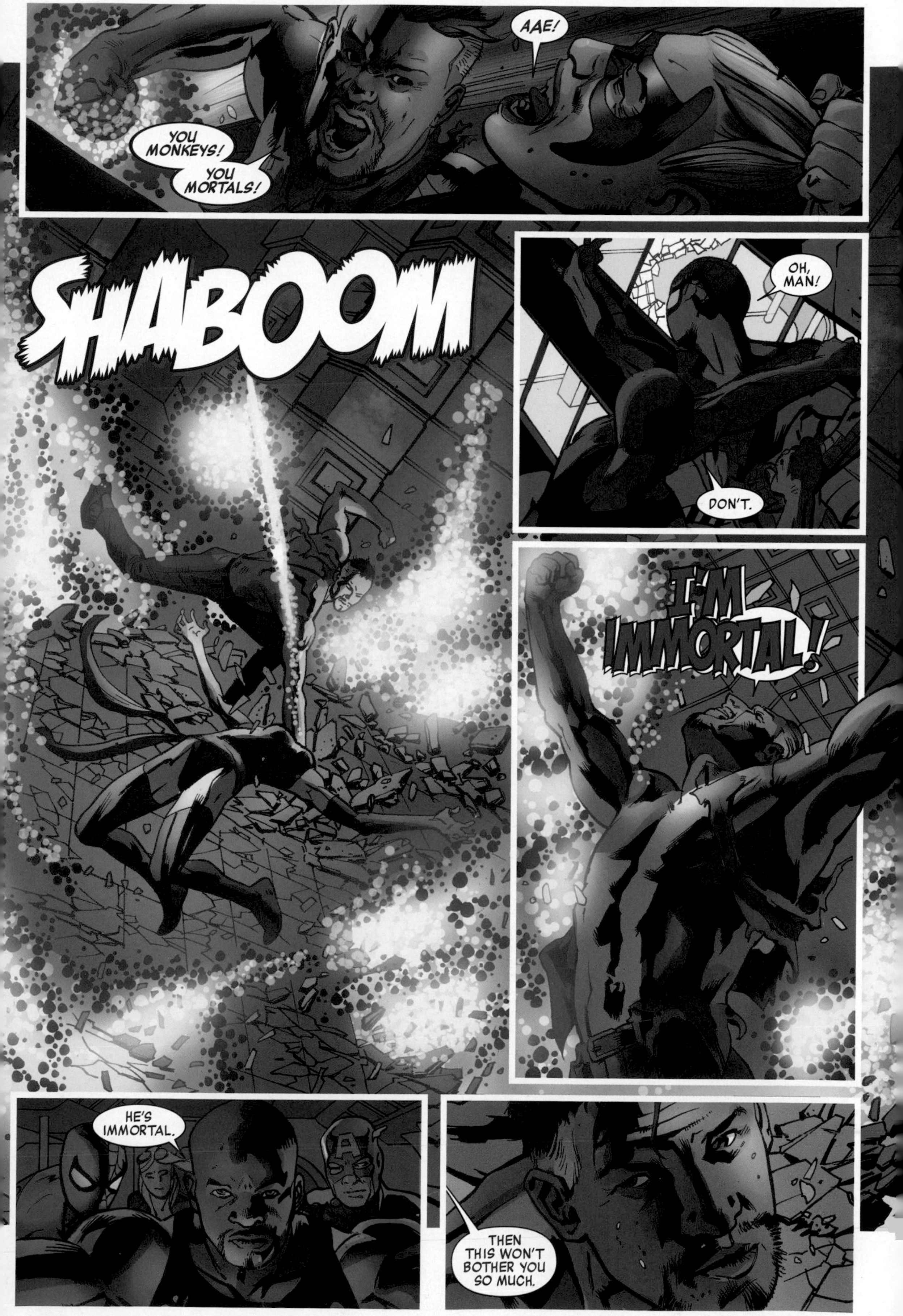
AAE!
YOU MONKEYS!
YOU MORTALS!
SHABOOM
OH, MAN!
DON'T.
I'M IMMORTAL!
HE'S IMMORTAL.
THEN THIS WON'T BOTHER YOU SO MUCH.

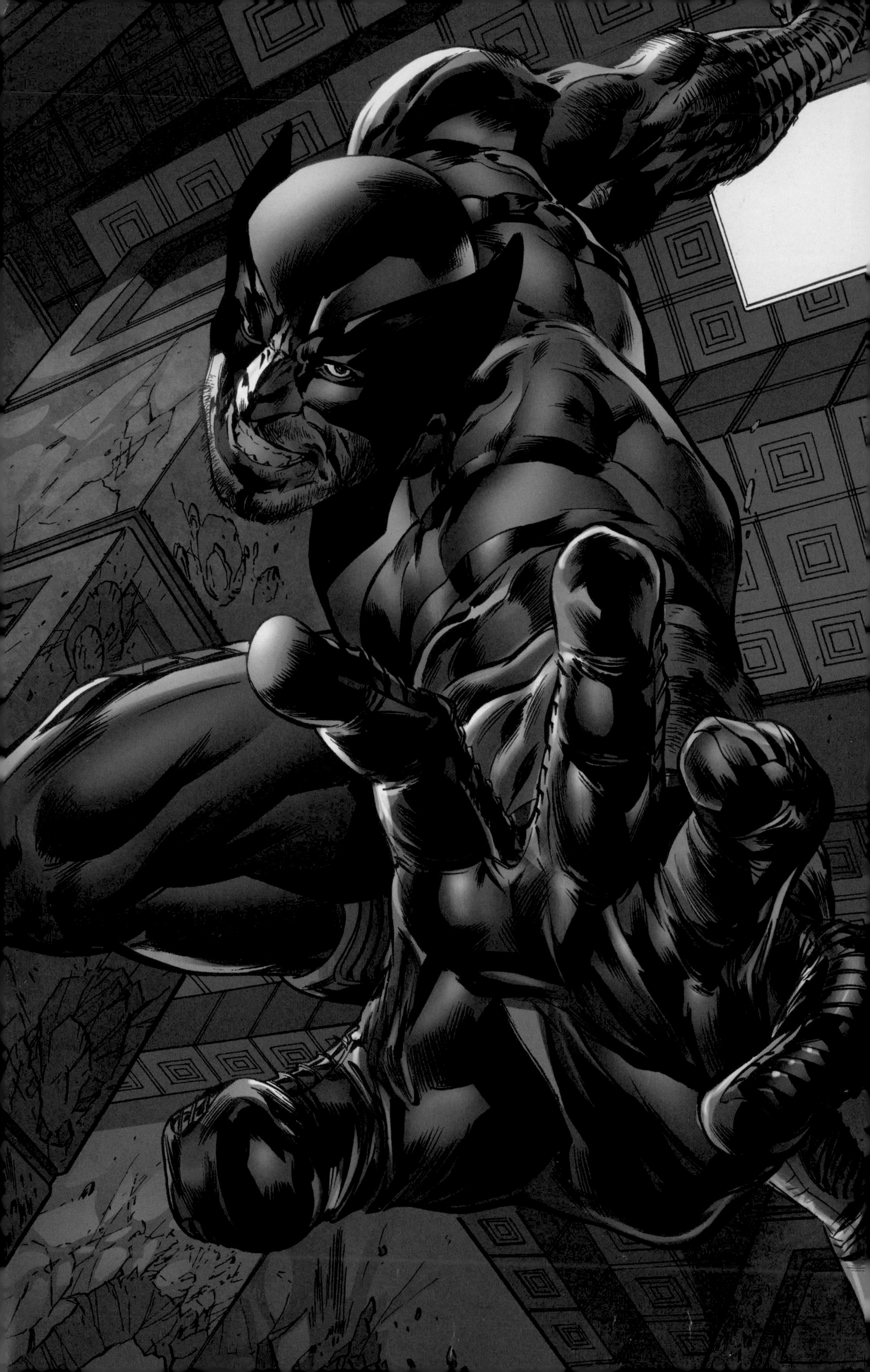

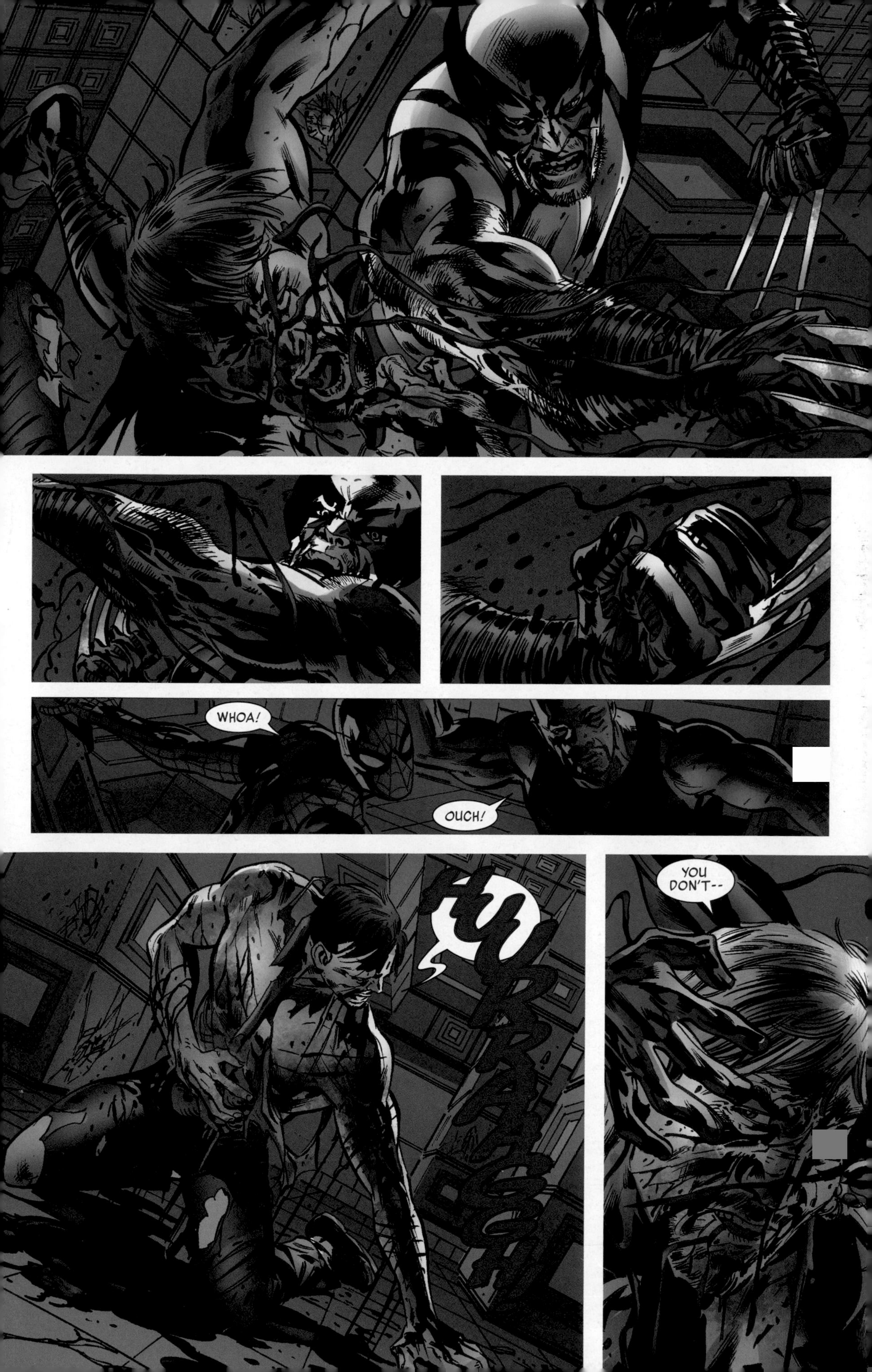
WHOA!
OUCH!
HYAAAAH
YOU DON'T--

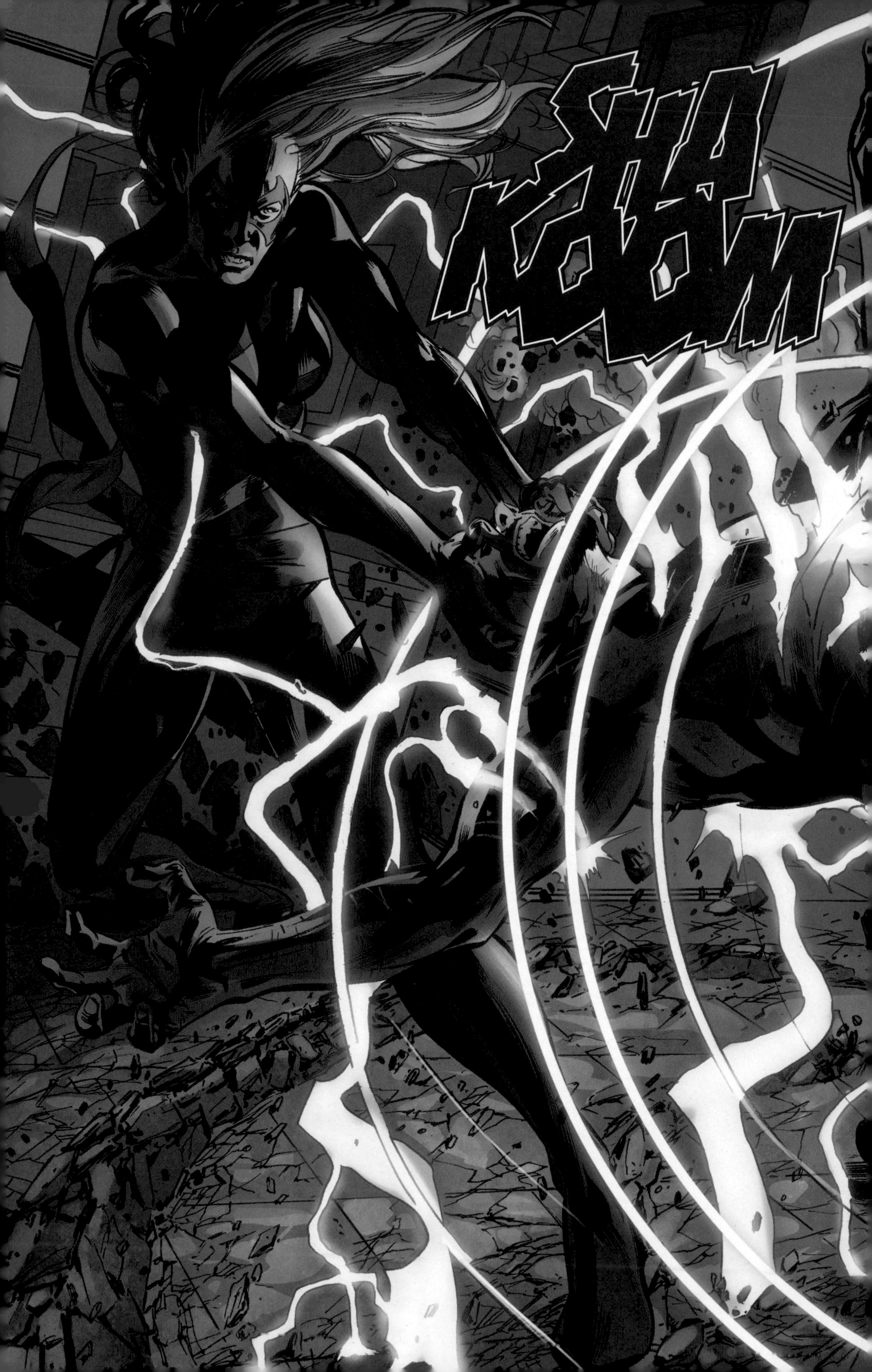

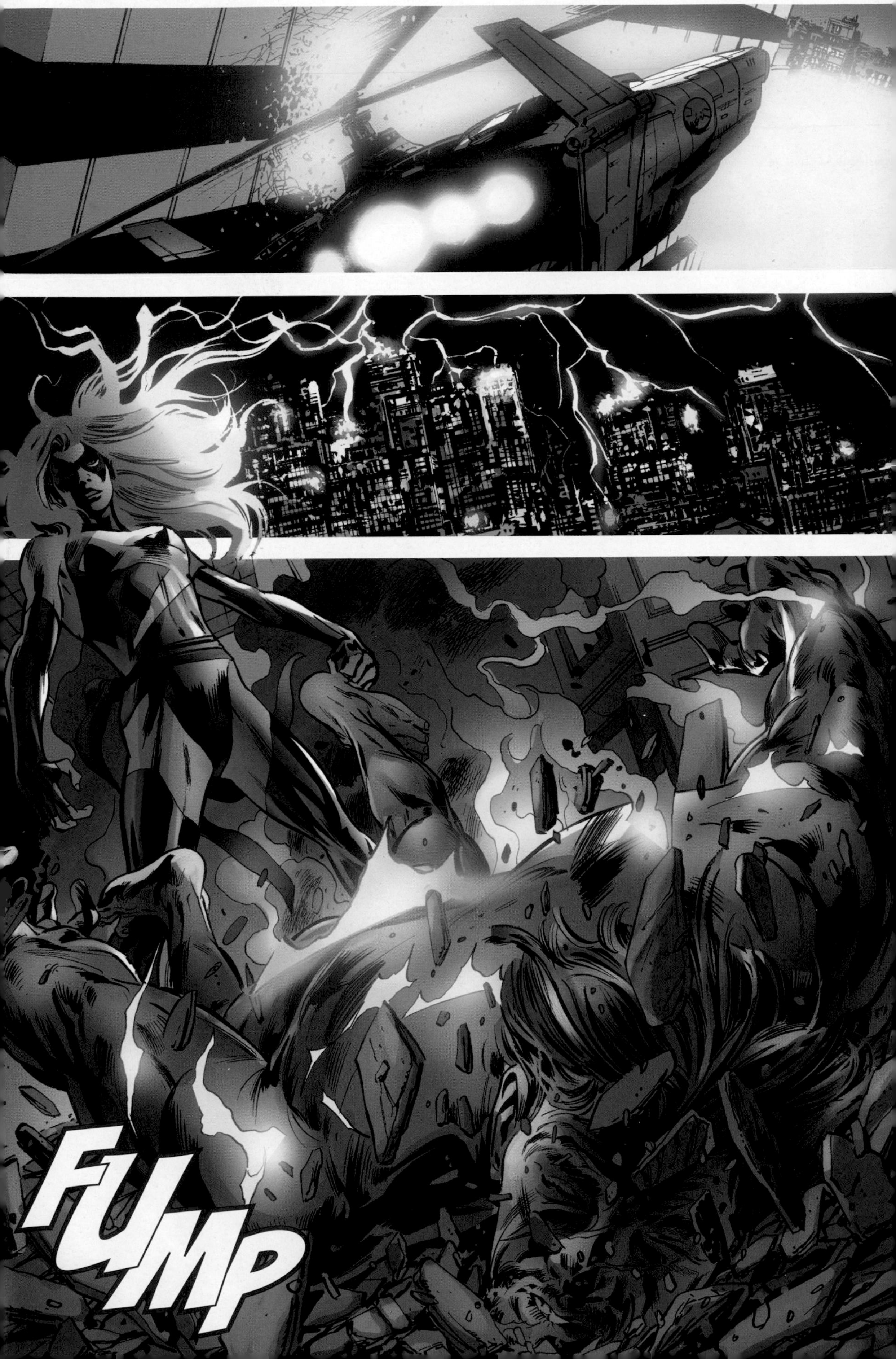
FUMP

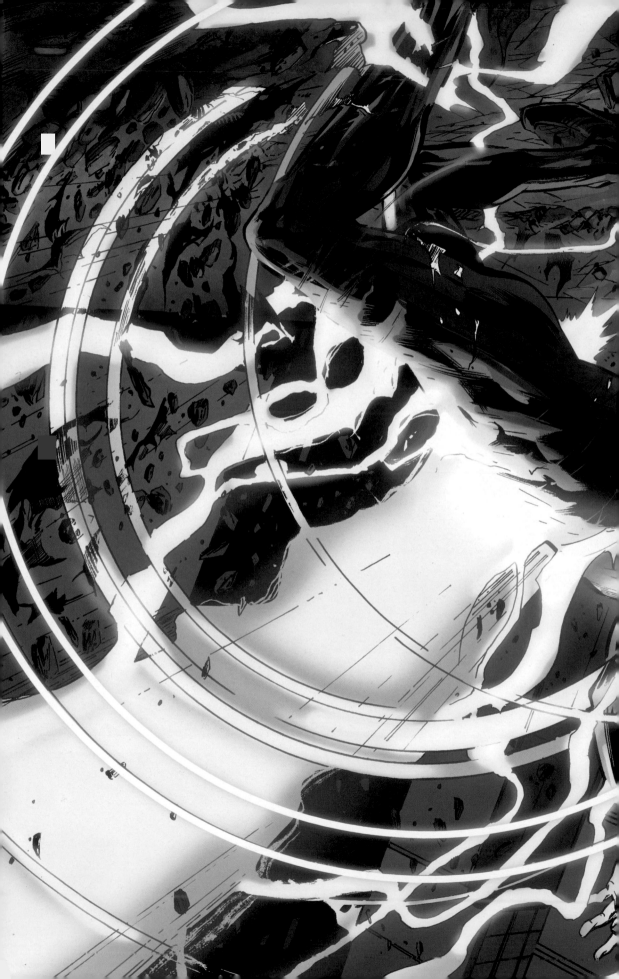

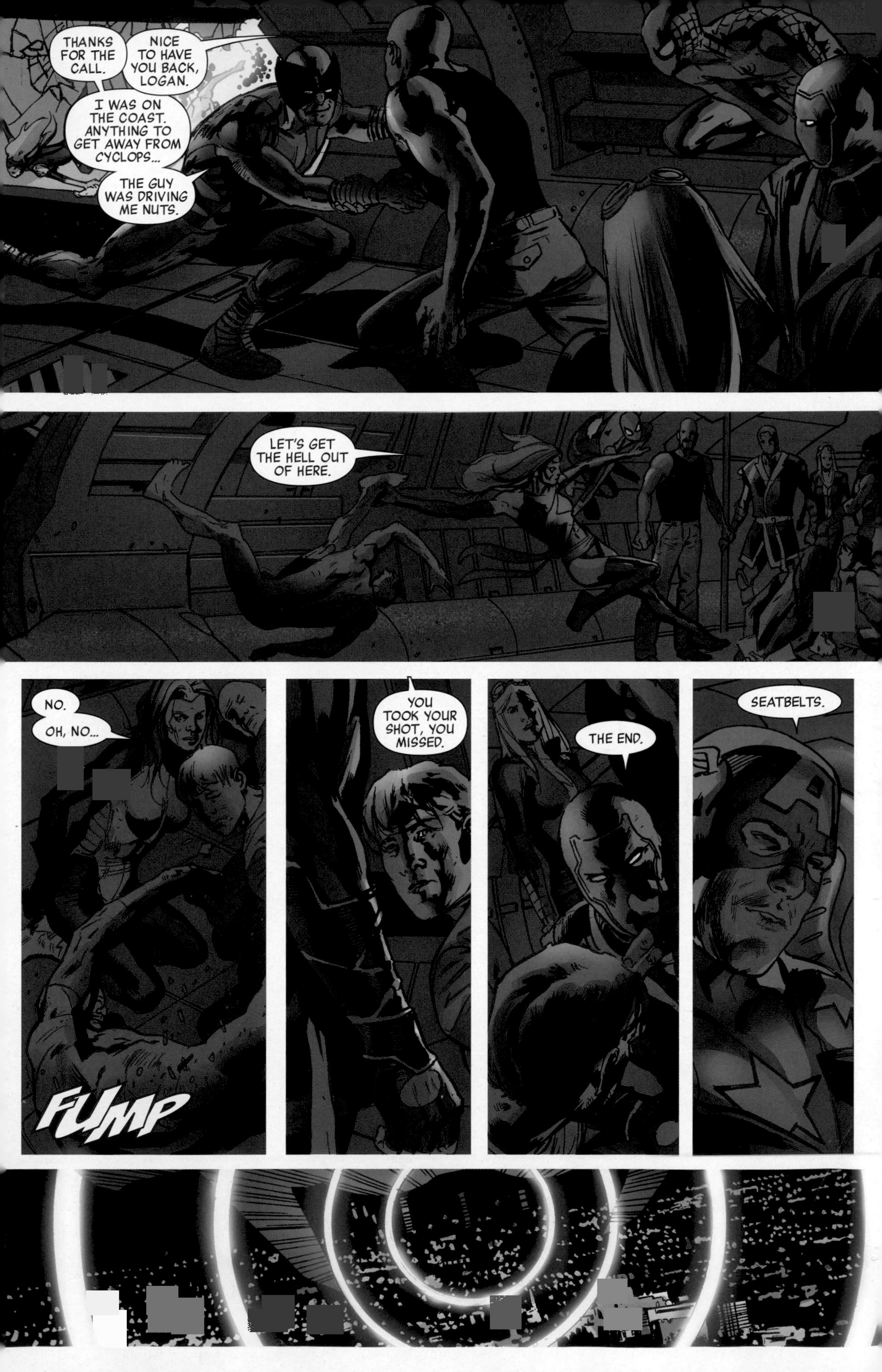
THANKS FOR THE CALL.
NICE TO HAVE YOU BACK, LOGAN.
I WAS ON THE COAST. ANYTHING TO GET AWAY FROM CYCLOPS...
THE GUY WAS DRIVING ME NUTS.
LET'S GET THE HELL OUT OF HERE.
NO.
OH, NO...
FUMP
YOU TOOK YOUR SHOT, YOU MISSED.
THE END.
SEATBELTS.

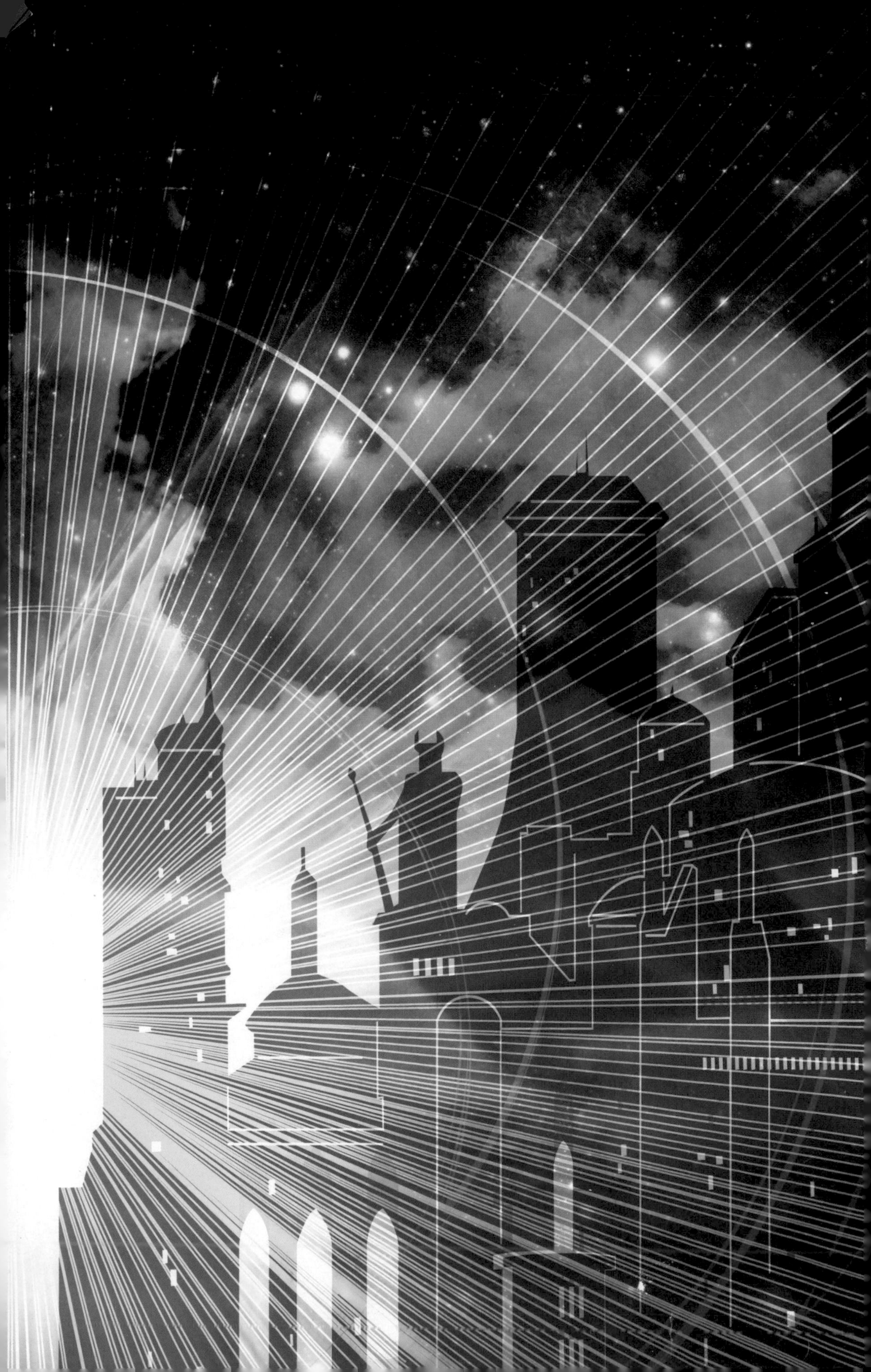

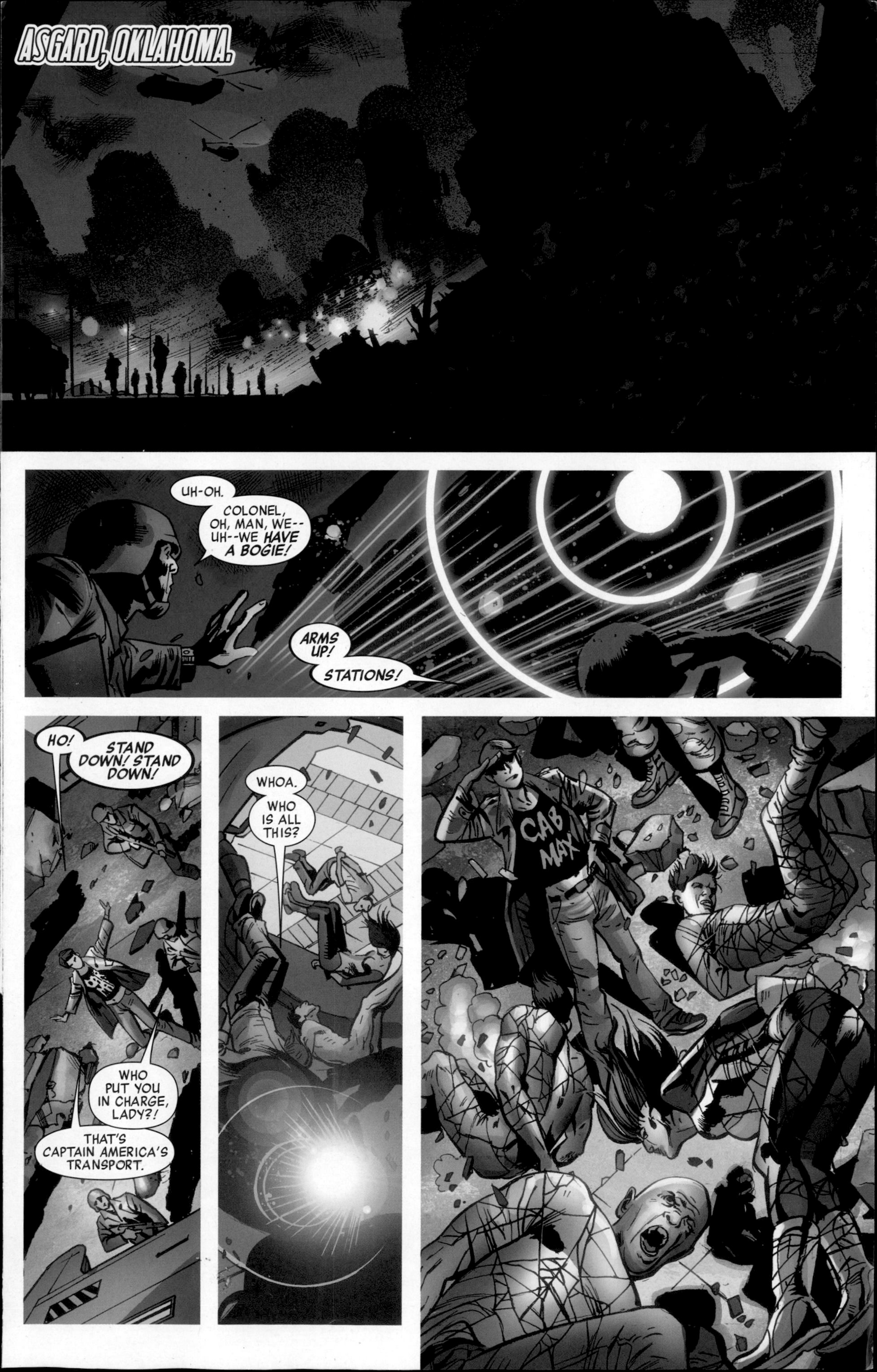
ASGARD, OKLAHOMA.
UH-OH.
COLONEL, OH, MAN, WE-- UH--WE HAVE A BOGIE!
ARMS UP!
STATIONS!
HO!
STAND DOWN! STAND DOWN!
WHO PUT YOU IN CHARGE, LADY?!
THAT'S CAPTAIN AMERICA'S TRANSPORT.
WHOA.
WHO IS ALL THIS?
CAB MAX

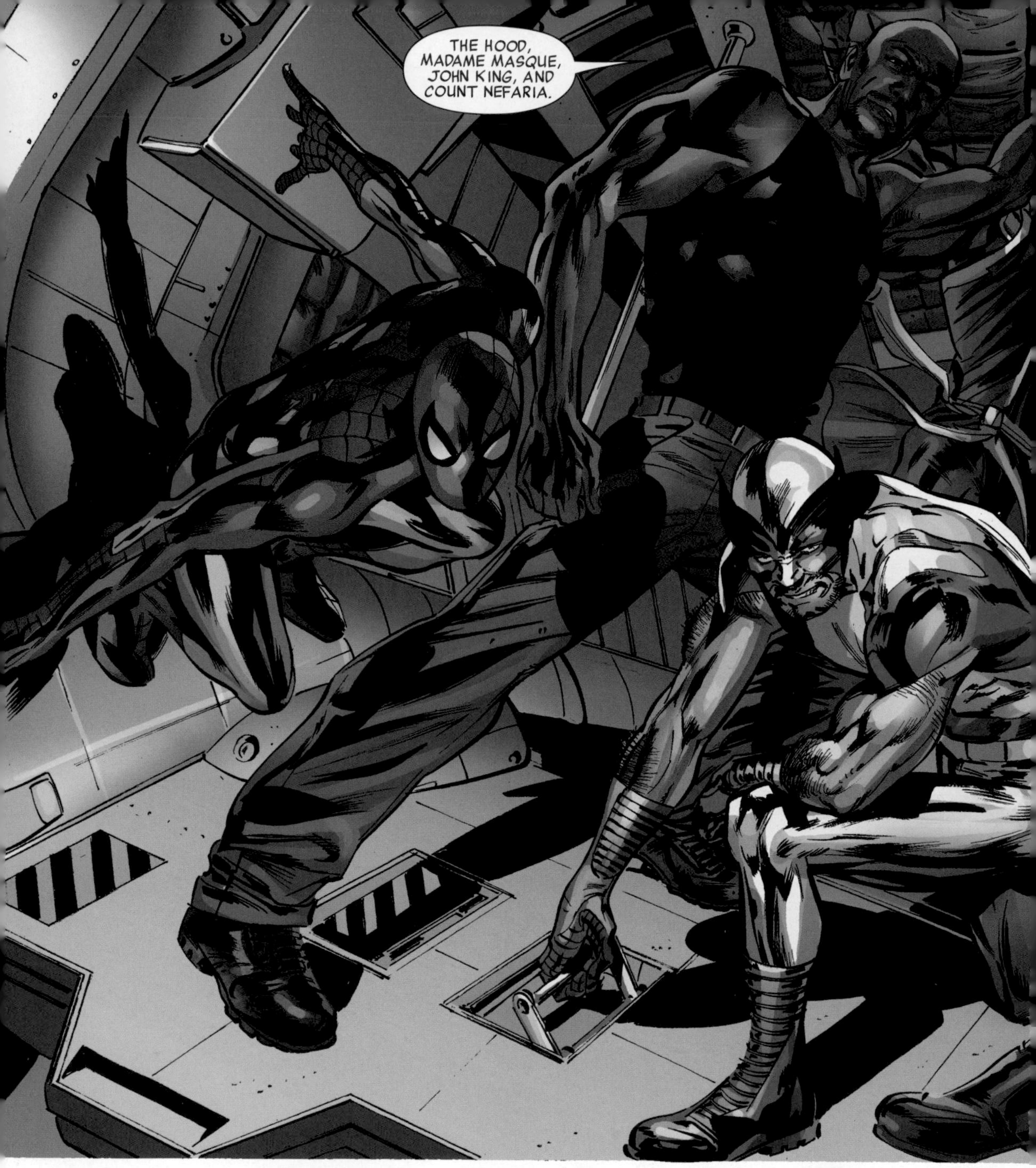
THE HOOD, MADAME MASQUE, JOHN KING, AND COUNT NEFARIA.

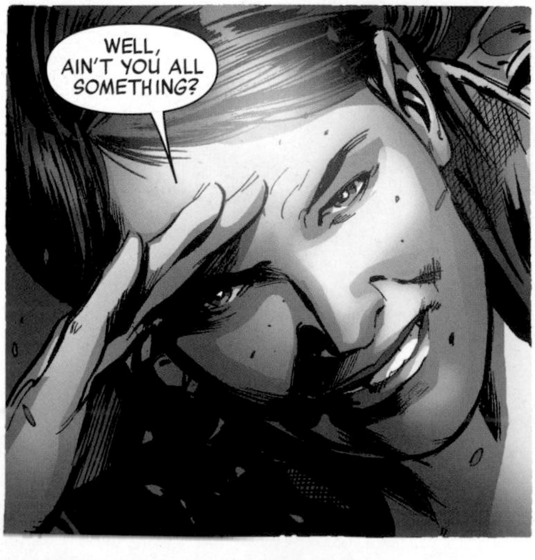
WELL, AIN'T YOU ALL SOMETHING?

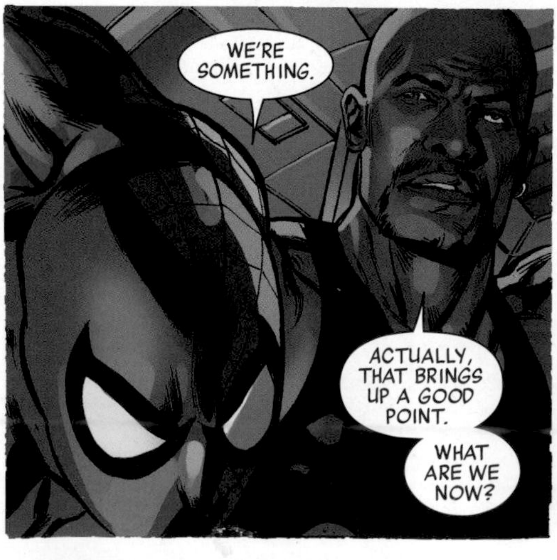
WE'RE SOMETHING.
ACTUALLY, THAT BRINGS UP A GOOD POINT.
WHAT ARE WE NOW?

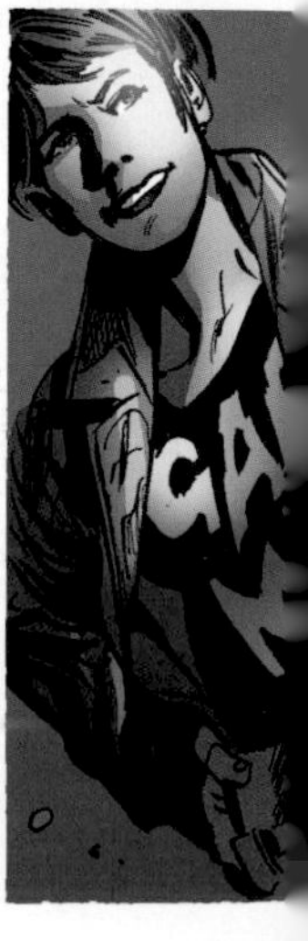

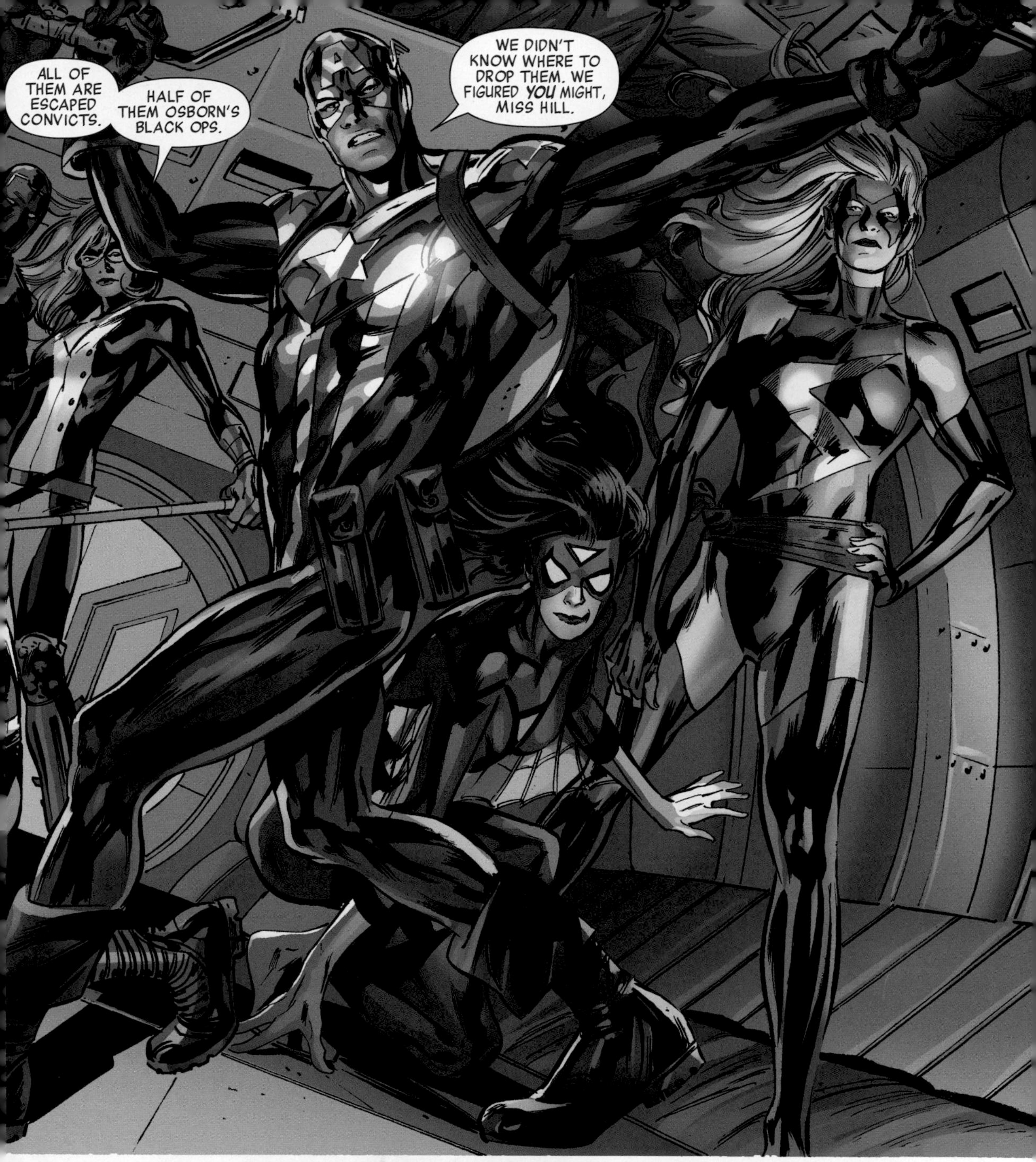
ALL OF THEM ARE ESCAPED CONVICTS.
HALF OF THEM OSBORN'S BLACK OPS.
WE DIDN'T KNOW WHERE TO DROP THEM. WE FIGURED **YOU** MIGHT, MISS HILL.

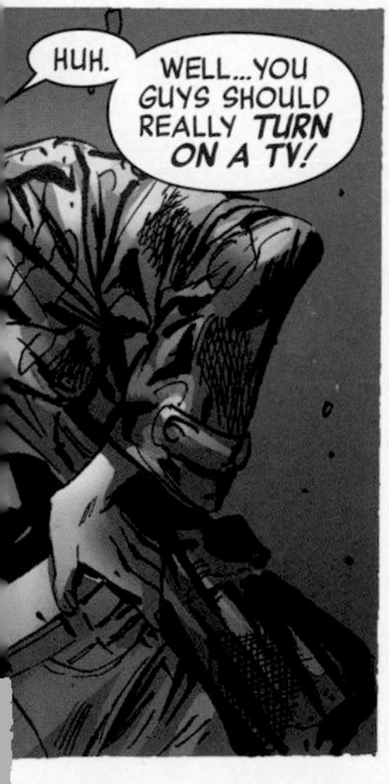
HUH.
WELL...YOU GUYS SHOULD REALLY **TURN ON A TV!**

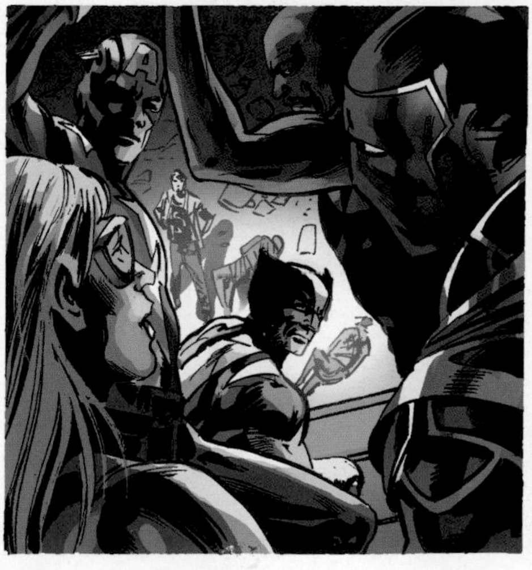

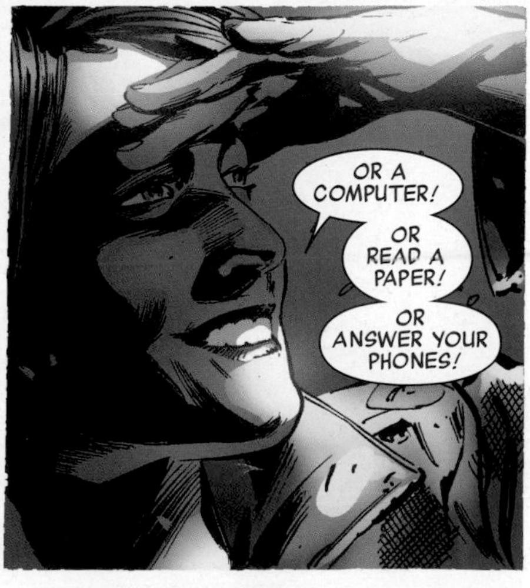
OR A COMPUTER!
OR READ A PAPER!
OR ANSWER YOUR PHONES!

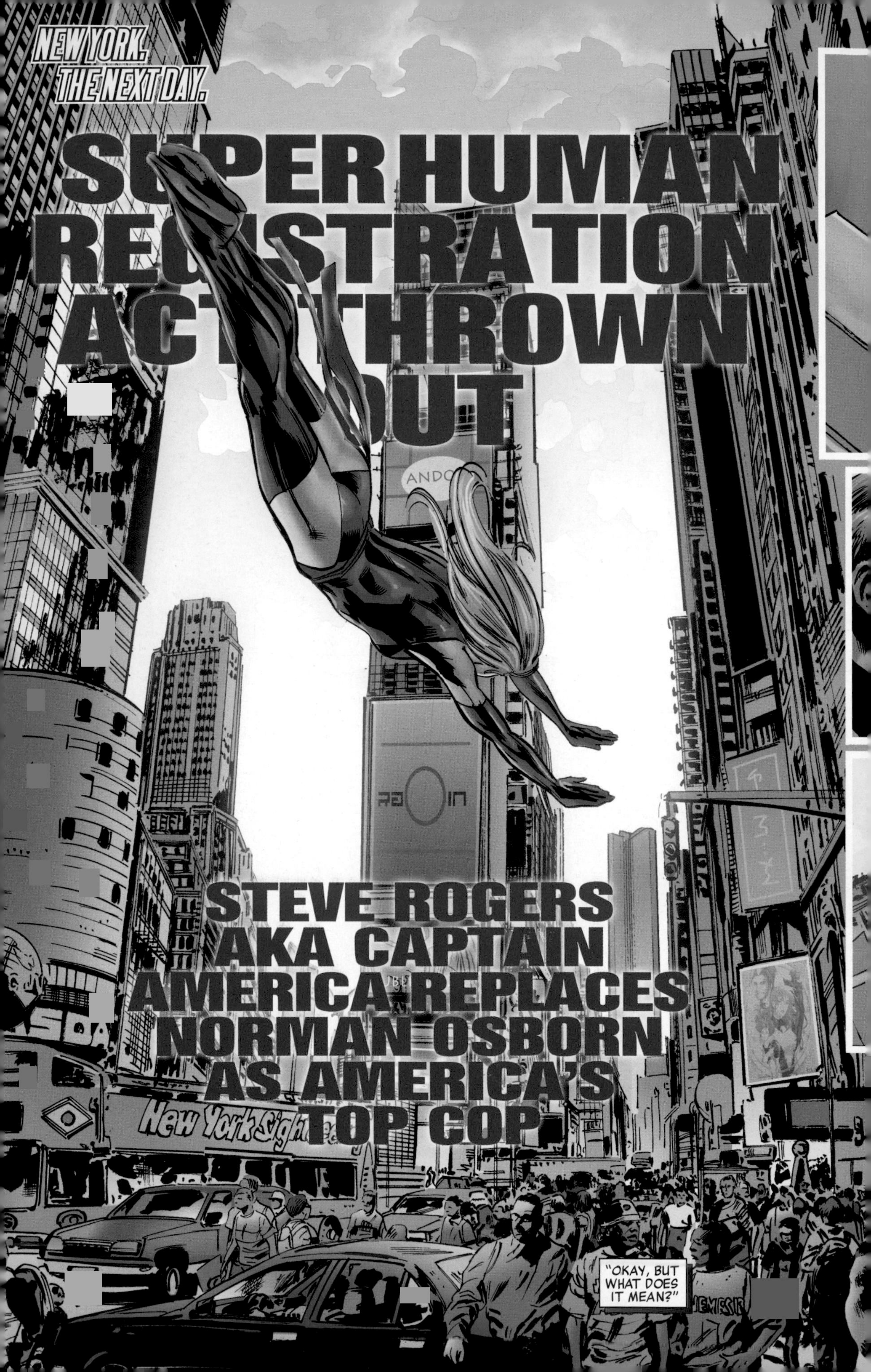
NEW YORK.
THE NEXT DAY.
SUPERHUMAN REGISTRATION ACT THROWN OUT
STEVE ROGERS AKA CAPTAIN AMERICA REPLACES NORMAN OSBORN AS AMERICA'S TOP COP
"OKAY, BUT WHAT DOES IT MEAN?"

IT MEANS IT'S OVER.

THE PRESIDENT OF THE UNITED STATES TOOK THE SUPERHUMAN REGISTRATION ACT AND HE TOSSED IT.

IT'S. DONE.

JUST LIKE *THAT?*

HE ASKED ME TO BE AMERICA'S NEXT TOP COP.

I SAID I HAD A *LIST* OF DEMANDS. *THAT* WAS THE FIRST ONE.

YOU ARE ALL...FREE MEN. FREE WOMEN.

YOU'RE THE NEW NORMAN OSBORN?!

I'M THE NEW *NICK FURY.*

HA HA!

AND I CAN'T TELL YOU HOW IMPRESSED HE--WE *ALL* WERE--WITH LAST NIGHT'S LITTLE ADVENTURE.

IT WAS ABOVE AND BEYOND. THAT WAS A *BIG WIN.*

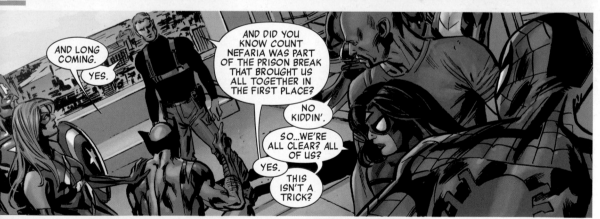

AND LONG COMING.

YES.

AND DID YOU KNOW COUNT NEFARIA WAS PART OF THE PRISON BREAK THAT BROUGHT US ALL TOGETHER IN THE FIRST PLACE?

NO KIDDIN'.

SO...WE'RE ALL CLEAR? ALL OF US?

YES.

THIS ISN'T A TRICK?

TRICK? I WOULDN'T TRICK YOU.

HE KNOWS WHERE TO FIND US.

TRUE. BUT I AM HERE TO SAY... NO MORE HIDING. IT'S OVER.

YOU WON.

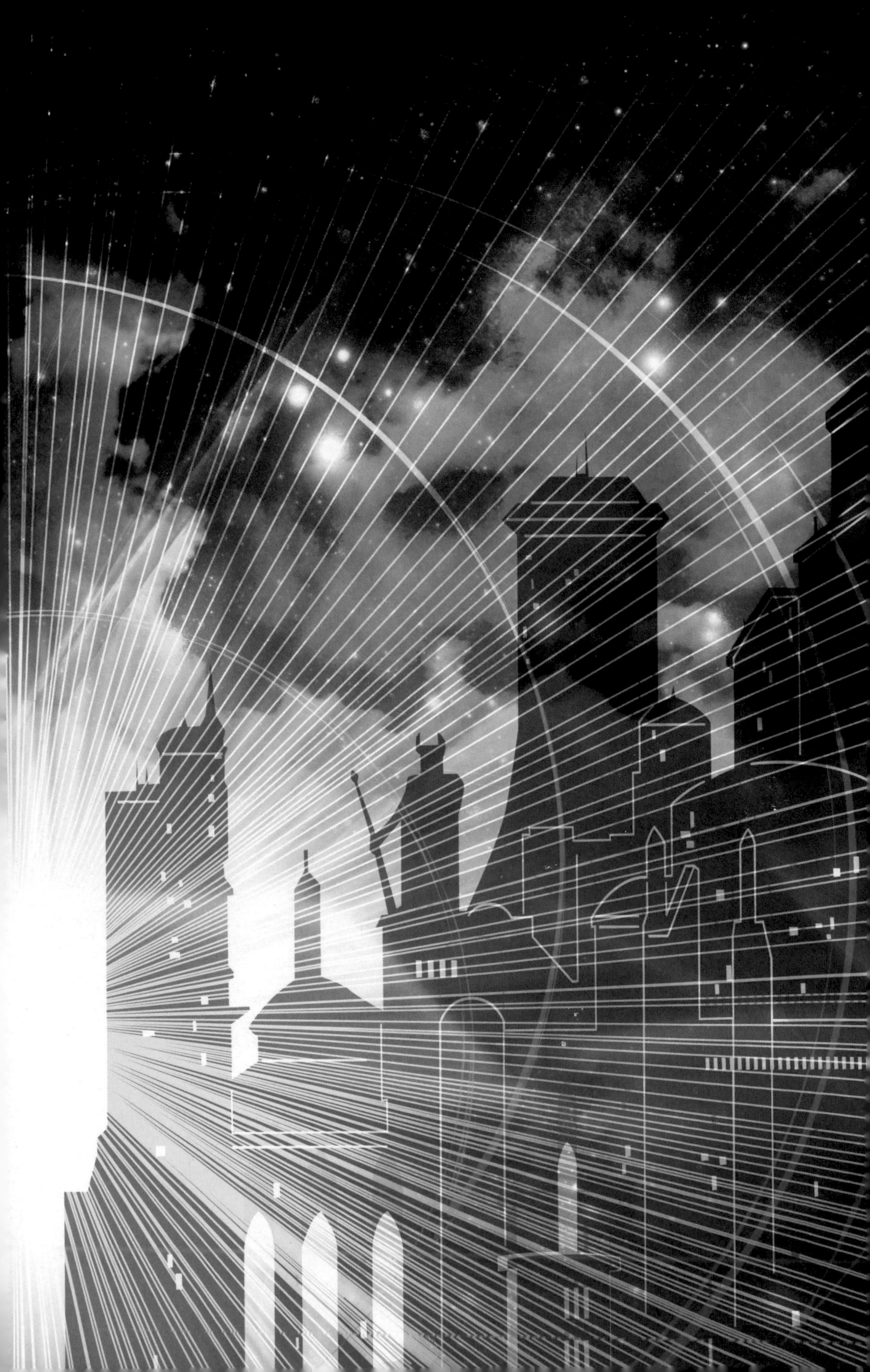

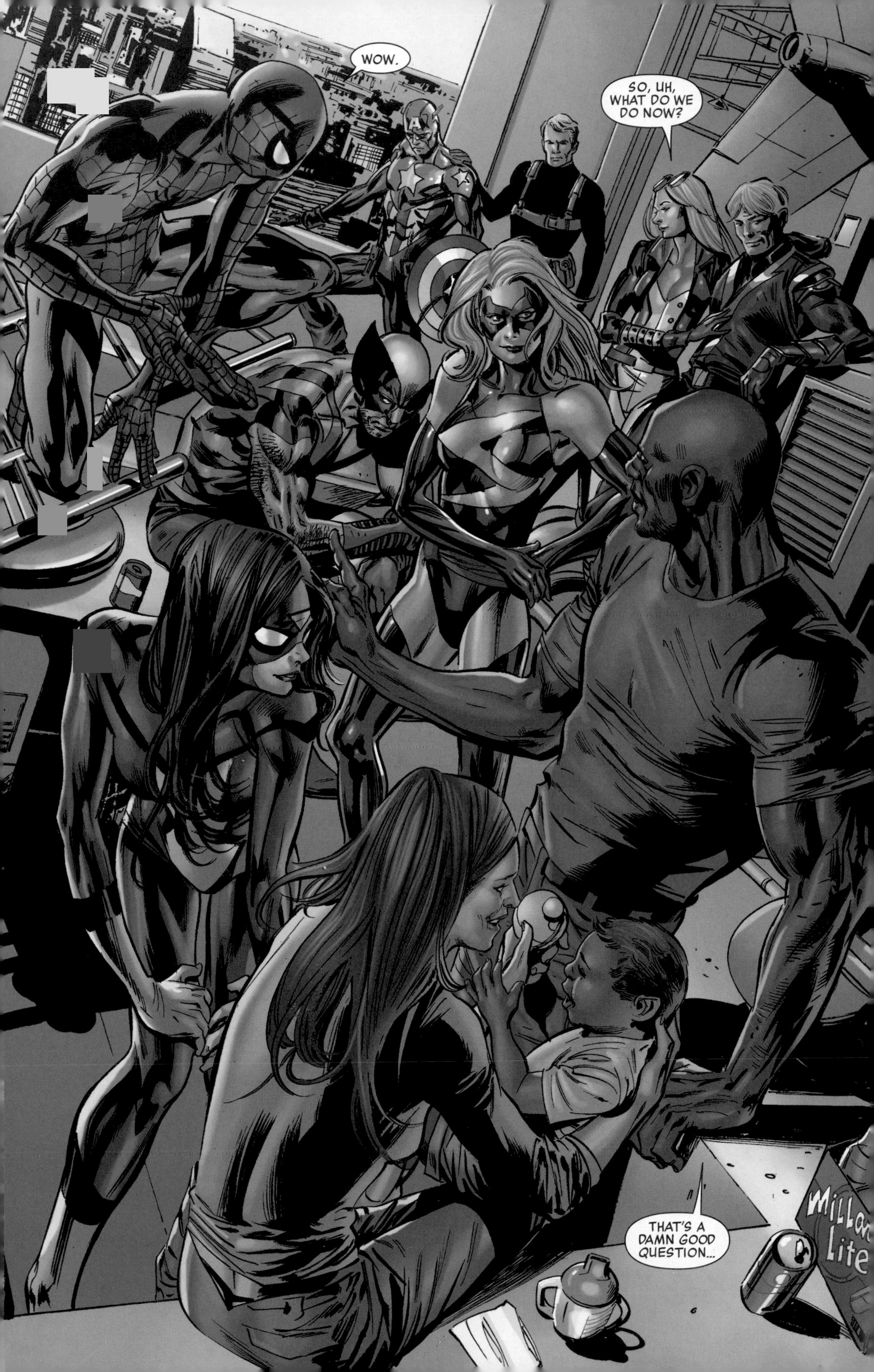
WOW.
SO, UH, WHAT DO WE DO NOW?
THAT'S A DAMN GOOD QUESTION...
Millar Lite

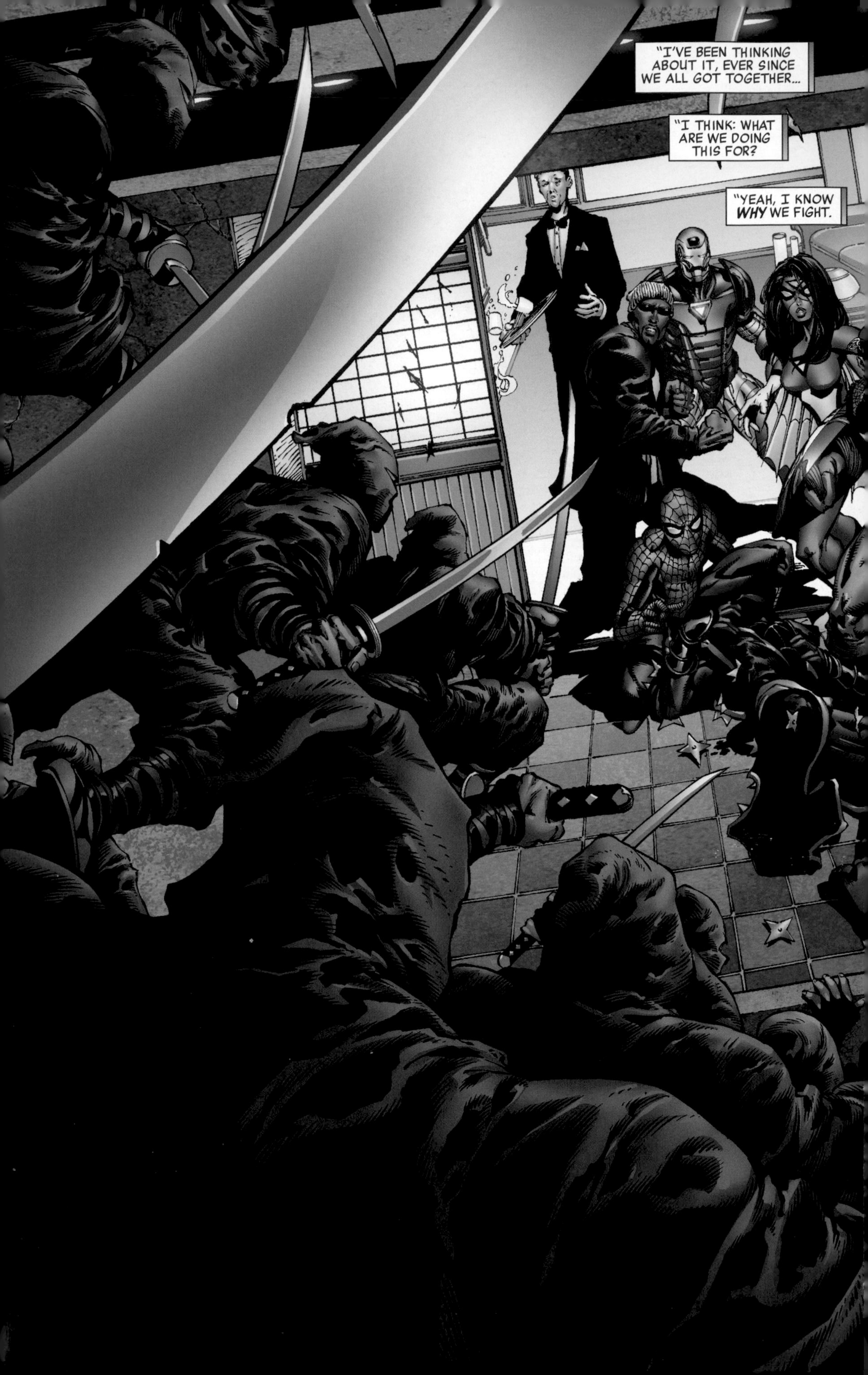

"I'VE BEEN THINKING ABOUT IT, EVER SINCE WE ALL GOT TOGETHER...
"I THINK: WHAT ARE WE DOING THIS FOR?
"YEAH, I KNOW WHY WE FIGHT.

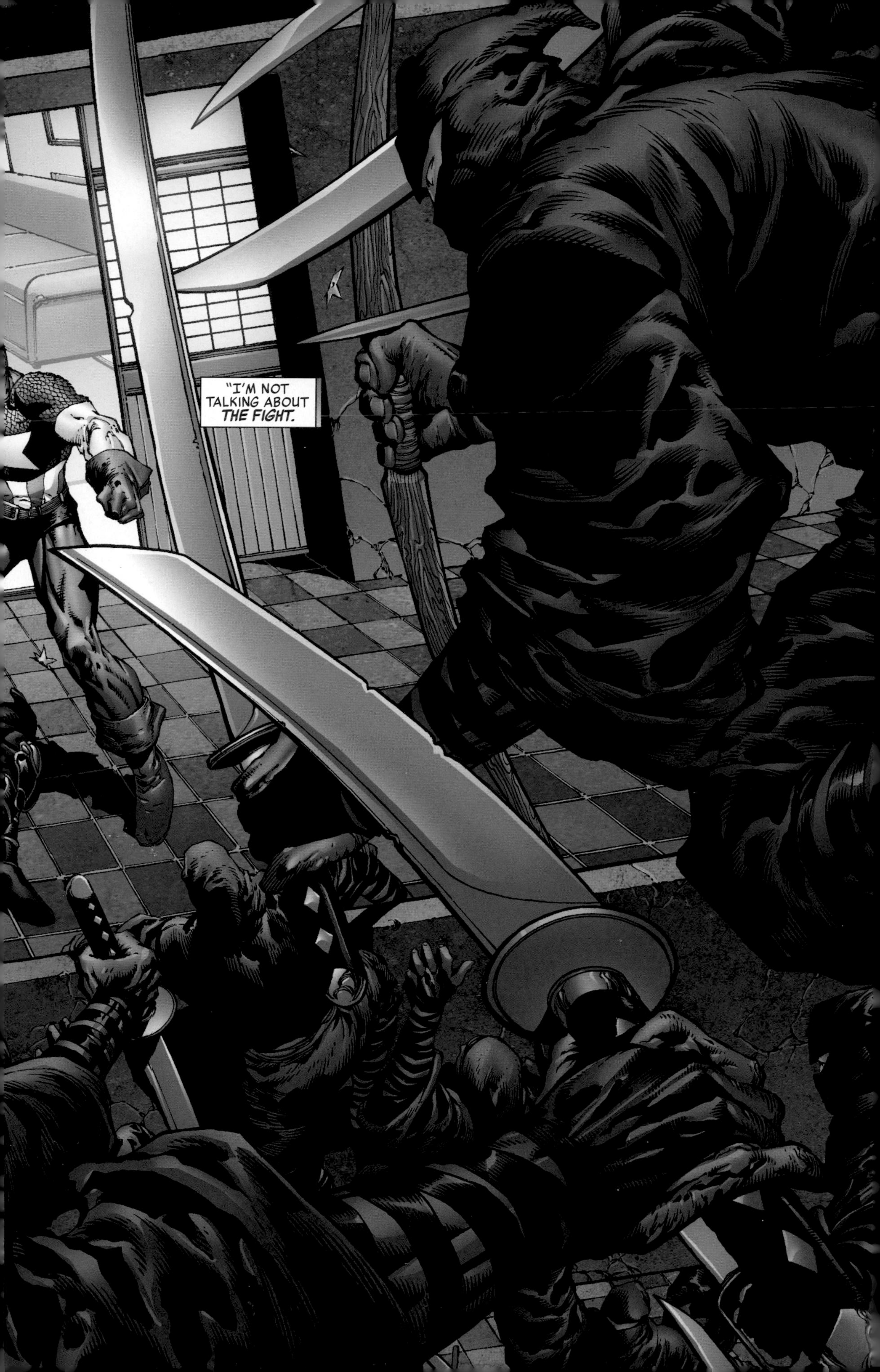
"I'M NOT TALKING ABOUT THE FIGHT.

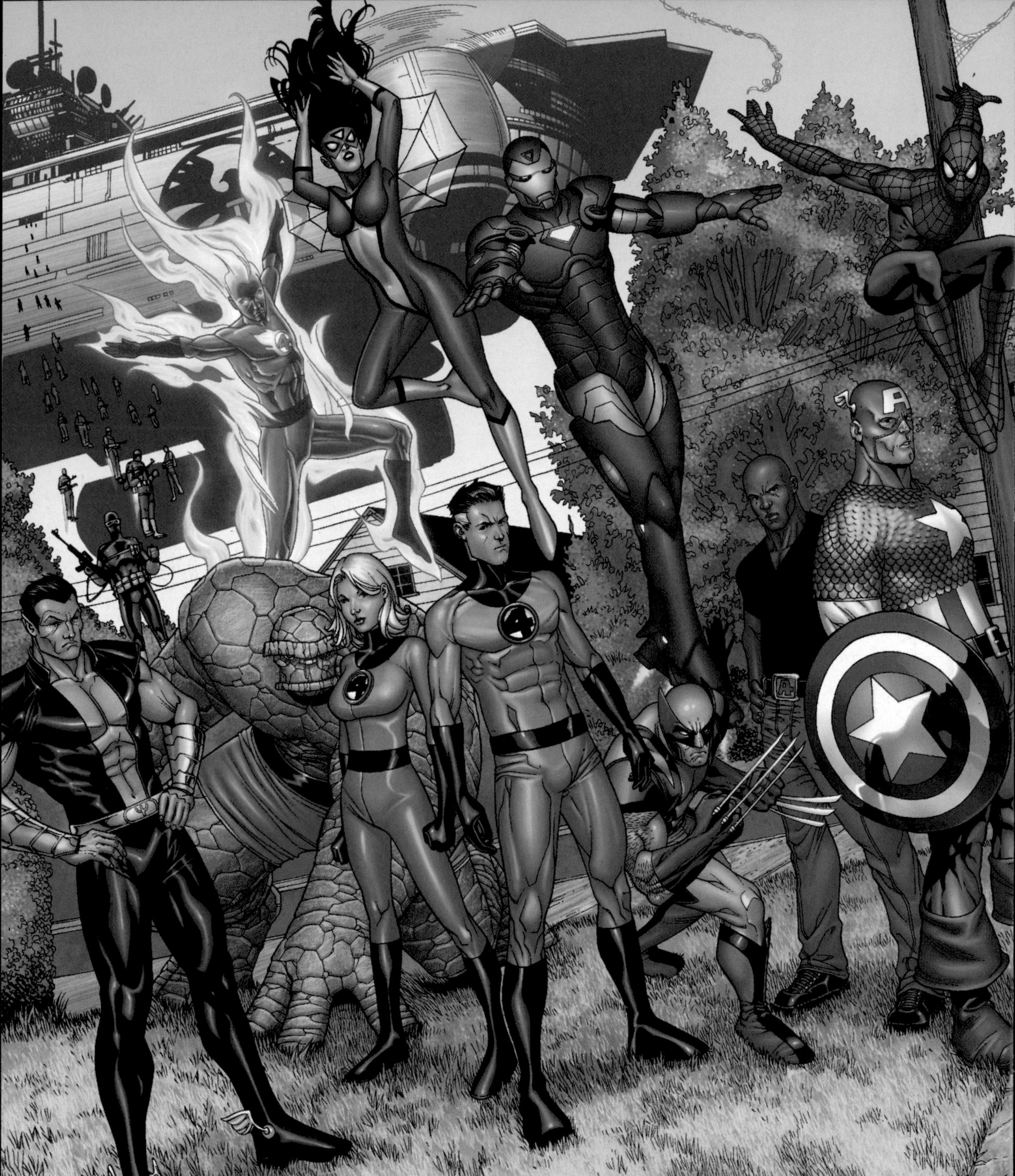

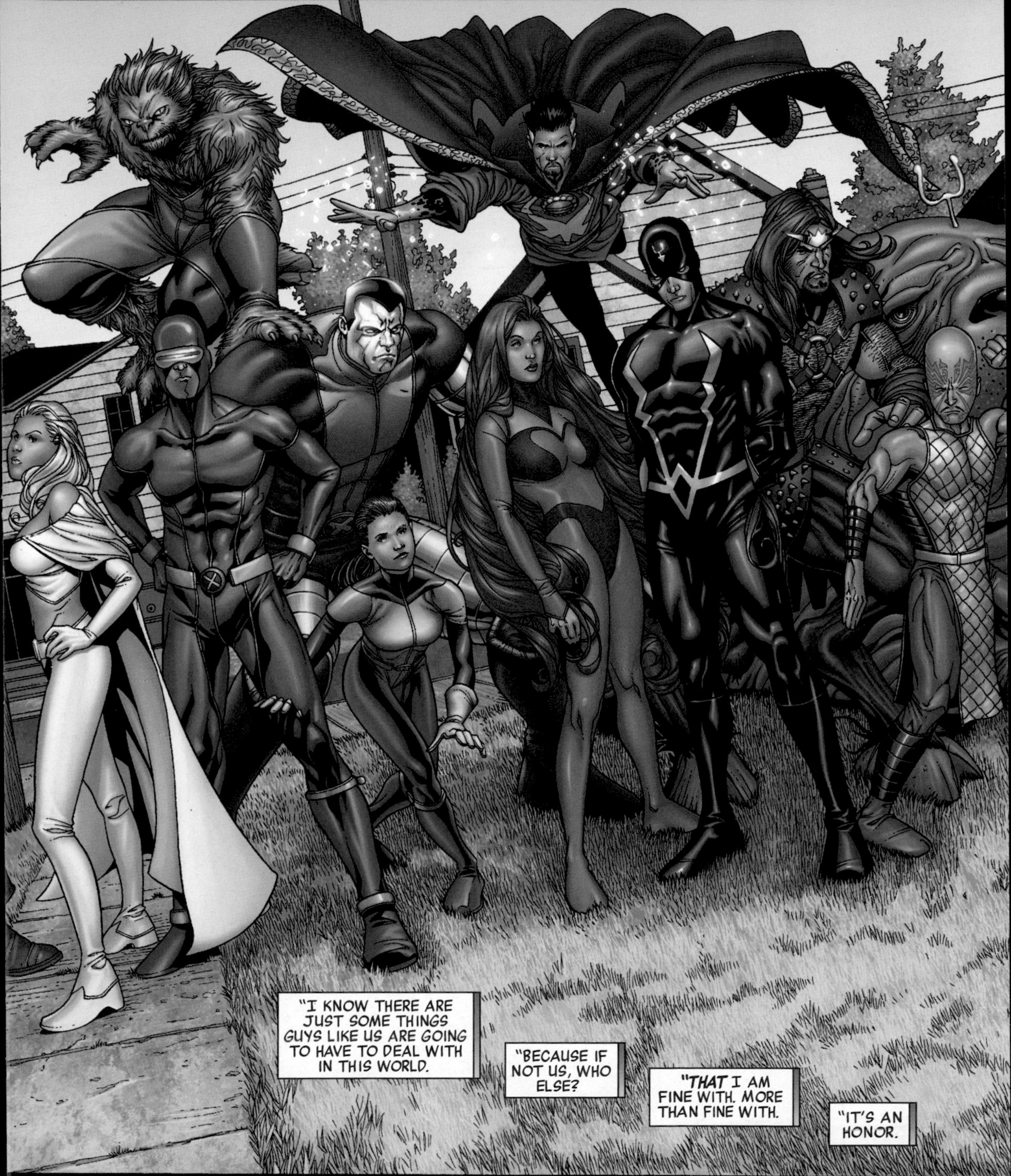
"I KNOW THERE ARE JUST SOME THINGS GUYS LIKE US ARE GOING TO HAVE TO DEAL WITH IN THIS WORLD.
"BECAUSE IF NOT US, WHO ELSE?
"THAT I AM FINE WITH. MORE THAN FINE WITH.
"IT'S AN HONOR.

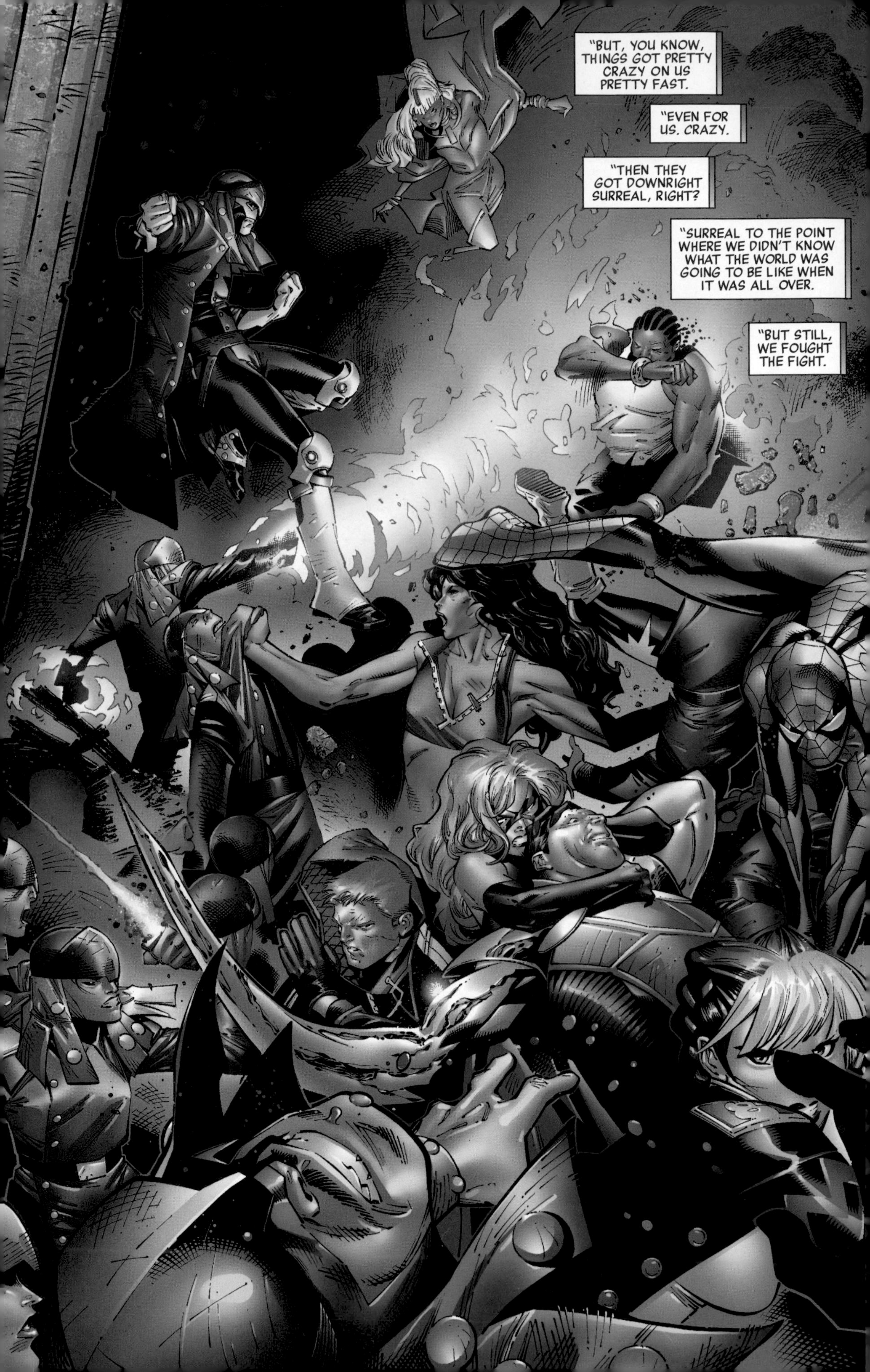
"BUT, YOU KNOW, THINGS GOT PRETTY CRAZY ON US PRETTY FAST.
"EVEN FOR US. CRAZY.
"THEN THEY GOT DOWNRIGHT SURREAL, RIGHT?
"SURREAL TO THE POINT WHERE WE DIDN'T KNOW WHAT THE WORLD WAS GOING TO BE LIKE WHEN IT WAS ALL OVER.
"BUT STILL, WE FOUGHT THE FIGHT.

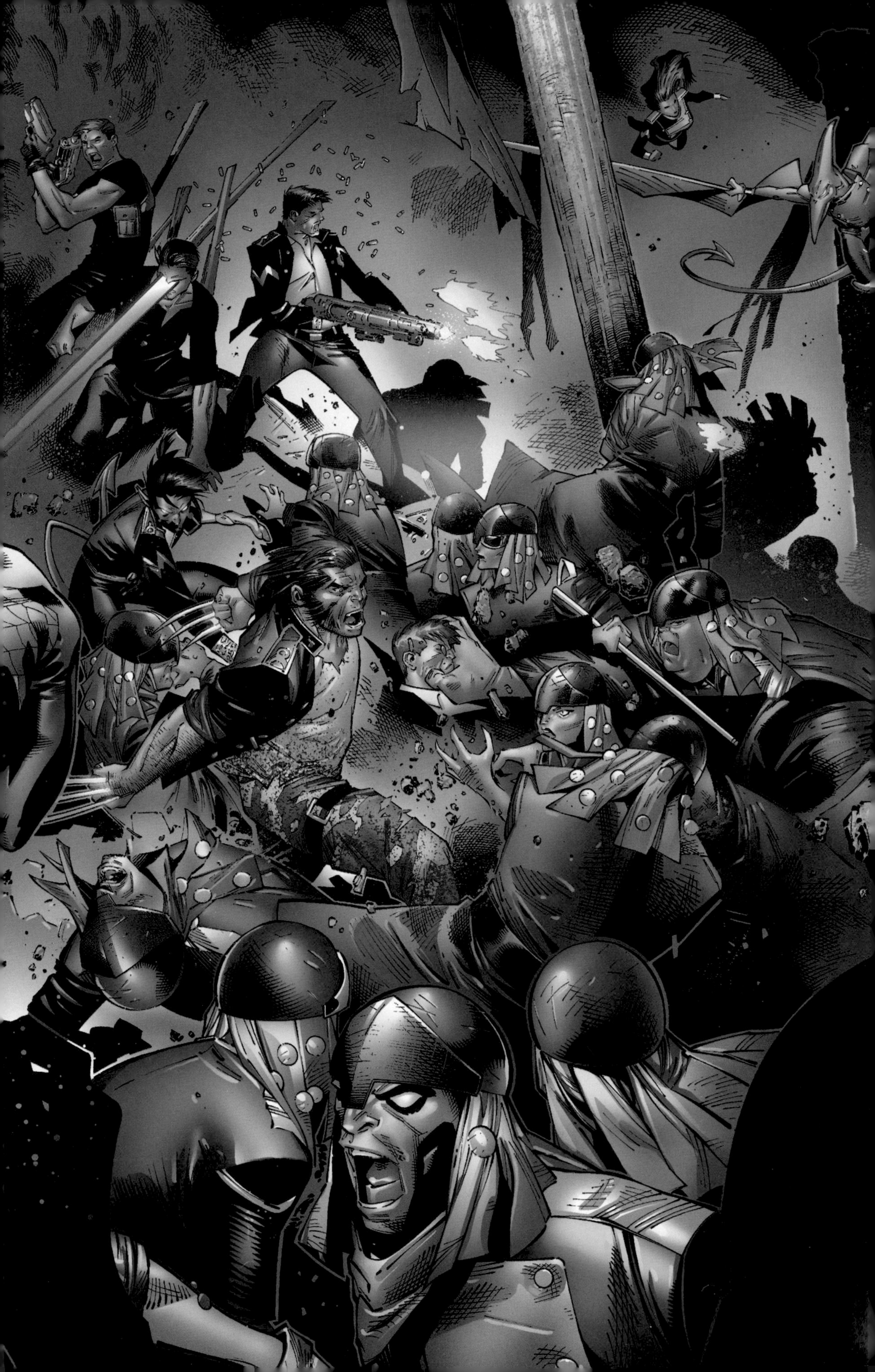

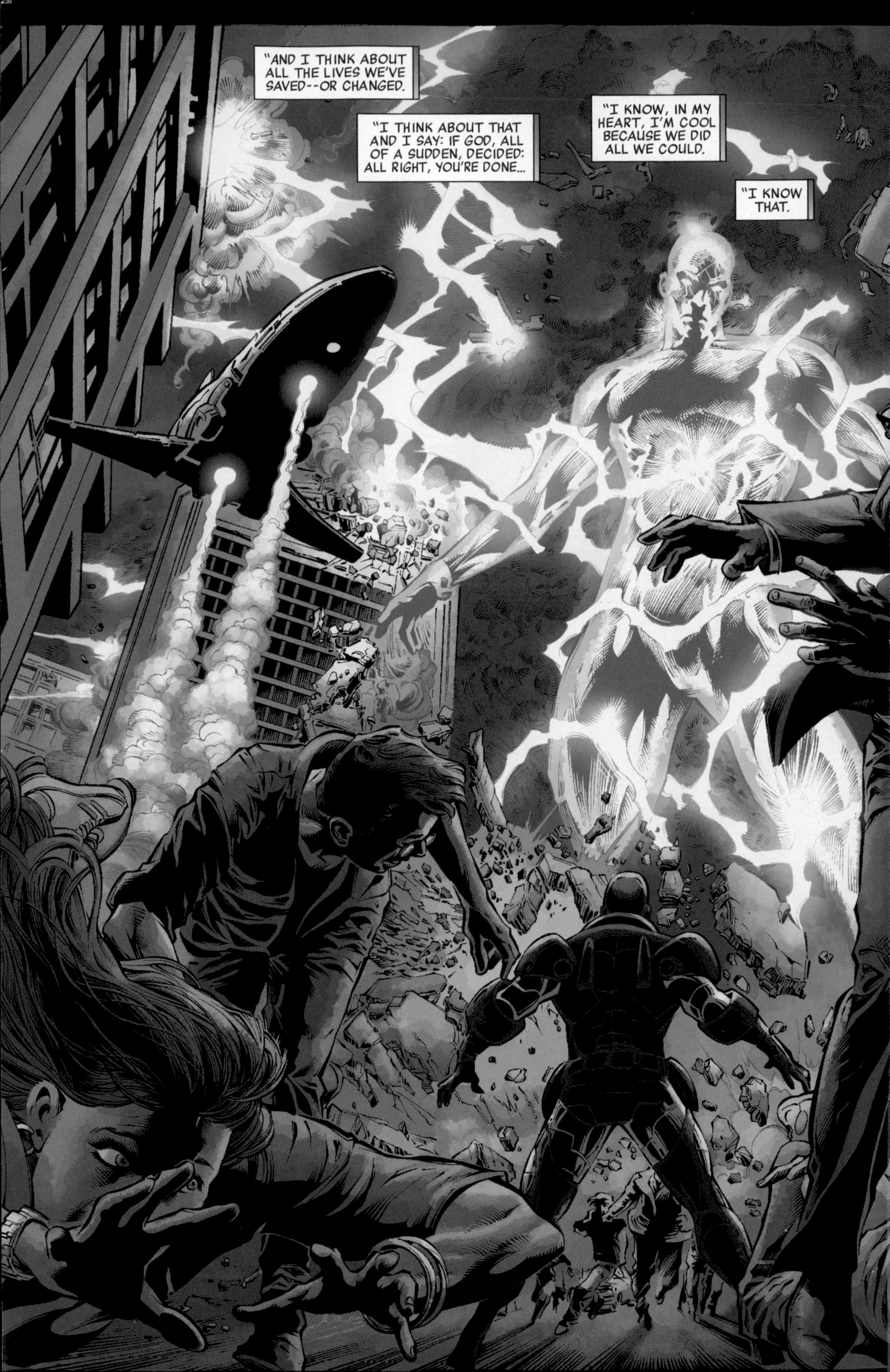
"AND I THINK ABOUT ALL THE LIVES WE'VE SAVED--OR CHANGED.
"I THINK ABOUT THAT AND I SAY: IF GOD, ALL OF A SUDDEN, DECIDED: ALL RIGHT, YOU'RE DONE...
"I KNOW, IN MY HEART, I'M COOL BECAUSE WE DID ALL WE COULD.
"I KNOW THAT.

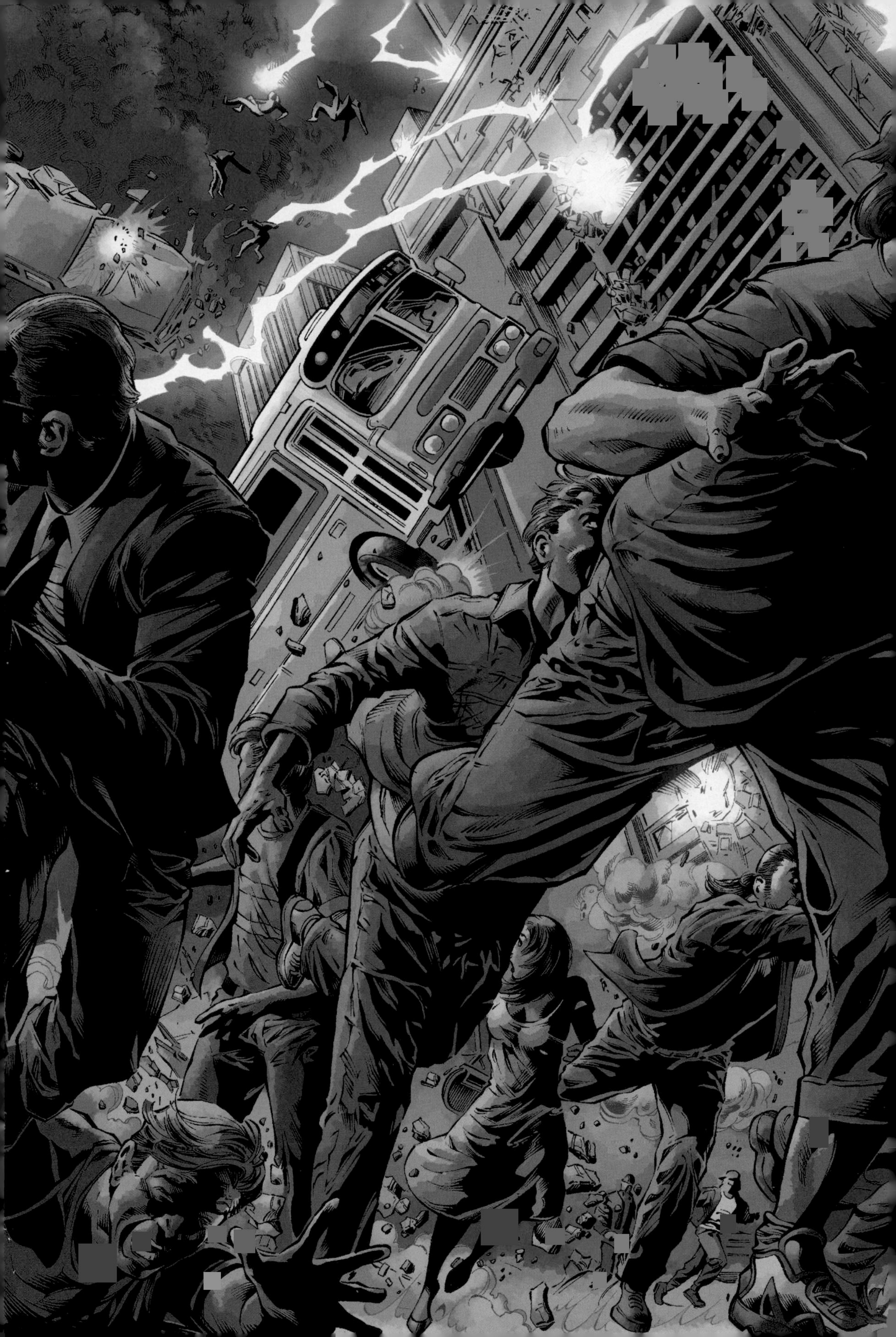

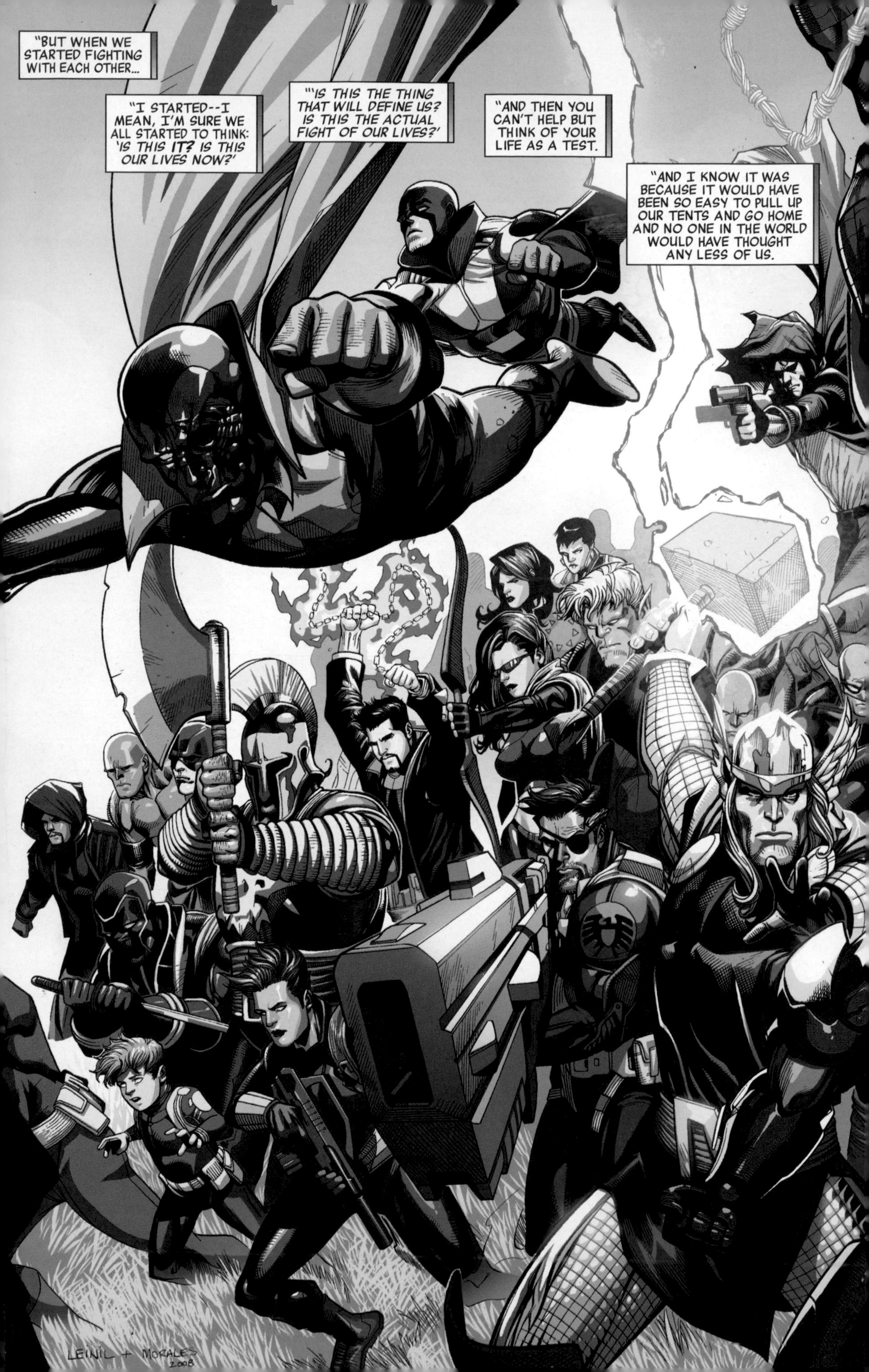
"BUT WHEN WE STARTED FIGHTING WITH EACH OTHER...
"I STARTED--I MEAN, I'M SURE WE ALL STARTED TO THINK: 'IS THIS IT? IS THIS OUR LIVES NOW?'
"'IS THIS THE THING THAT WILL DEFINE US? IS THIS THE ACTUAL FIGHT OF OUR LIVES?'
"AND THEN YOU CAN'T HELP BUT THINK OF YOUR LIFE AS A TEST.
"AND I KNOW IT WAS BECAUSE IT WOULD HAVE BEEN SO EASY TO PULL UP OUR TENTS AND GO HOME AND NO ONE IN THE WORLD WOULD HAVE THOUGHT ANY LESS OF US.
LEINIL + MORALES 2008

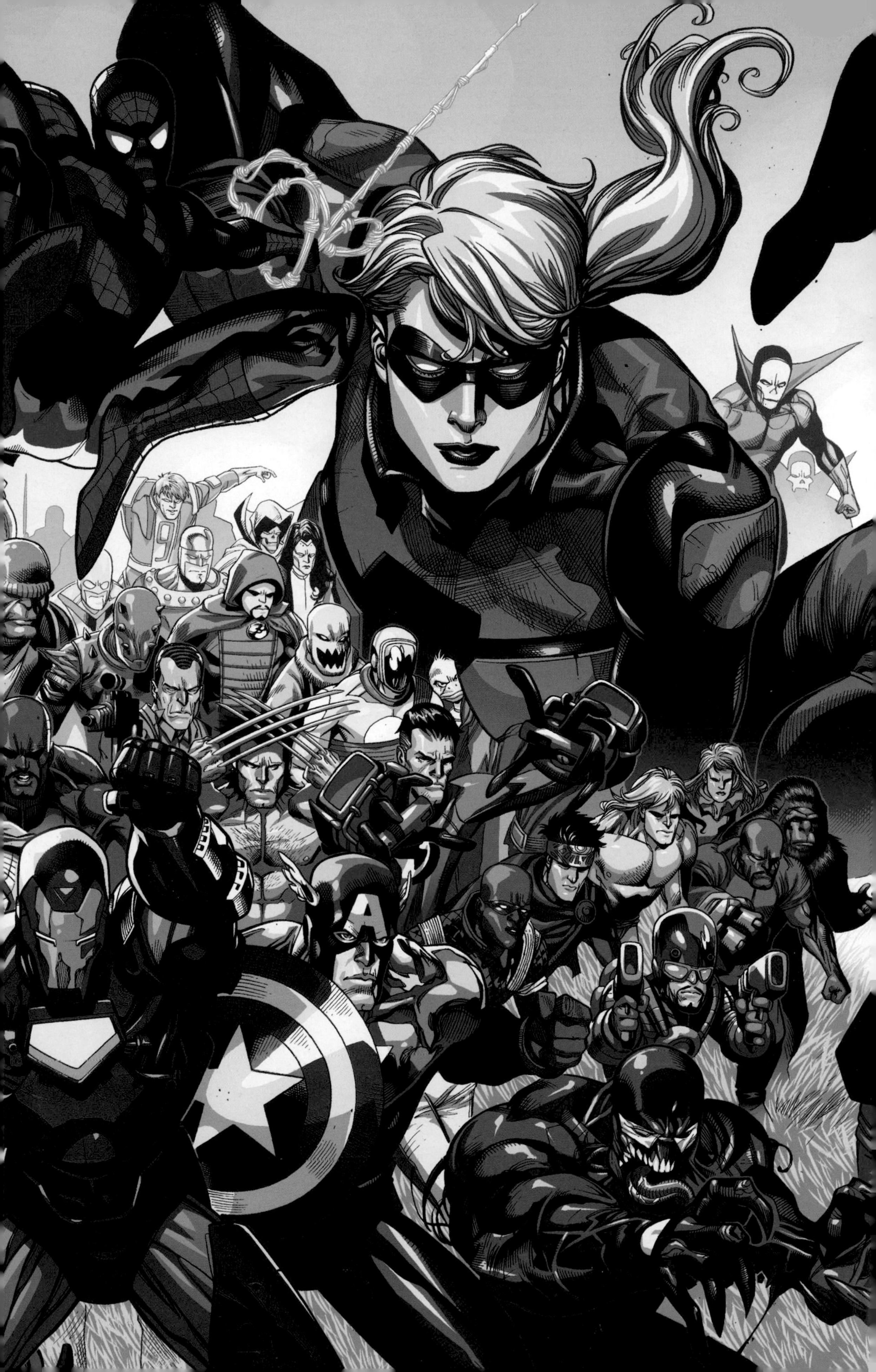

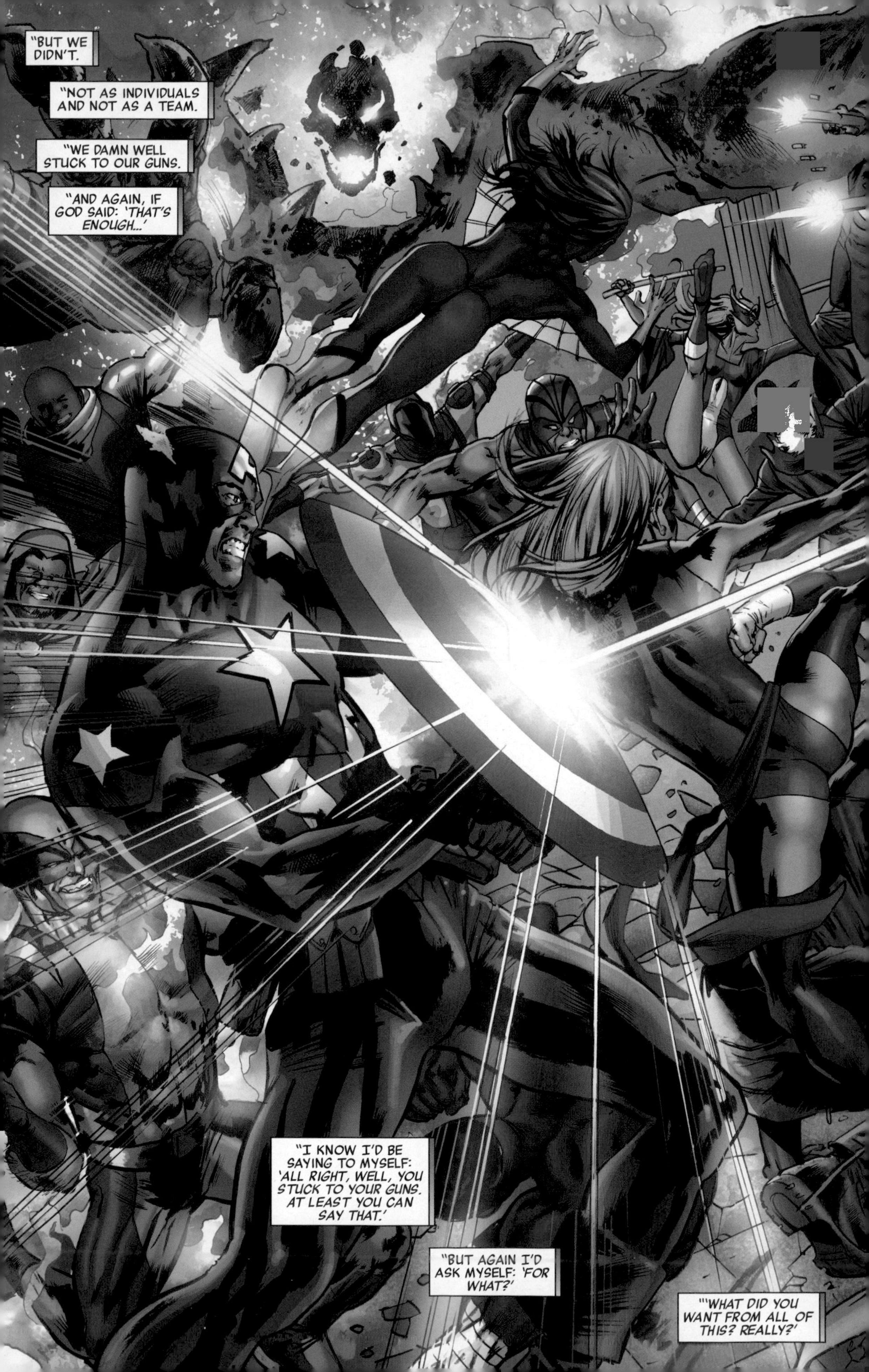
"BUT WE DIDN'T.
"NOT AS INDIVIDUALS AND NOT AS A TEAM.
"WE DAMN WELL STUCK TO OUR GUNS.
"AND AGAIN, IF GOD SAID: 'THAT'S ENOUGH...'
"I KNOW I'D BE SAYING TO MYSELF: 'ALL RIGHT, WELL, YOU STUCK TO YOUR GUNS. AT LEAST YOU CAN SAY THAT.'
"BUT AGAIN I'D ASK MYSELF: 'FOR WHAT?'
"'WHAT DID YOU WANT FROM ALL OF THIS? REALLY?'

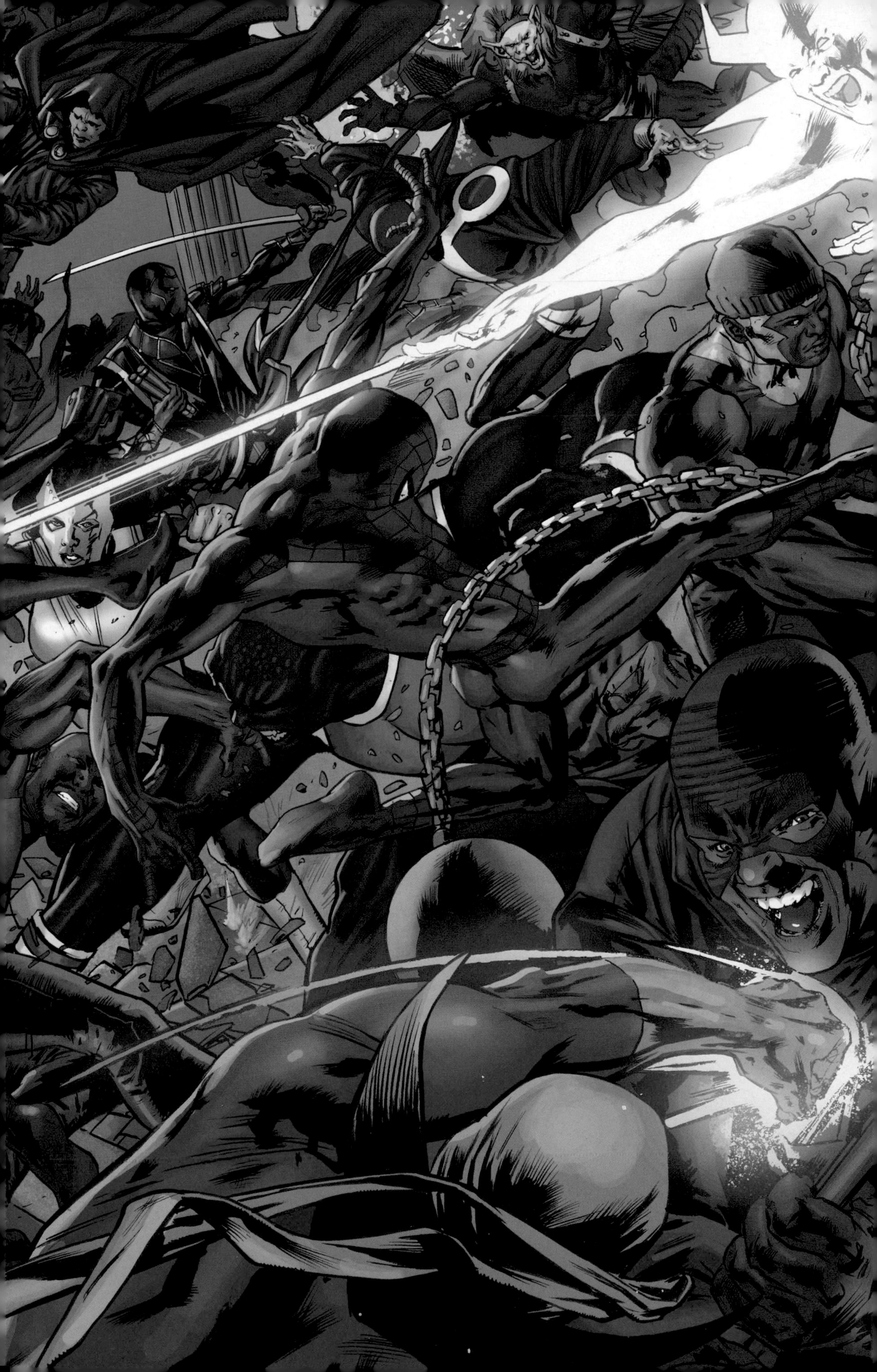

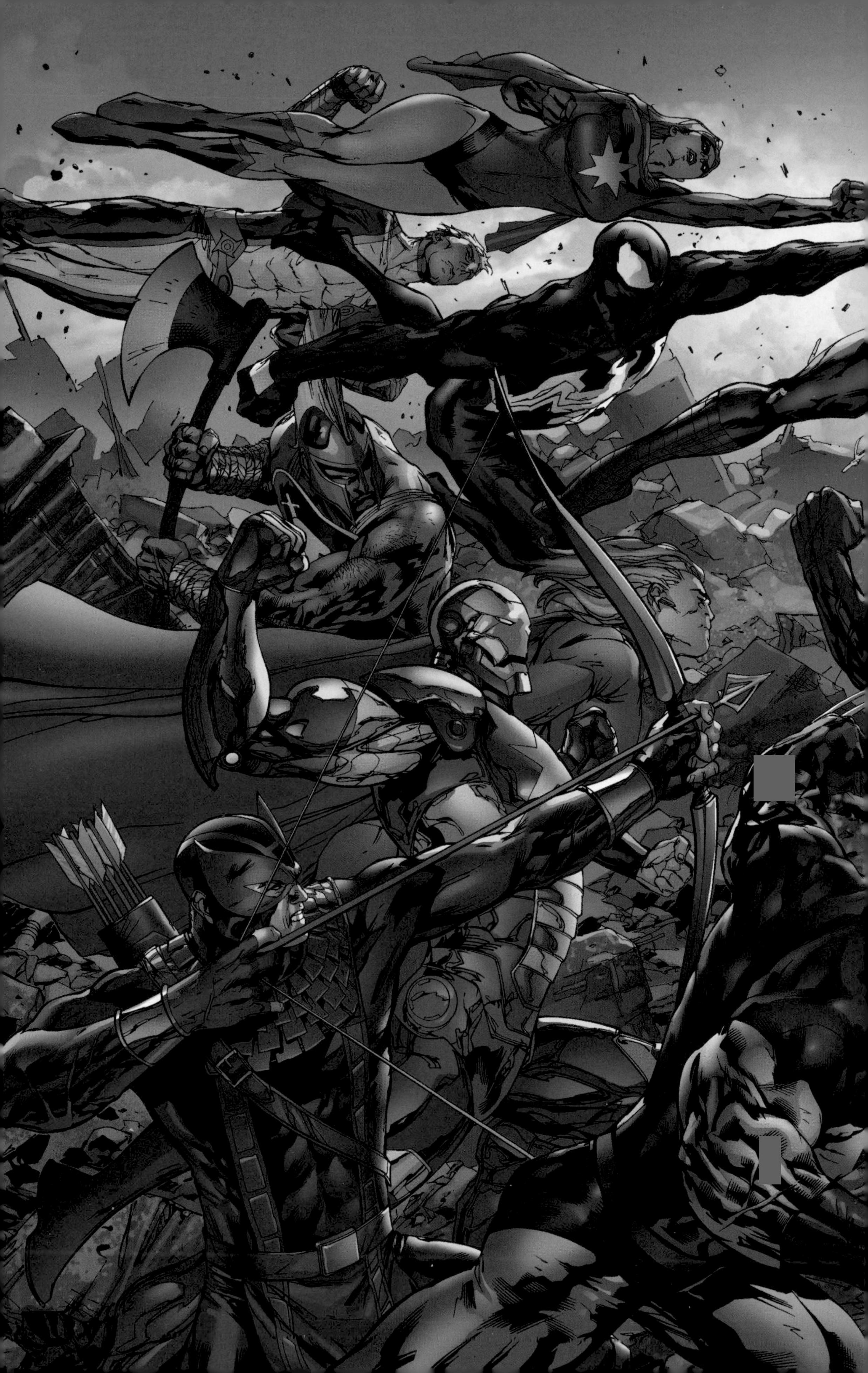

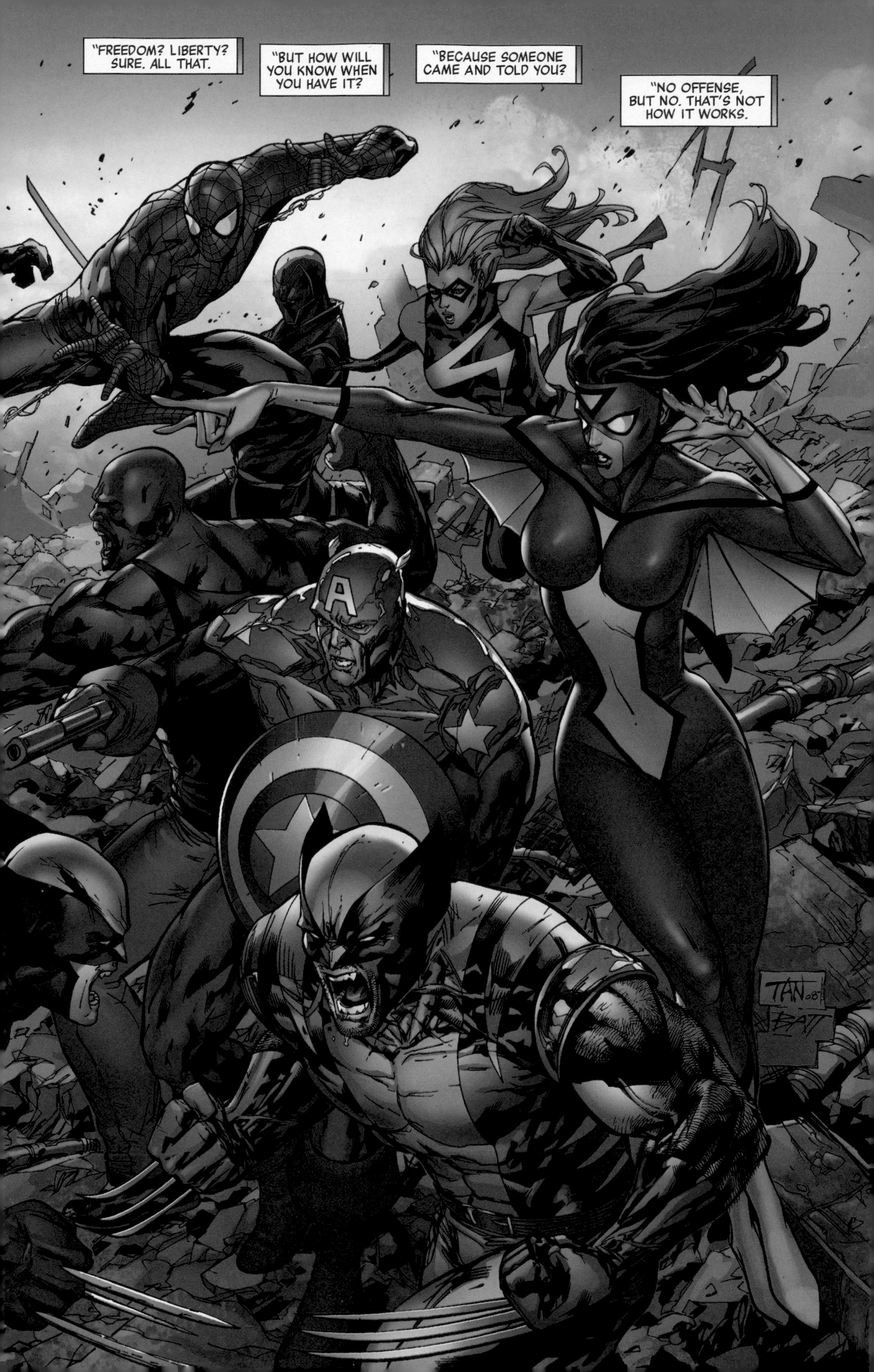
"FREEDOM? LIBERTY? SURE. ALL THAT.
"BUT HOW WILL YOU KNOW WHEN YOU HAVE IT?
"BECAUSE SOMEONE CAME AND TOLD YOU?
"NO OFFENSE, BUT NO. THAT'S NOT HOW IT WORKS.
TAN '08
BATT

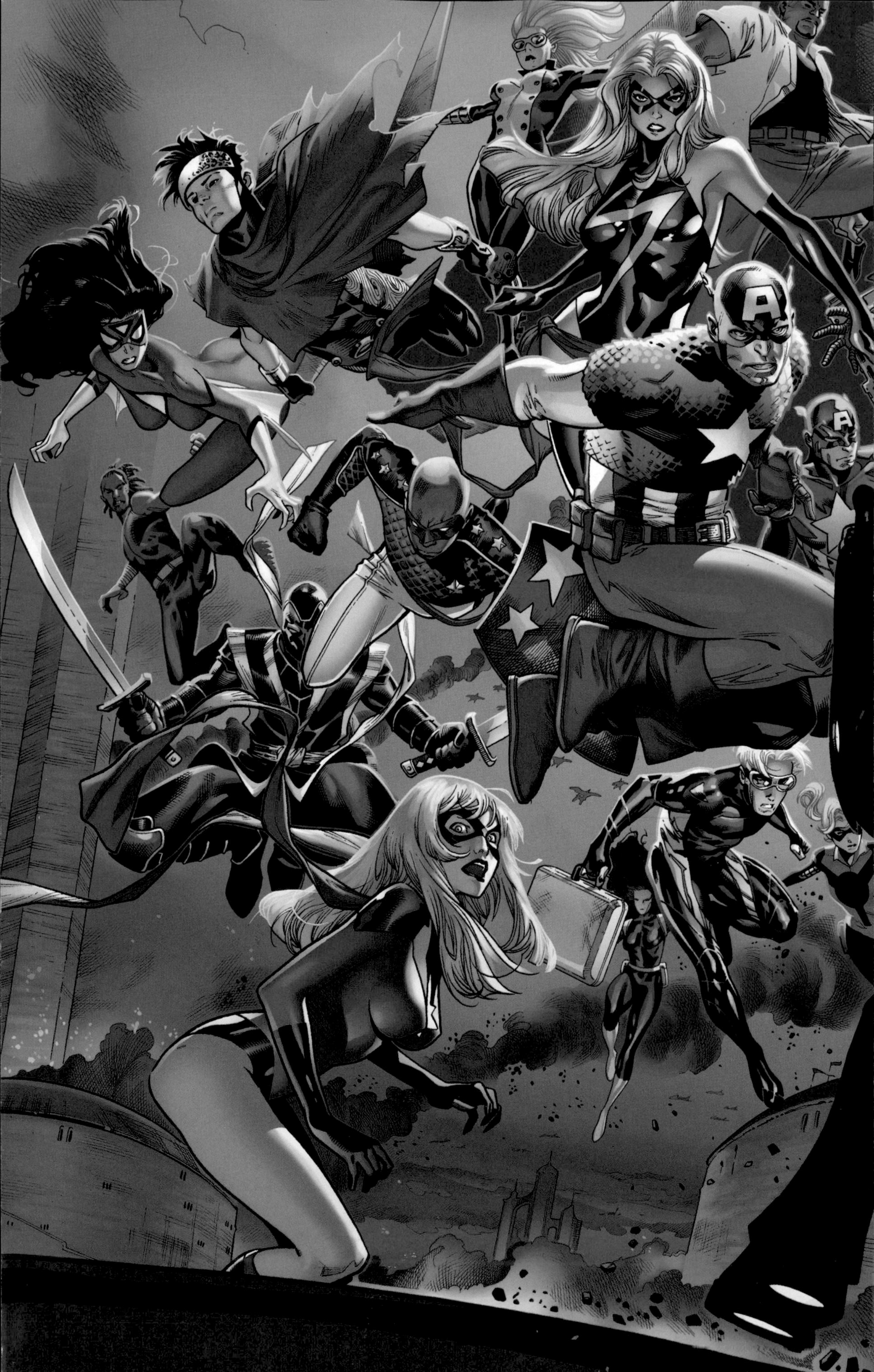

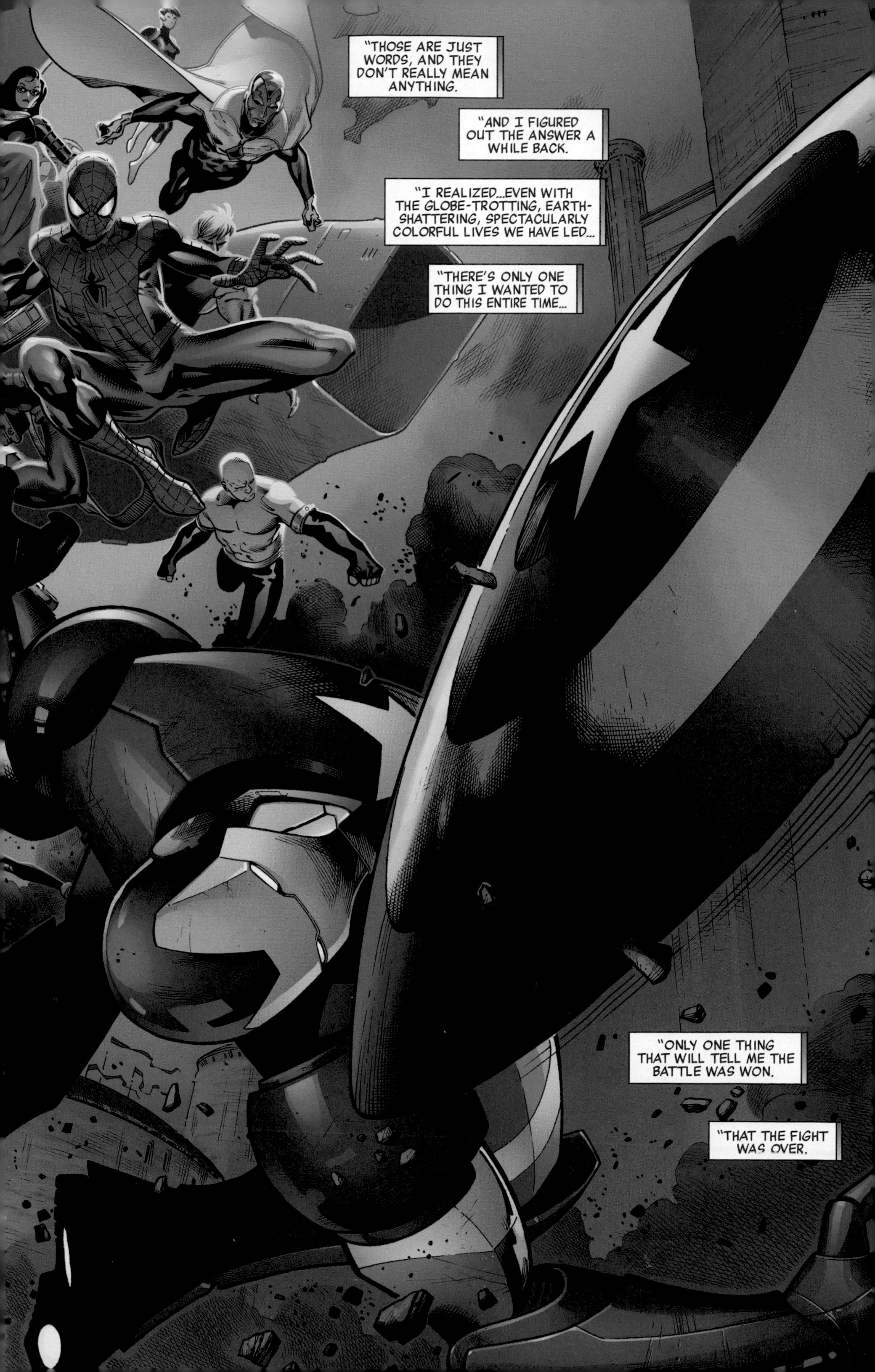
"THOSE ARE JUST WORDS, AND THEY DON'T REALLY MEAN ANYTHING.
"AND I FIGURED OUT THE ANSWER A WHILE BACK.
"I REALIZED...EVEN WITH THE GLOBE-TROTTING, EARTH-SHATTERING, SPECTACULARLY COLORFUL LIVES WE HAVE LED...
"THERE'S ONLY ONE THING I WANTED TO DO THIS ENTIRE TIME...
"ONLY ONE THING THAT WILL TELL ME THE BATTLE WAS WON.
"THAT THE FIGHT WAS OVER.

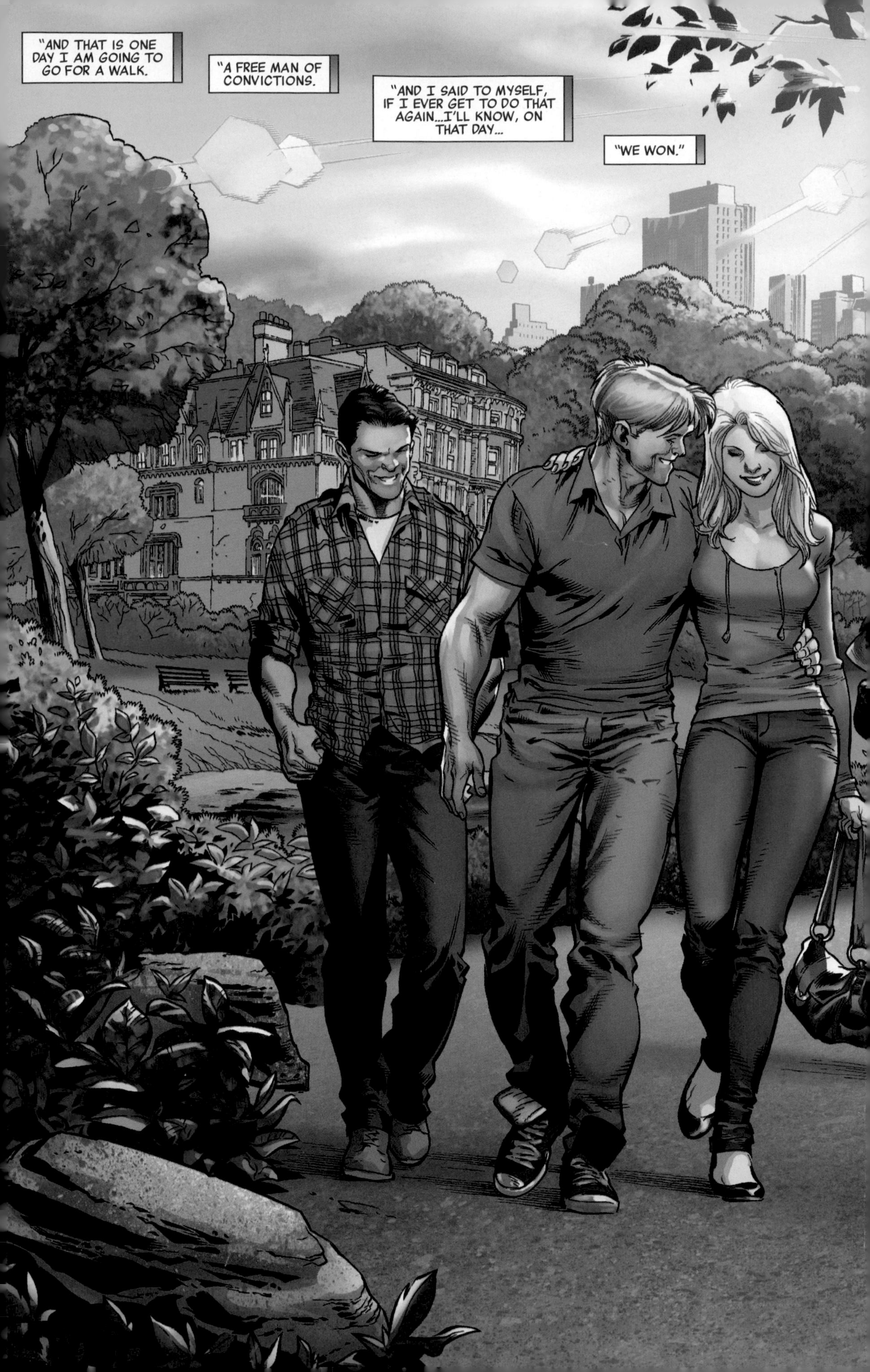
"AND THAT IS ONE DAY I AM GOING TO GO FOR A WALK.
"A FREE MAN OF CONVICTIONS.
"AND I SAID TO MYSELF, IF I EVER GET TO DO THAT AGAIN...I'LL KNOW, ON THAT DAY...
"WE WON."

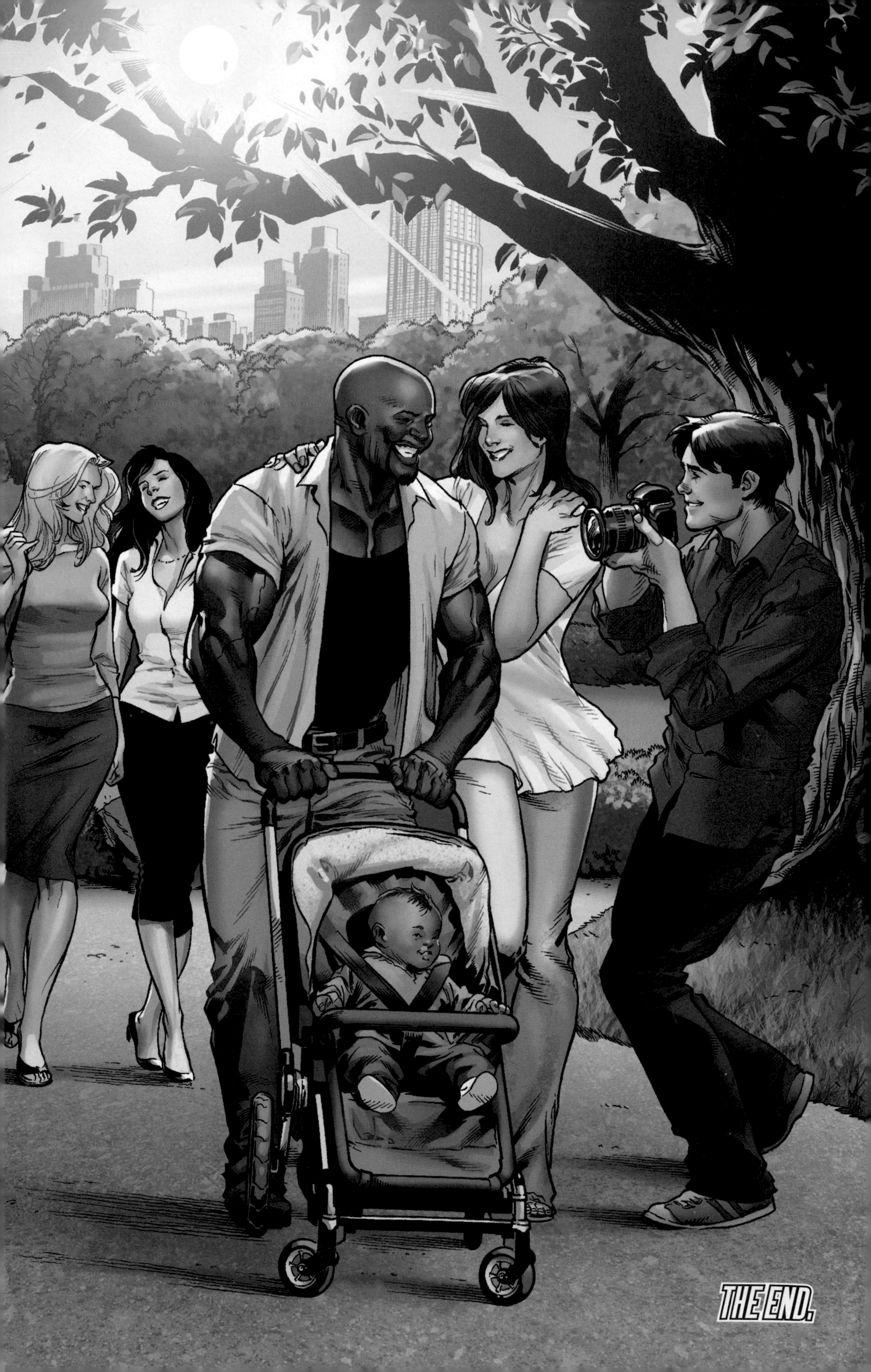
THE END.

DARK REIGN: THE LIST — AVNEGERS VARIANTS

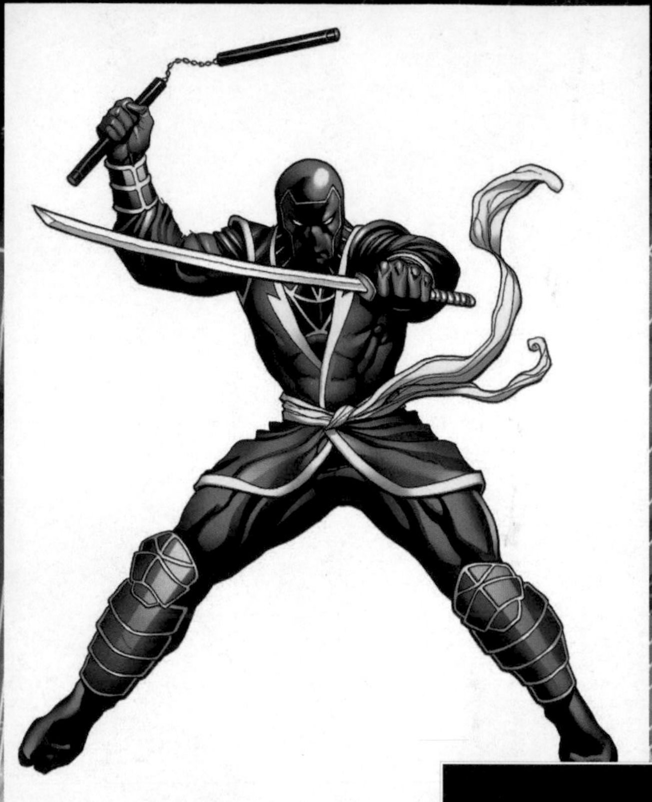

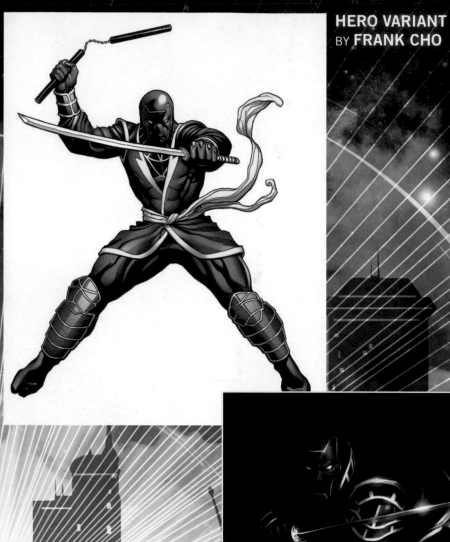

HERO VARIANT
BY FRANK CHO

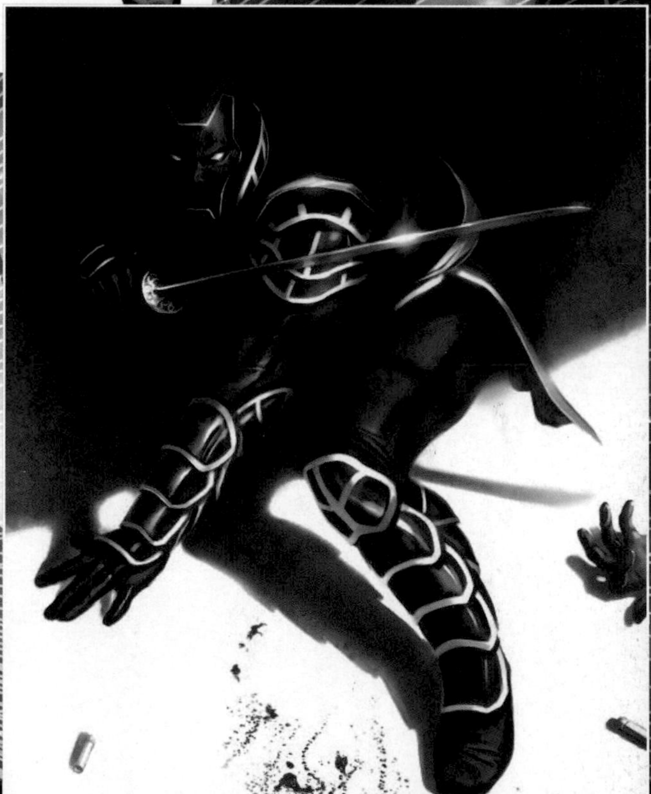

2ND PRINTING VARIANT BY MARKO DJURDJEVIC